# FAIRY TAIL

61

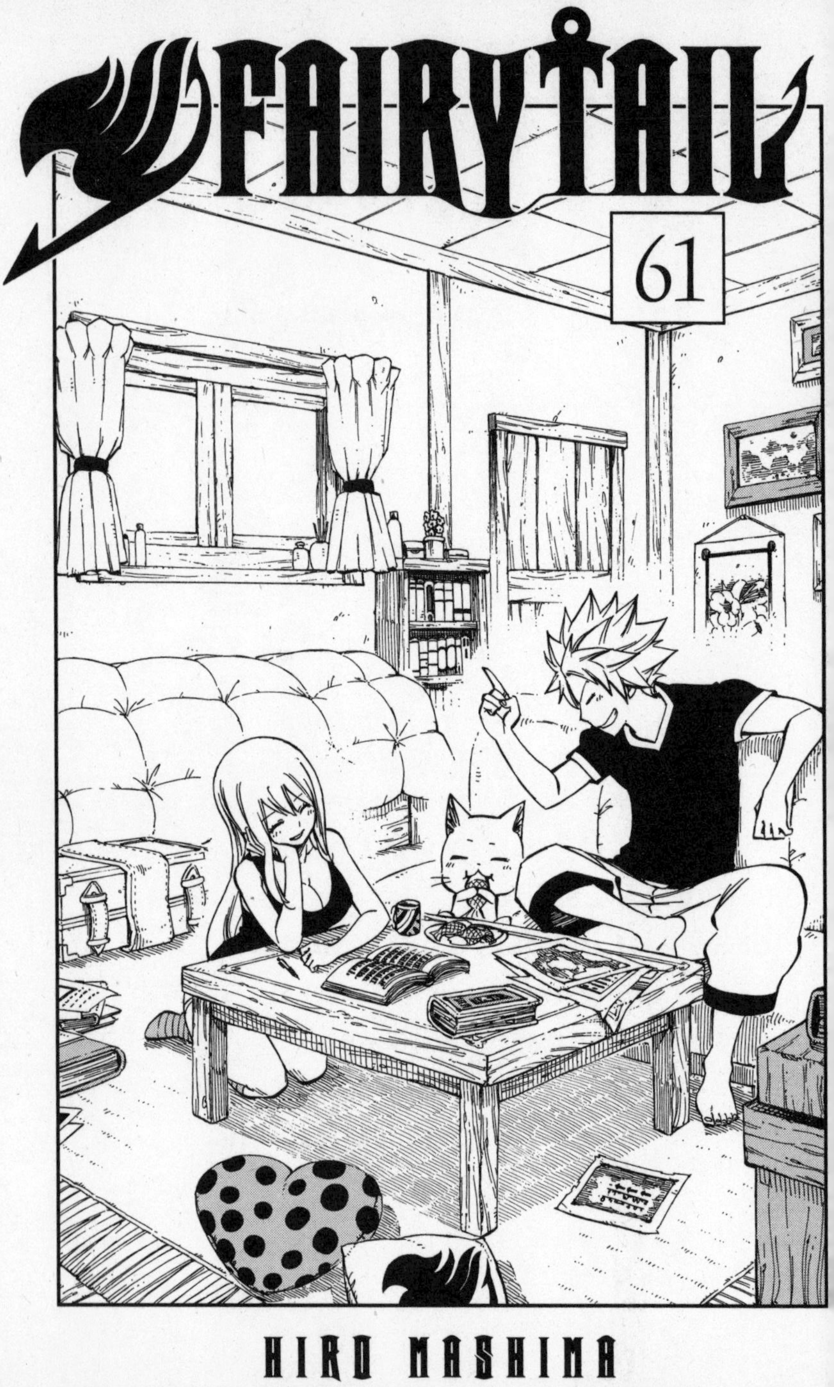

HIRO MASHIMA

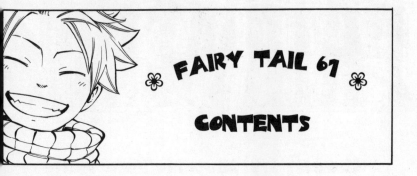

# FAIRY TAIL 61

# CONTENTS

# FAIRY TAIL

フェアリーテイル

## Chapter 519: Show Me Your Smile

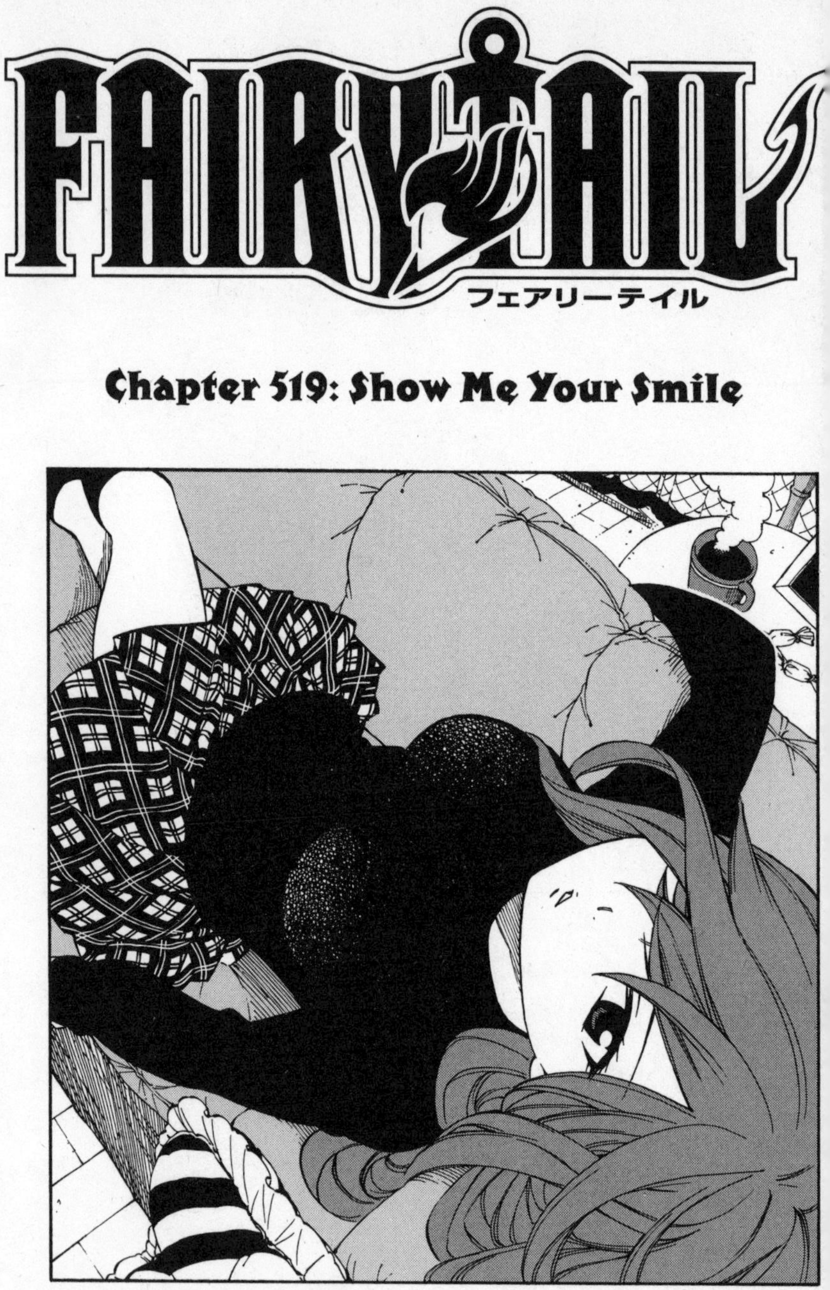

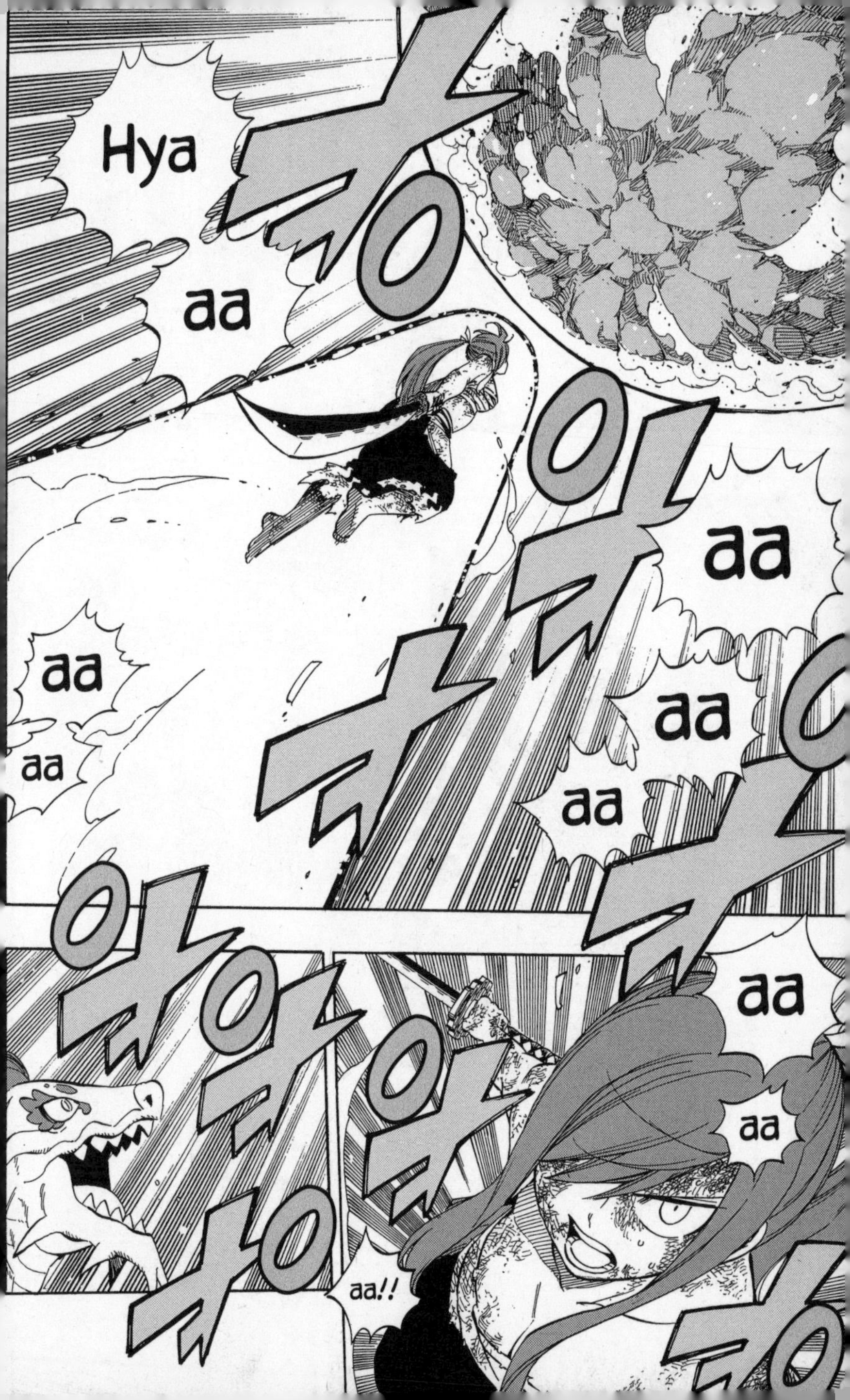
Hya
aa
aa
aa
aa
aa
aa
aa
aa
aa!!

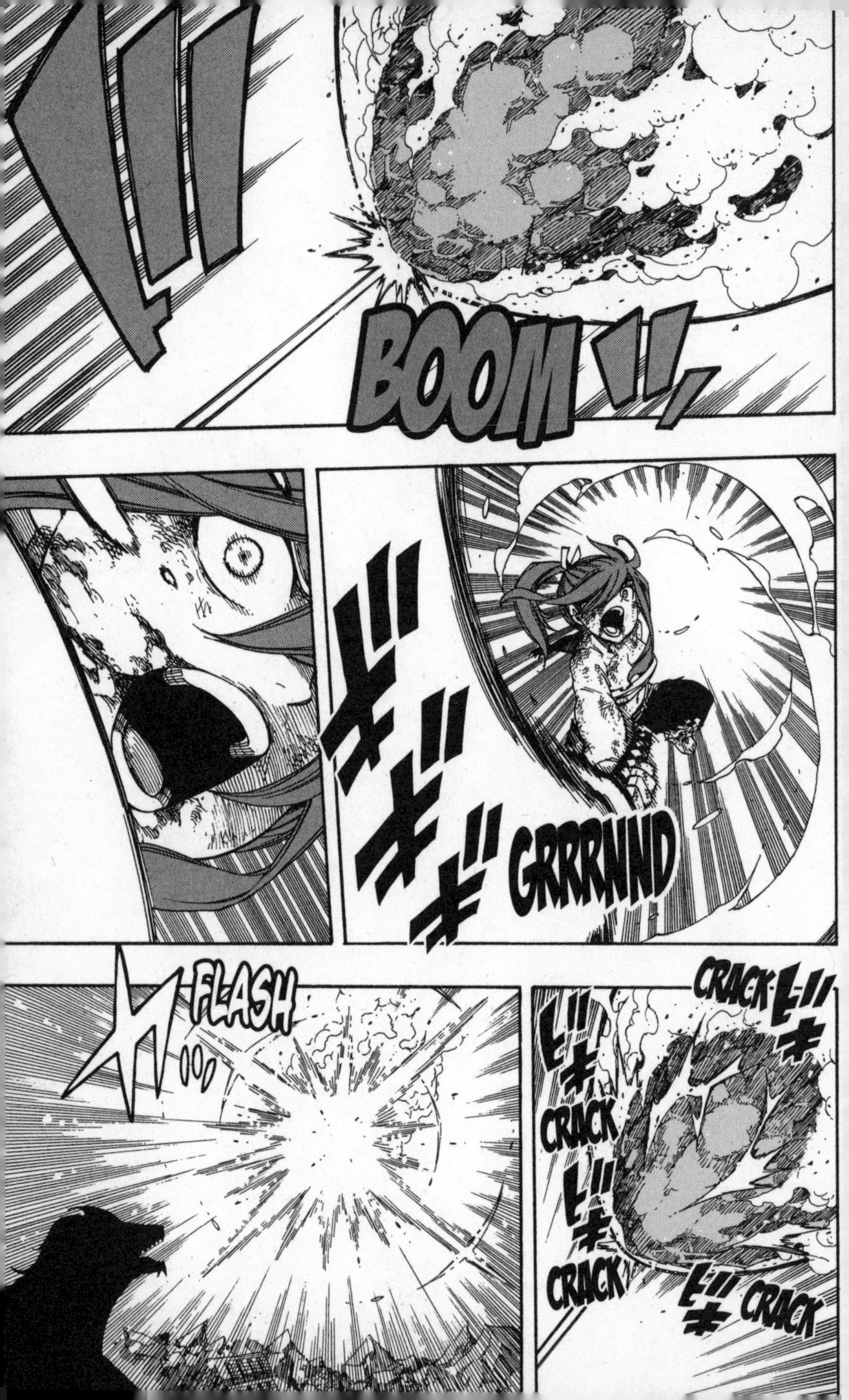
BOOM
GRRRNND
CRACK
CRACK
CRACK
CRACK
FLASH

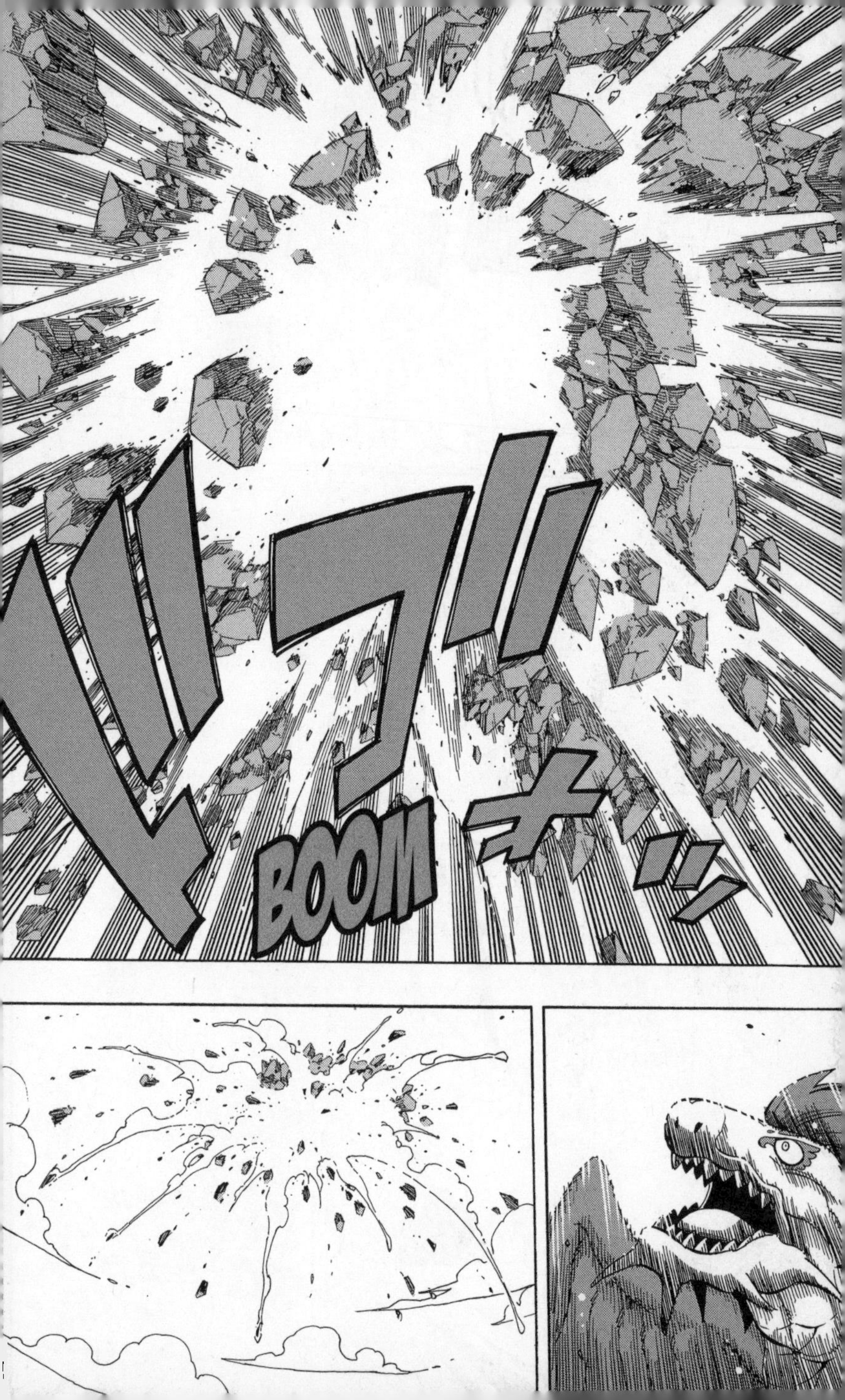
BOOM

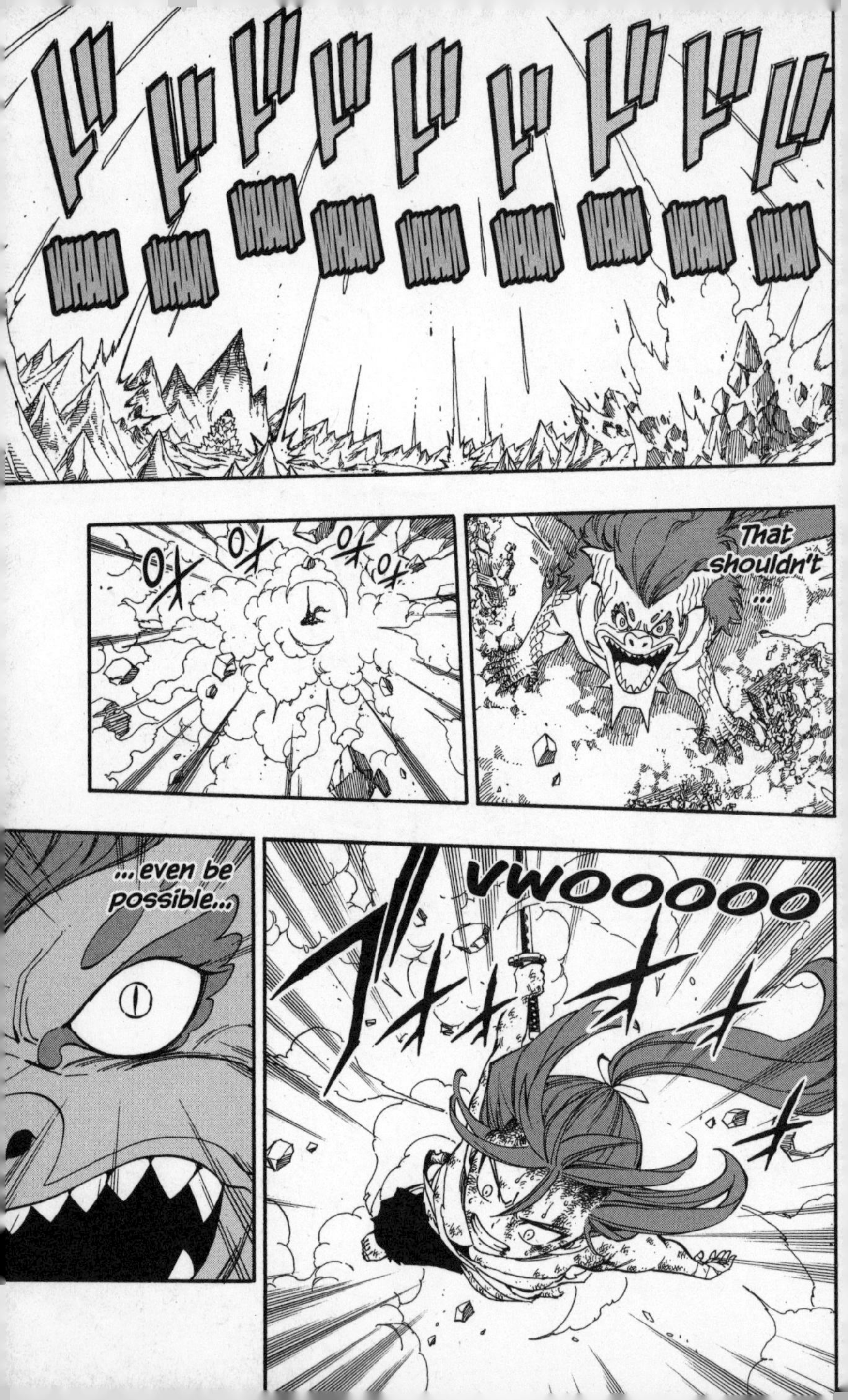
VWAM
VWAM
VWAM
VWAM
VWAM
VWAM
VWAM
VWAM
VWAM
That shouldn't ...
... even be possible...
VWOOOOOO

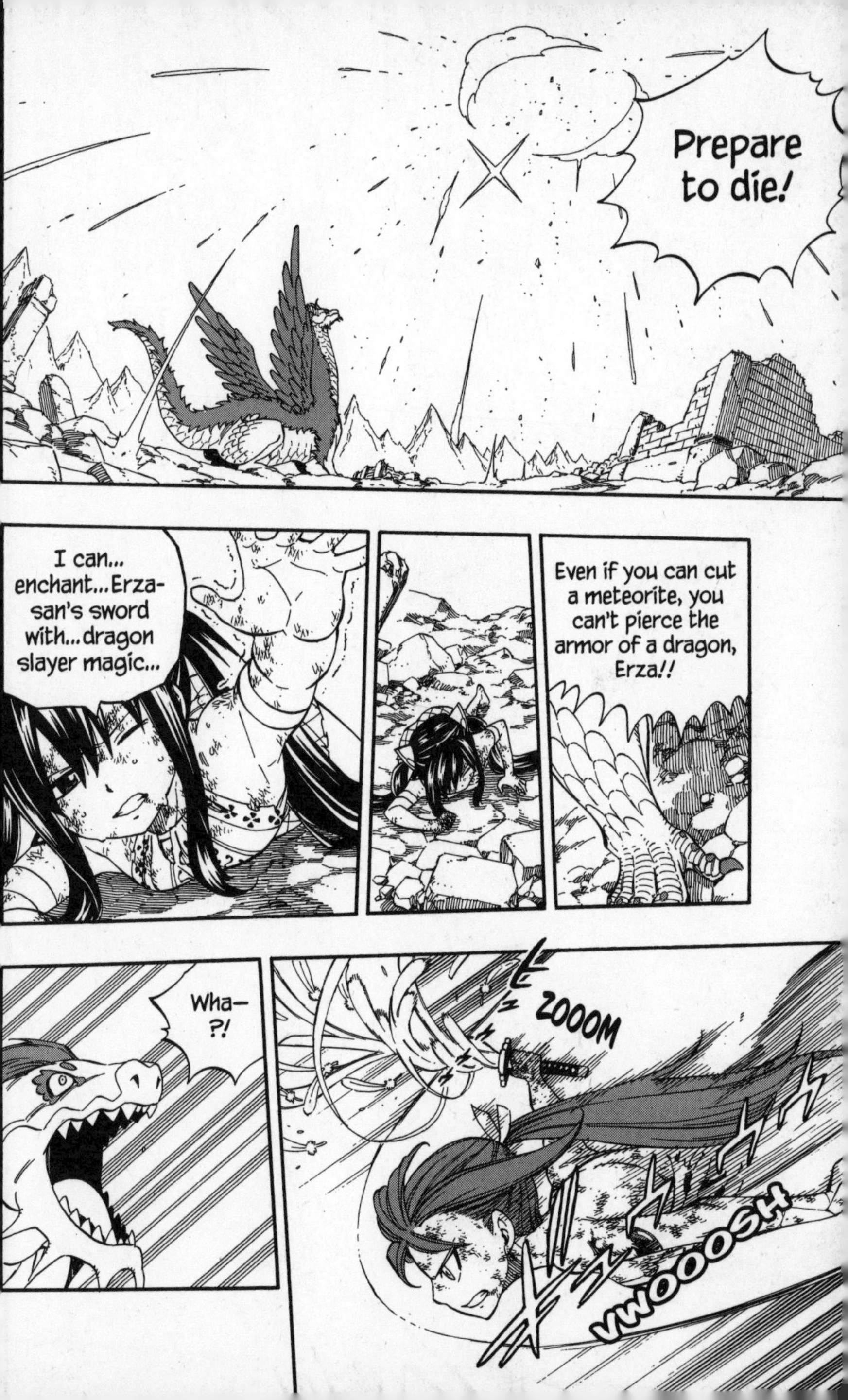
Prepare to die!
Even if you can cut a meteorite, you can't pierce the armor of a dragon, Erza!!
I can... enchant...Erza-san's sword with...dragon slayer magic...
ZOOOM
VWOOOSH
Wha-?!

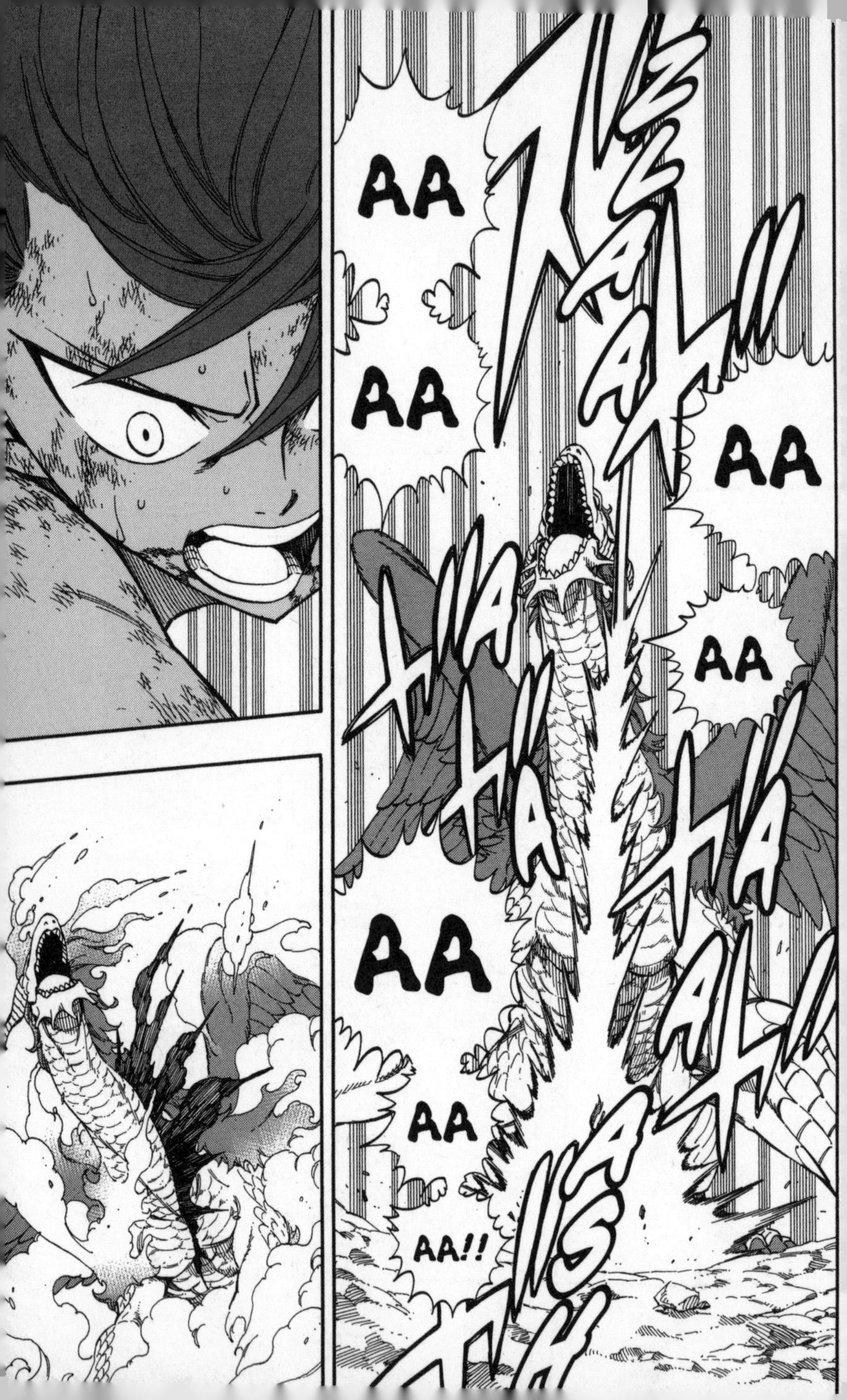
AA
AA
AA
AA
AA
AA
AA!!

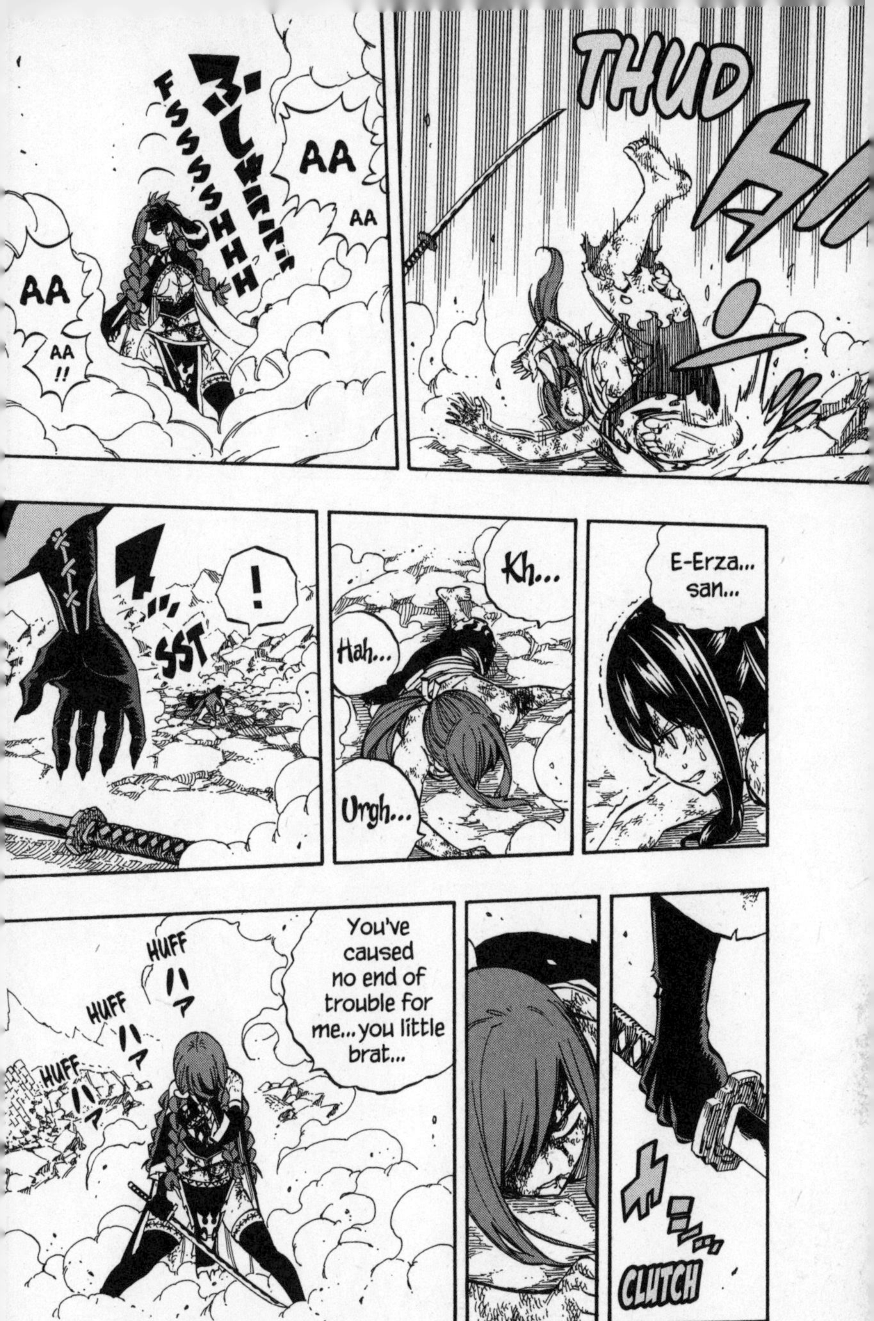
THUD
AA
AA
FSSSSHHH
AA
AA!!
E-Erza... san...
Kh...
Hah...
Urgh...
!
SST
CLUTCH
You've caused no end of trouble for me...you little brat...
HUFF
HUFF
HUFF

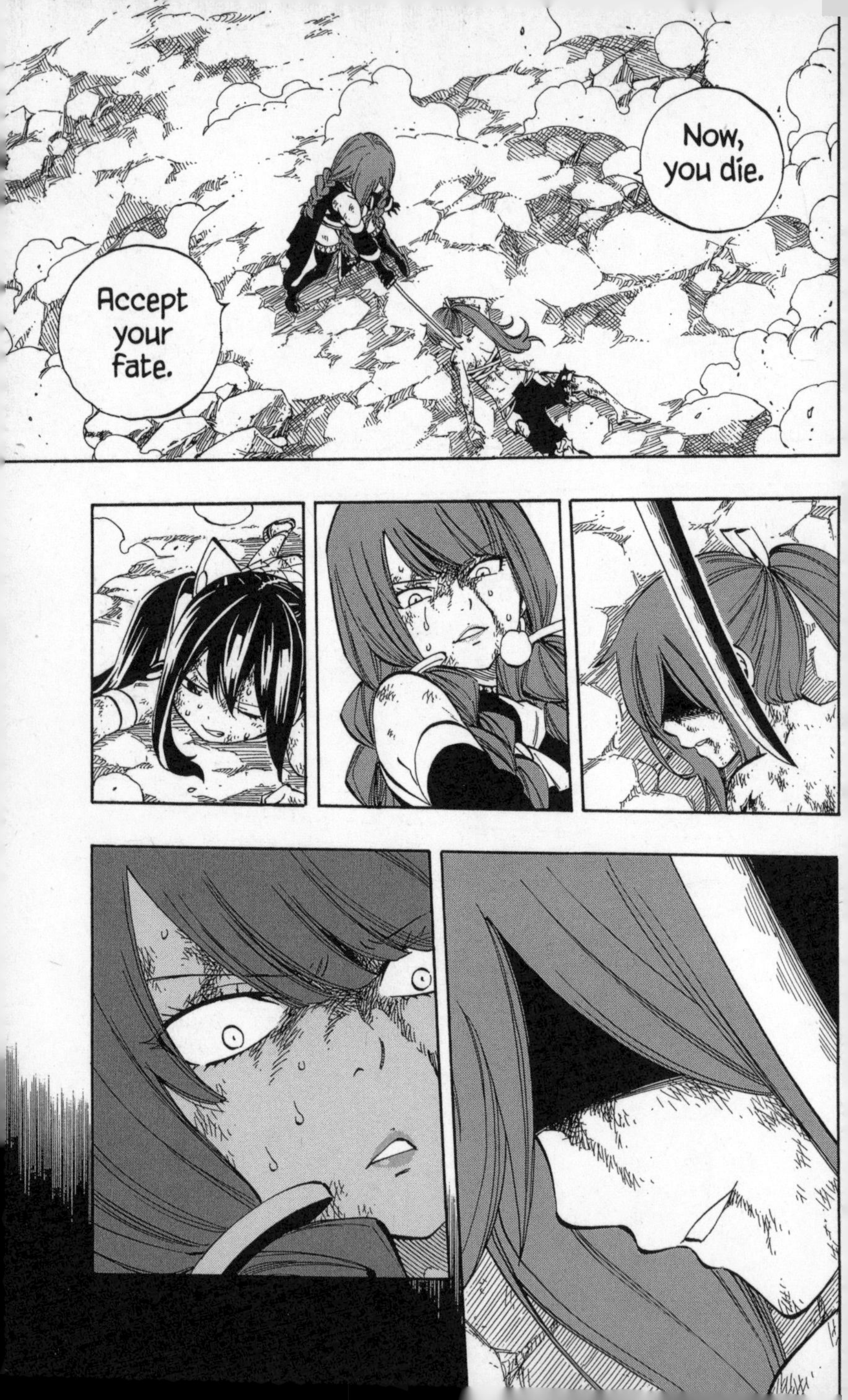
Now, you die.
Accept your fate.

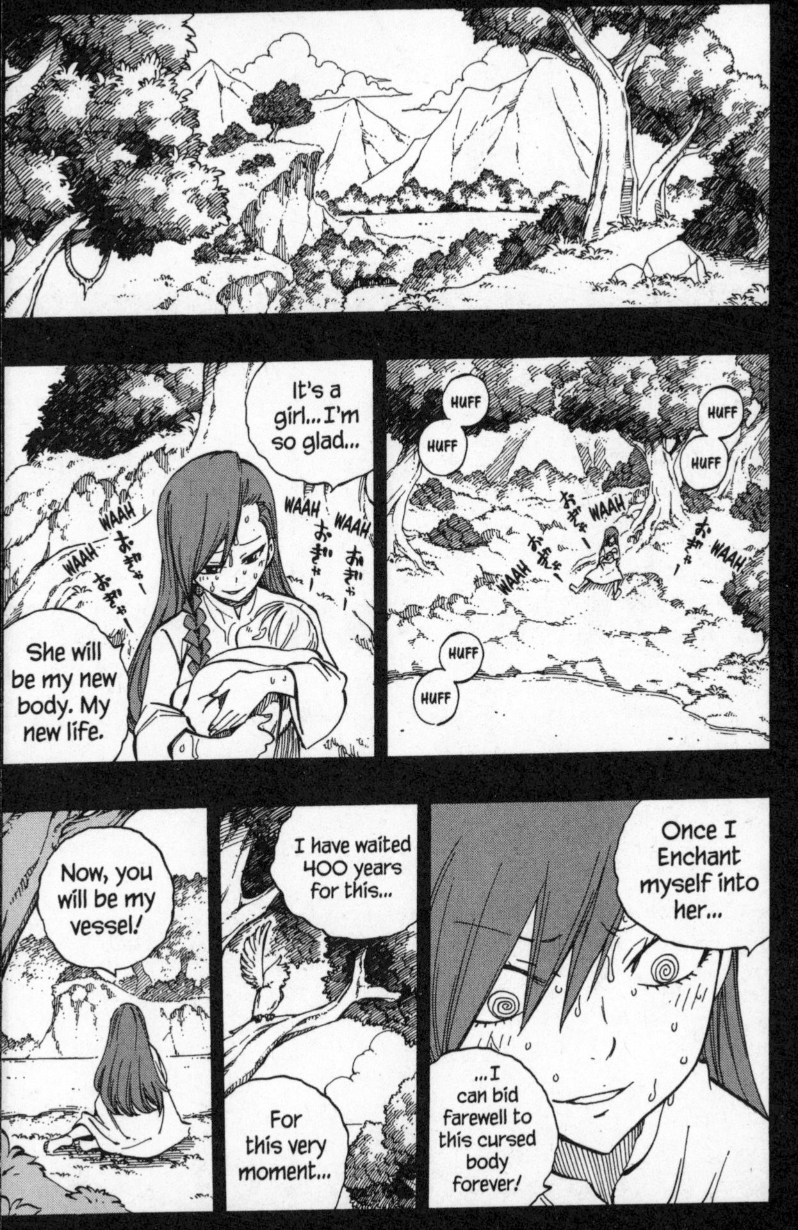
HUFF
HUFF
HUFF
HUFF
WAAH
おぎゃー
WAAH
おぎゃー
WAAH
おぎゃー
HUFF
HUFF
It's a girl...I'm so glad...
WAAH
おぎゃー
WAAH
おぎゃー
WAAH
おぎゃー
WAAH
おぎゃー
She will be my new body. My new life.
Once I Enchant myself into her...
...I can bid farewell to this cursed body forever!
I have waited 400 years for this...
For this very moment...
Now, you will be my vessel!

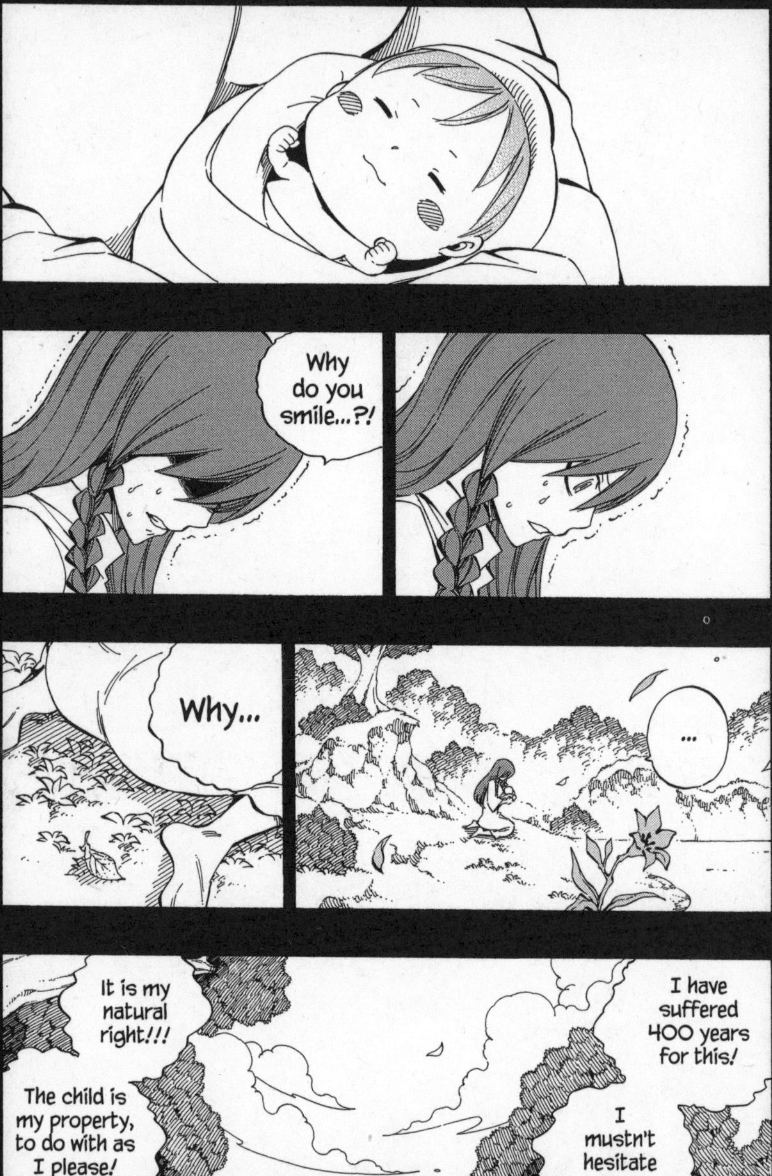
Why do you smile...?!
...
Why...
I have suffered 400 years for this!
It is my natural right!!!
The child is my property, to do with as I please!
I mustn't hesitate now!

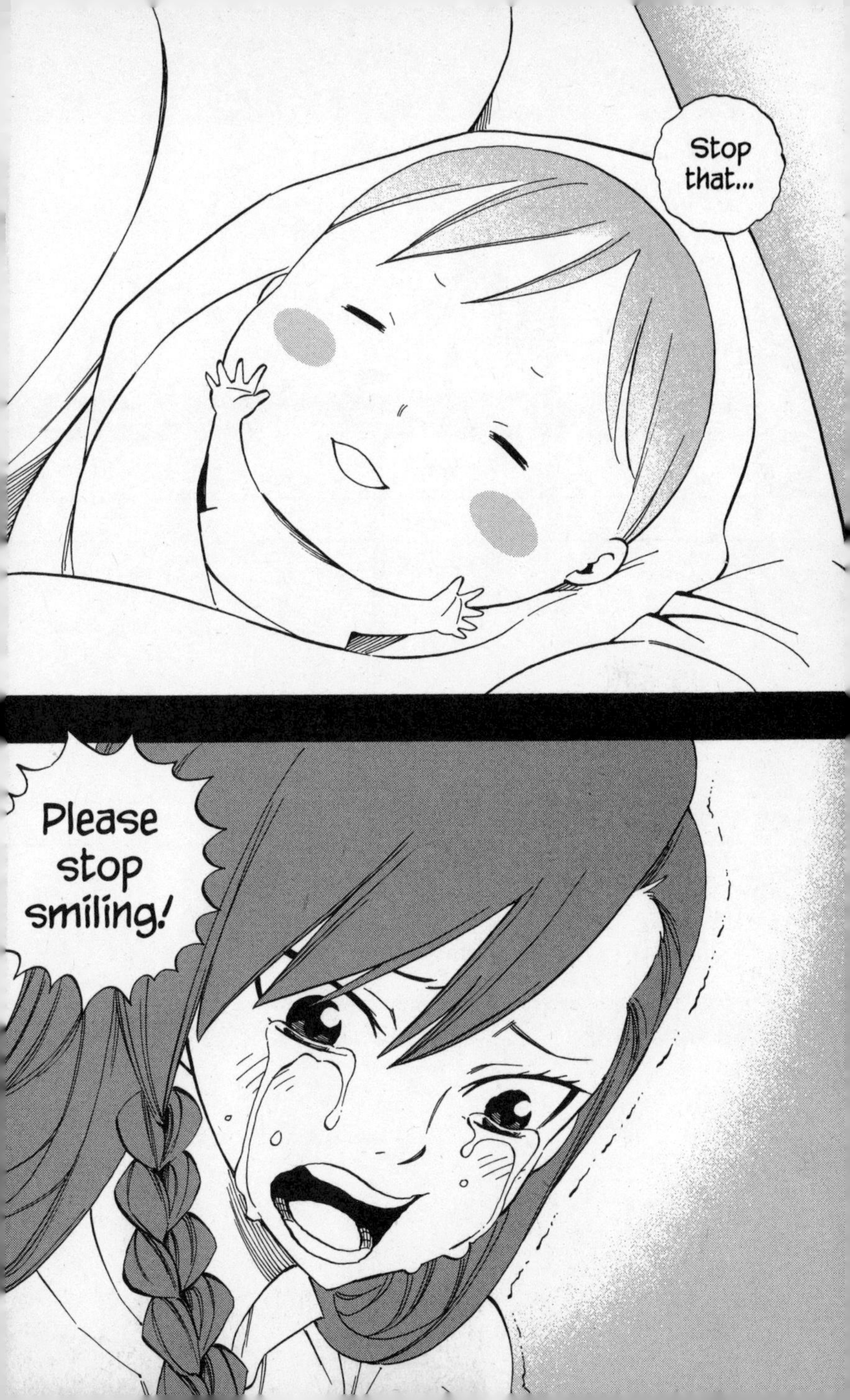
Stop that...
Please stop smiling!

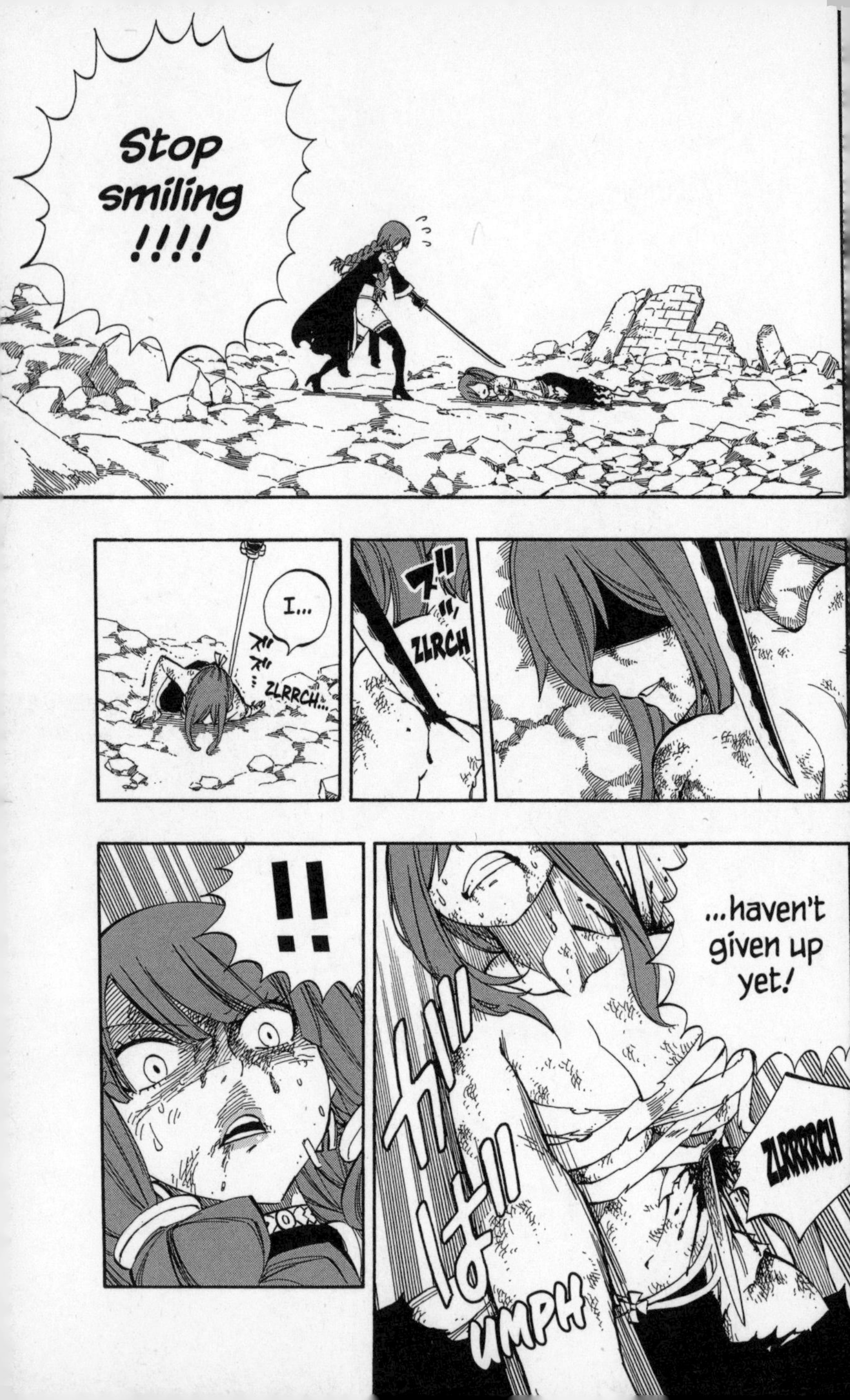
Stop smiling !!!!
ZLRCH
I...
ZLRRCH...
...haven't given up yet!
ZLRRRRCH
UMPH
!!

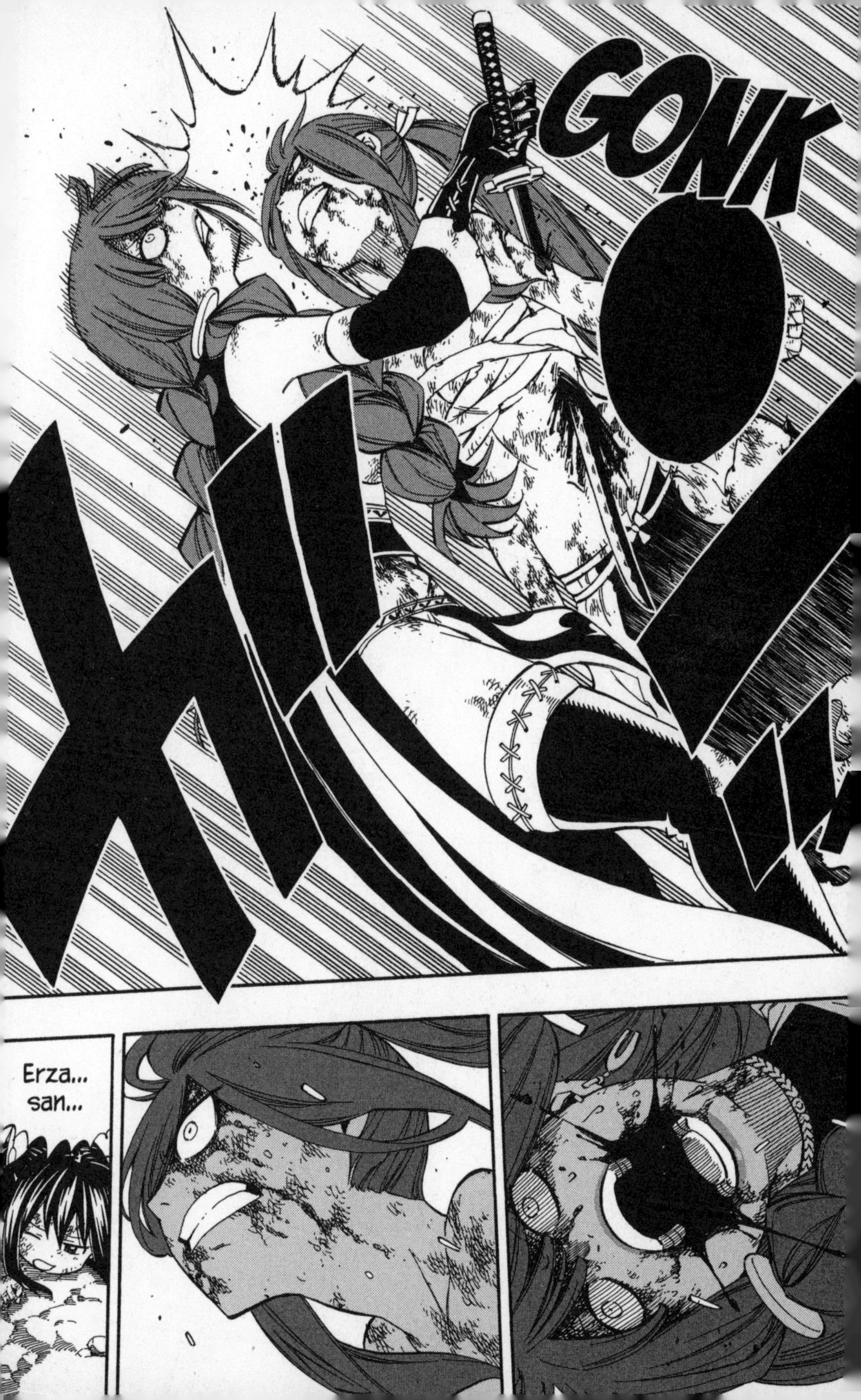
GONK
Erza...
san...

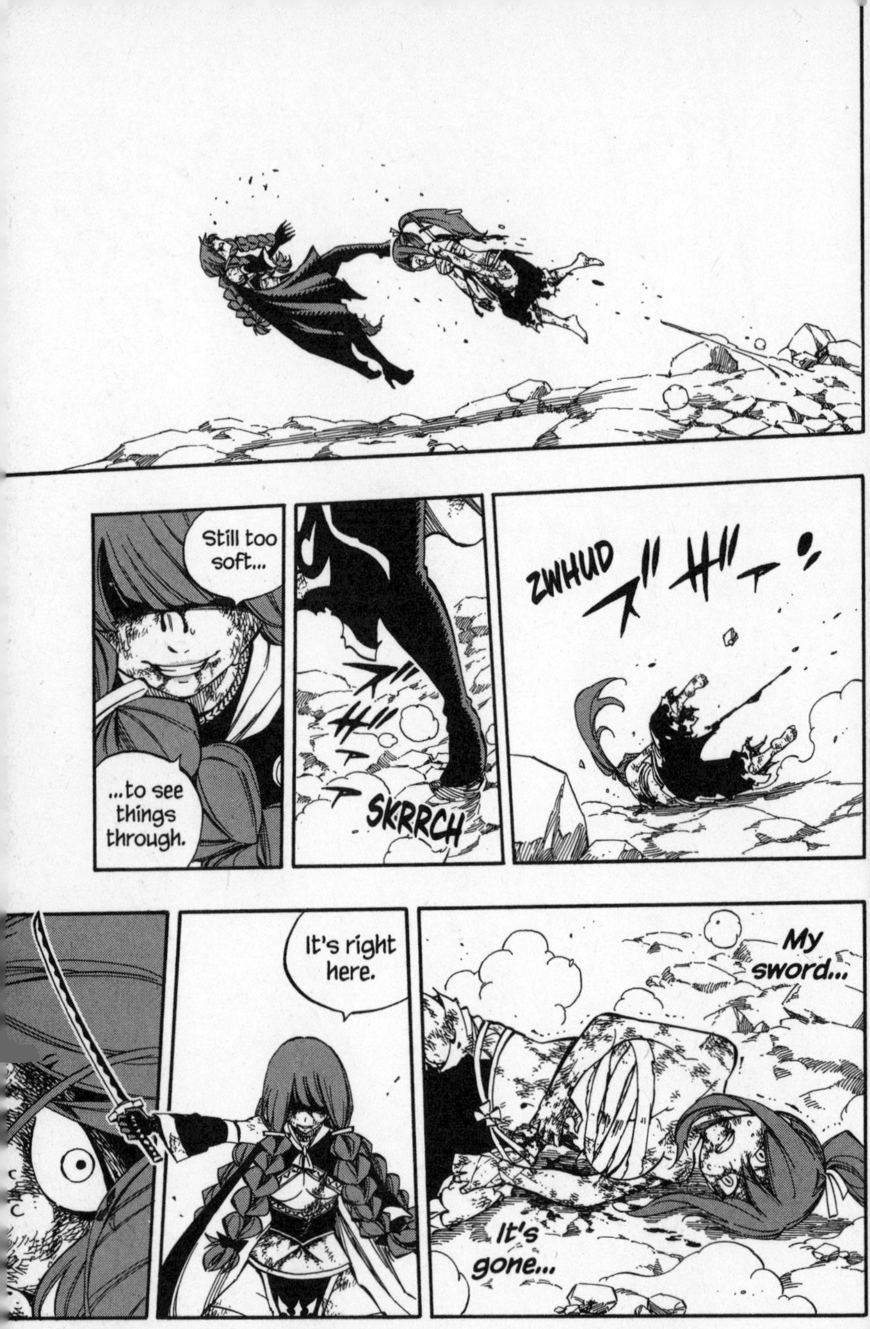
ZWHUD
SKRRCH
Still too soft...
...to see things through.
My sword...
It's gone...
It's right here.

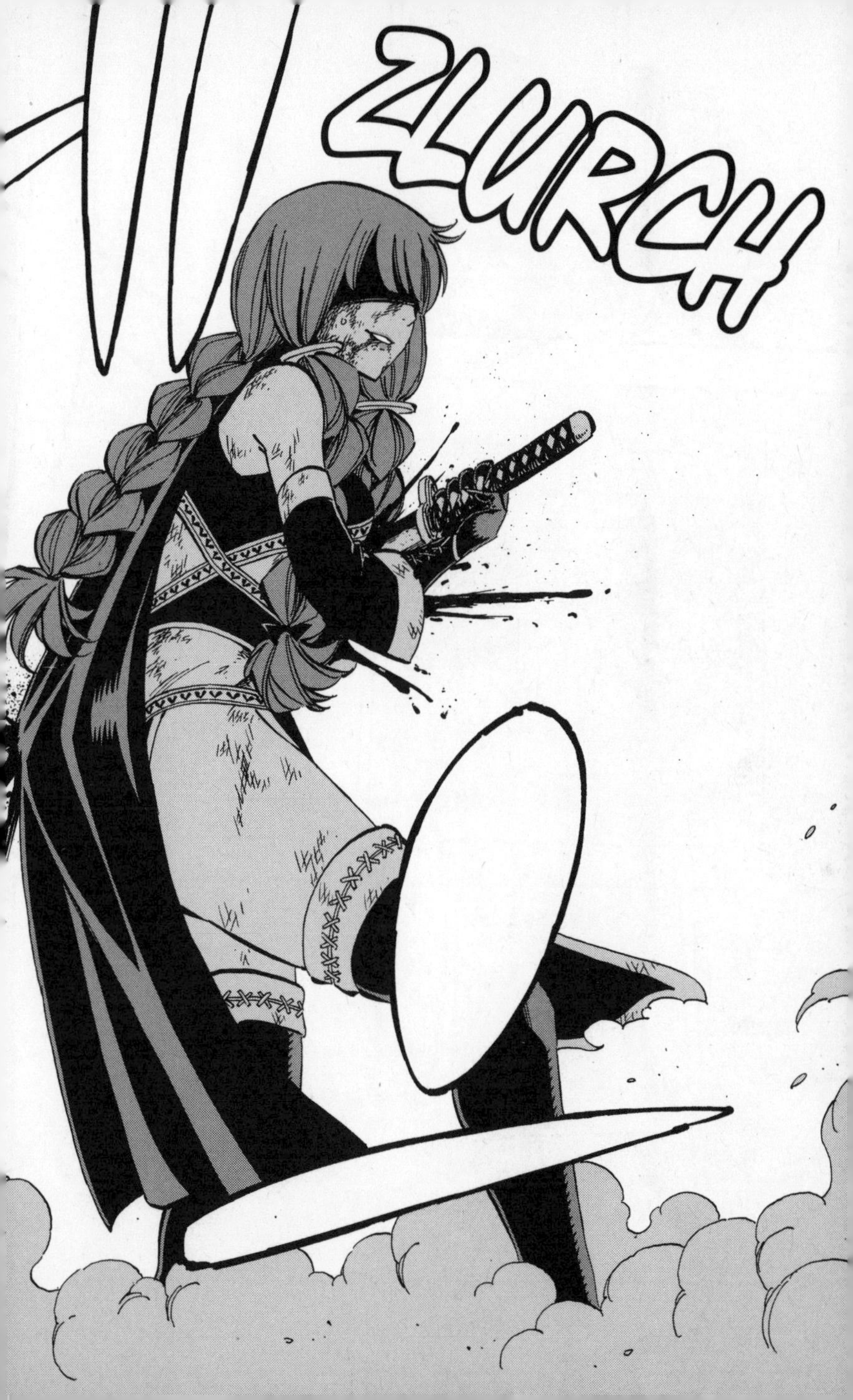
ZLURCH

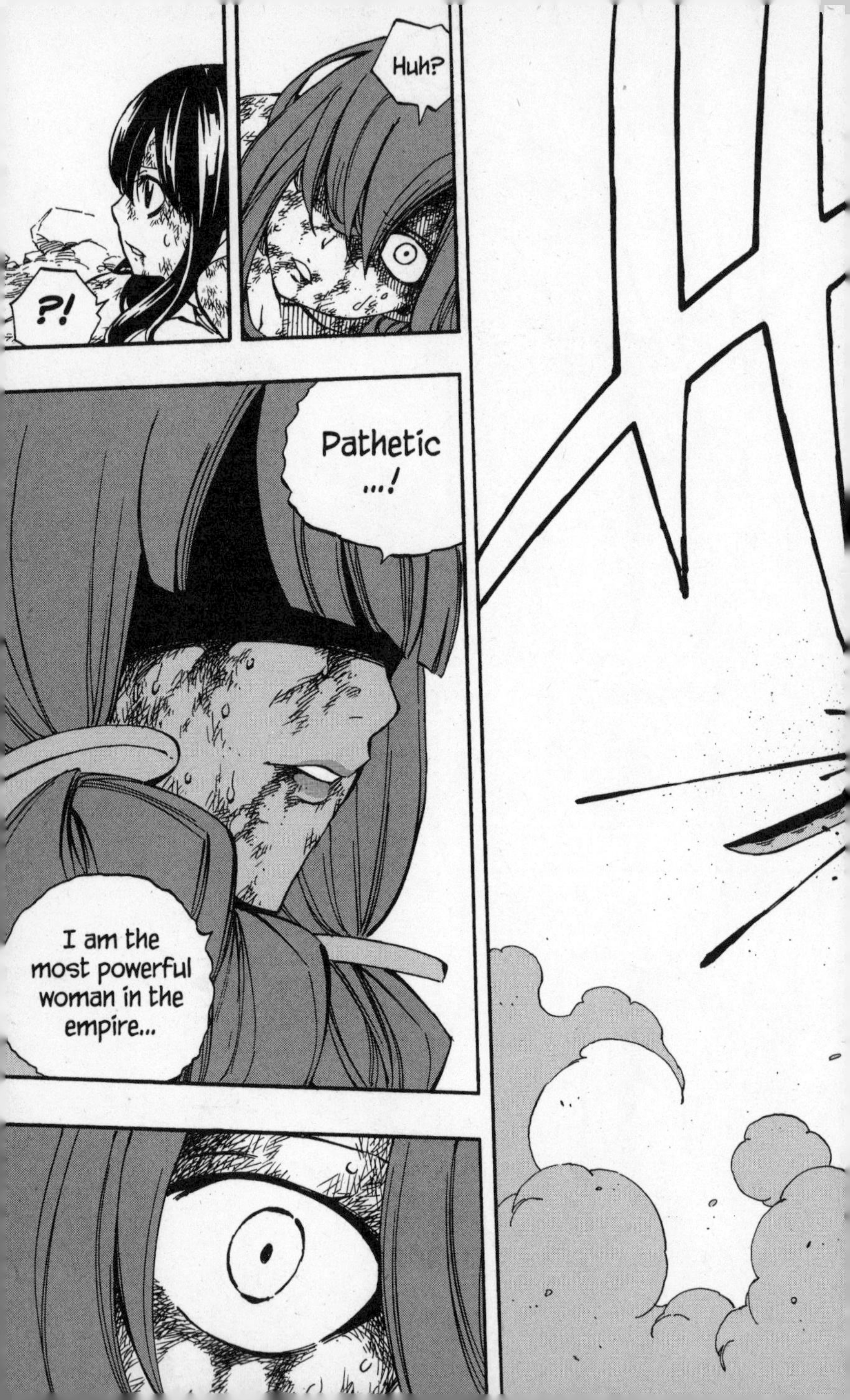
Huh?
?!
Pathetic ...!
I am the most powerful woman in the empire...

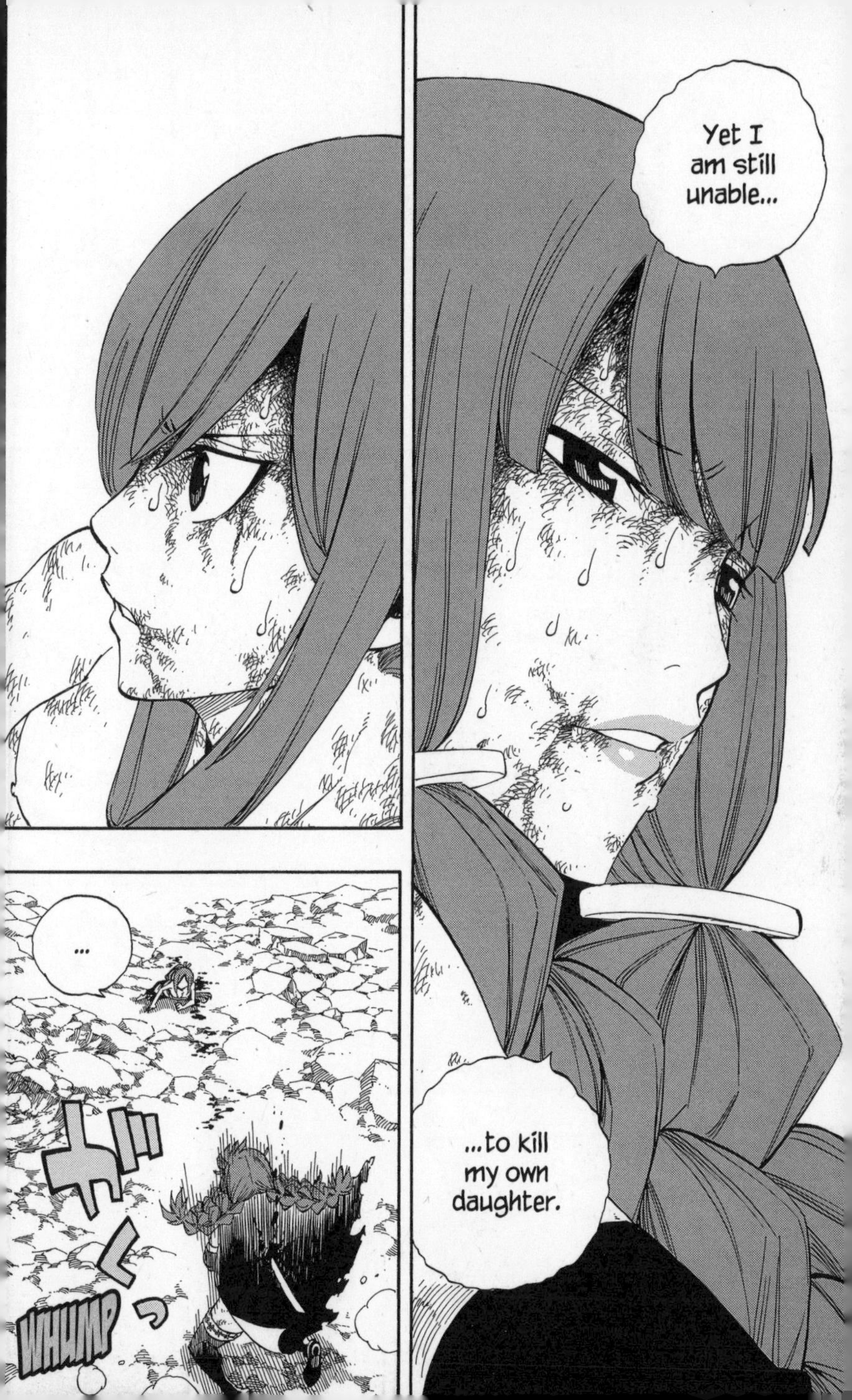
Yet I am still unable...
...to kill my own daughter.
...
WHUMP

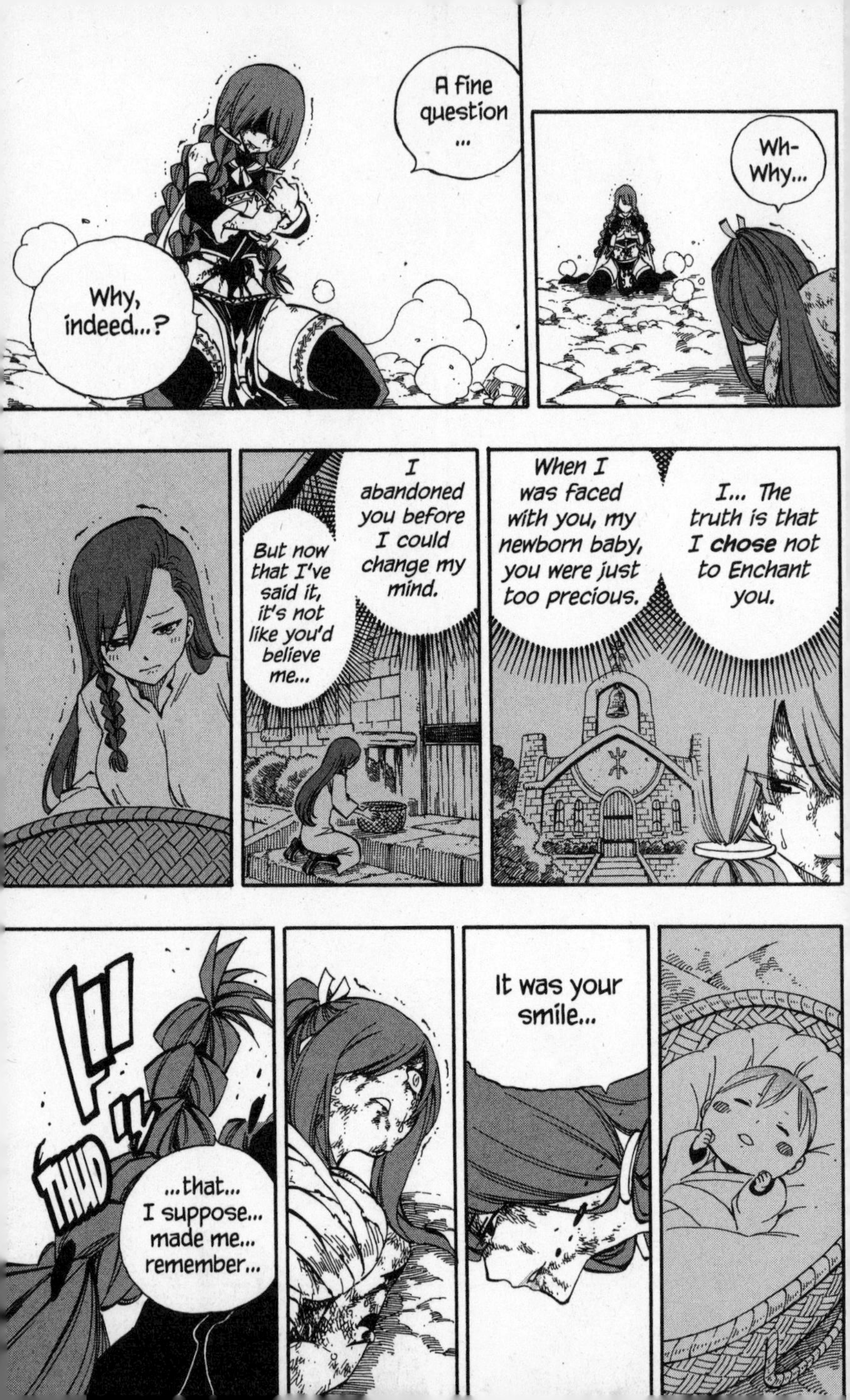
Wh- Why...
A fine question ...
Why, indeed...?
I... The truth is that I **chose** not to Enchant you.
When I was faced with you, my newborn baby, you were just too precious.
I abandoned you before I could change my mind.
But now that I've said it, it's not like you'd believe me...
It was your smile...
!!
THUD
...that... I suppose... made me... remember...

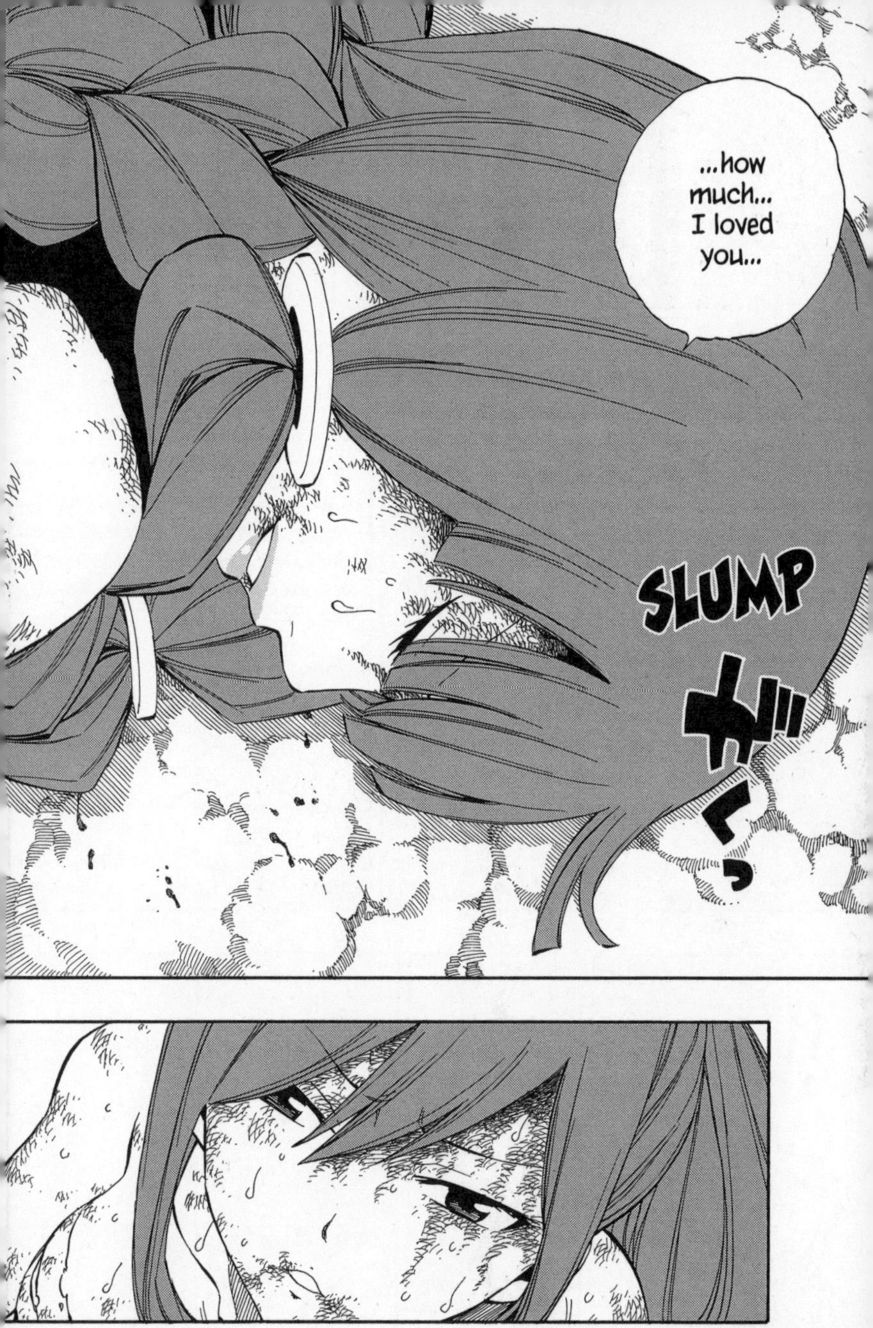
...how much... I loved you...
SLUMP

# FAIRY TAIL
フェアリーテイル

## Chapter 520: Dragon or Demon

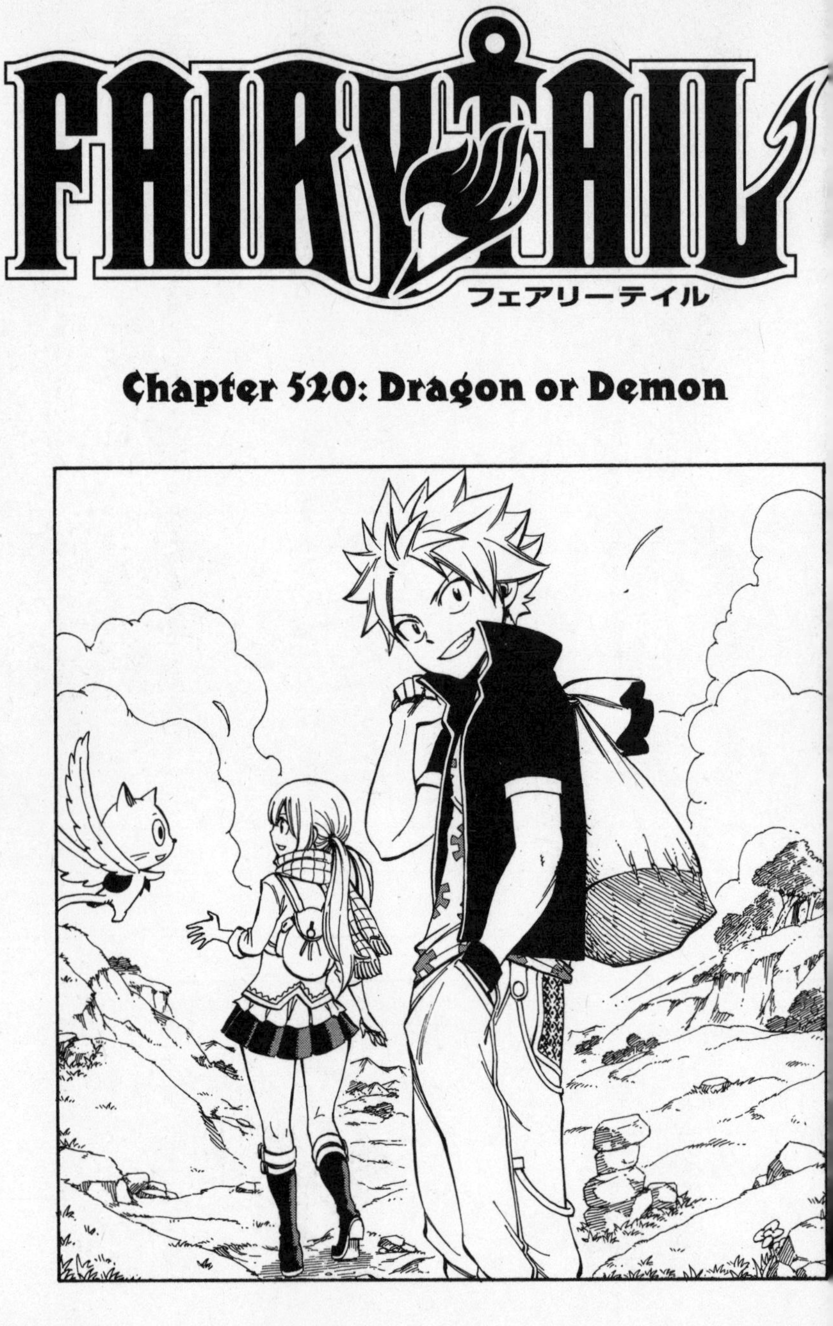

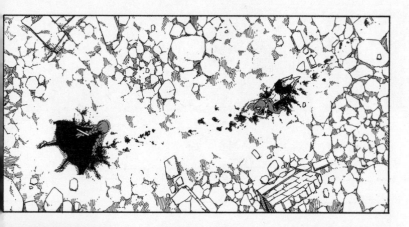

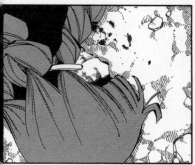

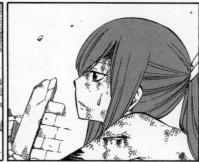

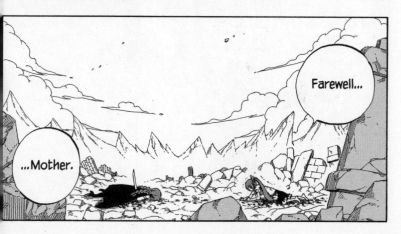

Farewell...

...Mother.

24

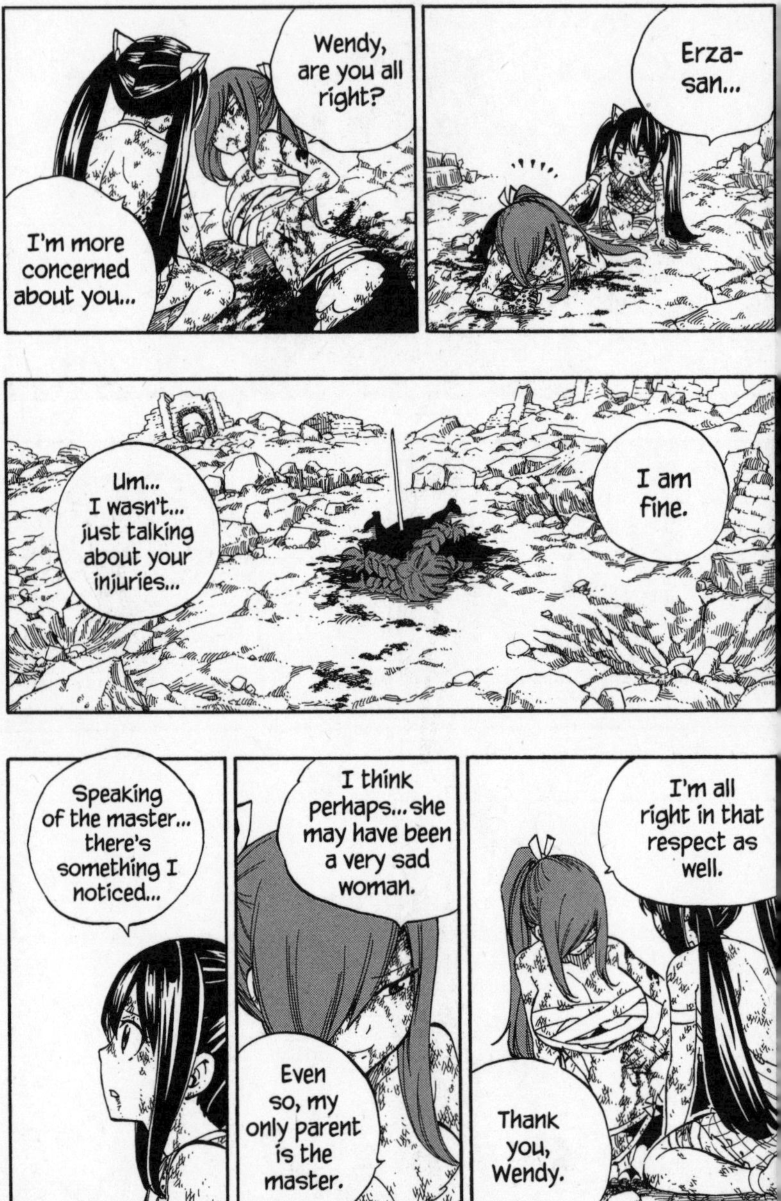

Erza-san...
Wendy, are you all right?
I'm more concerned about you...
I am fine.
Um... I wasn't... just talking about your injuries...
I'm all right in that respect as well.
Thank you, Wendy.
I think perhaps...she may have been a very sad woman.
Even so, my only parent is the master.
Speaking of the master... there's something I noticed...

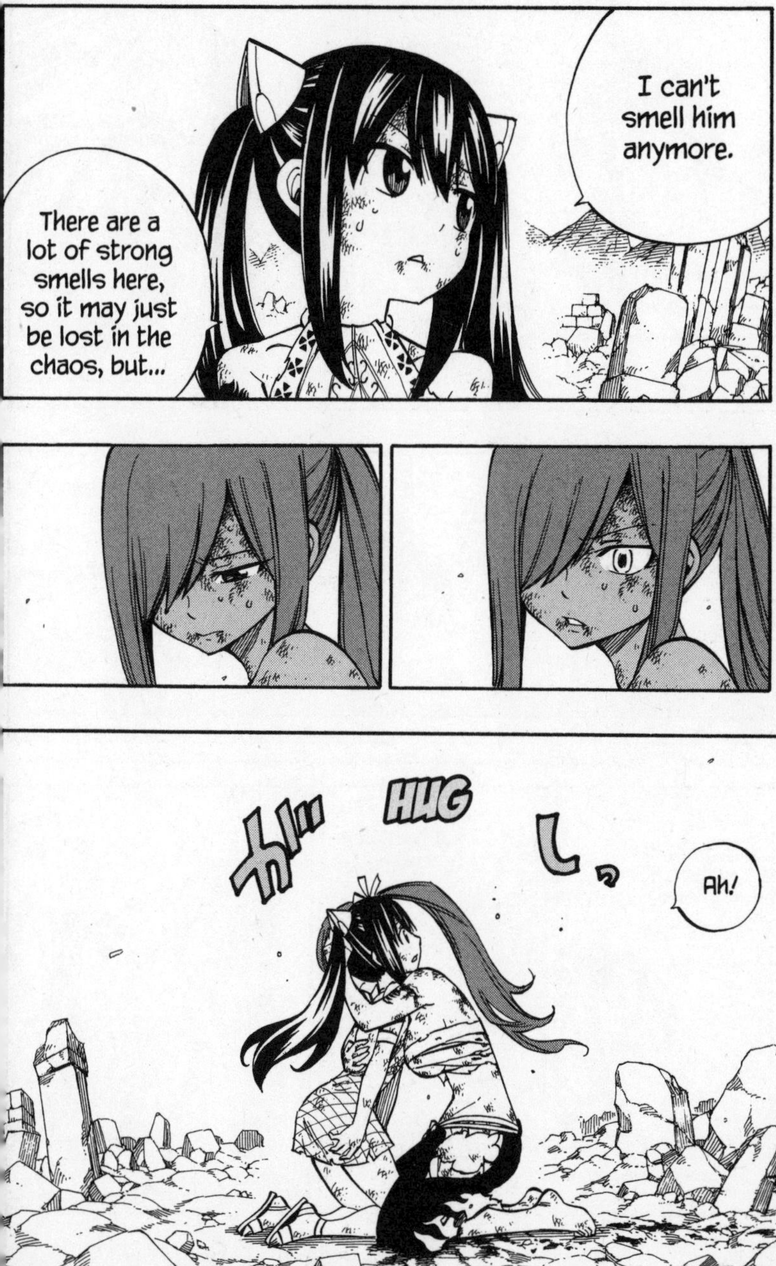
I can't smell him anymore.
There are a lot of strong smells here, so it may just be lost in the chaos, but...
Ah!
HUG

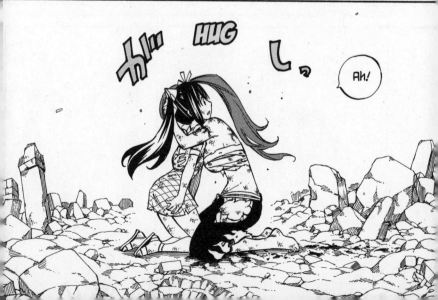

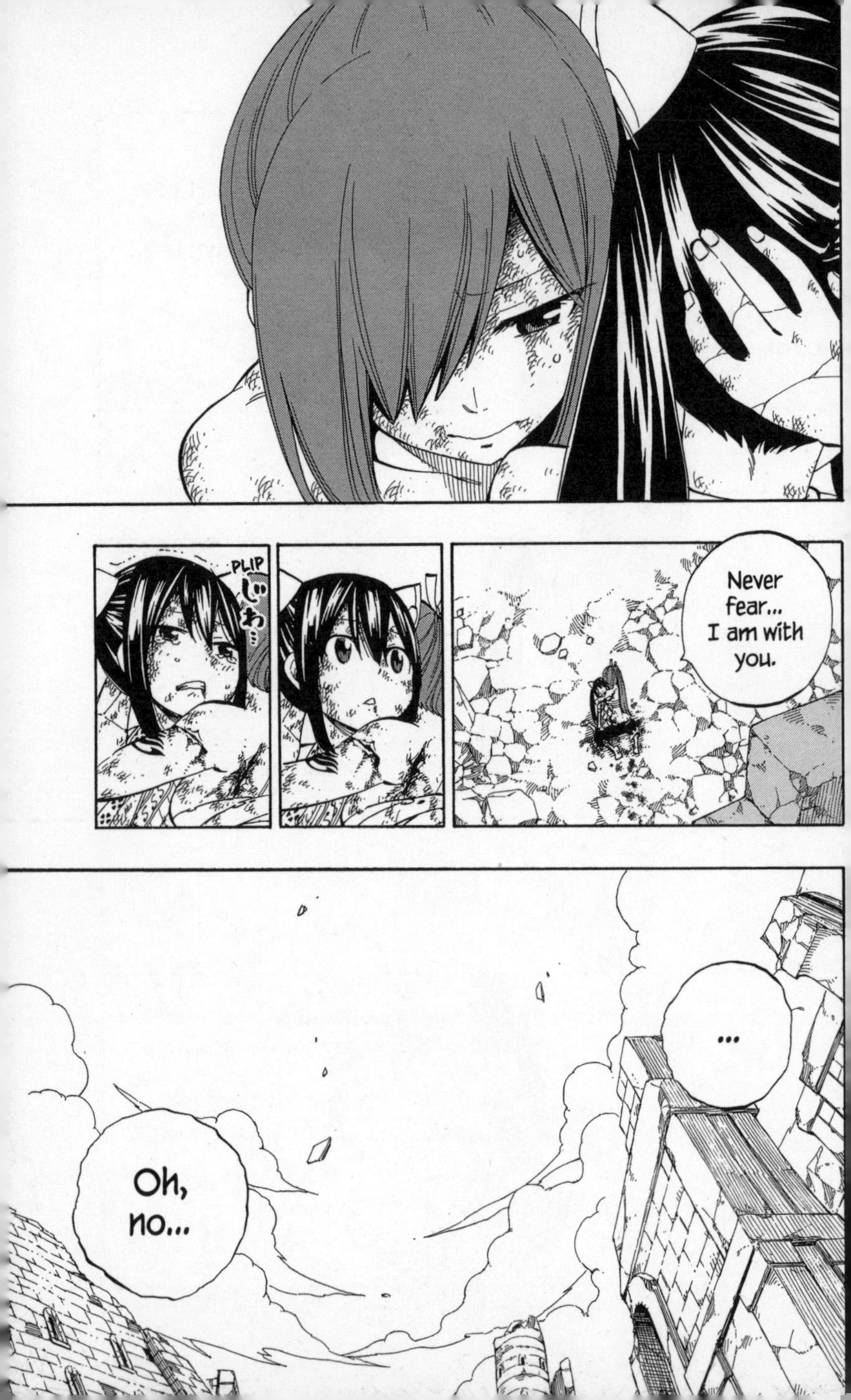
Never fear... I am with you.
PLIP
じわ…
...
Oh, no...

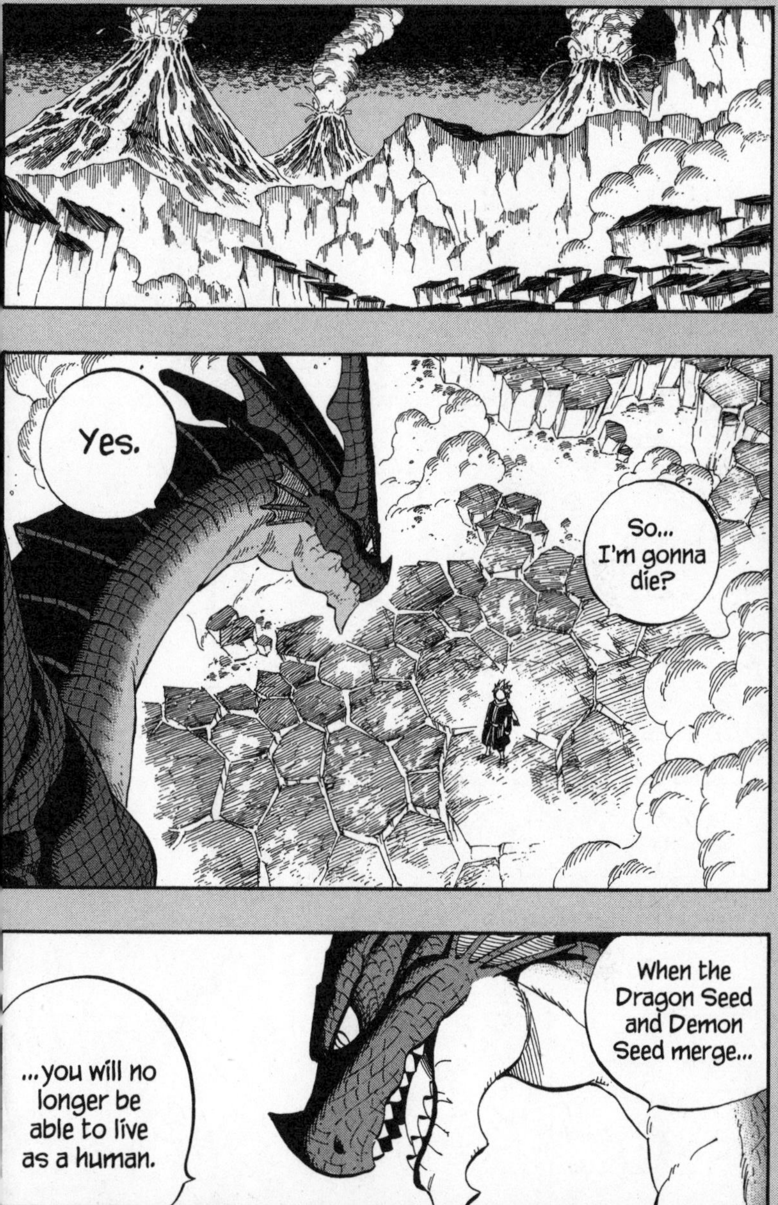
So... I'm gonna die?
Yes.
When the Dragon Seed and Demon Seed merge...
...you will no longer be able to live as a human.

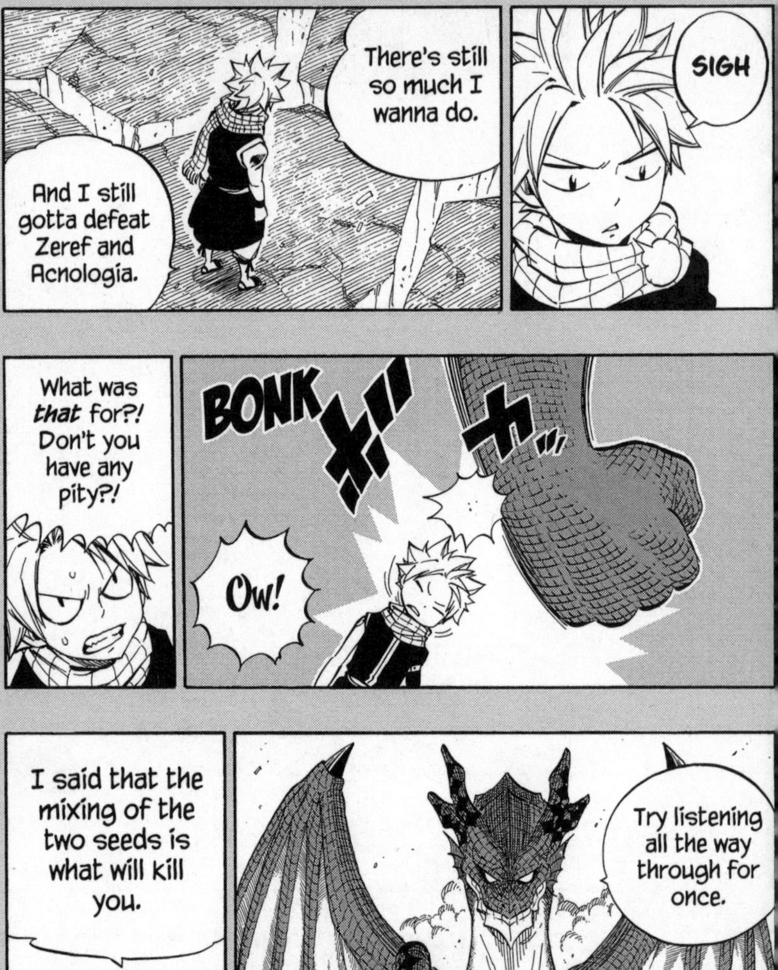
SIGH
There's still so much I wanna do.
And I still gotta defeat Zeref and Acnologia.
BONK
Ow!
What was *that* for?! Don't you have any pity?!
Try listening all the way through for once.
?
I said that the mixing of the two seeds is what will kill you.

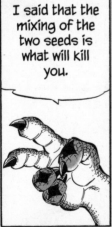

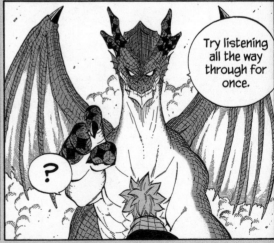

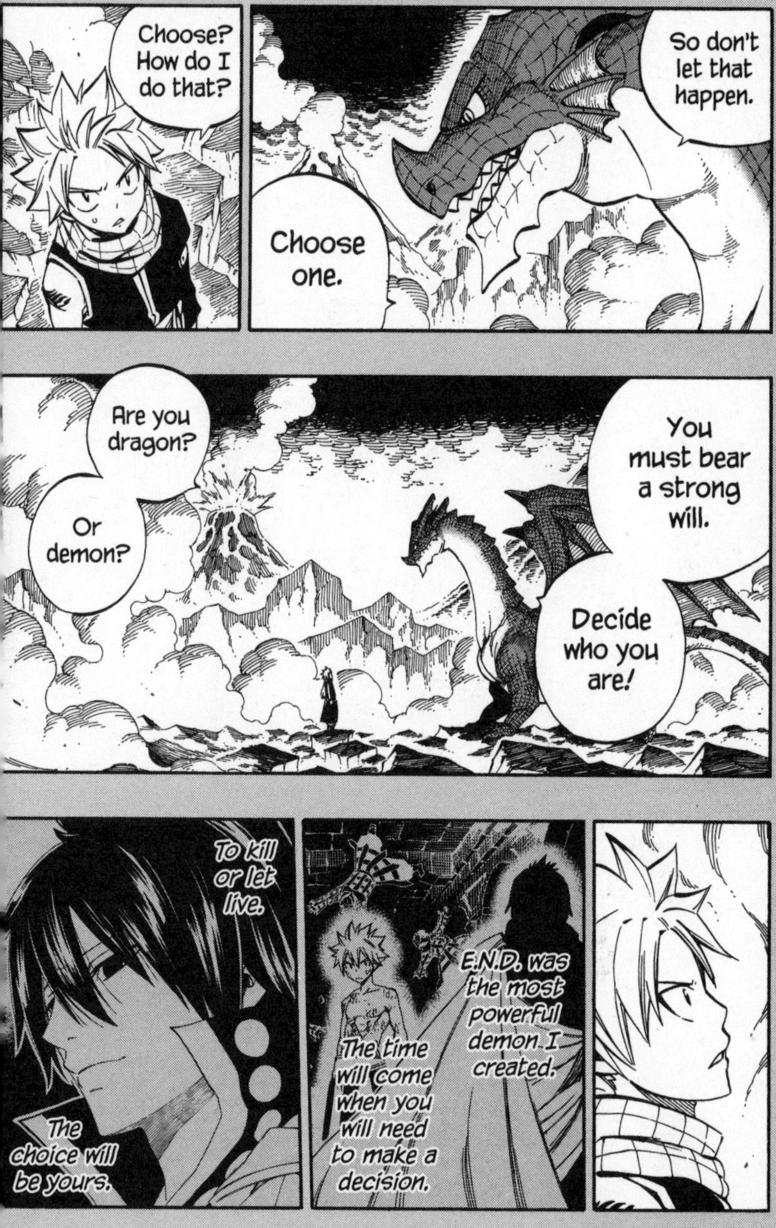
So don't let that happen.
Choose one.
Choose? How do I do that?
You must bear a strong will.
Decide who you are!
Are you dragon?
Or demon?
E.N.D. was the most powerful demon I created.
The time will come when you will need to make a decision.
To kill or let live.
The choice will be yours.

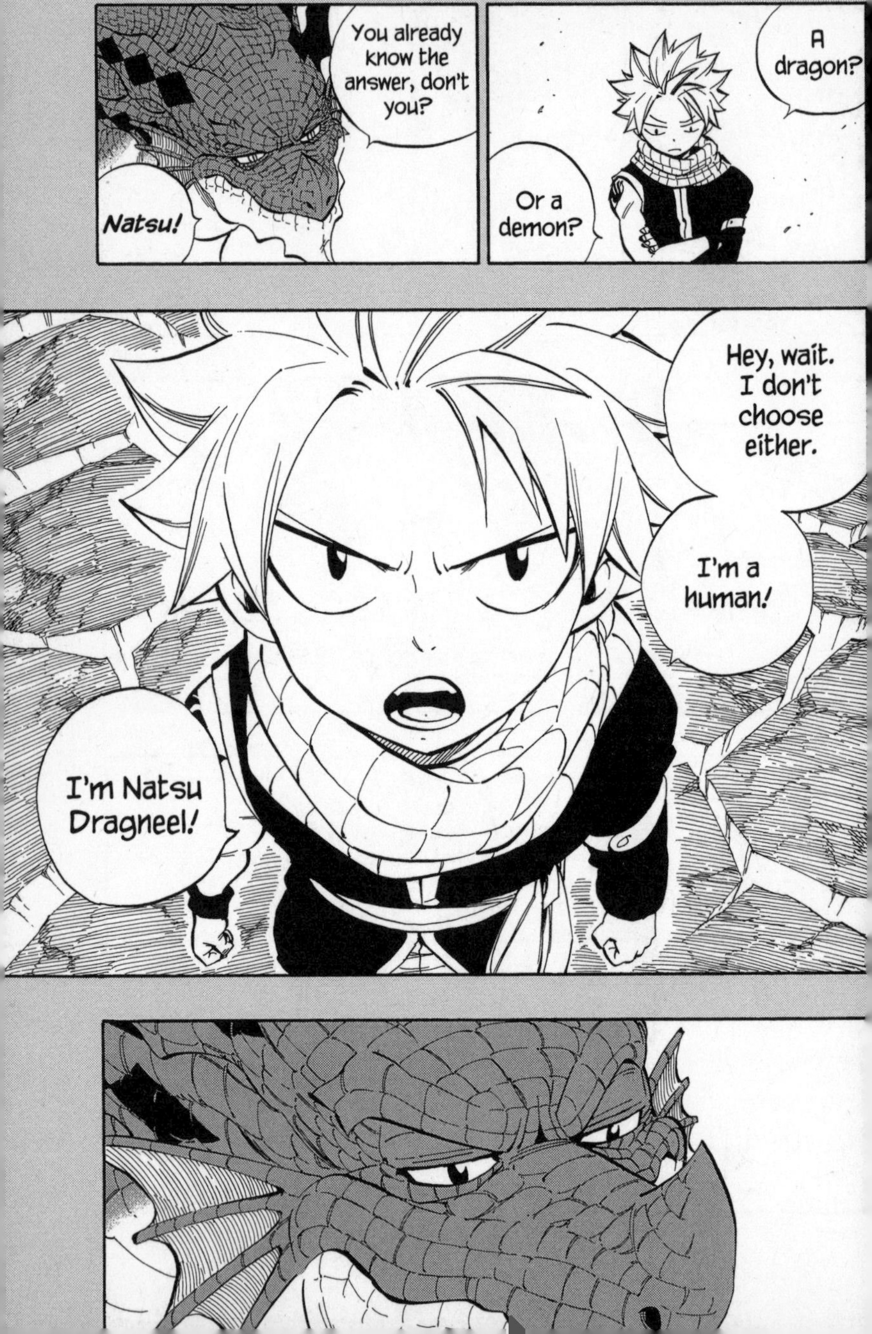
A dragon?
Or a demon?
You already know the answer, don't you?
Natsu!
Hey, wait. I don't choose either.
I'm a human!
I'm Natsu Dragneel!

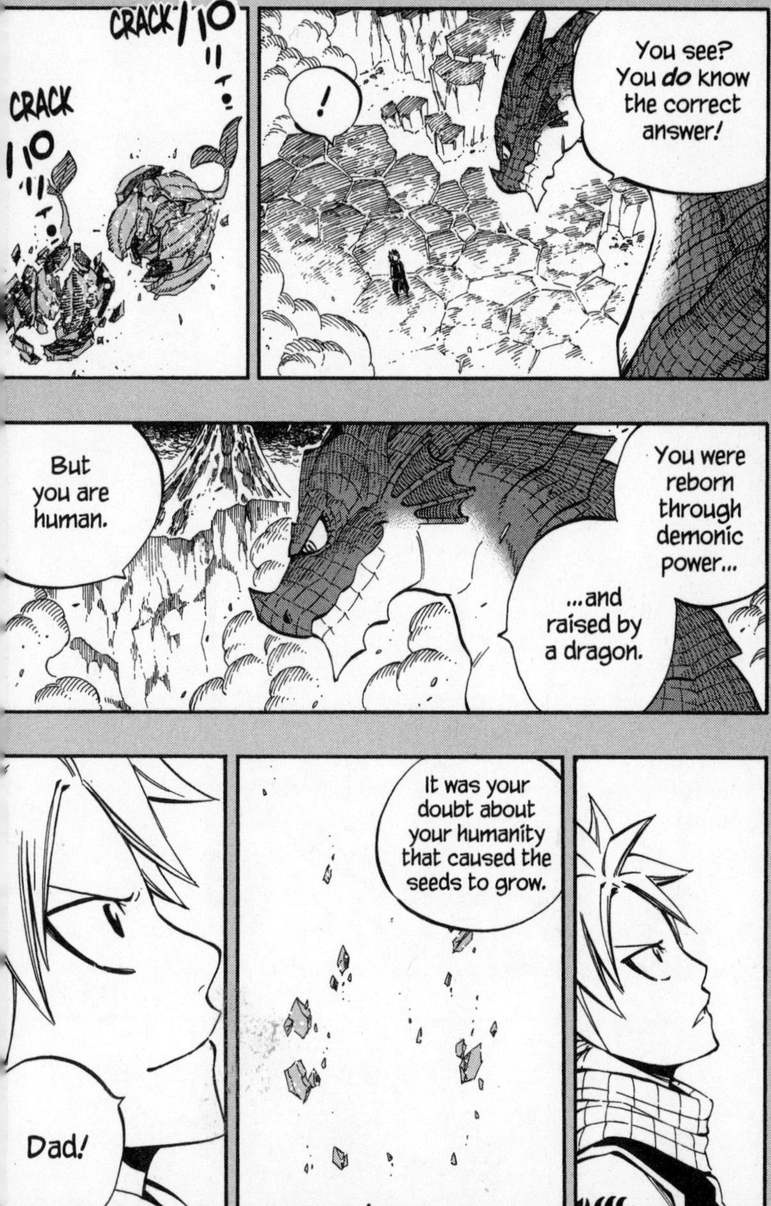
You see? You do know the correct answer!
!
CRACK
CRACK
You were reborn through demonic power...
...and raised by a dragon.
But you are human.
It was your doubt about your humanity that caused the seeds to grow.
Dad!

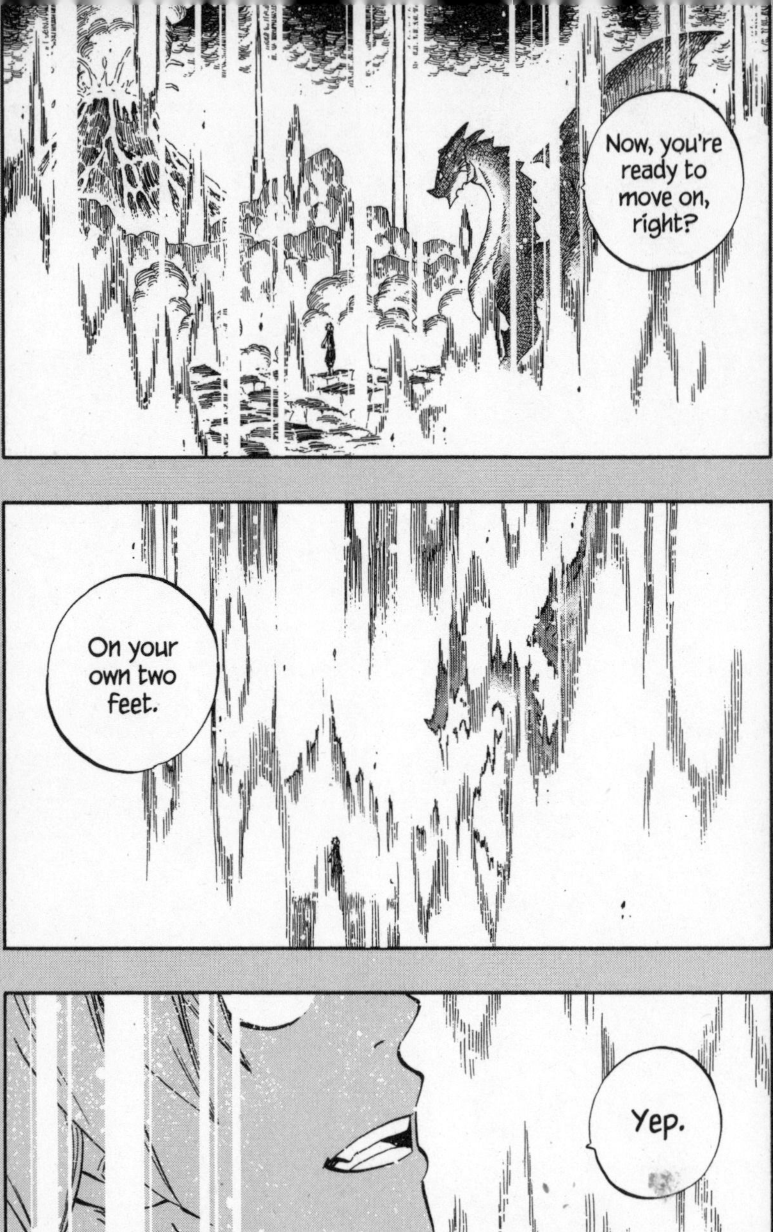
Now, you're ready to move on, right?
On your own two feet.
Yep.

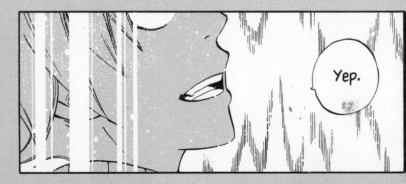

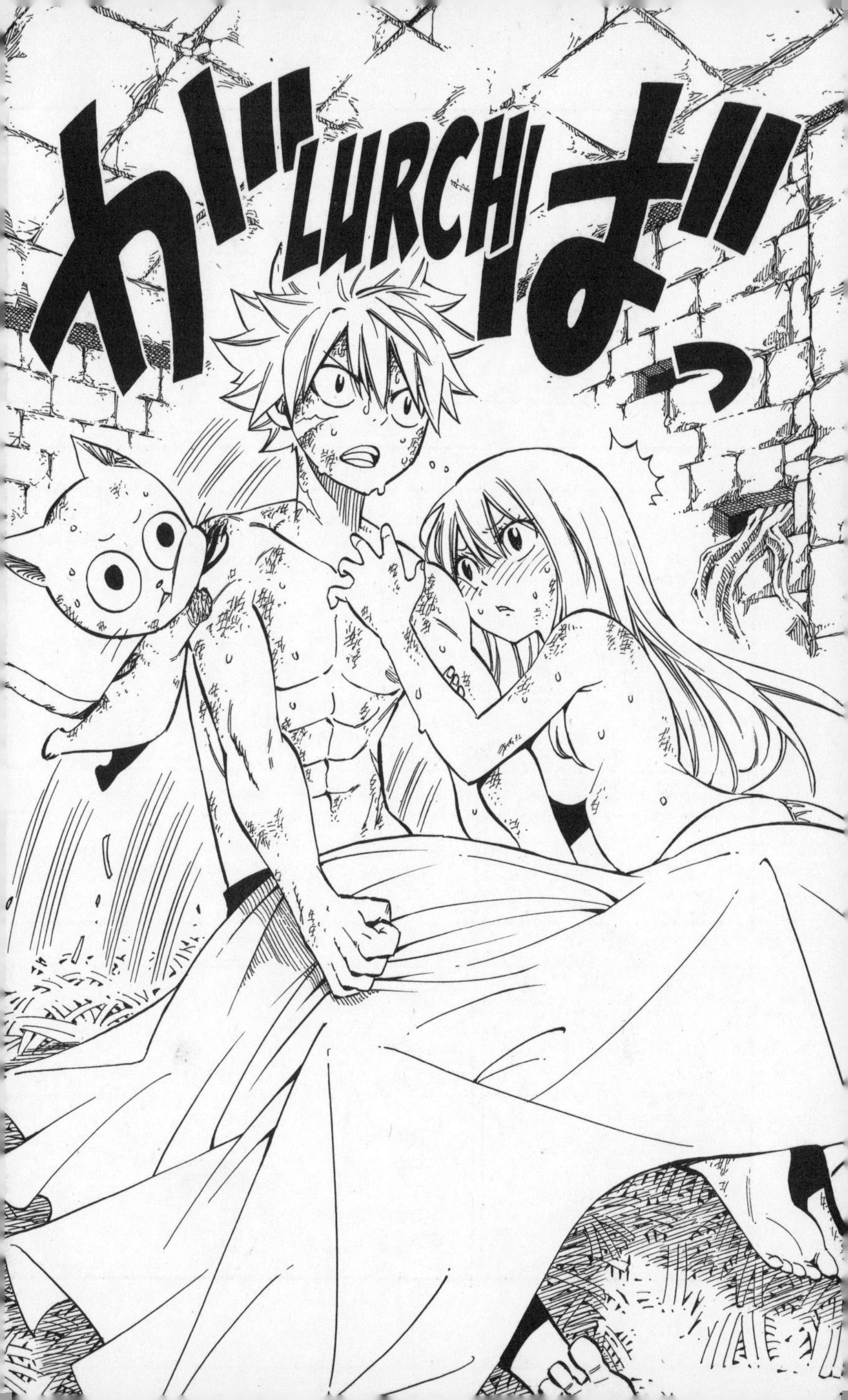
LURCH!

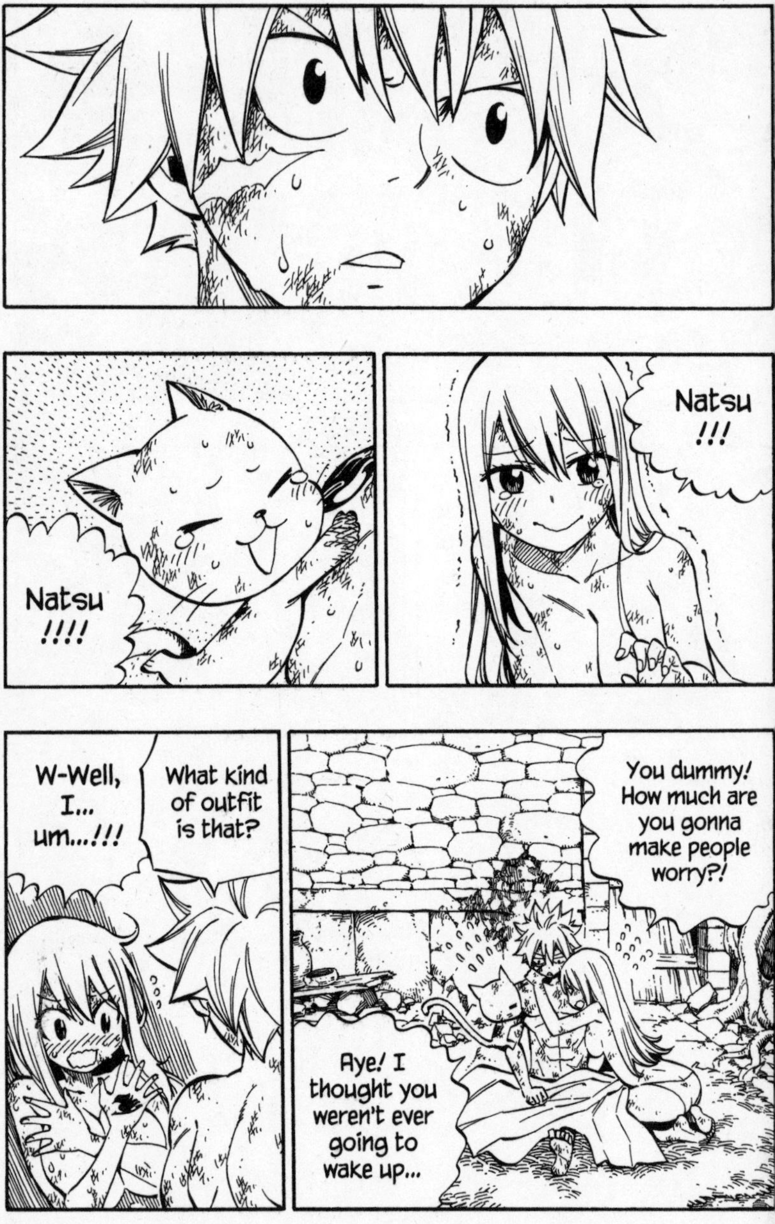
Natsu !!!
Natsu !!!!
You dummy! How much are you gonna make people worry?!
Aye! I thought you weren't ever going to wake up...
What kind of outfit is that?
W-Well, I... um...!!!

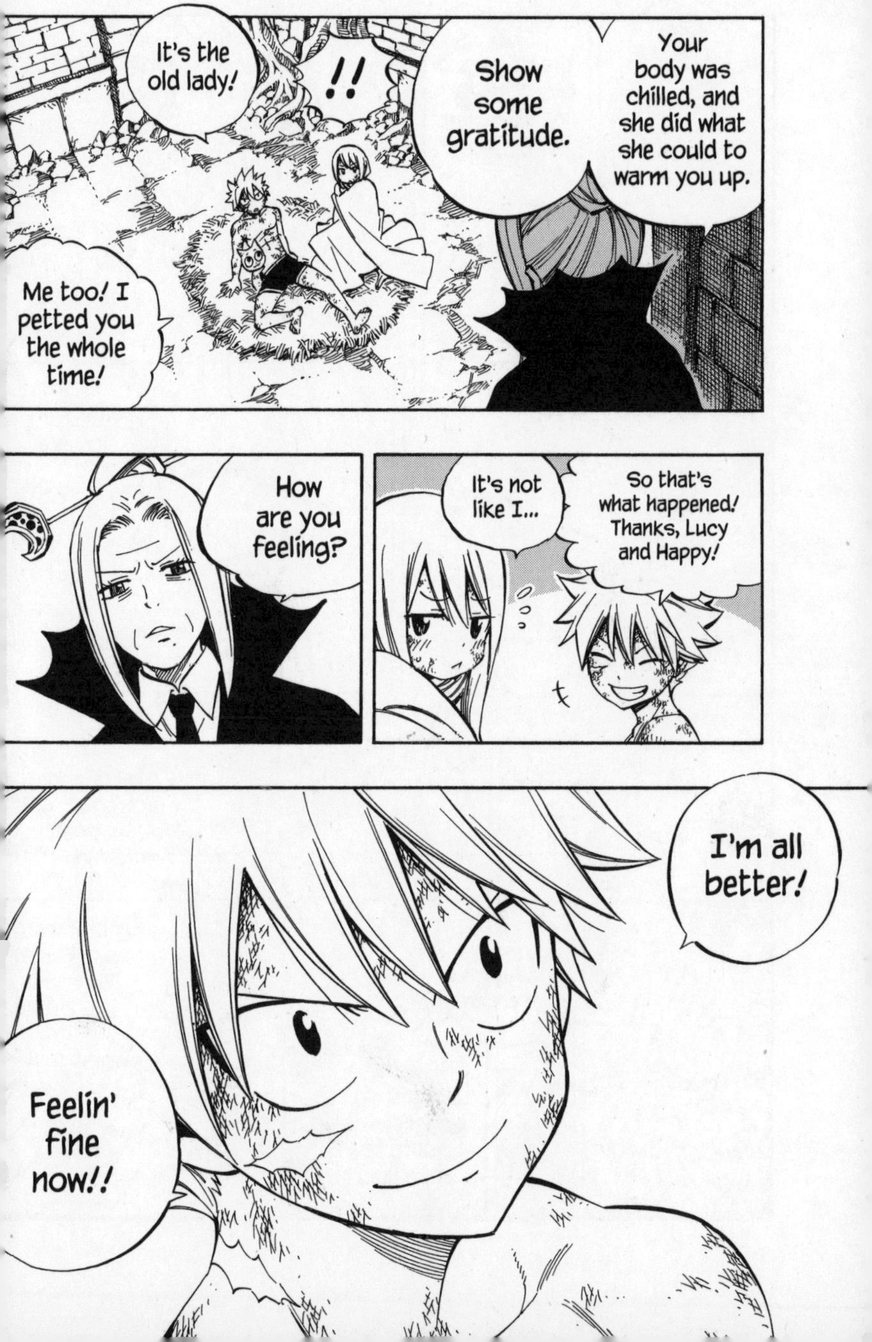
Your body was chilled, and she did what she could to warm you up.
Show some gratitude.
!!
It's the old lady!
Me too! I petted you the whole time!
So that's what happened! Thanks, Lucy and Happy!
It's not like I...
How are you feeling?
I'm all better!
Feelin' fine now!!

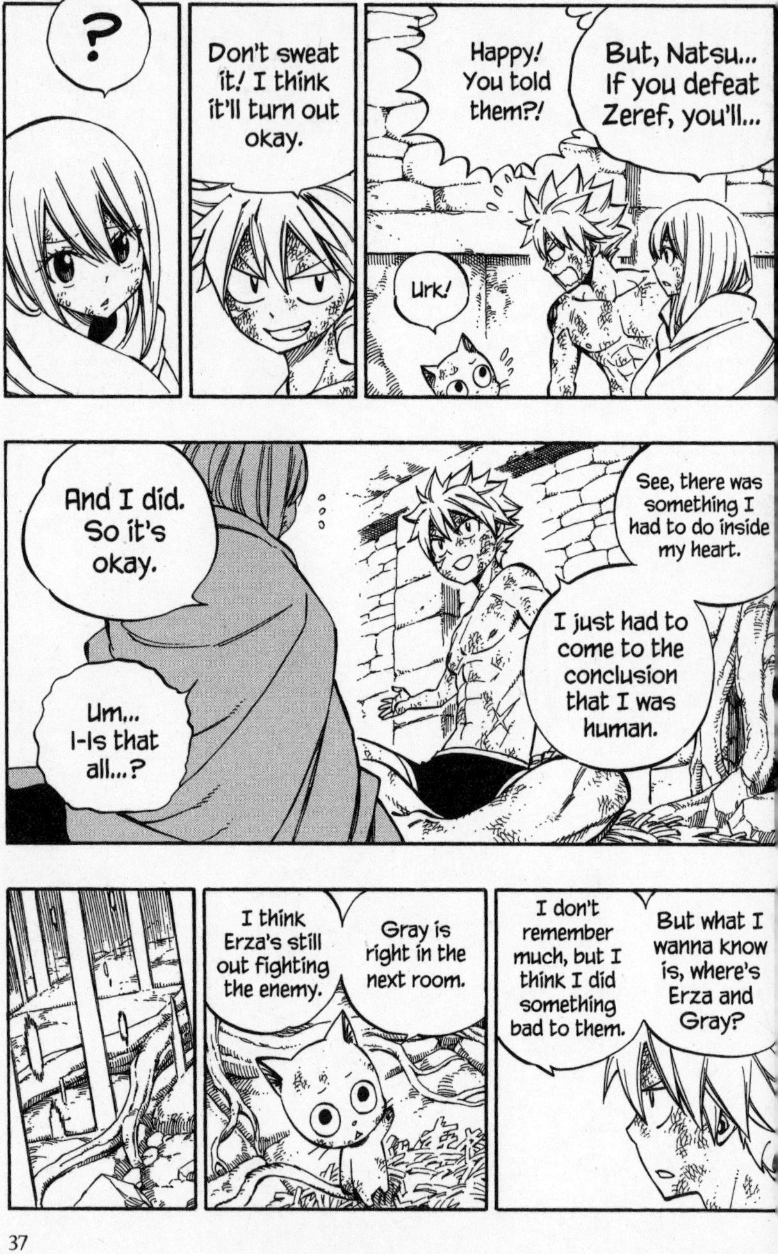
But, Natsu... If you defeat Zeref, you'll...
Happy! You told them?!
Urk!
Don't sweat it! I think it'll turn out okay.
?
See, there was something I had to do inside my heart.
I just had to come to the conclusion that I was human.
And I did. So it's okay.
Um... I-Is that all...?
But what I wanna know is, where's Erza and Gray?
I don't remember much, but I think I did something bad to them.
Gray is right in the next room.
I think Erza's still out fighting the enemy.

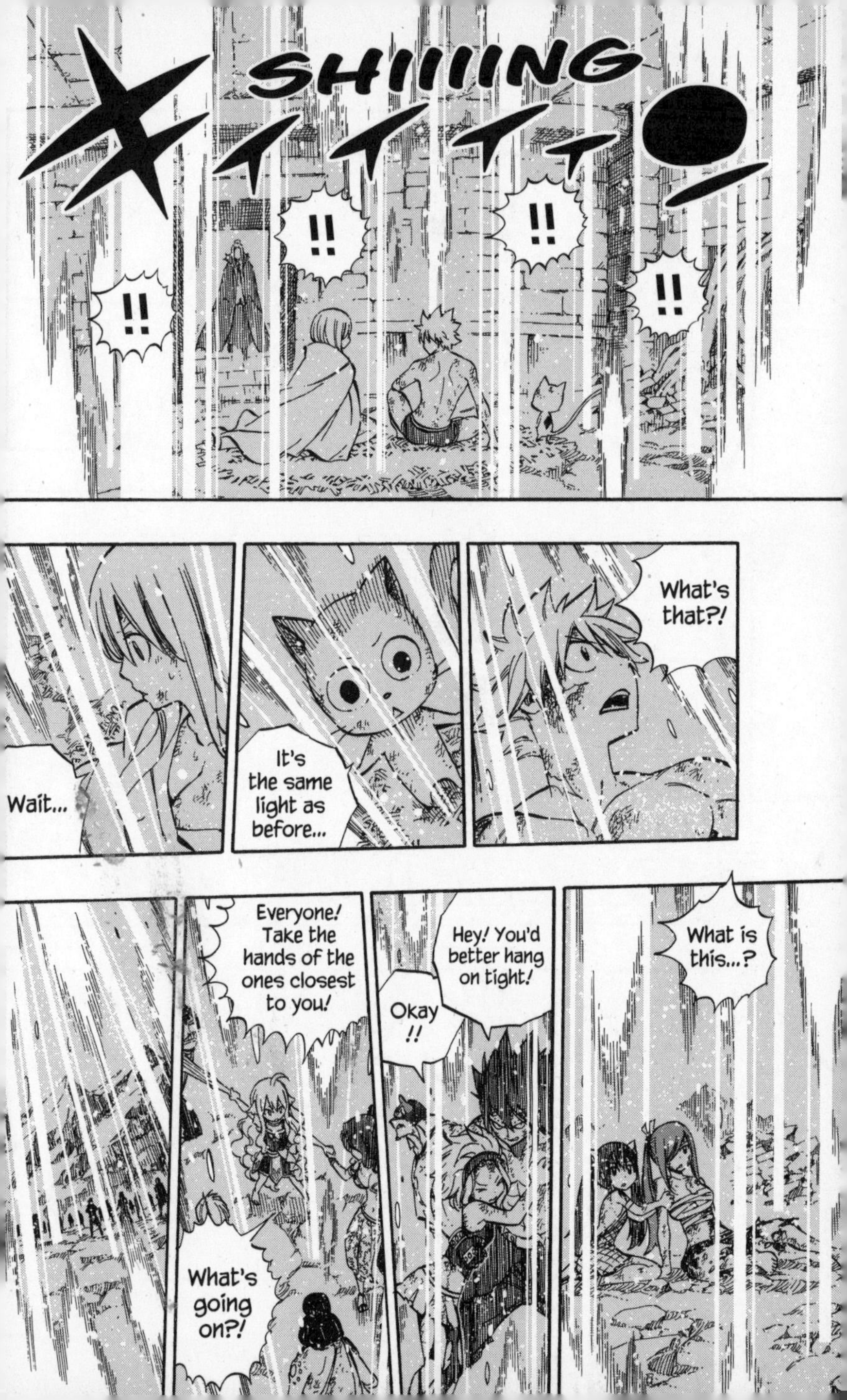
SHIIIING
!!
!!
!!
!!
What's that?!
It's the same light as before...
Wait...
What is this...?
Hey! You'd better hang on tight!
Okay!!
Everyone! Take the hands of the ones closest to you!
What's going on?!

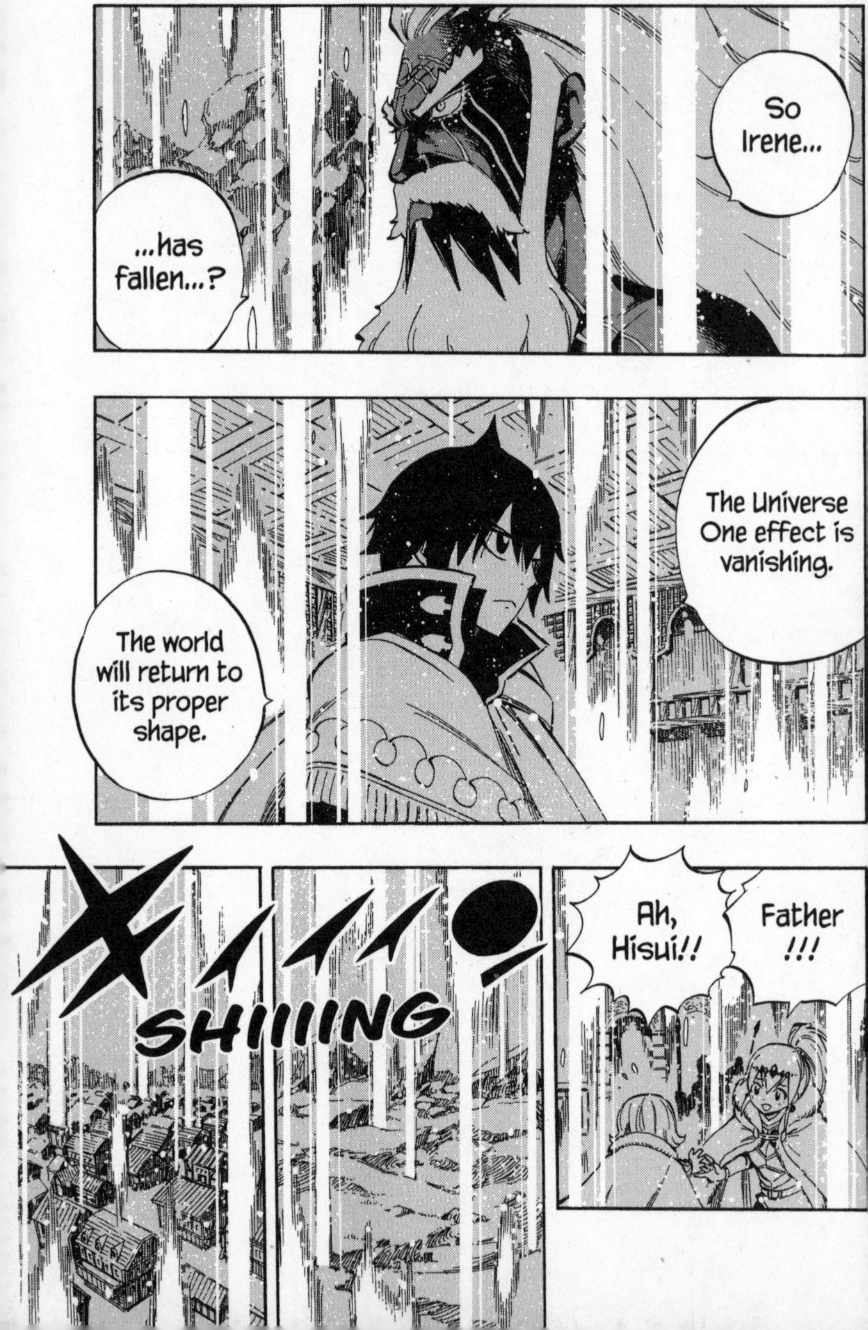
So Irene...
...has fallen...?
The Universe One effect is vanishing.
The world will return to its proper shape.
Father!!!
Ah, Hisui!!
SHIIIING

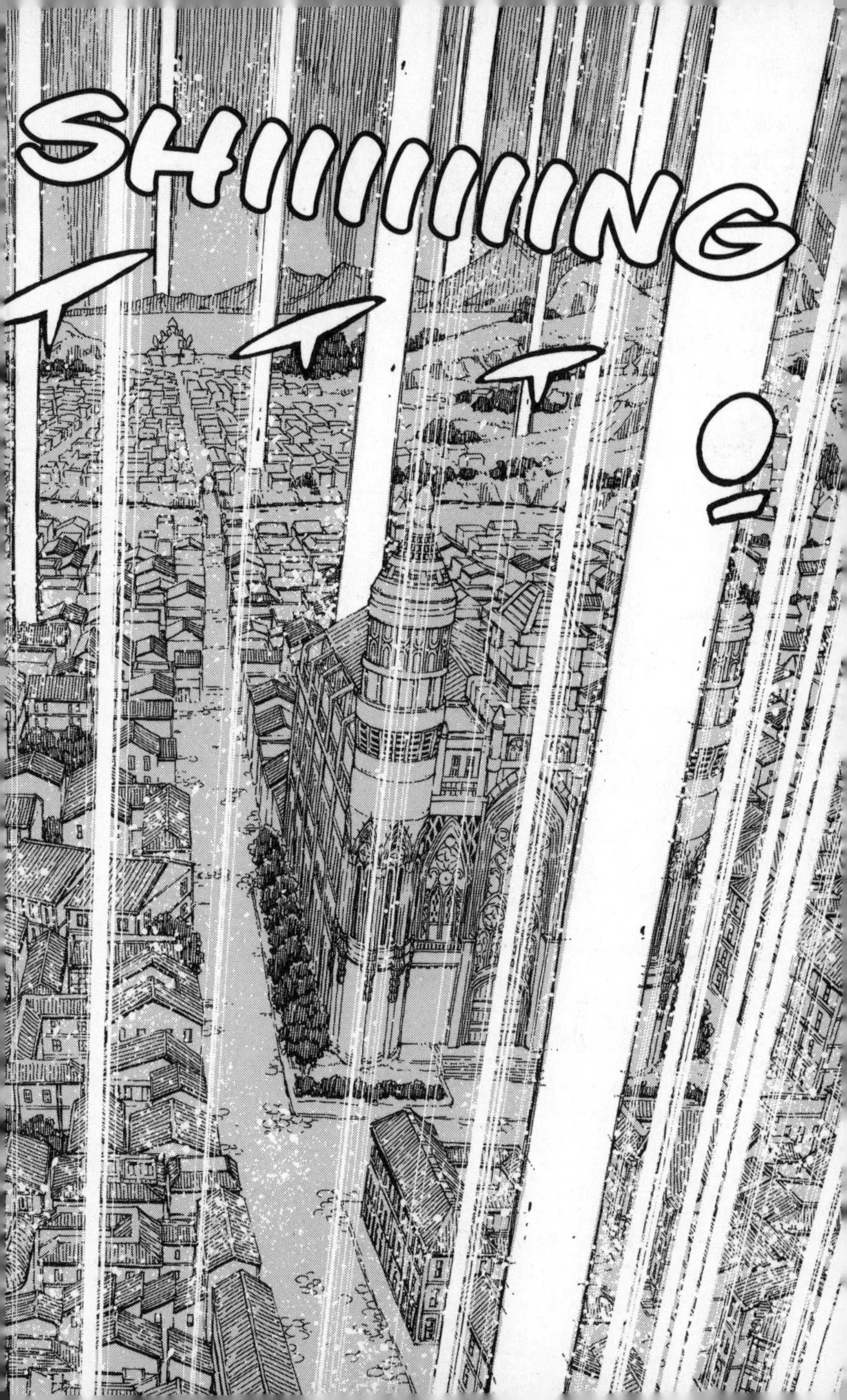
SHIIIIIIING

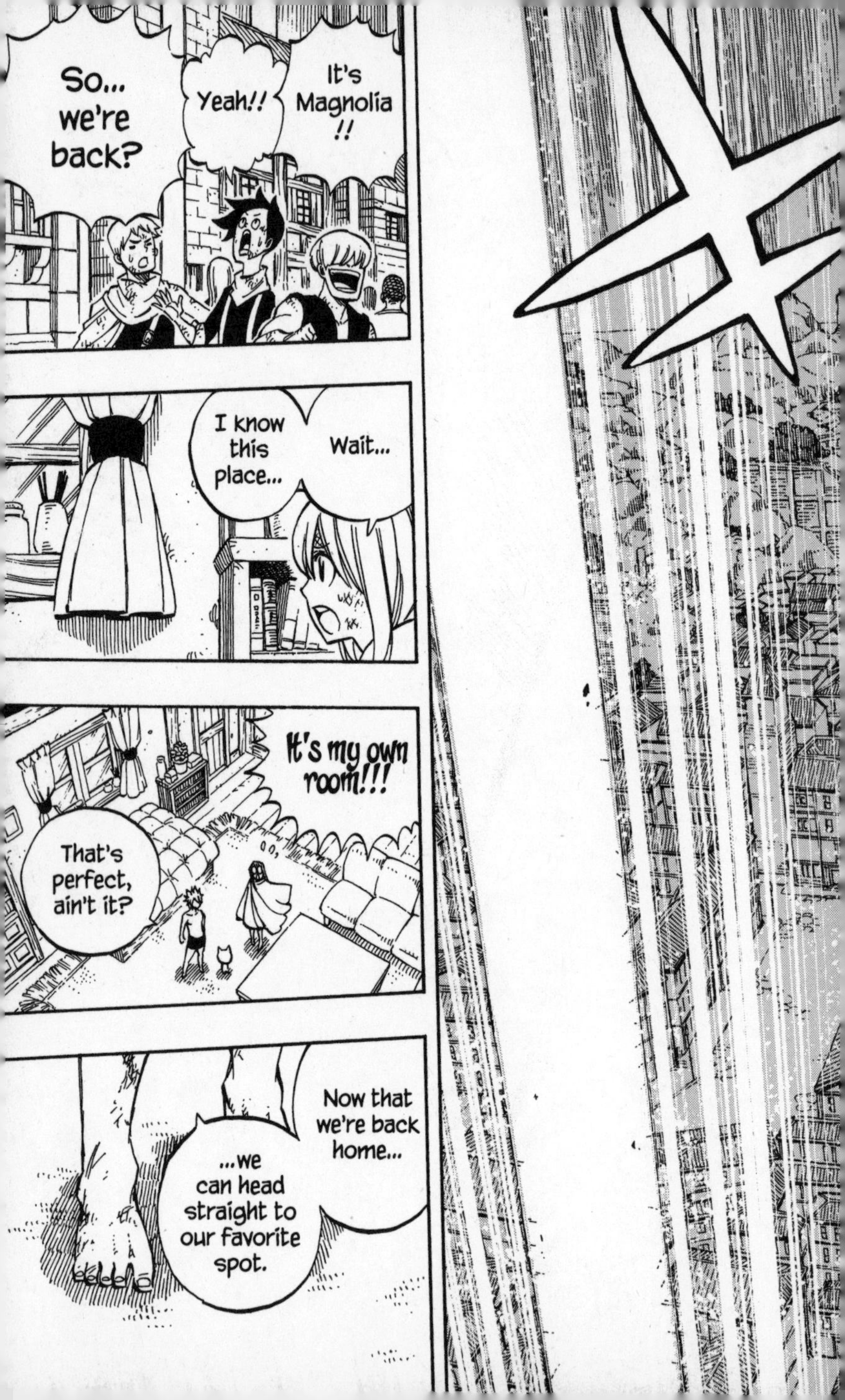
It's Magnolia!!
Yeah!!
So... we're back?
Wait...
I know this place...
It's my own room!!!
That's perfect, ain't it?
Now that we're back home...
...we can head straight to our favorite spot.

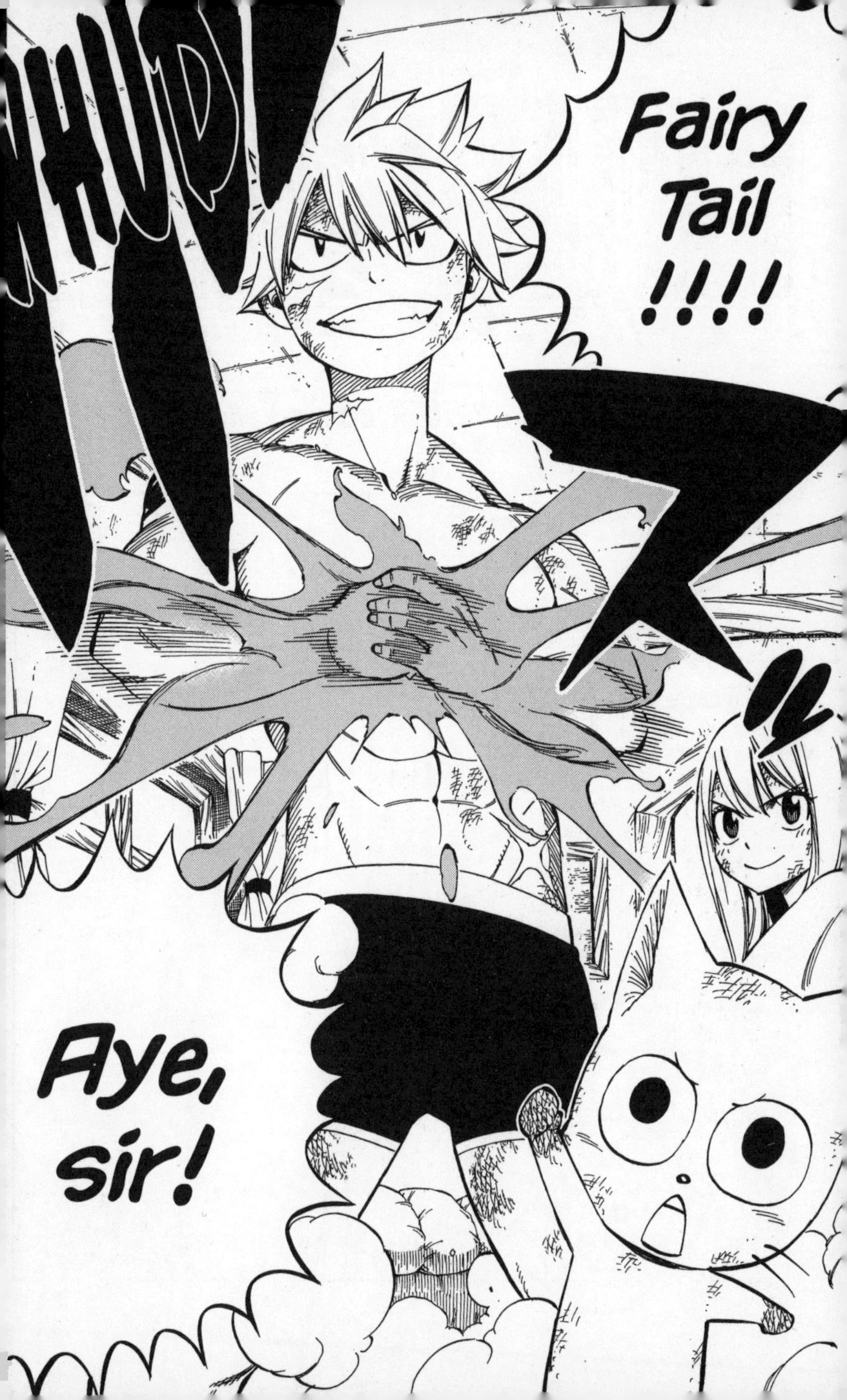
Fairy Tail !!!!
HUD!
!!
Aye, sir!

# FAIRY TAIL

フェアリーテイル

## Chapter 521: The Strongest Wizard

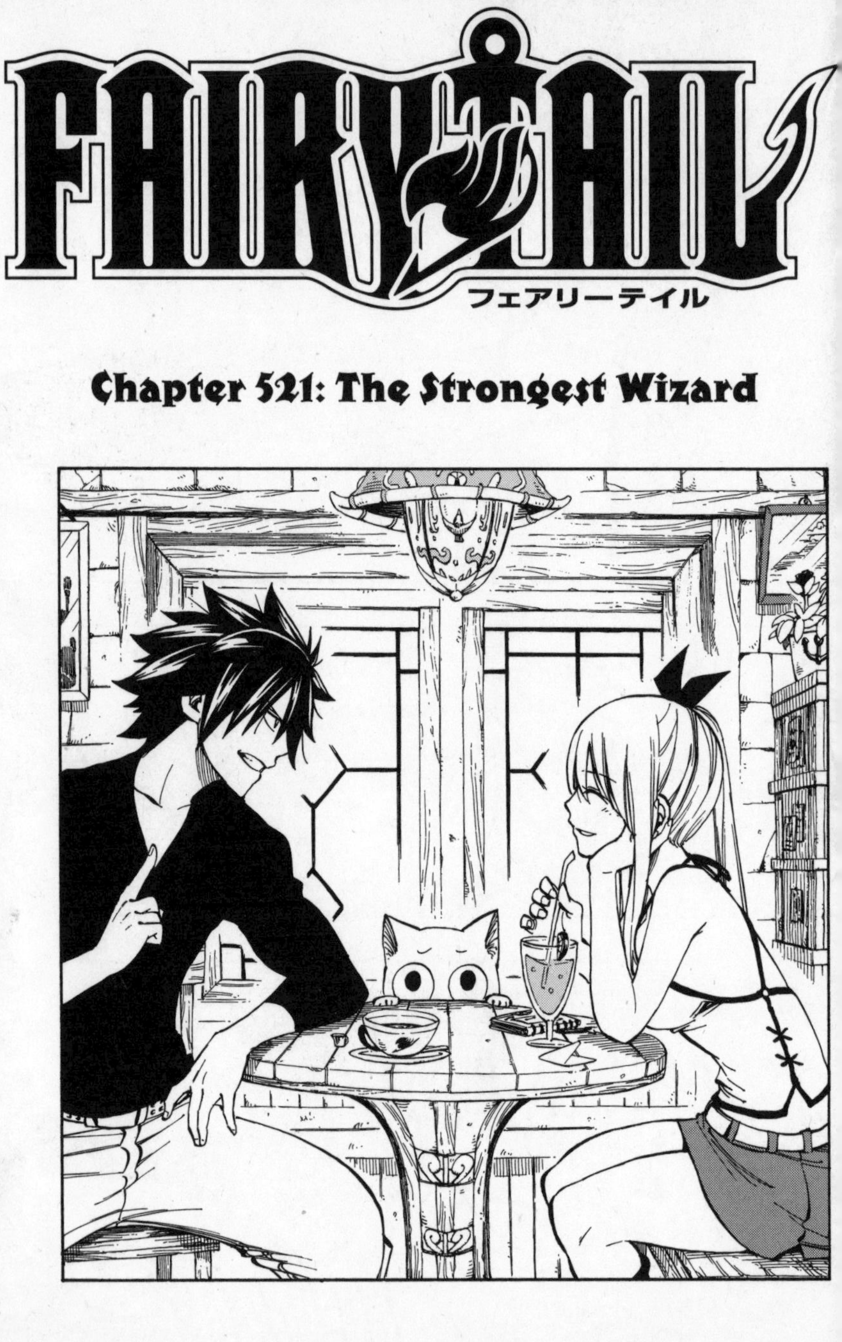

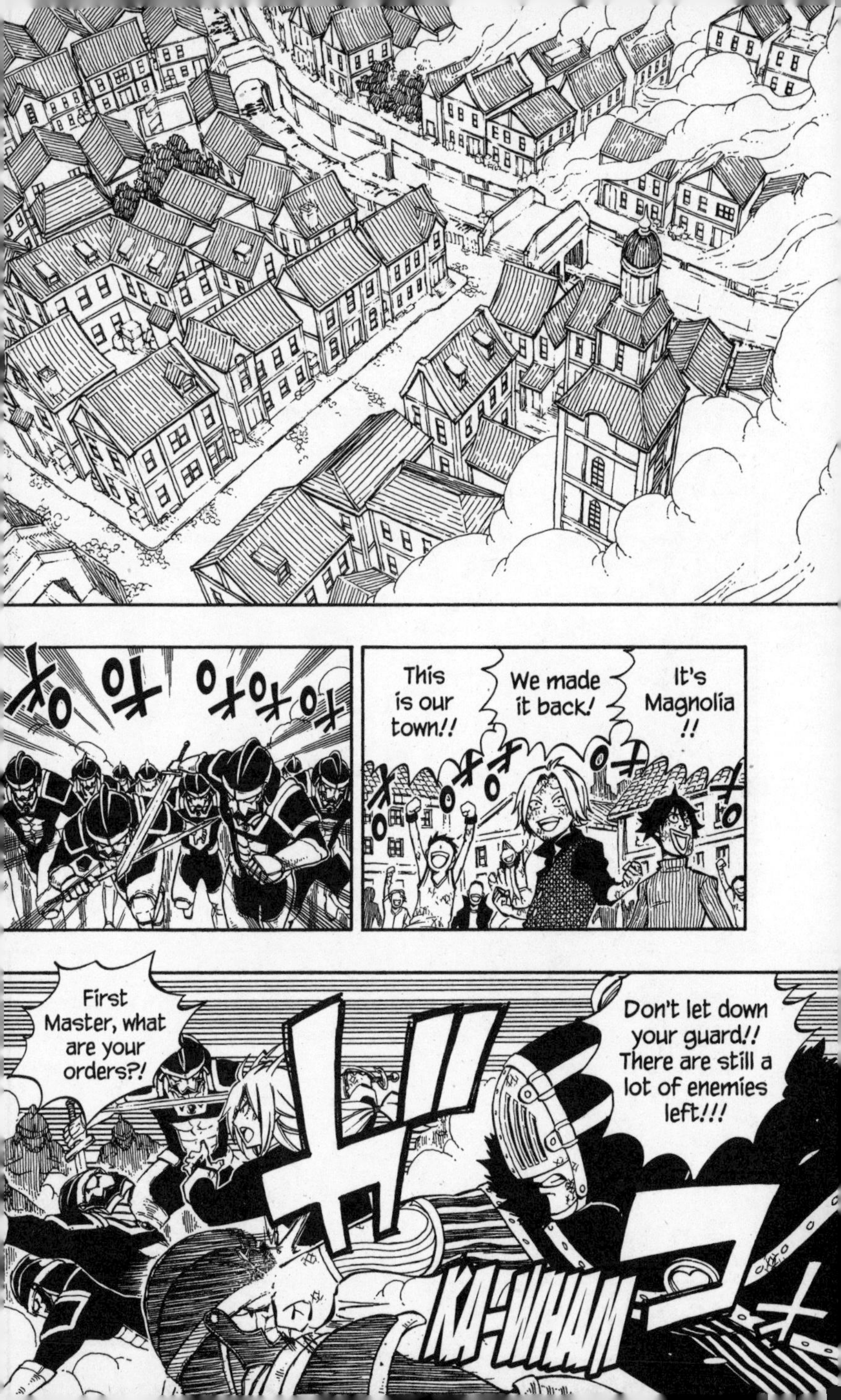
It's Magnolia!!
We made it back!
This is our town!!
Don't let down your guard!! There are still a lot of enemies left!!!
First Master, what are your orders?!
KA-WHAM

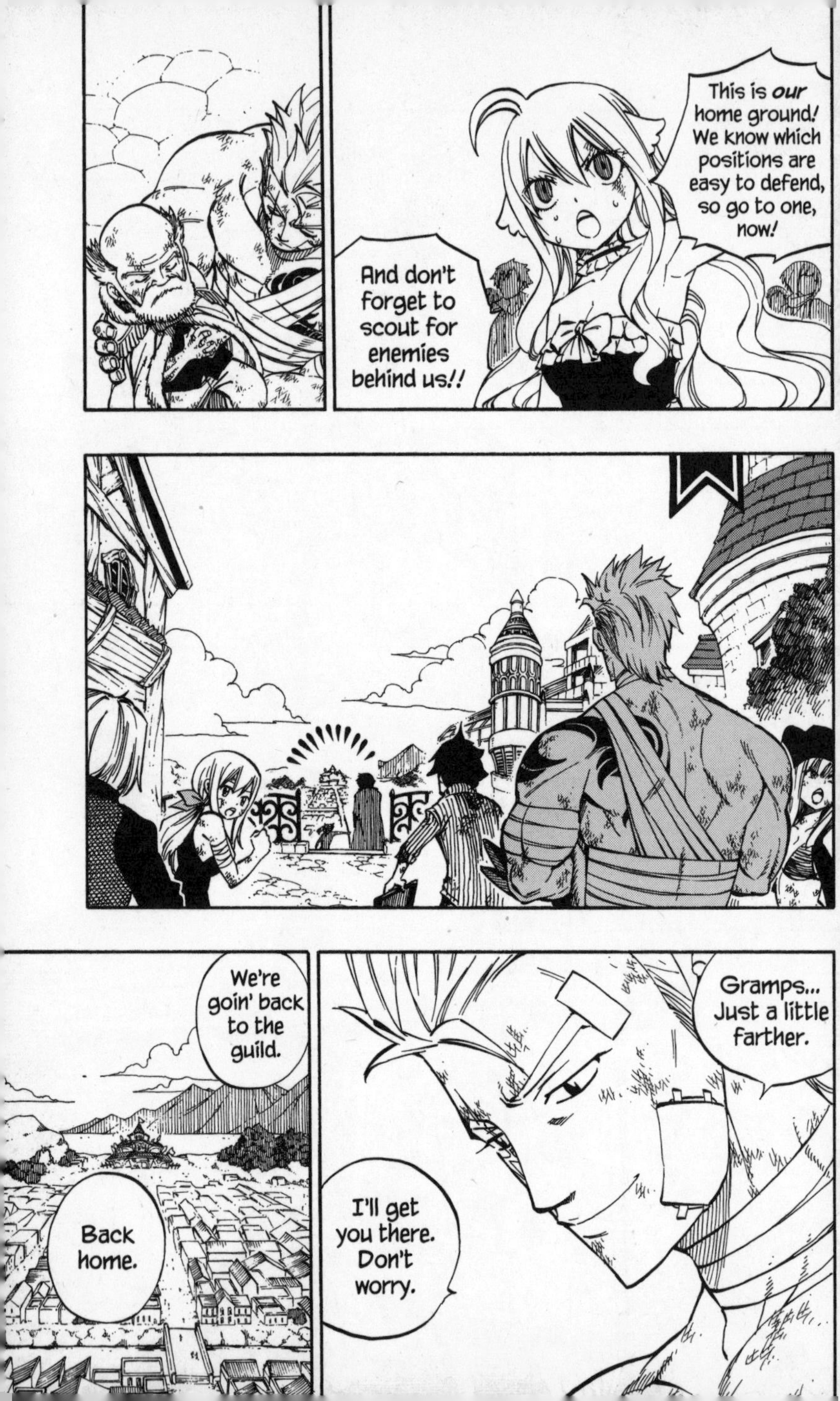
This is *our* home ground! We know which positions are easy to defend, so go to one, now!
And don't forget to scout for enemies behind us!!
Gramps... Just a little farther.
I'll get you there. Don't worry.
We're goin' back to the guild.
Back home.

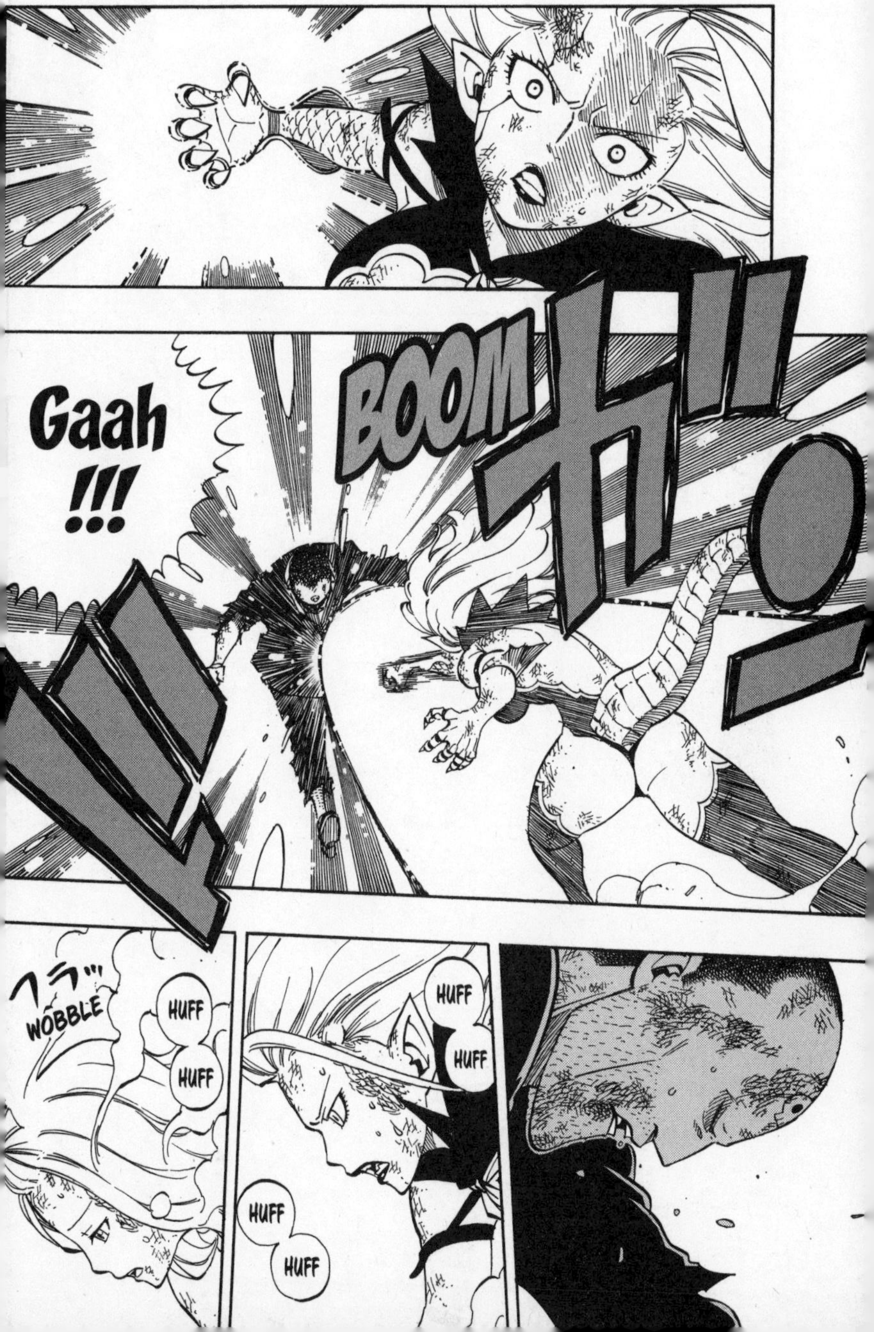
BOOM
Gaah !!!
HUFF
HUFF
HUFF
HUFF
HUFF
HUFF
WOBBLE

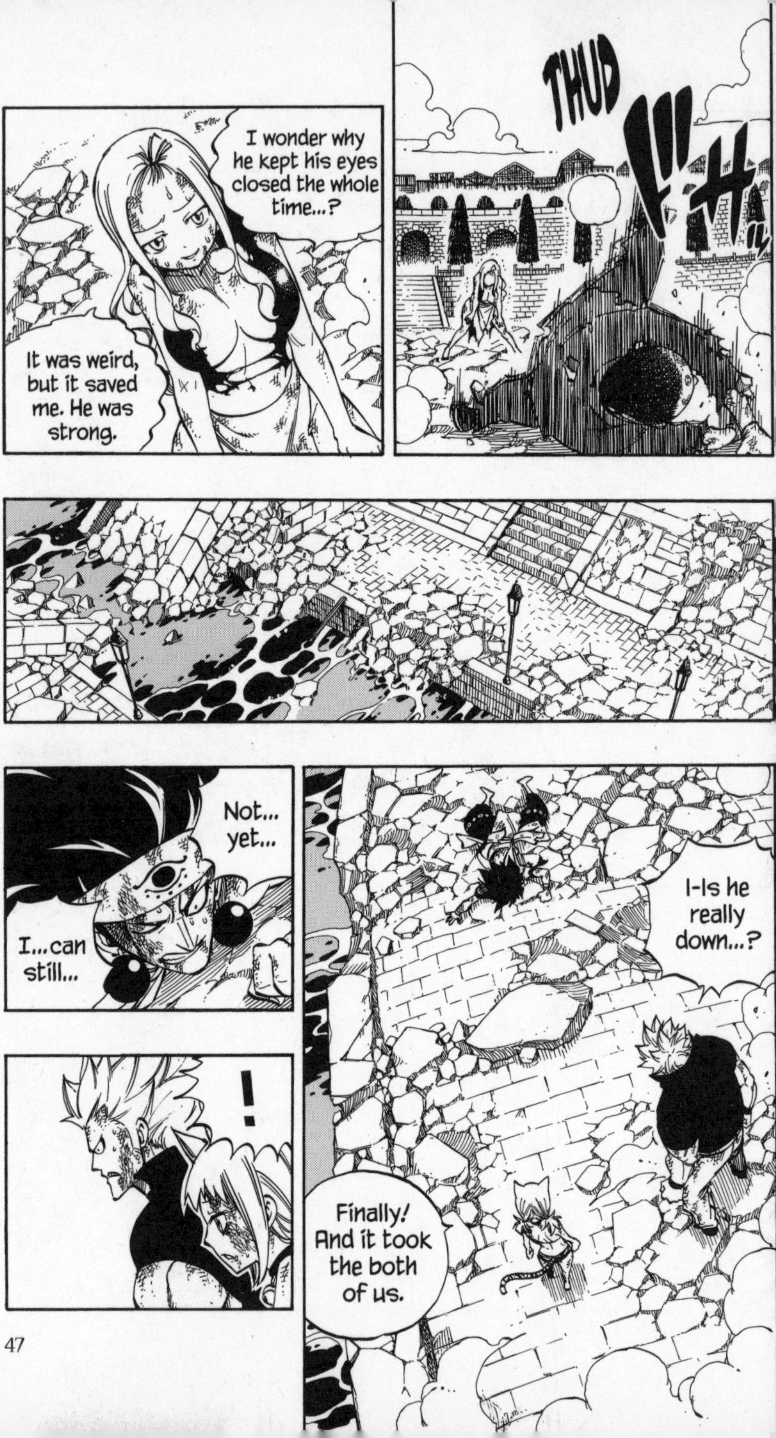
THUD
ドサッ
I wonder why he kept his eyes closed the whole time...?
It was weird, but it saved me. He was strong.
I-Is he really down...?
Finally! And it took the both of us.
Not... yet...
I...can still...
!

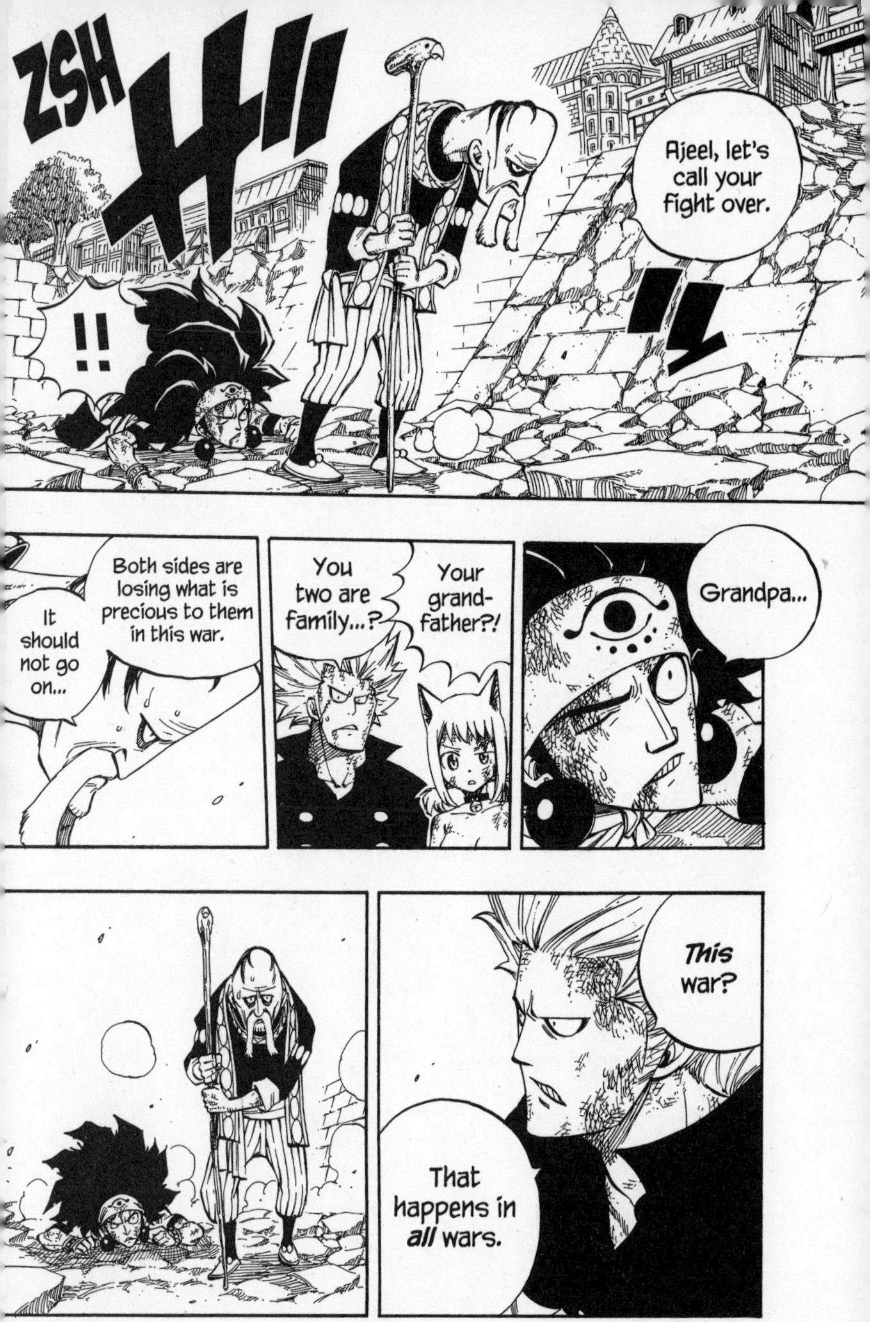
Ajeel, let's call your fight over.
ZSH
!!
Grandpa...
Your grand-father?!
You two are family...?
Both sides are losing what is precious to them in this war.
It should not go on...
*This* war?
That happens in *all* wars.

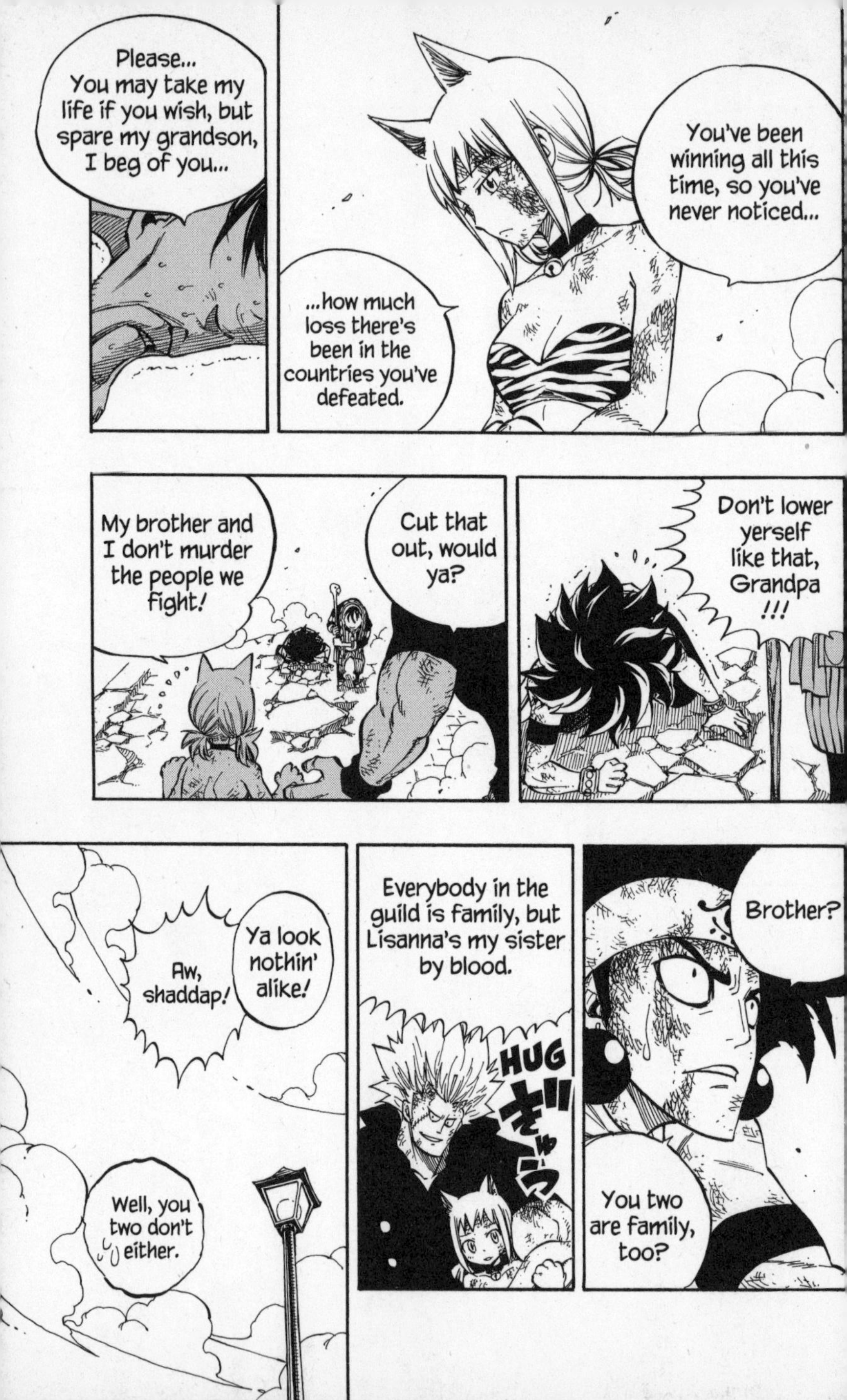
You've been winning all this time, so you've never noticed...
...how much loss there's been in the countries you've defeated.
Please... You may take my life if you wish, but spare my grandson, I beg of you...
Don't lower yerself like that, Grandpa!!!
Cut that out, would ya?
My brother and I don't murder the people we fight!
Brother?
You two are family, too?
Everybody in the guild is family, but Lisanna's my sister by blood.
HUG
Ya look nothin' alike!
Aw, shaddap!
Well, you two don't either.

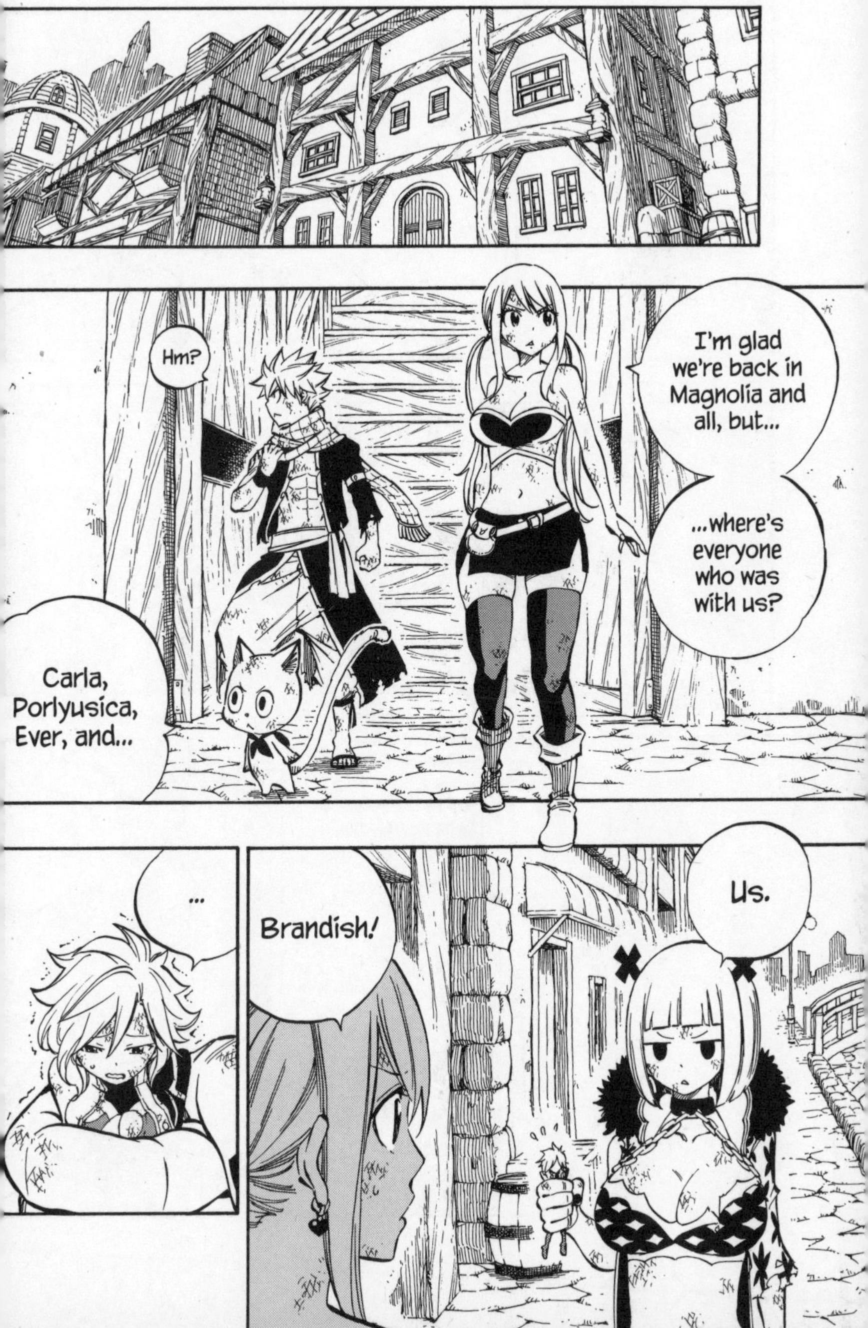
I'm glad we're back in Magnolia and all, but...
...where's everyone who was with us?
Hm?
Carla, Porlyusica, Ever, and...
Us.
Brandish!
...

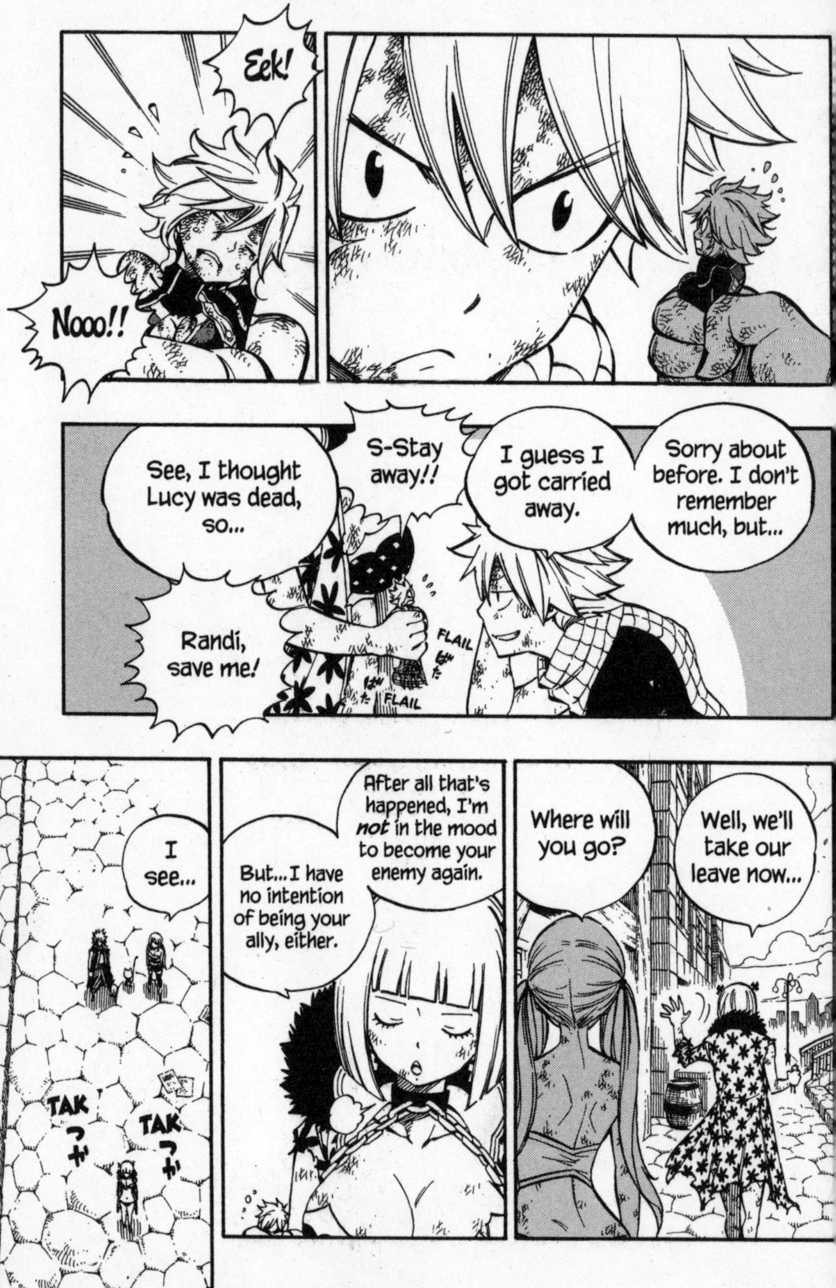
Eek!
Nooo!!
Sorry about before. I don't remember much, but...
I guess I got carried away.
S-Stay away!!
See, I thought Lucy was dead, so...
FLAIL
FLAIL
Randi, save me!
Well, we'll take our leave now...
Where will you go?
After all that's happened, I'm *not* in the mood to become your enemy again.
But...I have no intention of being your ally, either.
I see...
TAK
TAK

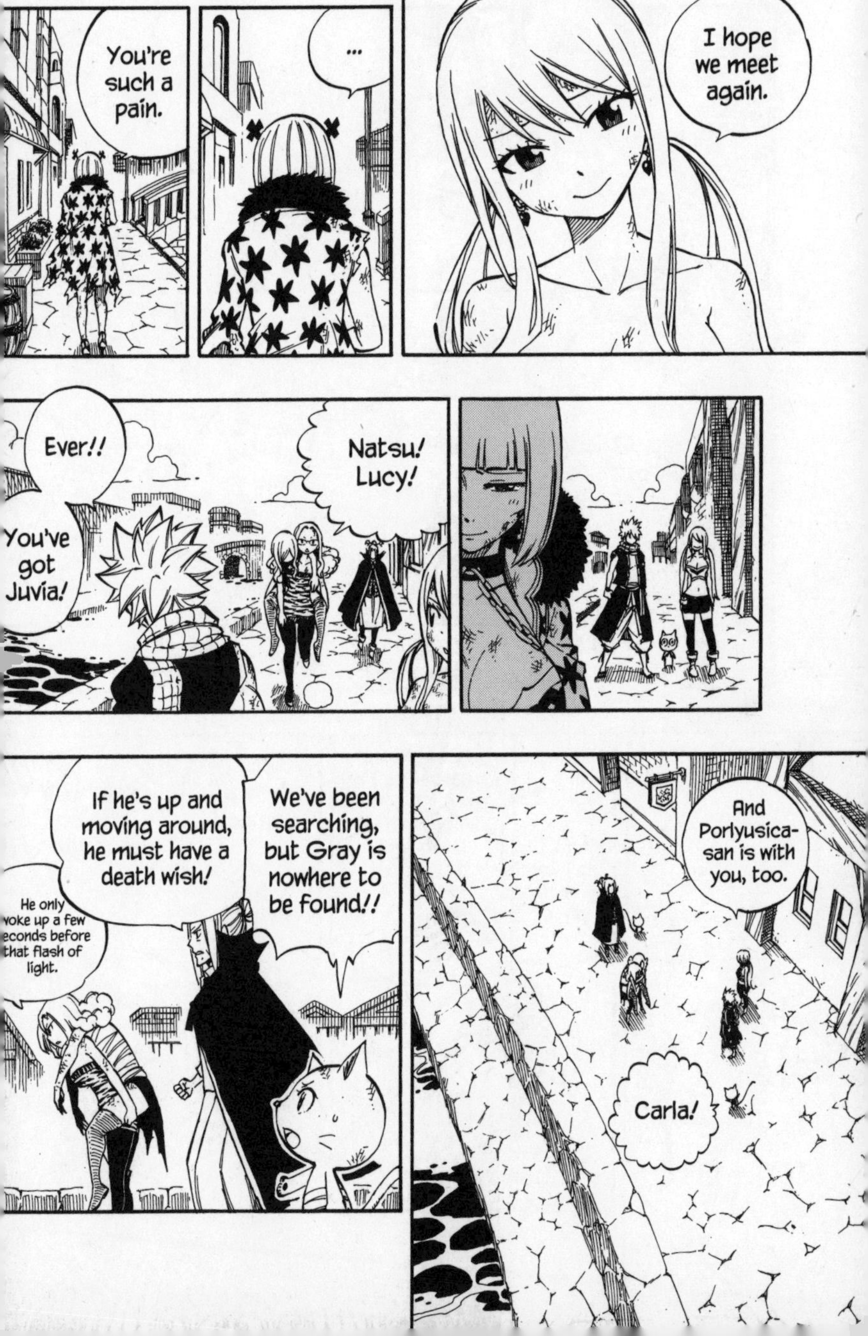

I hope we meet again.
...
You're such a pain.
Natsu! Lucy!
Ever!!
You've got Juvia!
And Porlyusica-san is with you, too.
Carla!
We've been searching, but Gray is nowhere to be found!!
If he's up and moving around, he must have a death wish!
He only voke up a few econds before that flash of light.

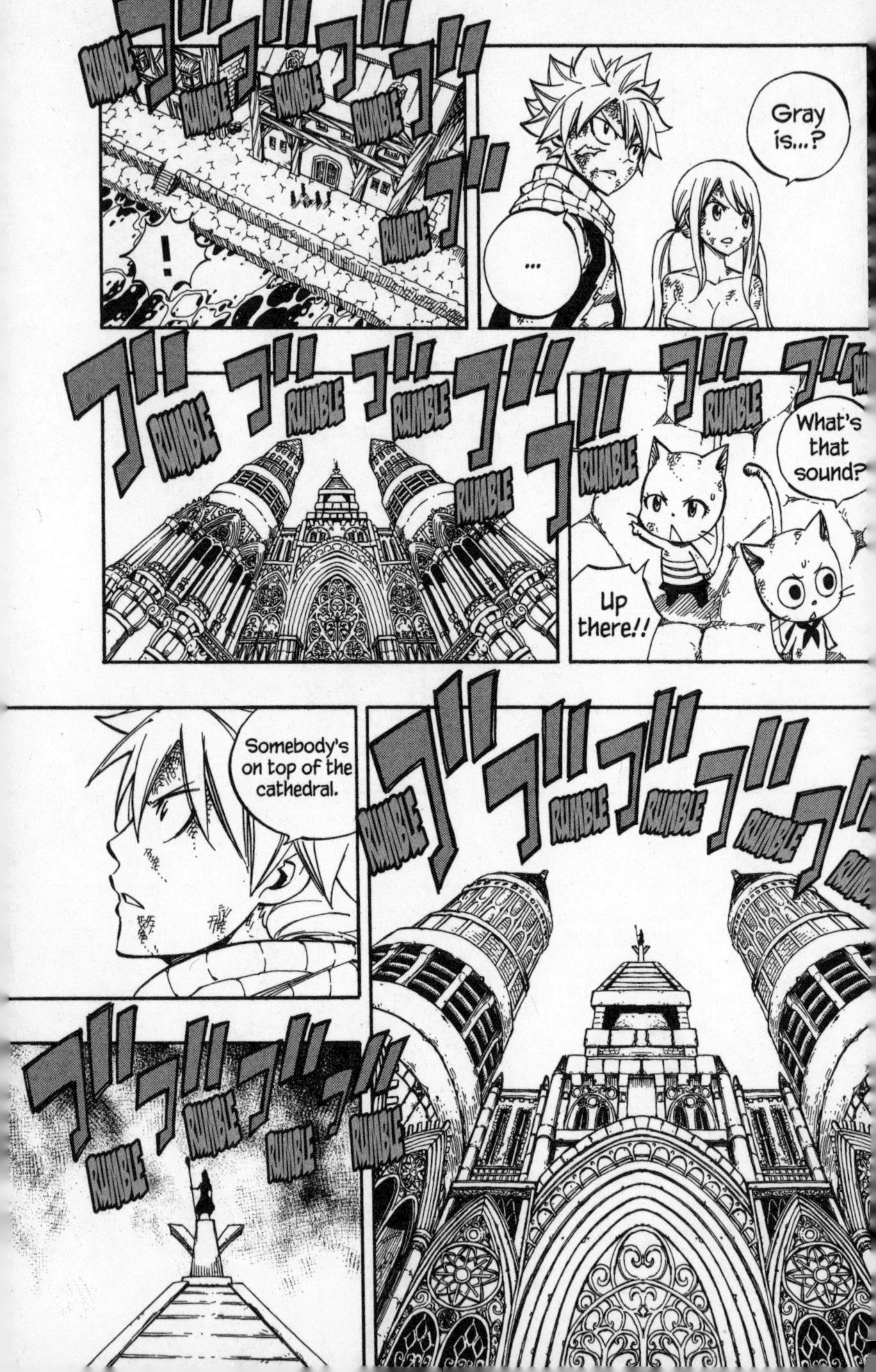
Gray is...?
...
RUMBLE RUMBLE RUMBLE RUMBLE RUMBLE
!
RUMBLE RUMBLE RUMBLE
What's that sound?
Up there!!
RUMBLE RUMBLE RUMBLE RUMBLE
RUMBLE RUMBLE RUMBLE RUMBLE RUMBLE
Somebody's on top of the cathedral.
RUMBLE RUMBLE RUMBLE RUMBLE

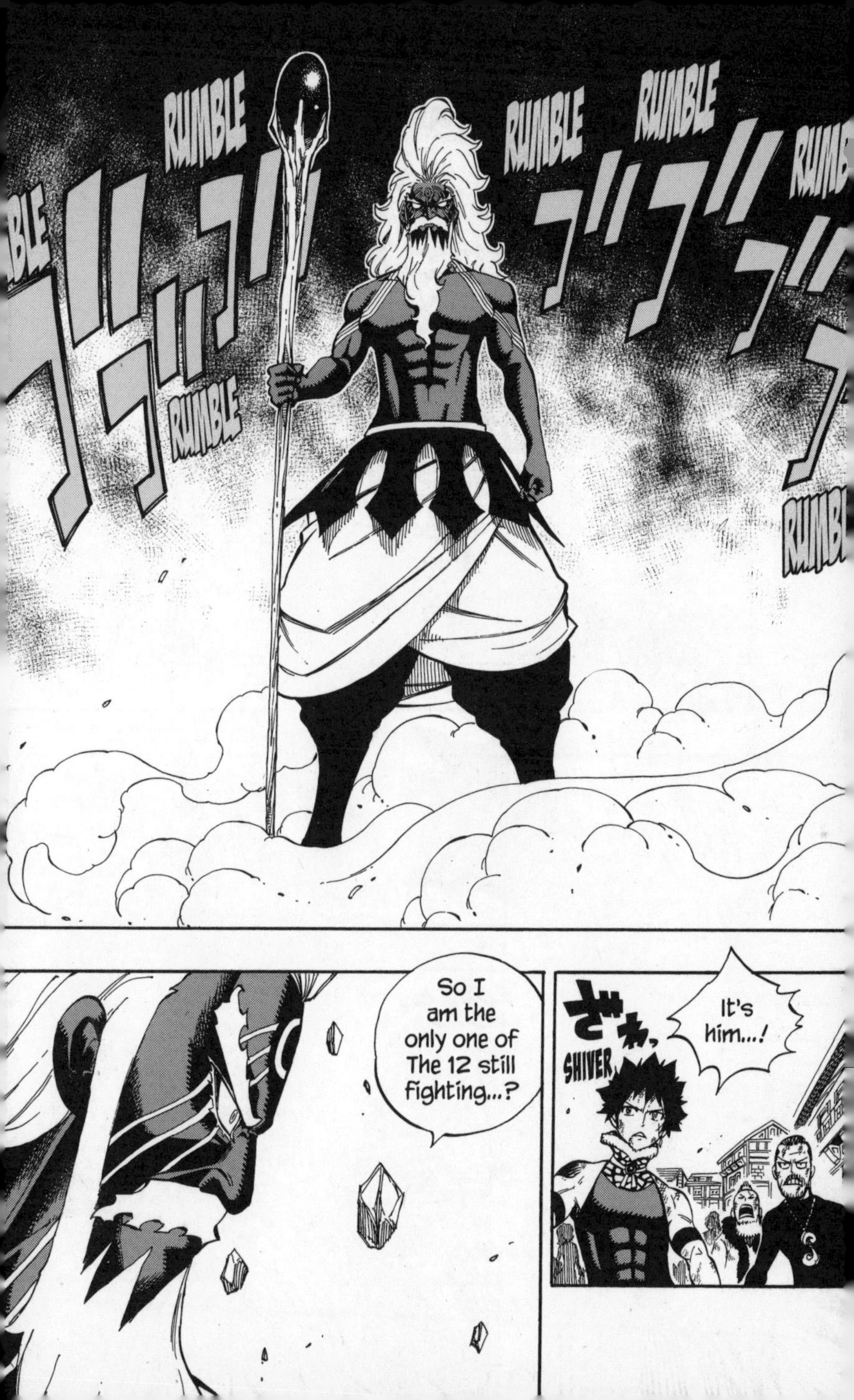
RUMB
RUMBLE
RUMBLE
RUMBLE
BLE
RUMBLE
RUMB
ざわ
SHIVER
It's him...!
So I am the only one of The 12 still fighting...?

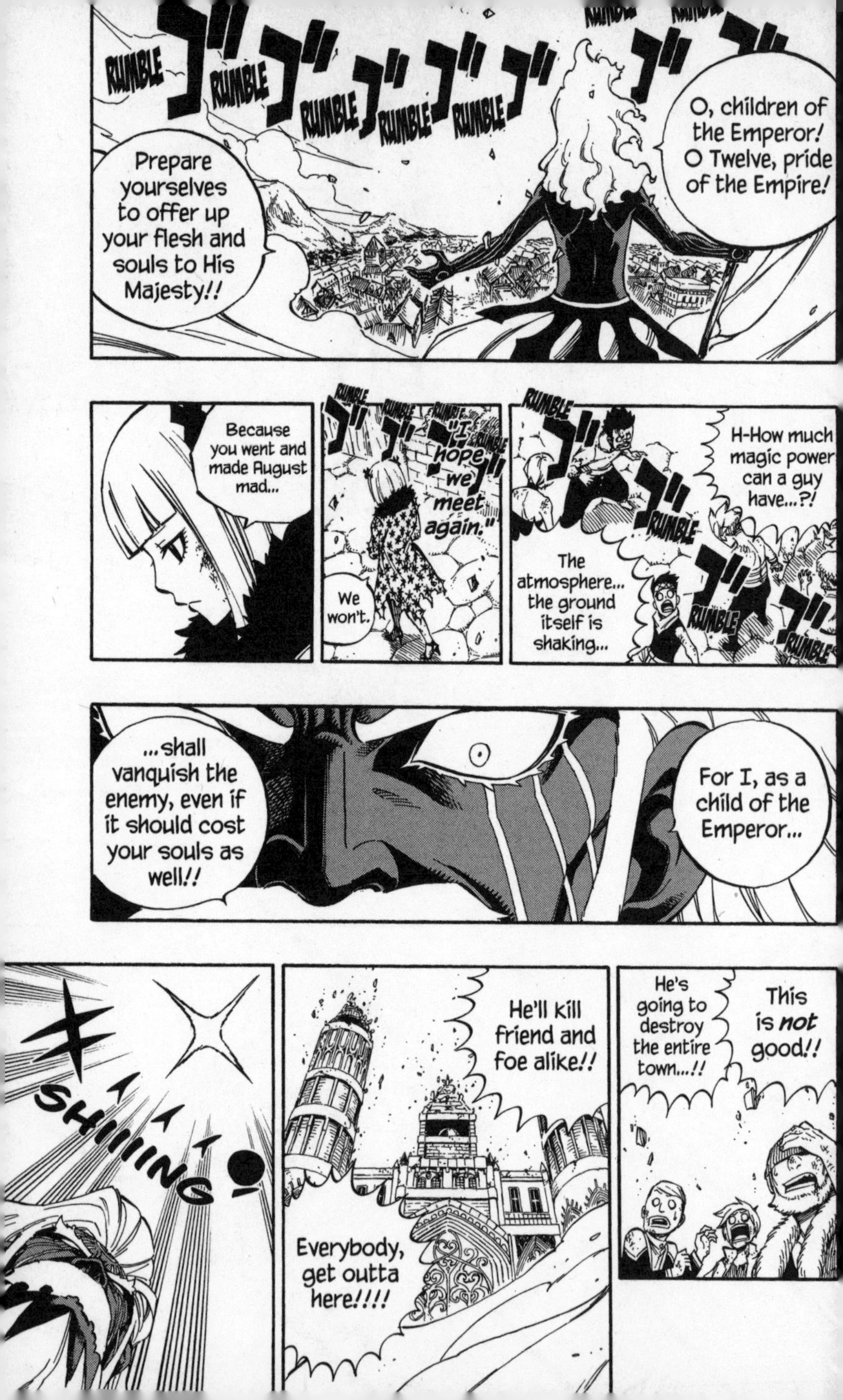
RUMBLE
O, children of the Emperor! O Twelve, pride of the Empire!
Prepare yourselves to offer up your flesh and souls to His Majesty!!
RUMBLE
H-How much magic power can a guy have...?!
The atmosphere... the ground itself is shaking...
RUMBLE
"I hope we meet again."
We won't.
Because you went and made August mad...
For I, as a child of the Emperor...
...shall vanquish the enemy, even if it should cost your souls as well!!
This is *not* good!!
He's going to destroy the entire town...!!
He'll kill friend and foe alike!!
Everybody, get outta here!!!!
SHIIIING

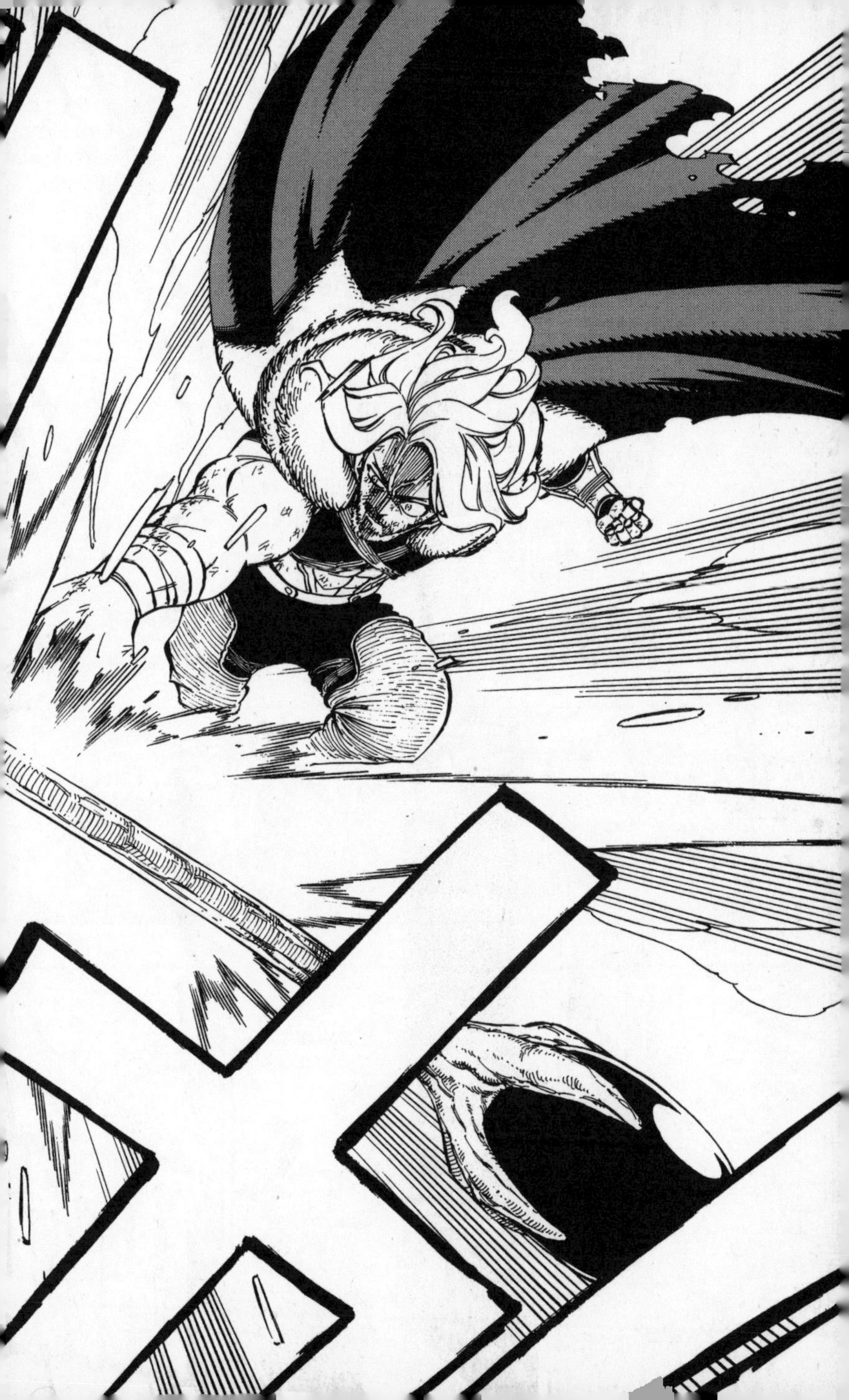

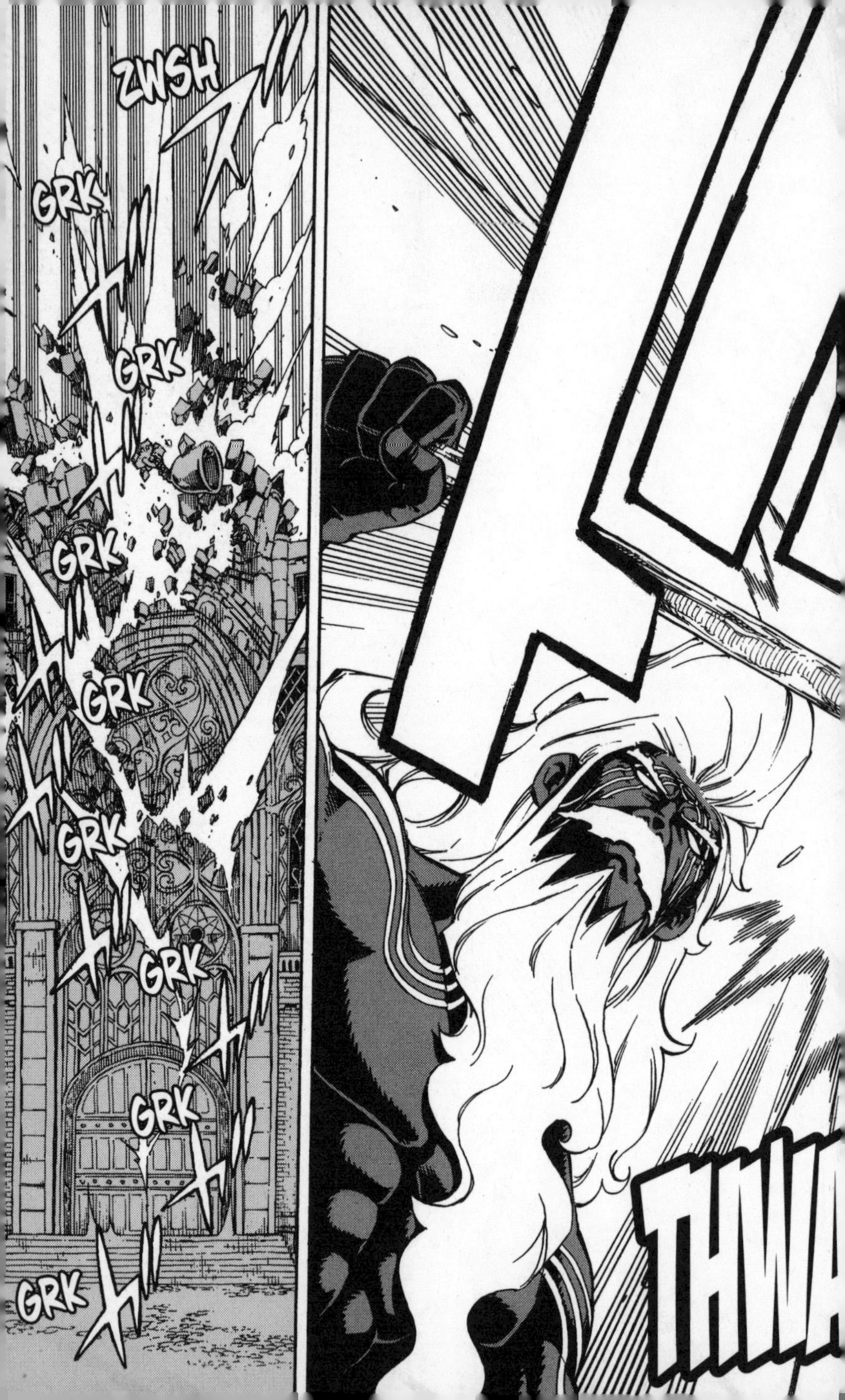
THWA
ZWSH
GRK
GRK
GRK
GRK
GRK
GRK
GRK
GRK

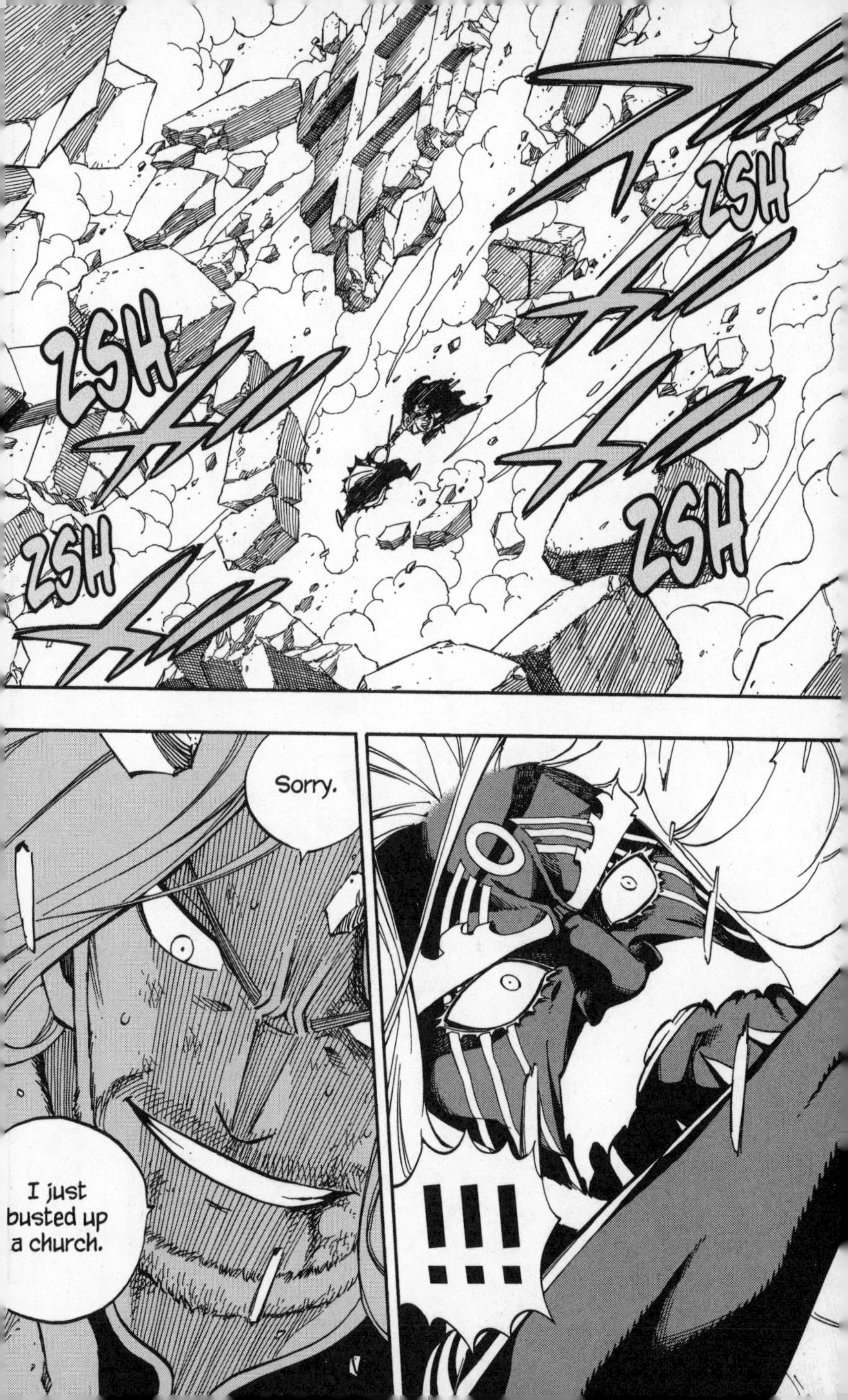
ZSH
ZSH
ZSH
ZSH
!!!
Sorry.
I just busted up a church.

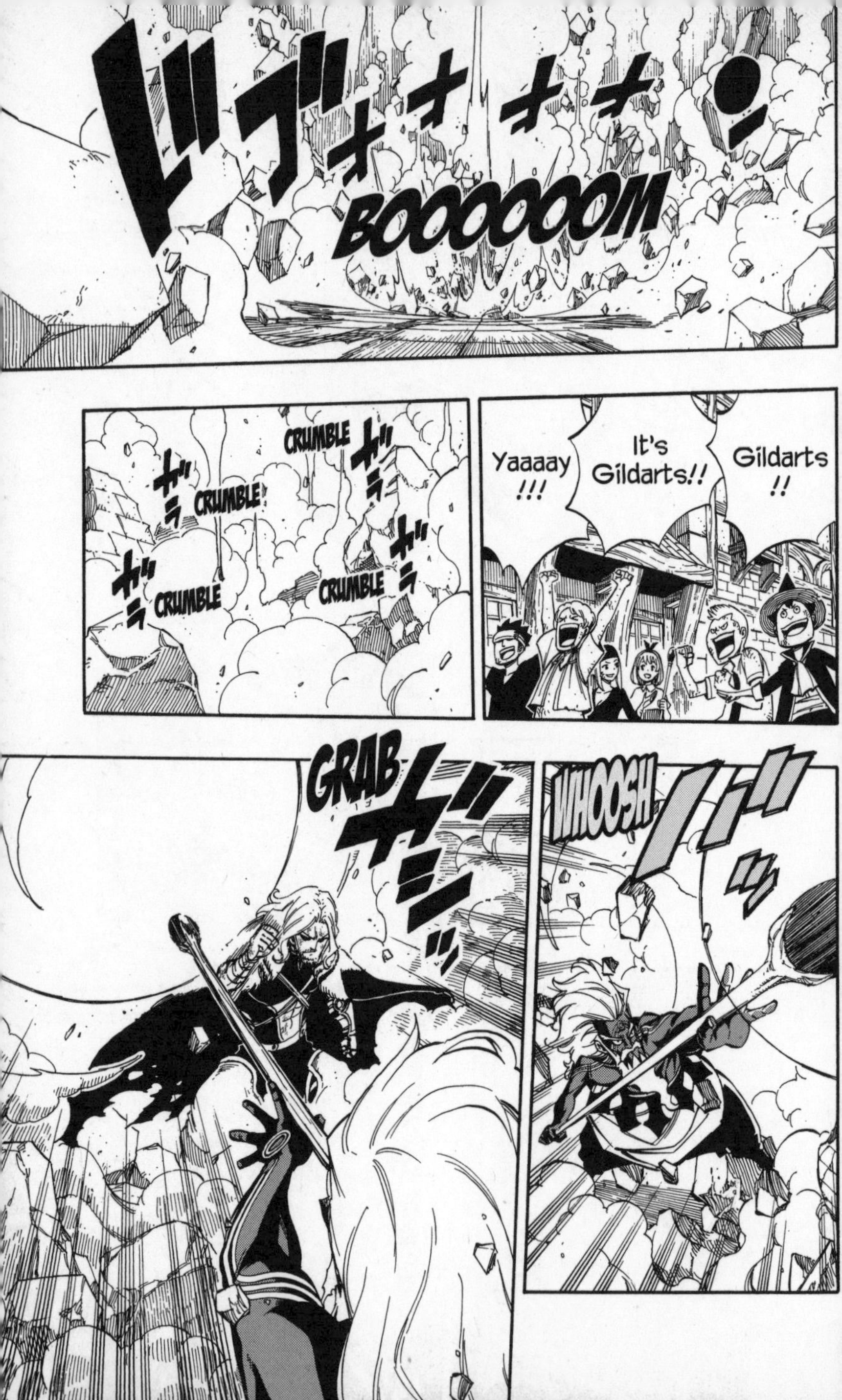
BOOOOOOM
Gildarts !!
It's Gildarts!!
Yaaaay !!!
CRUMBLE
CRUMBLE
CRUMBLE
CRUMBLE
WHOOSH
GRAB

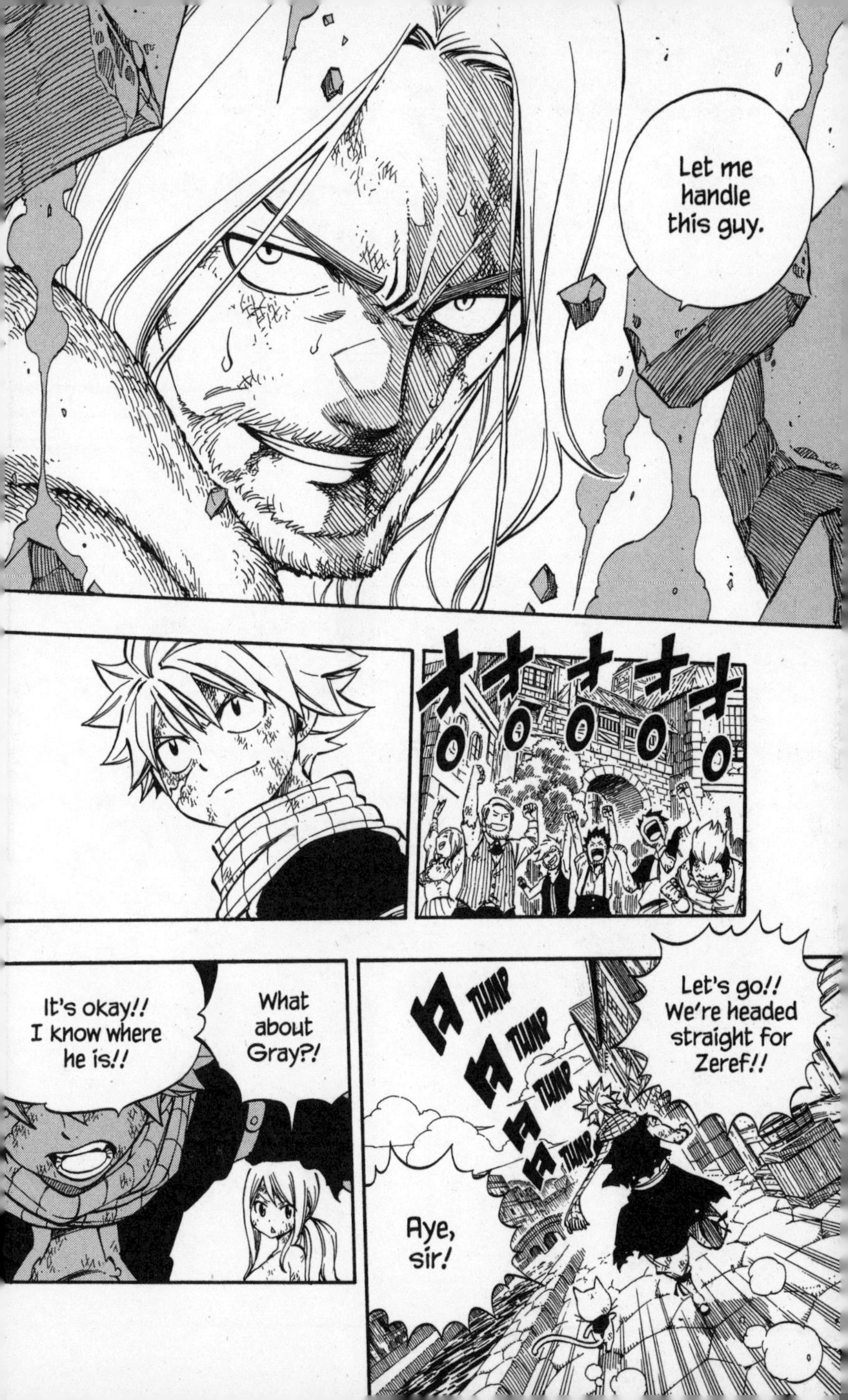
Let me handle this guy.
Let's go!! We're headed straight for Zeref!!
TUMP
TUMP
TUMP
TUMP
Aye, sir!
What about Gray?!
It's okay!! I know where he is!!

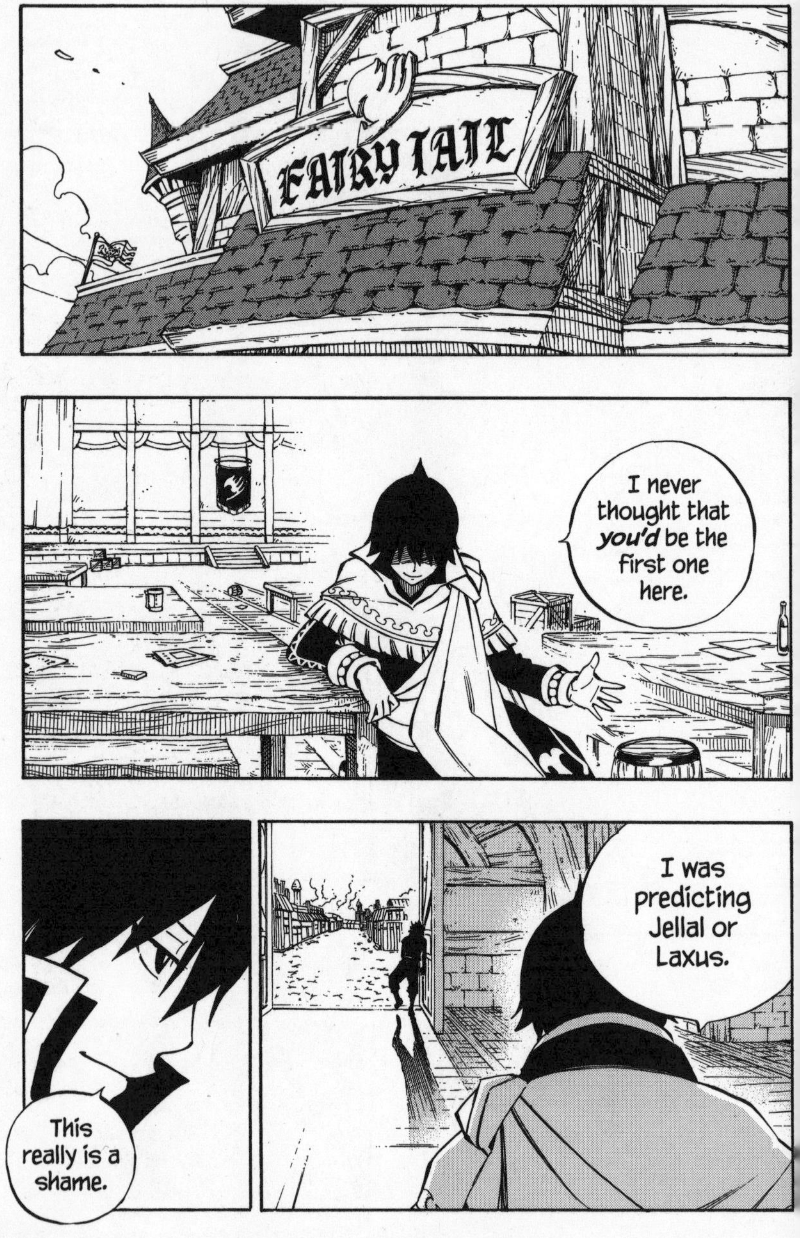
FAIRY TAIL
I never thought that *you'd* be the first one here.
I was predicting Jellal or Laxus.
This really is a shame.

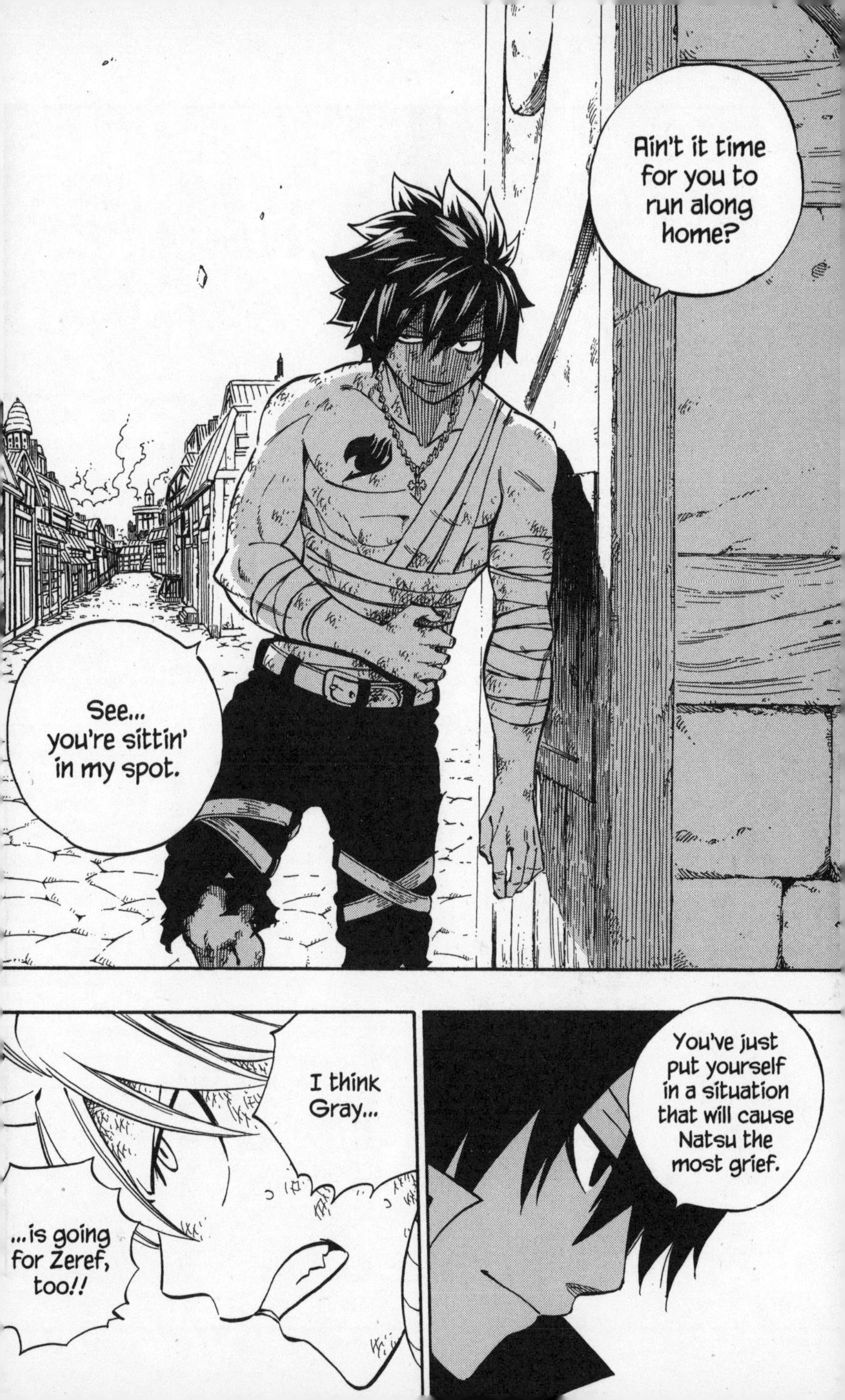
Ain't it time for you to run along home?
See... you're sittin' in my spot.
You've just put yourself in a situation that will cause Natsu the most grief.
I think Gray...
...is going for Zeref, too!!

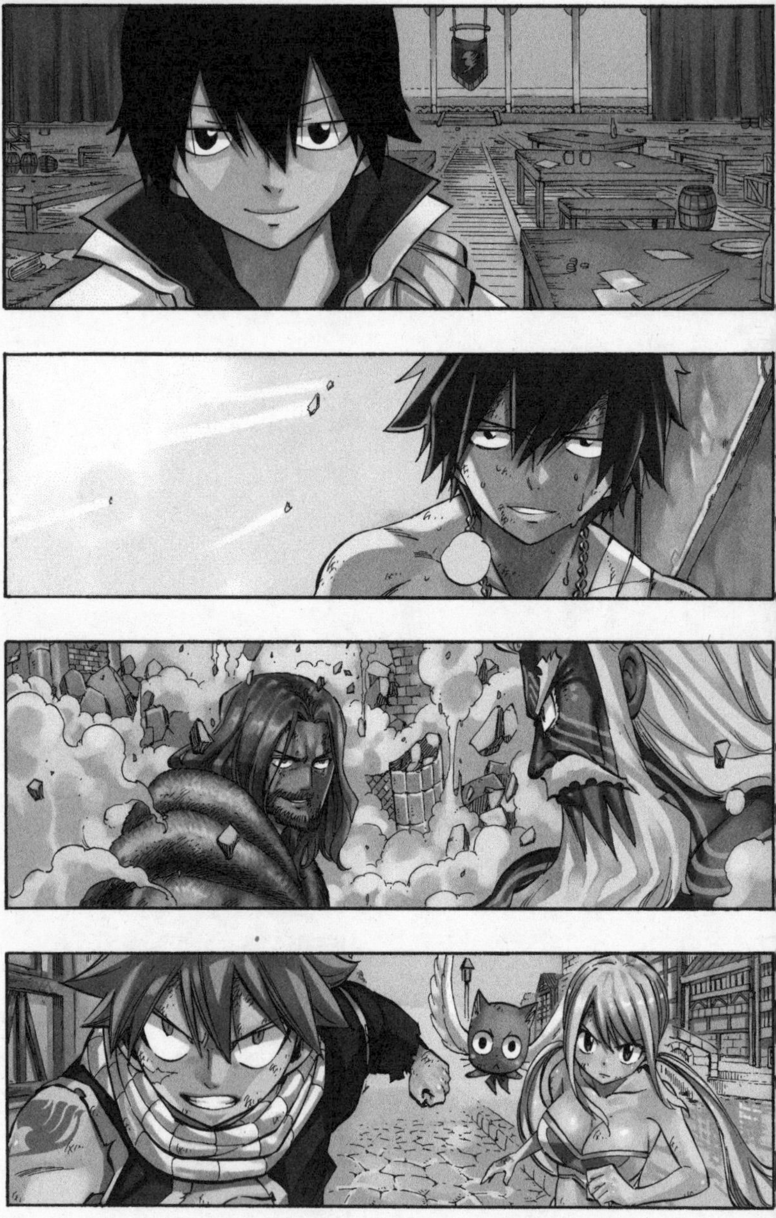

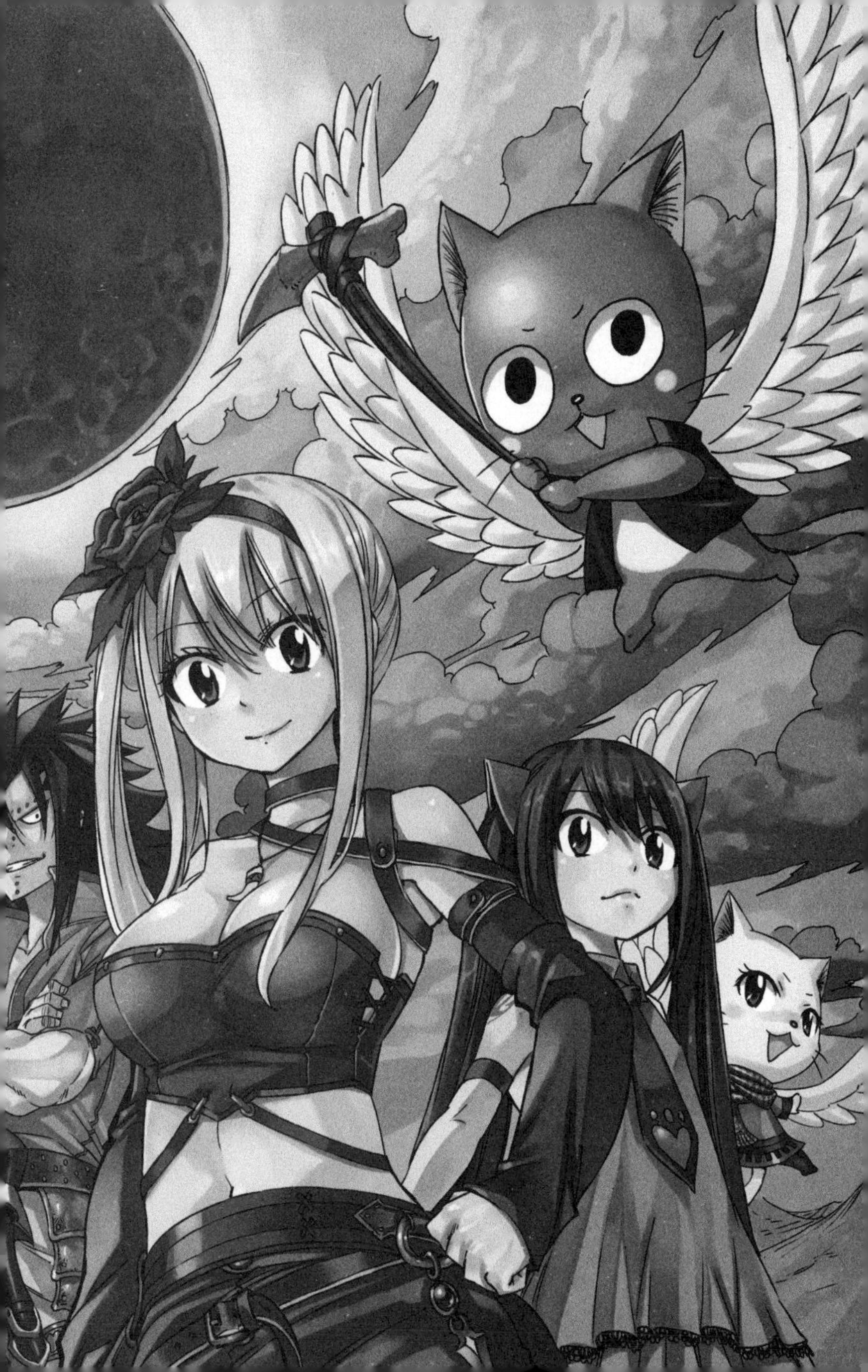

# Chapter 522: Gray's Trump Card

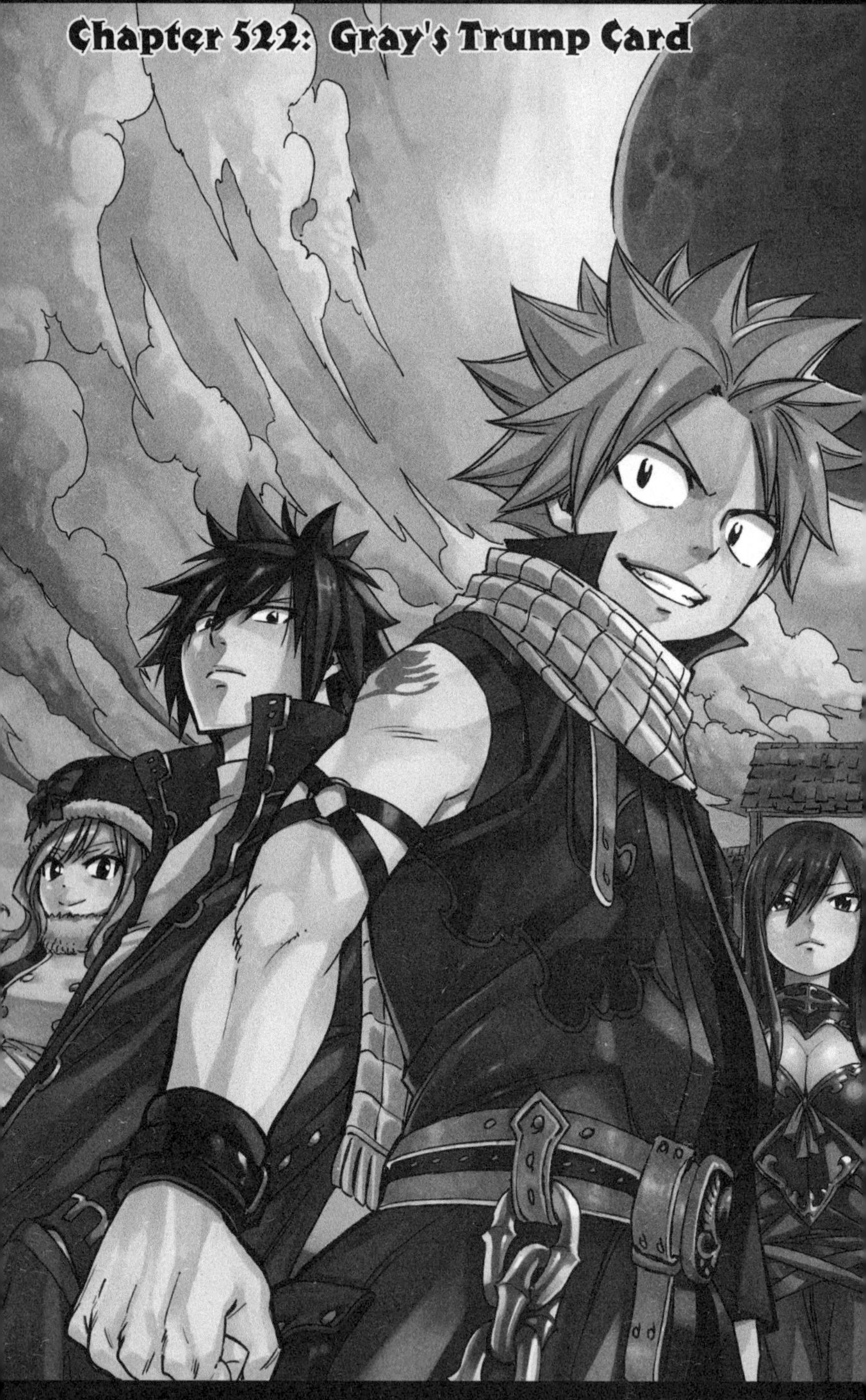

FAIRY TAIL
フェアリーテイル

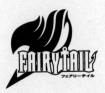

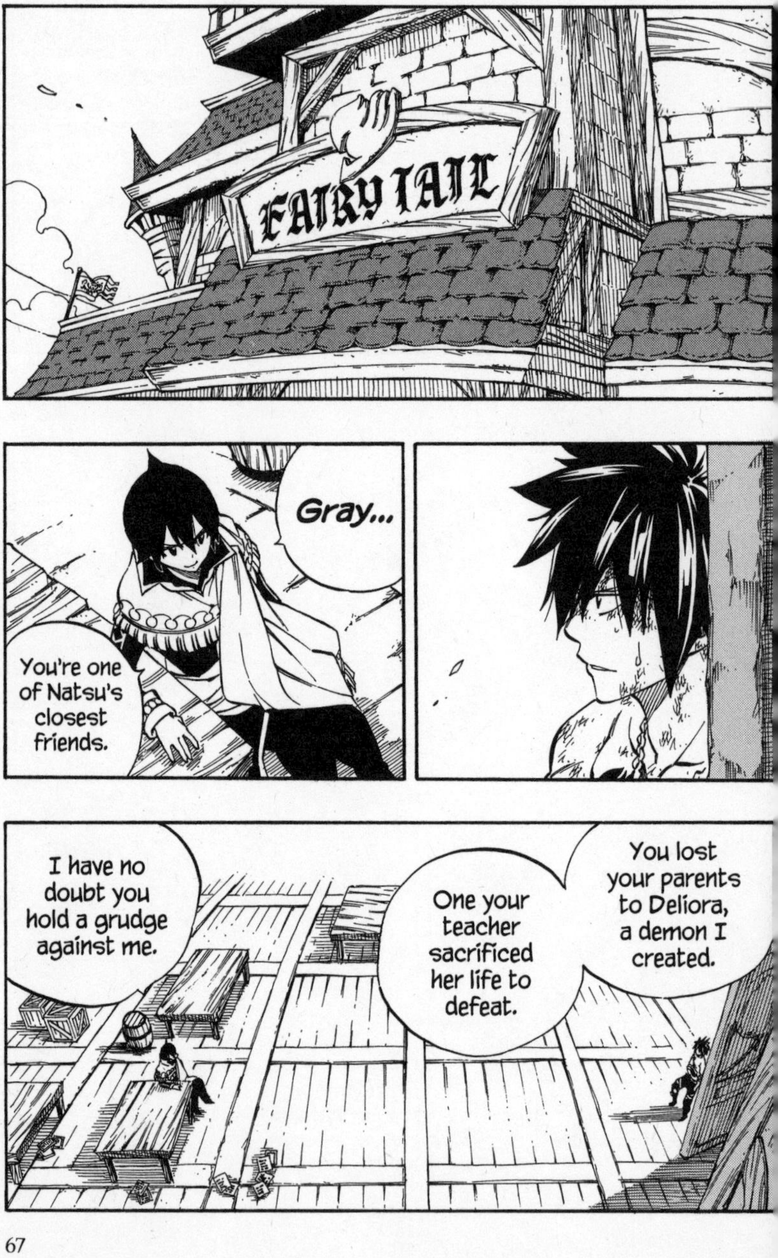
FAIRY TAIL
Gray...
You're one of Natsu's closest friends.
You lost your parents to Deliora, a demon I created.
One your teacher sacrificed her life to defeat.
I have no doubt you hold a grudge against me.

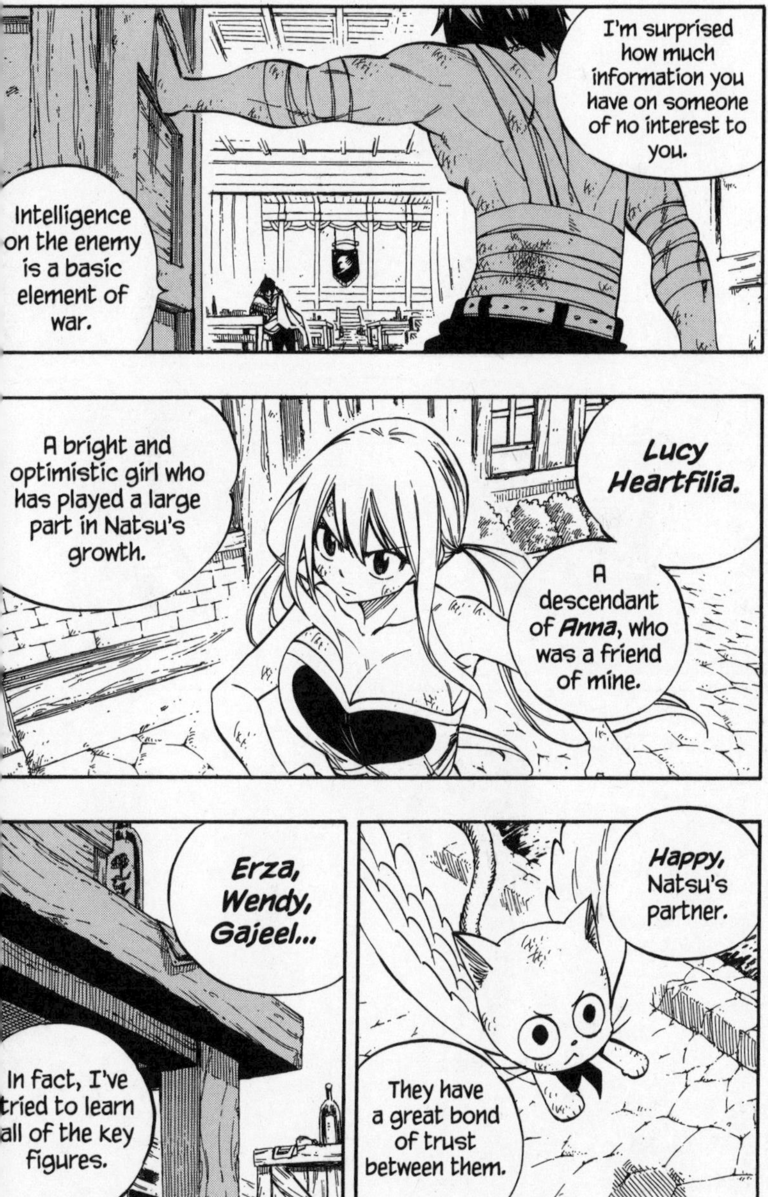
I'm surprised how much information you have on someone of no interest to you.
Intelligence on the enemy is a basic element of war.
*Lucy Heartfilia.*
A descendant of *Anna*, who was a friend of mine.
A bright and optimistic girl who has played a large part in Natsu's growth.
*Happy,* Natsu's partner.
They have a great bond of trust between them.
*Erza, Wendy, Gajeel...*
In fact, I've tried to learn all of the key figures.

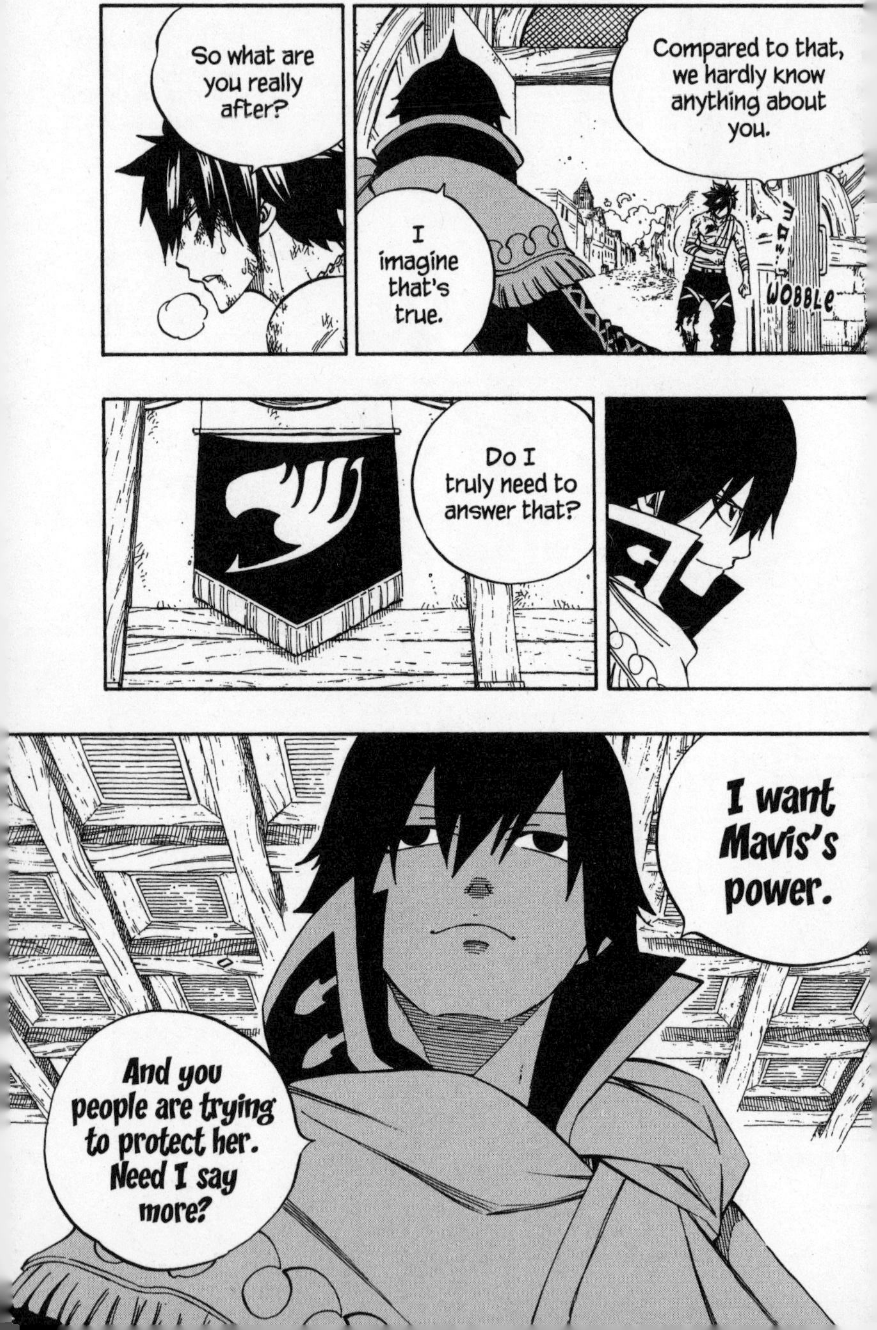

Compared to that, we hardly know anything about you.
WOBBLE
I imagine that's true.
So what are you really after?
Do I truly need to answer that?
I want Mavis's power.
And you people are trying to protect her. Need I say more?

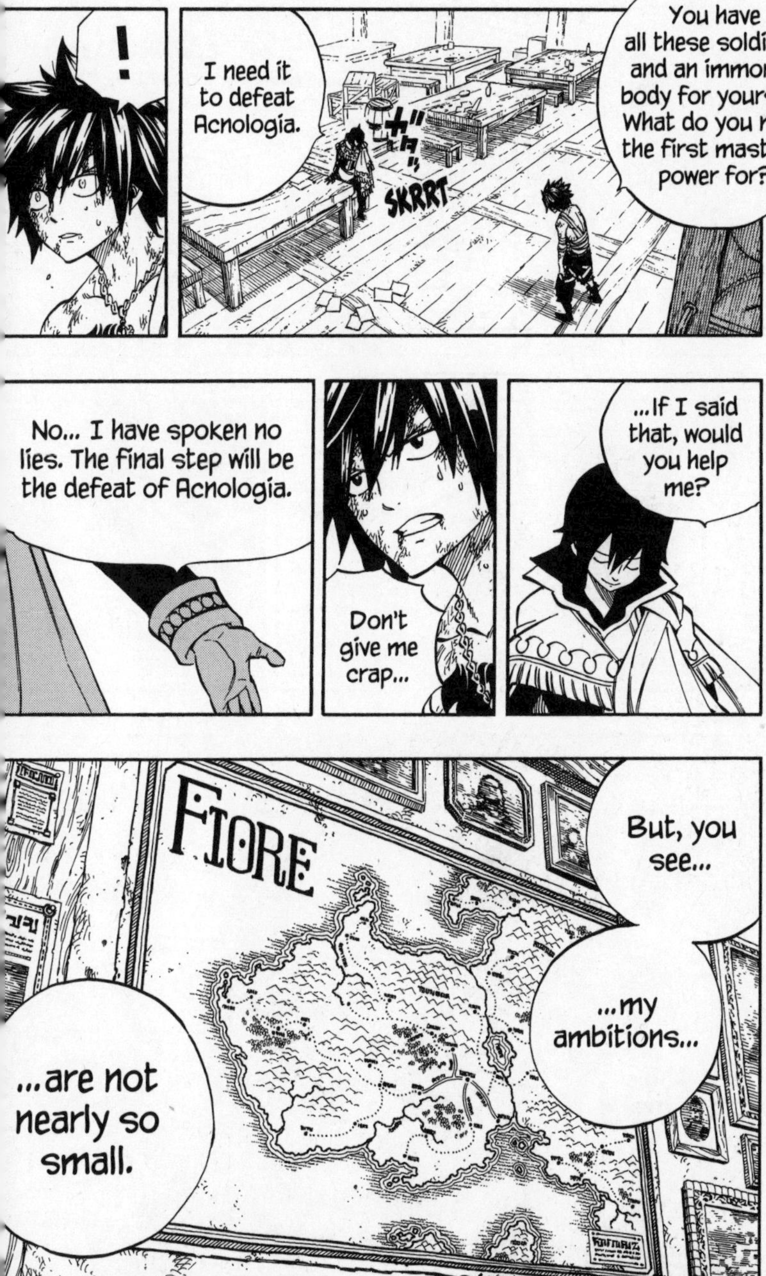
You have all these soldiers, and an immortal body for yourself. What do you need the first master's power for?
SKRRT
I need it to defeat Acnologia.
!
...If I said that, would you help me?
Don't give me crap...
No... I have spoken no lies. The final step will be the defeat of Acnologia.
FIORE
But, you see...
...my ambitions...
...are not nearly so small.

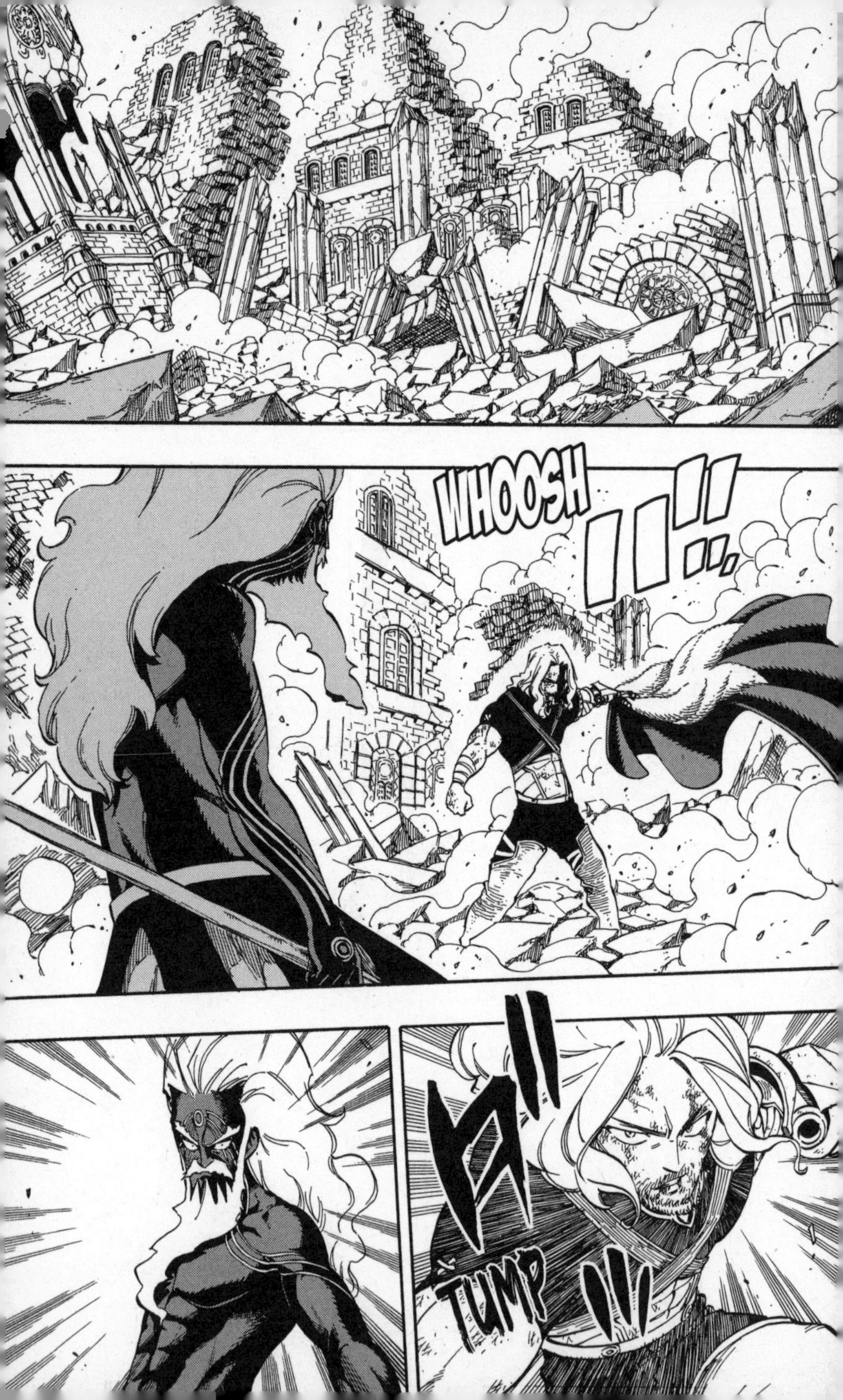
WHOOSH
TUMP

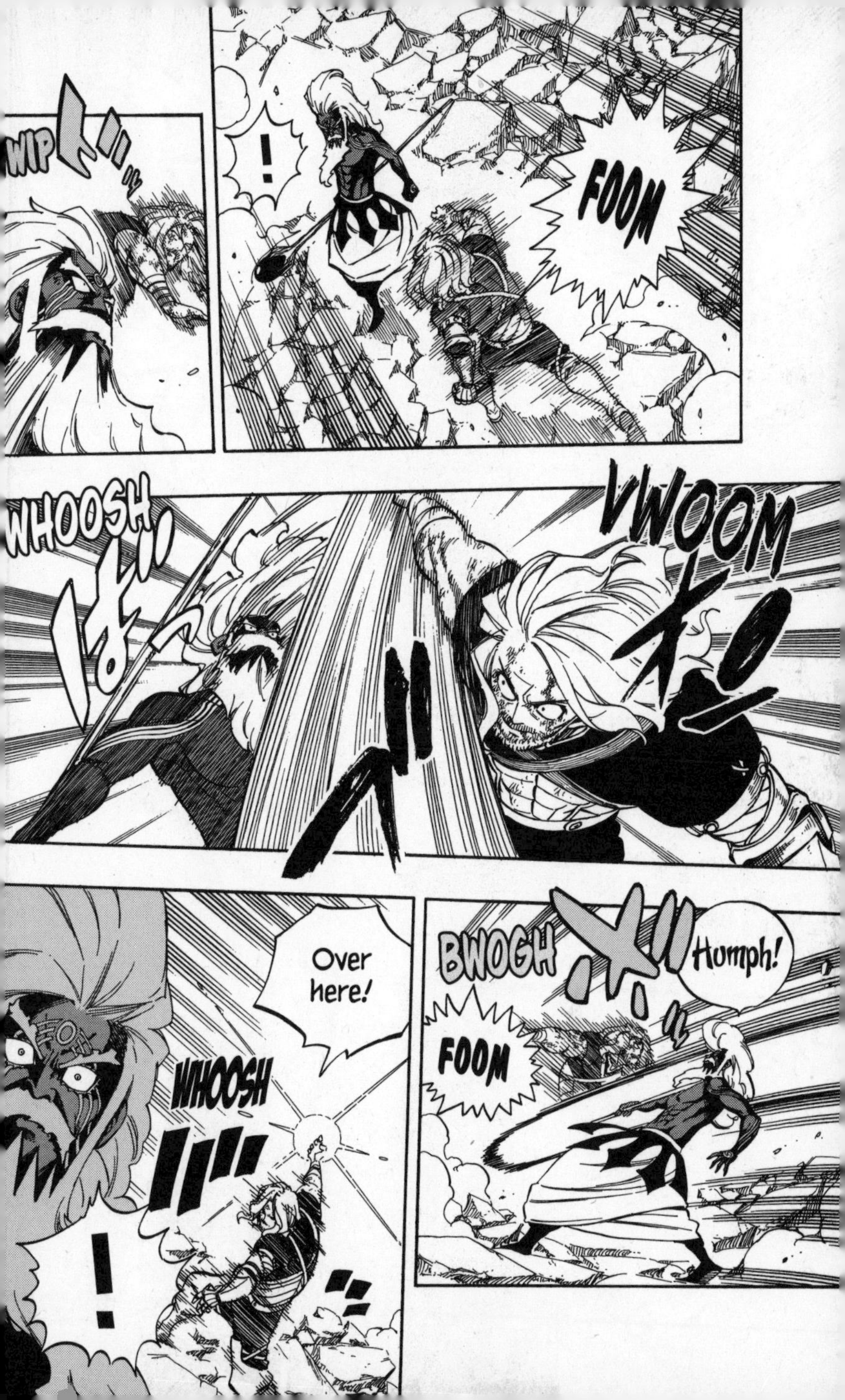
!
FOOM
WIP
VWOOM
WHOOSH
BWOGH
Humph!
FOOM
Over here!
WHOOSH
!

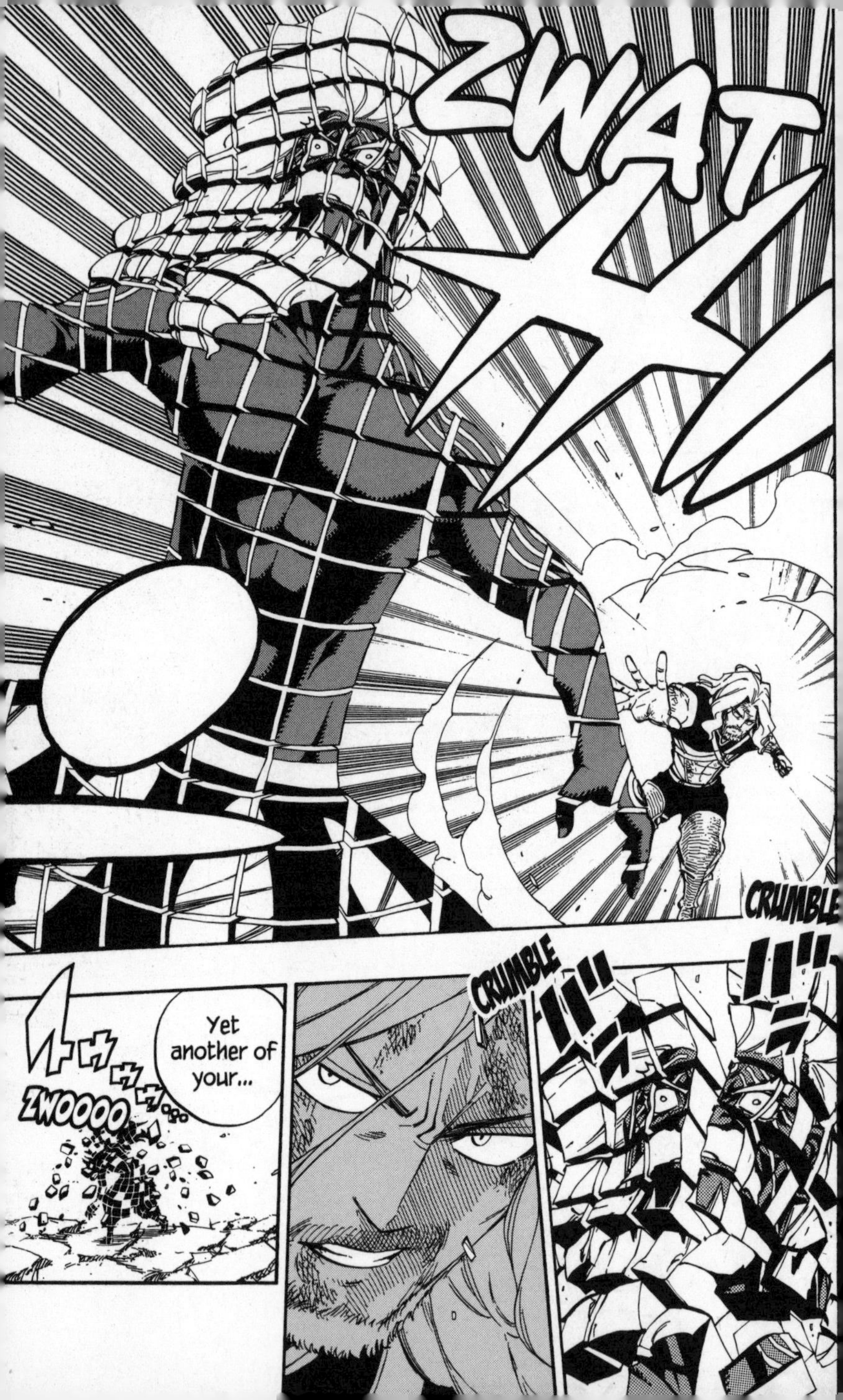
ZWAT
CRUMBLE
CRUMBLE
Yet another of your...
ZWOOOO

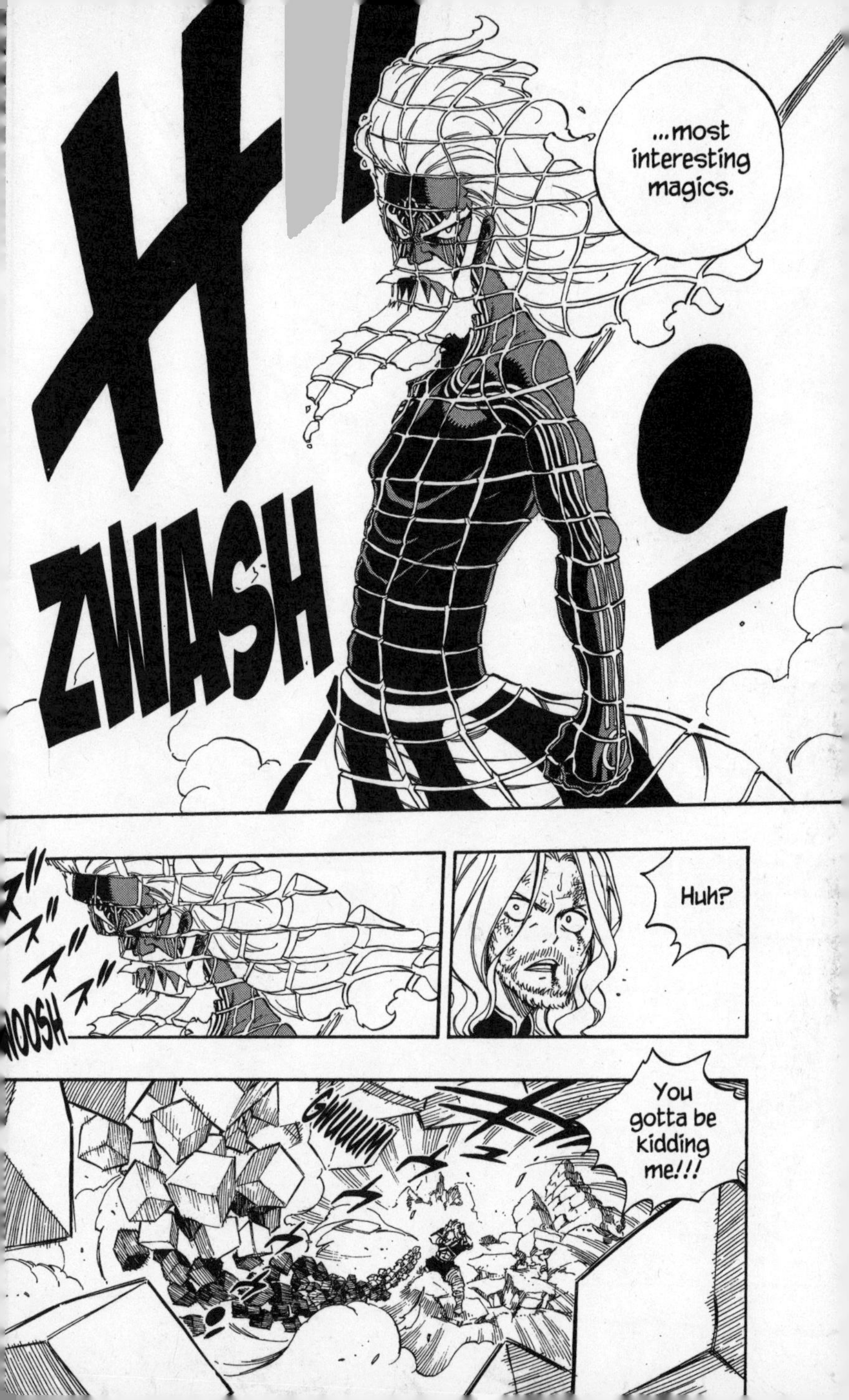
...most interesting magics.
ZWASH
Huh?
You gotta be kidding me!!!

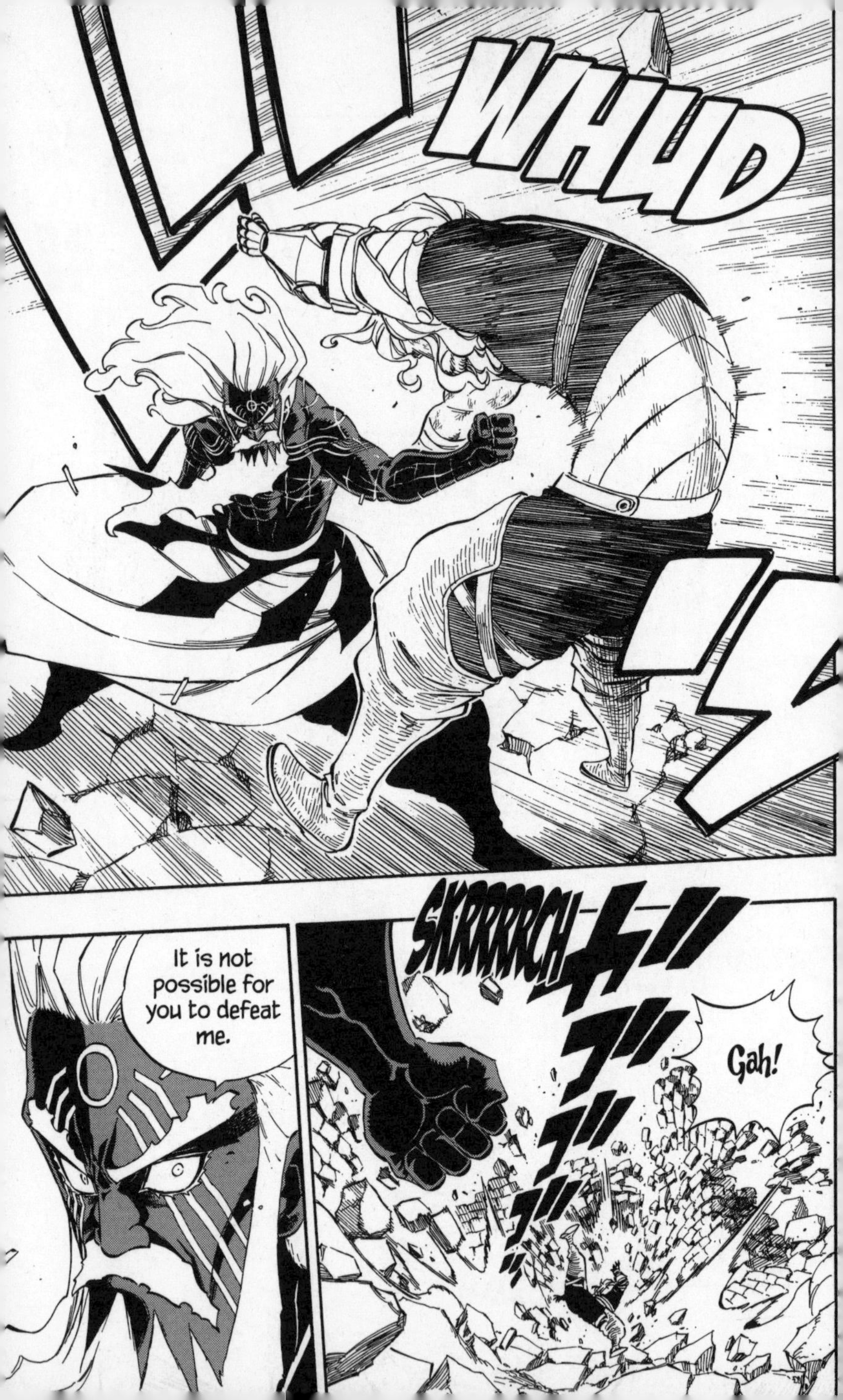
WHUD
SKRRRRCH
Gah!
It is not possible for you to defeat me.

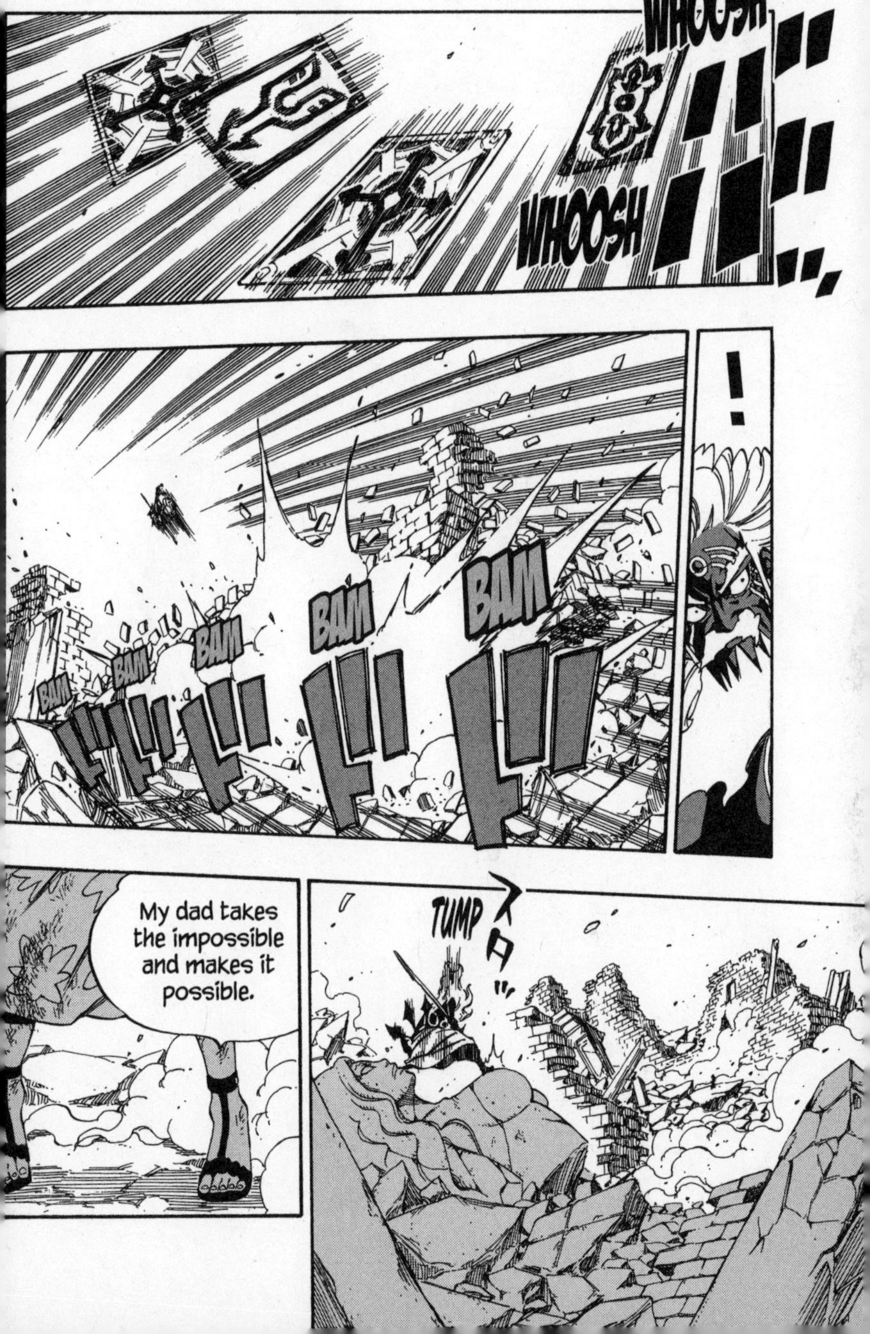
WHOOSH
WHOOSH
!
BAM
BAM
BAM
BAM
BAM
TUMP
My dad takes the impossible and makes it possible.

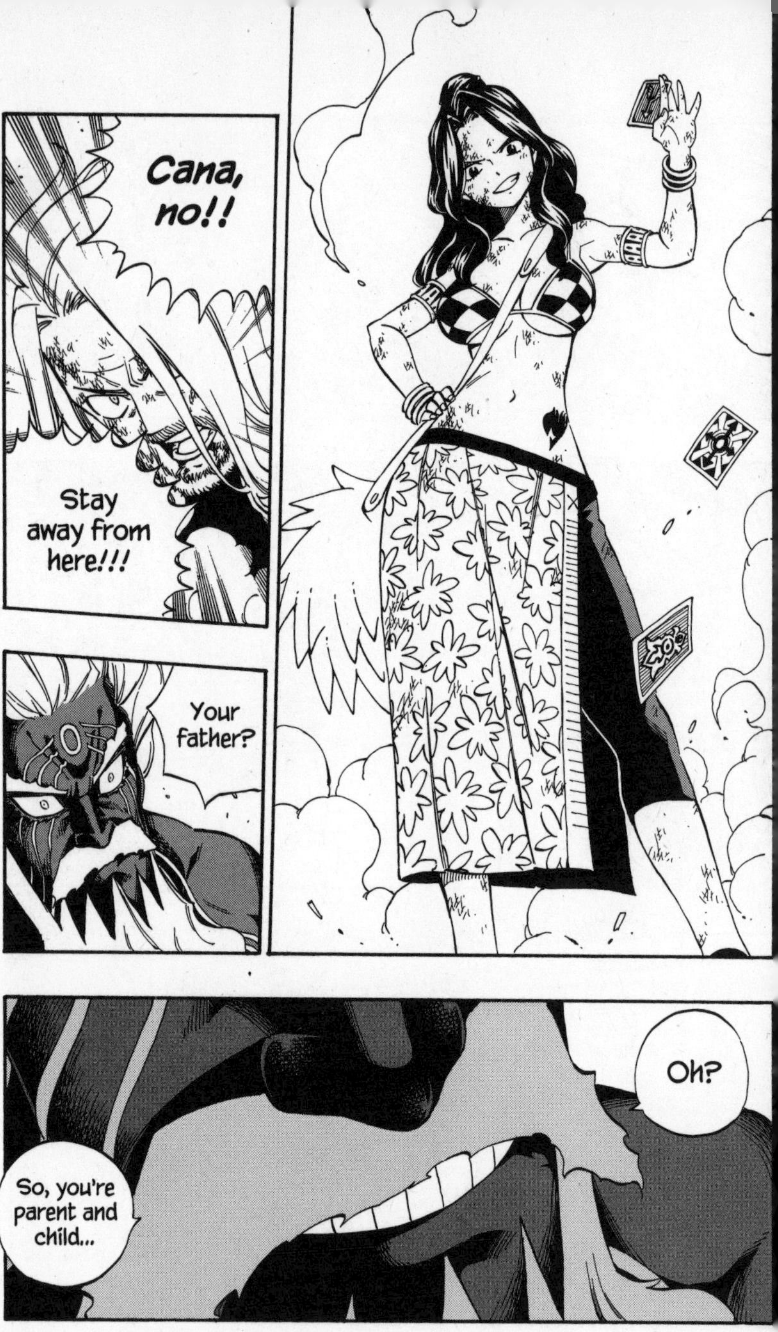
Cana, no!!
Stay away from here!!!
Your father?
Oh?
So, you're parent and child...

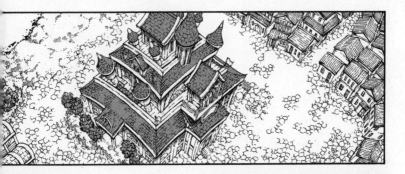

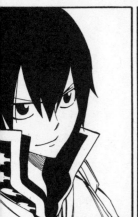

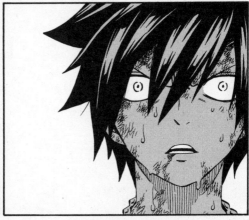

...
You're planning *what?!*
You are the first one to whom I have ever spoken of this.
It's likely even The 12 don't know.

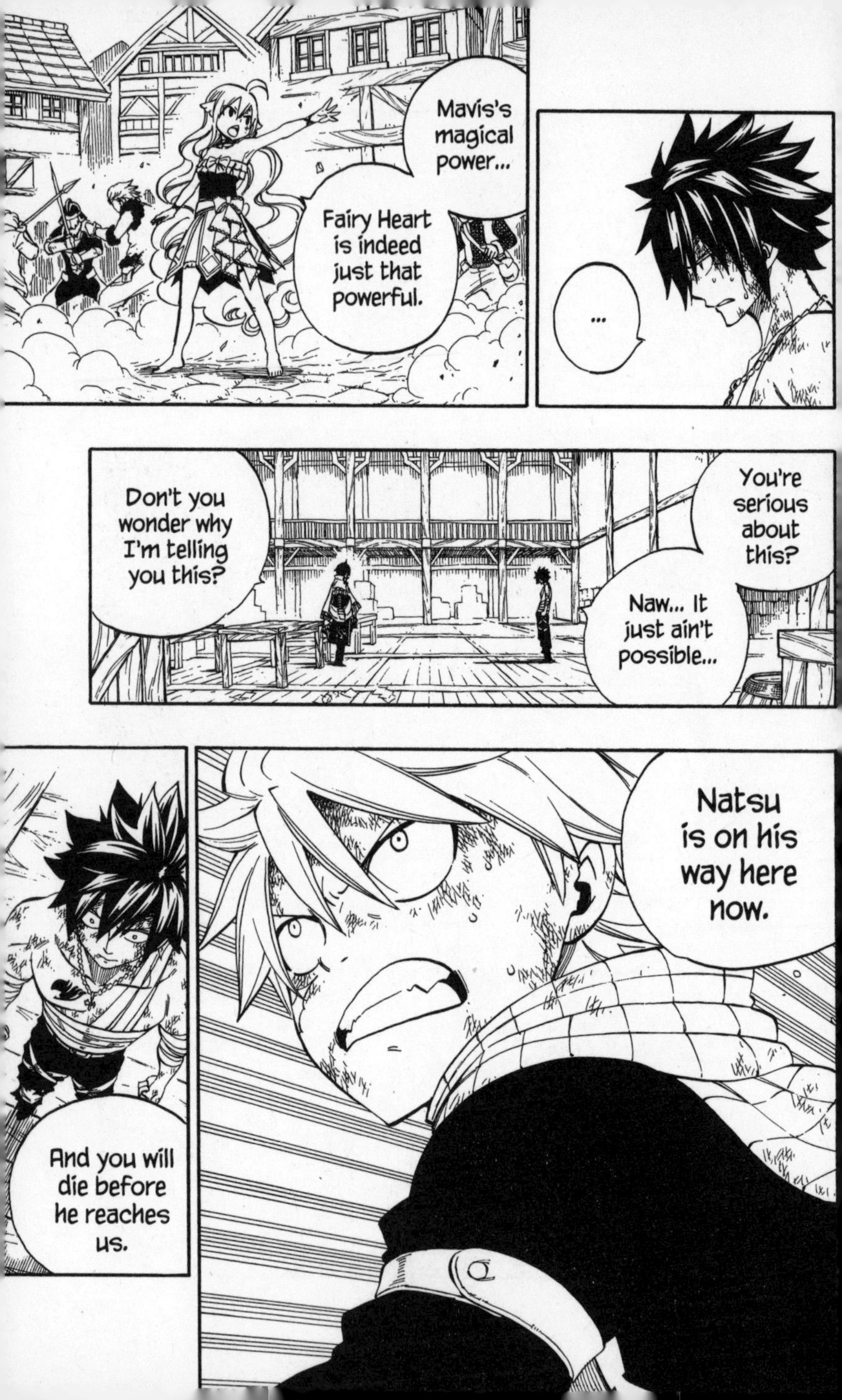
...
Mavis's magical power...
Fairy Heart is indeed just that powerful.
You're serious about this?
Naw... It just ain't possible...
Don't you wonder why I'm telling you this?
Natsu is on his way here now.
And you will die before he reaches us.

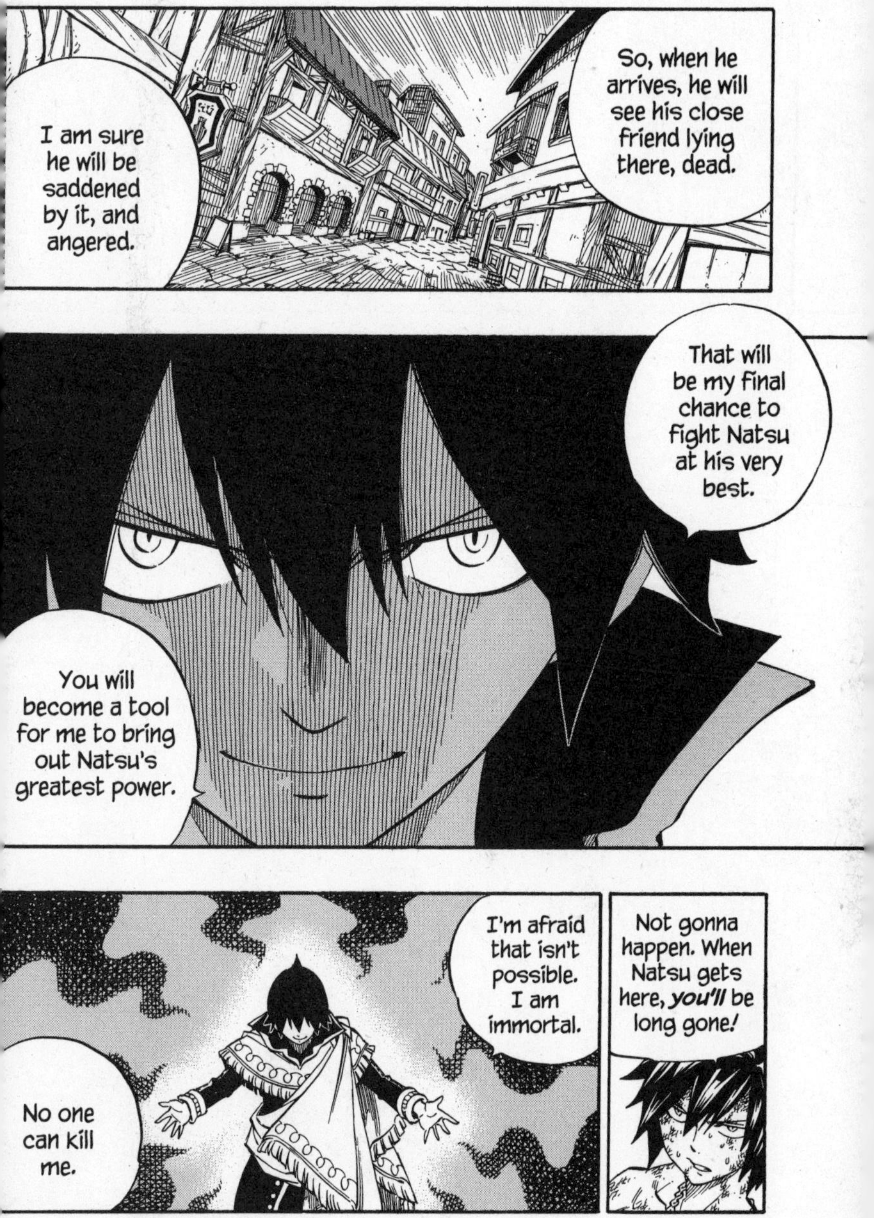
So, when he arrives, he will see his close friend lying there, dead.
I am sure he will be saddened by it, and angered.
That will be my final chance to fight Natsu at his very best.
You will become a tool for me to bring out Natsu's greatest power.
Not gonna happen. When Natsu gets here, *you'll* be long gone!
I'm afraid that isn't possible. I am immortal.
No one can kill me.

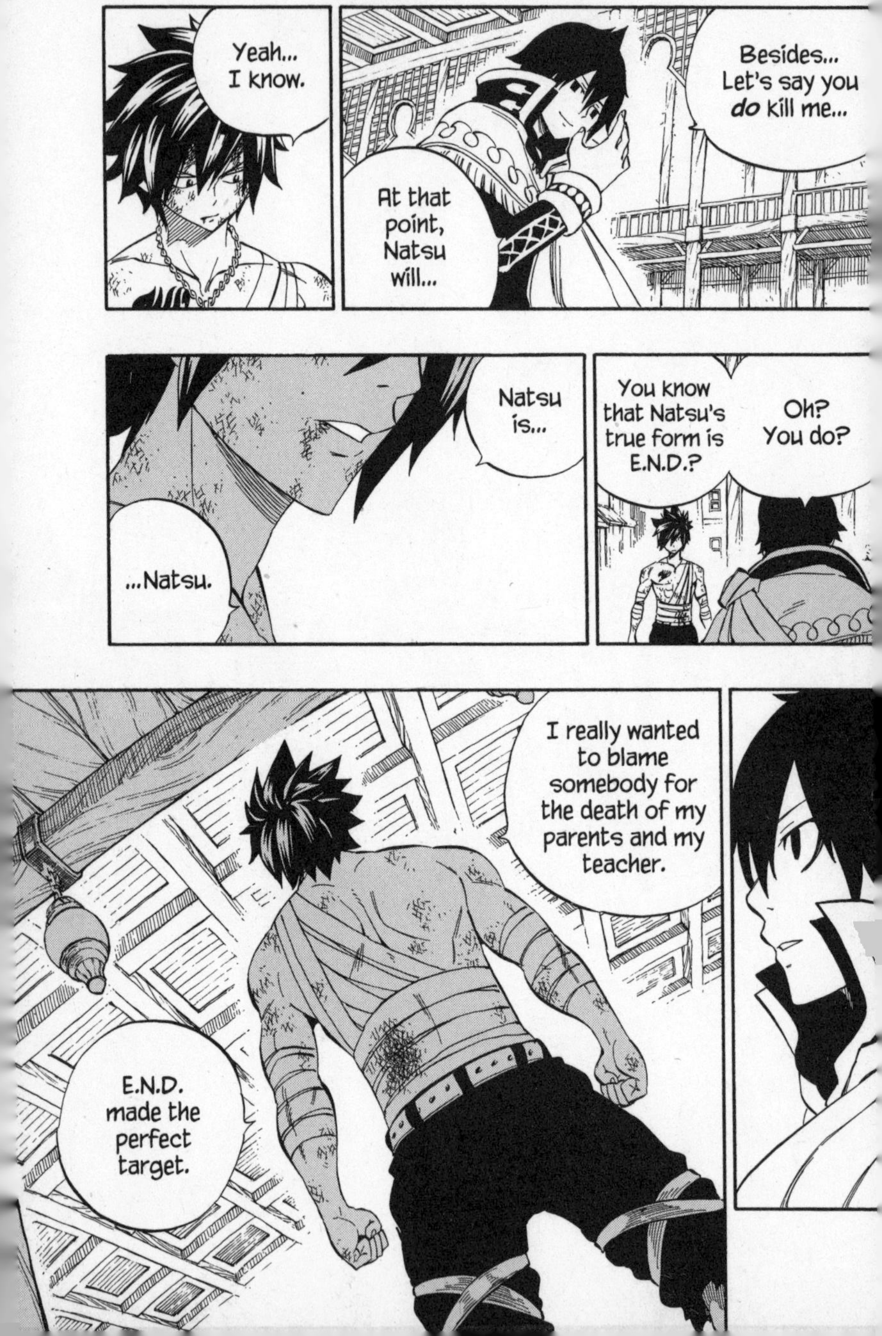
Besides... Let's say you *do* kill me...
At that point, Natsu will...
Yeah... I know.
Oh? You do?
You know that Natsu's true form is E.N.D.?
Natsu is...
...Natsu.
I really wanted to blame somebody for the death of my parents and my teacher.
E.N.D. made the perfect target.

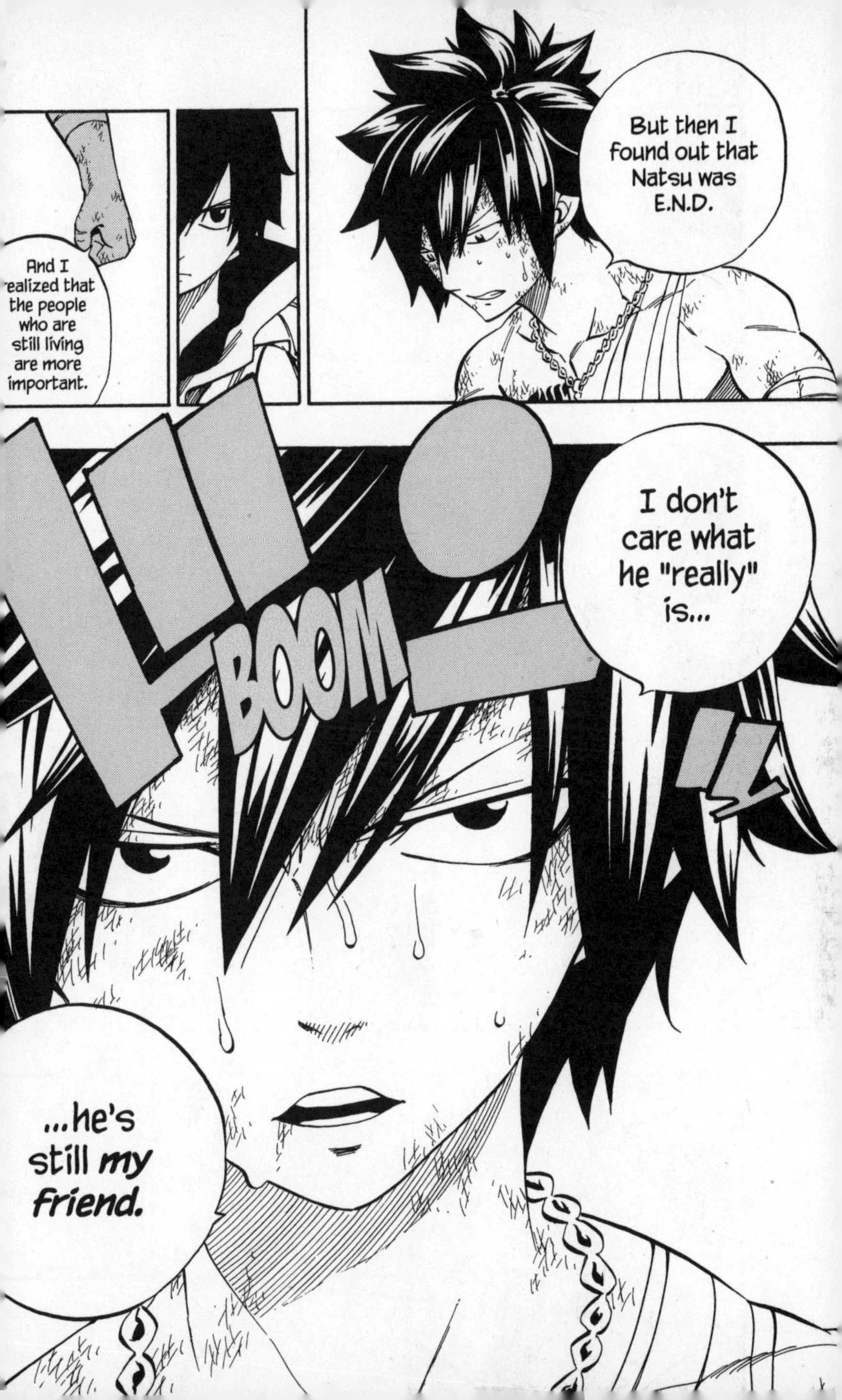
But then I found out that Natsu was E.N.D.
And I realized that the people who are still living are more important.
BOOM
I don't care what he "really" is...
...he's still *my* *friend.*

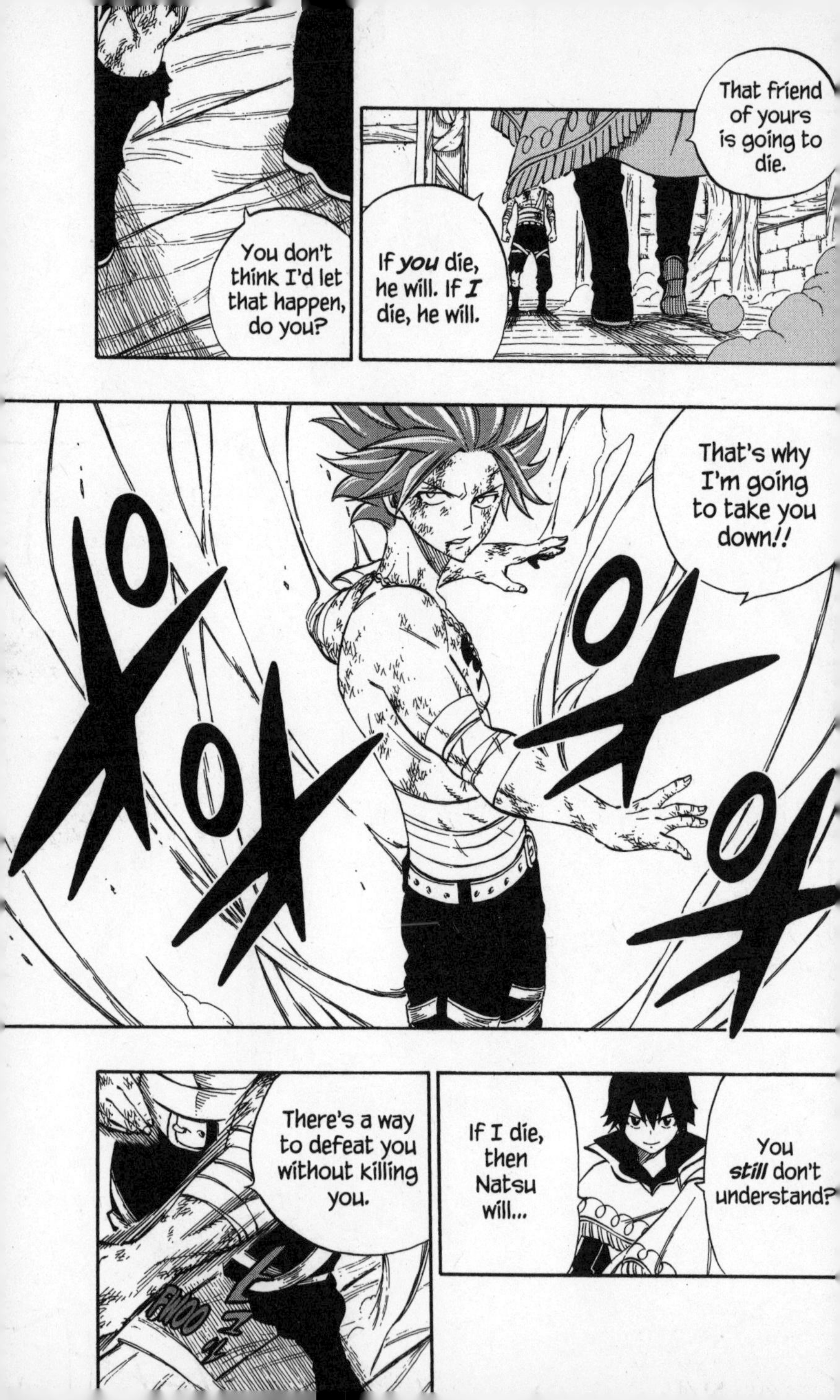
That friend of yours is going to die.
If *you* die, he will. If *I* die, he will.
You don't think I'd let that happen, do you?
That's why I'm going to take you down!!
You *still* don't understand?
If I die, then Natsu will...
There's a way to defeat you without killing you.
FWOO

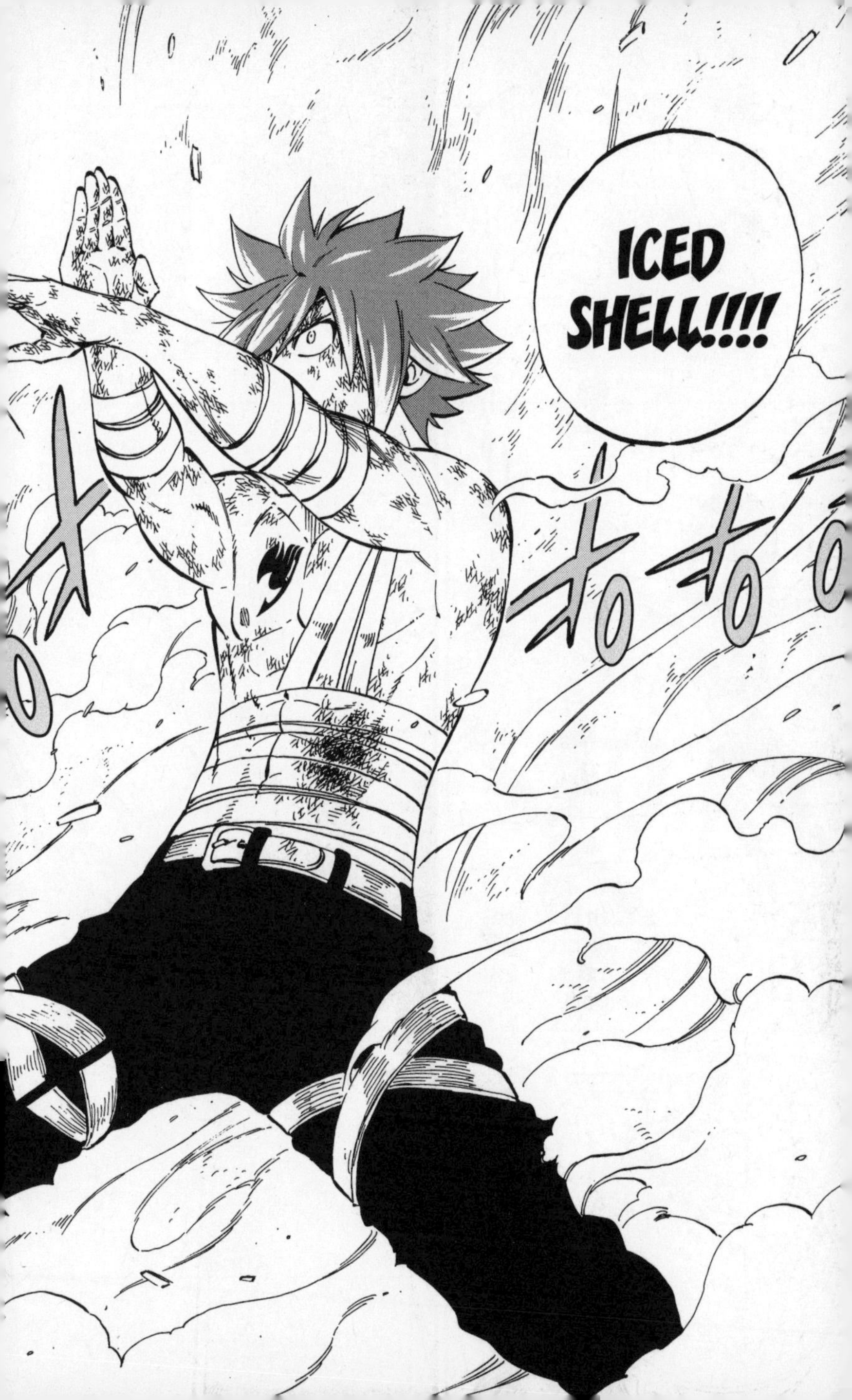
ICED SHELL!!!!

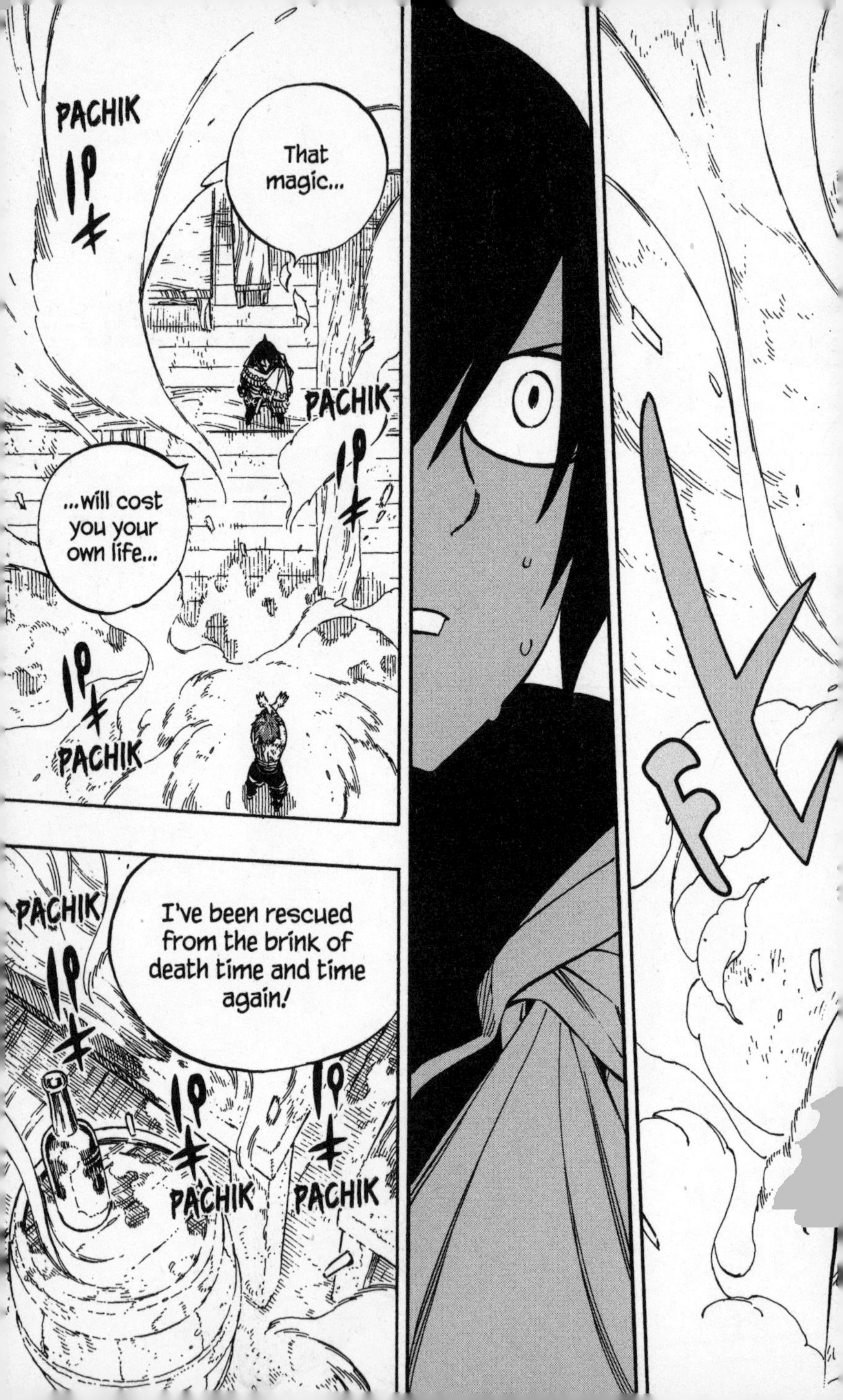
That magic...
PACHIK
PACHIK
...will cost you your own life...
PACHIK
I've been rescued from the brink of death time and time again!
PACHIK
PACHIK
PACHIK

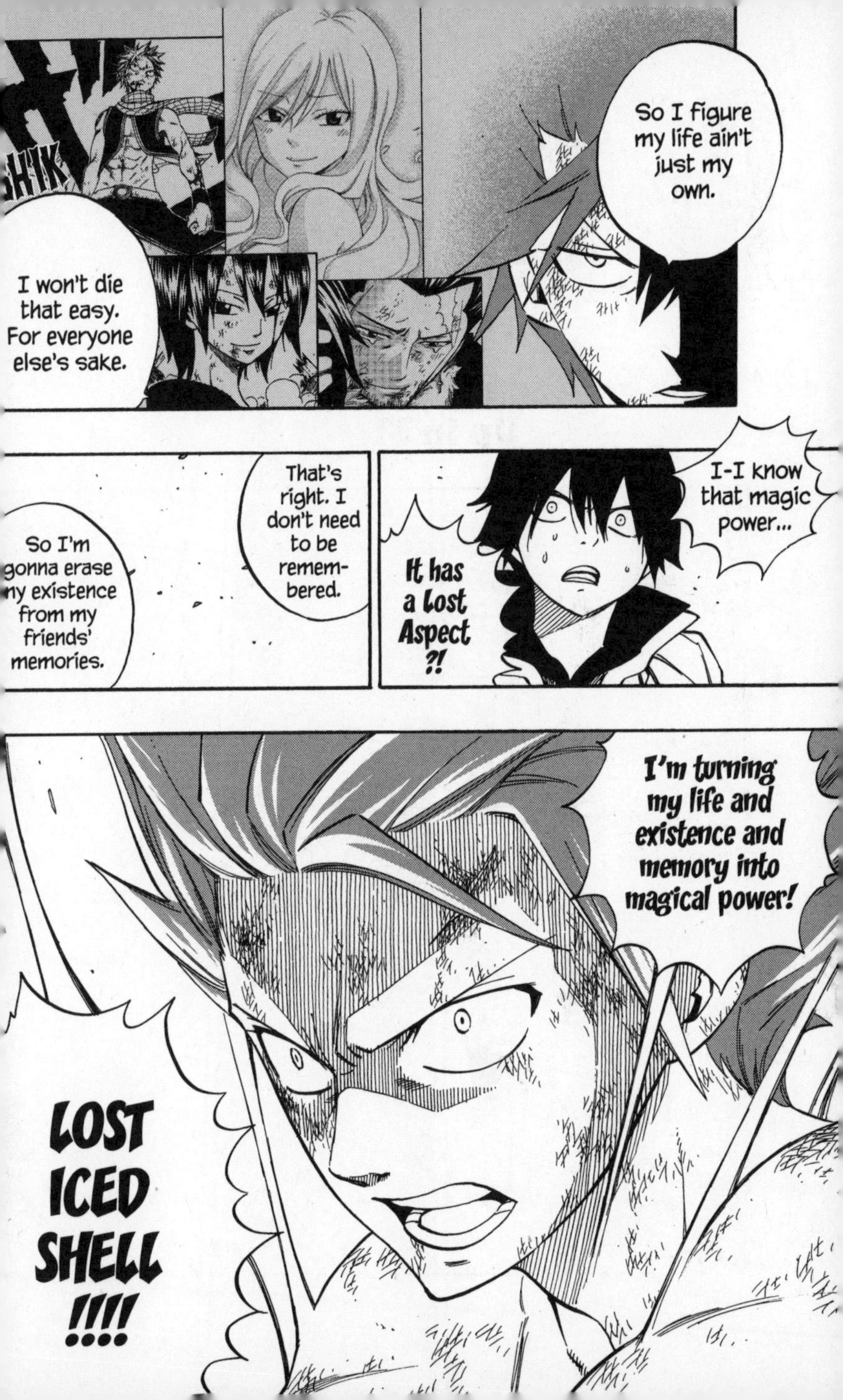

So I figure my life ain't just my own.
SHIK
I won't die that easy. For everyone else's sake.
I-I know that magic power...
It has a Lost Aspect?!
That's right. I don't need to be remembered.
So I'm gonna erase my existence from my friends' memories.
I'm turning my life and existence and memory into magical power!
LOST ICED SHELL!!!!

# FAIRY TAIL

フェアリーテイル

## Chapter 523: Is Destiny Going Up in Flames?

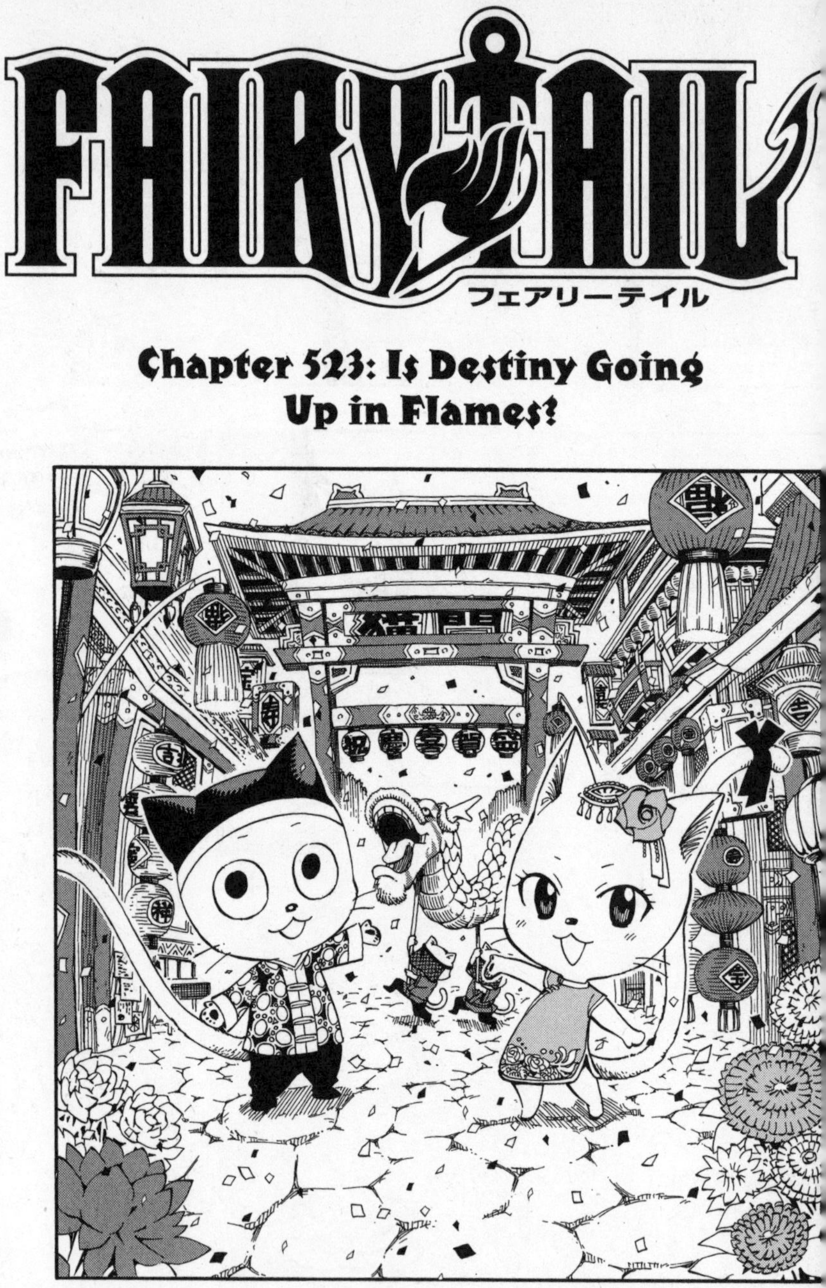

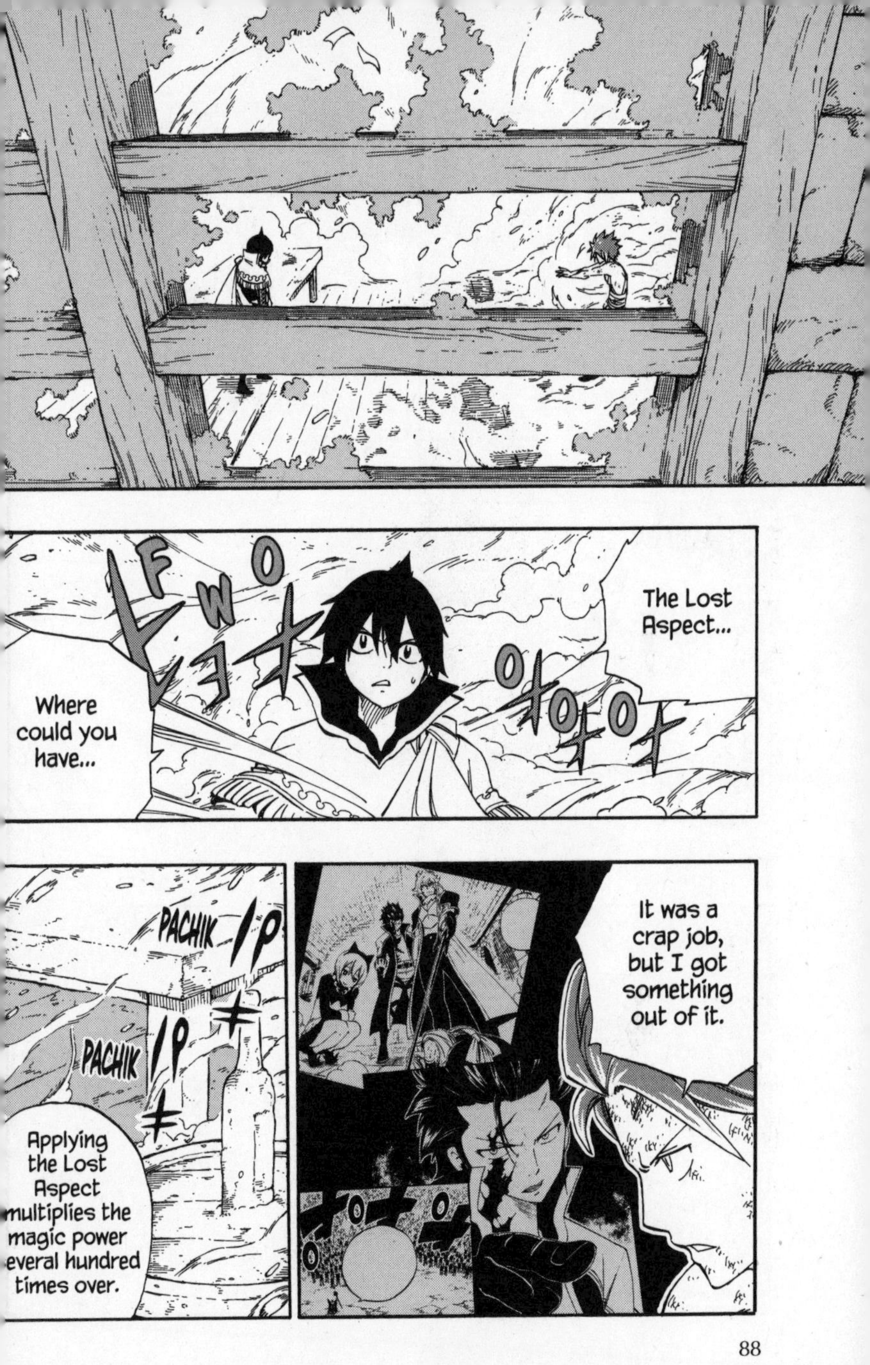
The Lost Aspect...
FWO
O O O
Where could you have...
It was a crap job, but I got something out of it.
PACHIK
PACHIK
Applying the Lost Aspect multiplies the magic power everal hundred times over.

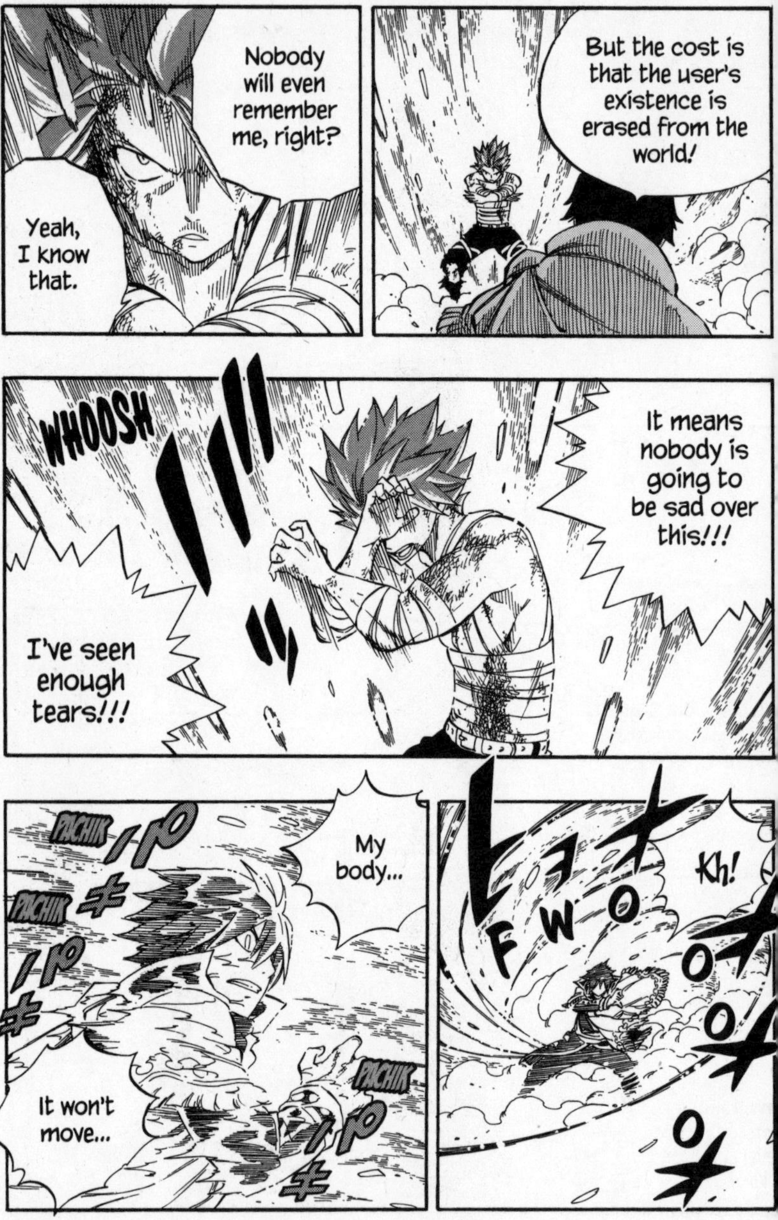

But the cost is that the user's existence is erased from the world!
Nobody will even remember me, right?
Yeah, I know that.
It means nobody is going to be sad over this!!!
WHOOSH
I've seen enough tears!!!
Kh!
FWOOOOOO
My body...
PACHIK
PACHIK
PACHIK
It won't move...

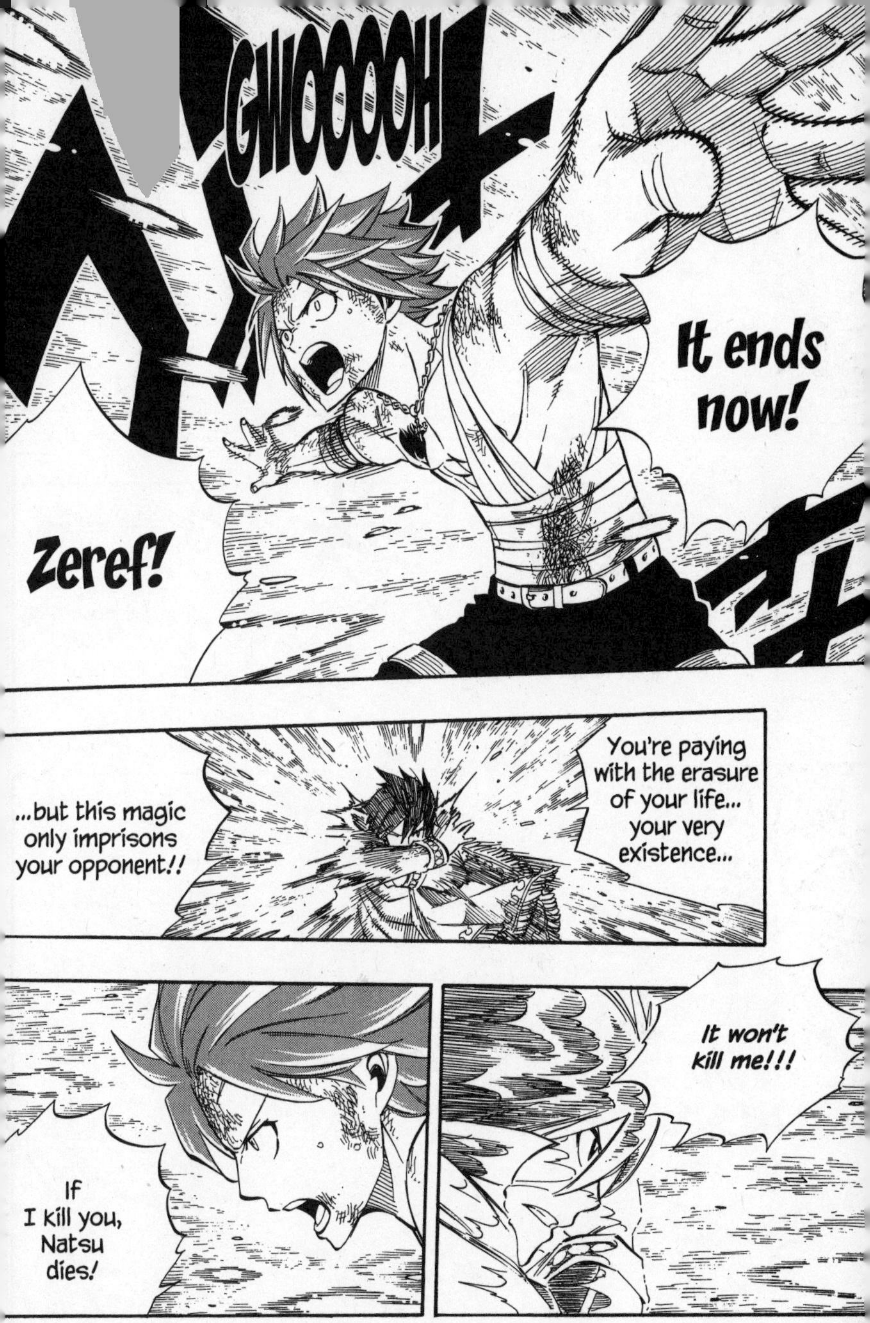
GWOOOOH!
It ends now!
Zeref!
You're paying with the erasure of your life... your very existence...
...but this magic only imprisons your opponent!!
It won't kill me!!!
If I kill you, Natsu dies!

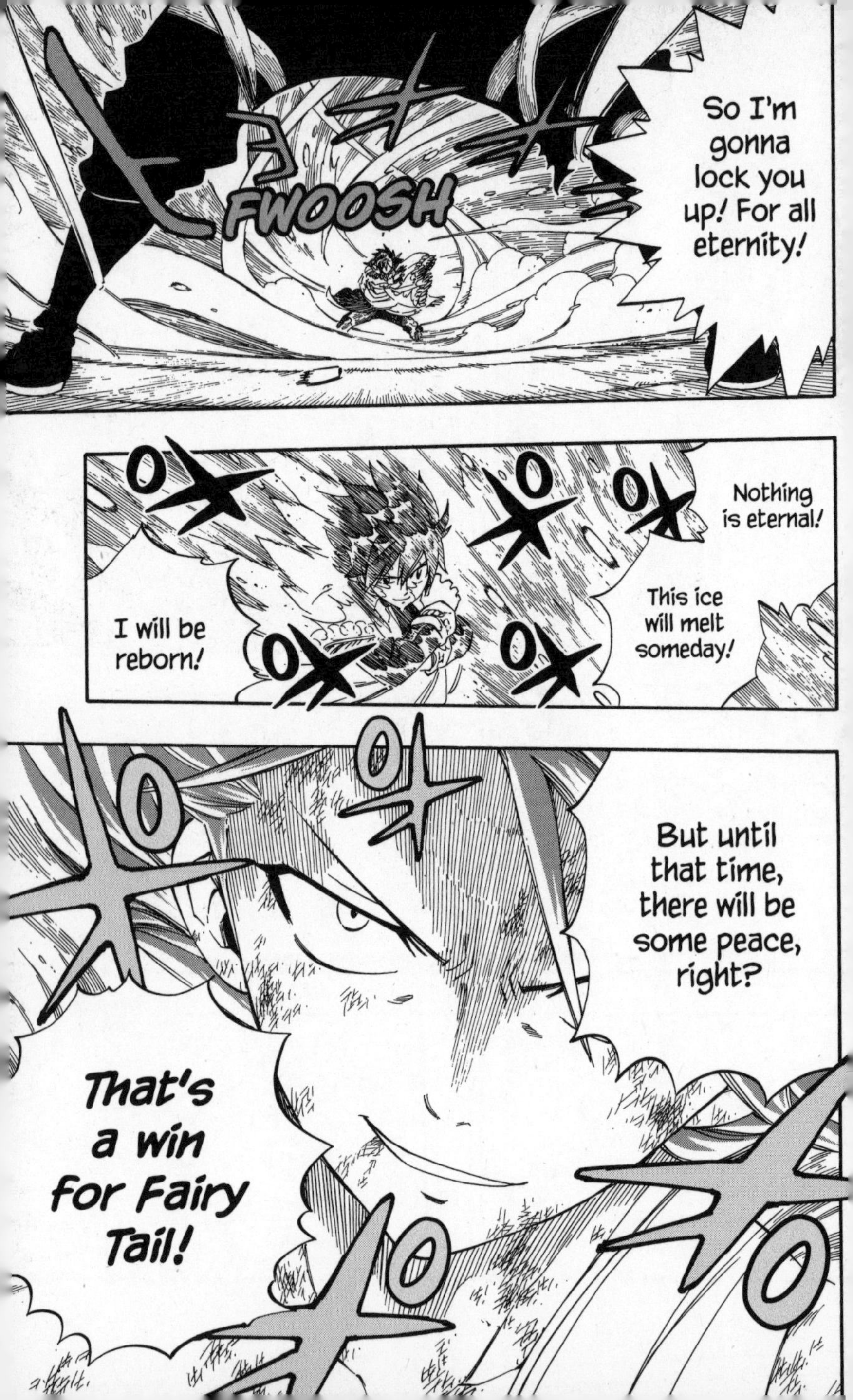
So I'm gonna lock you up! For all eternity!
FWOOSH
Nothing is eternal!
This ice will melt someday!
I will be reborn!
But until that time, there will be some peace, right?
That's a win for Fairy Tail!

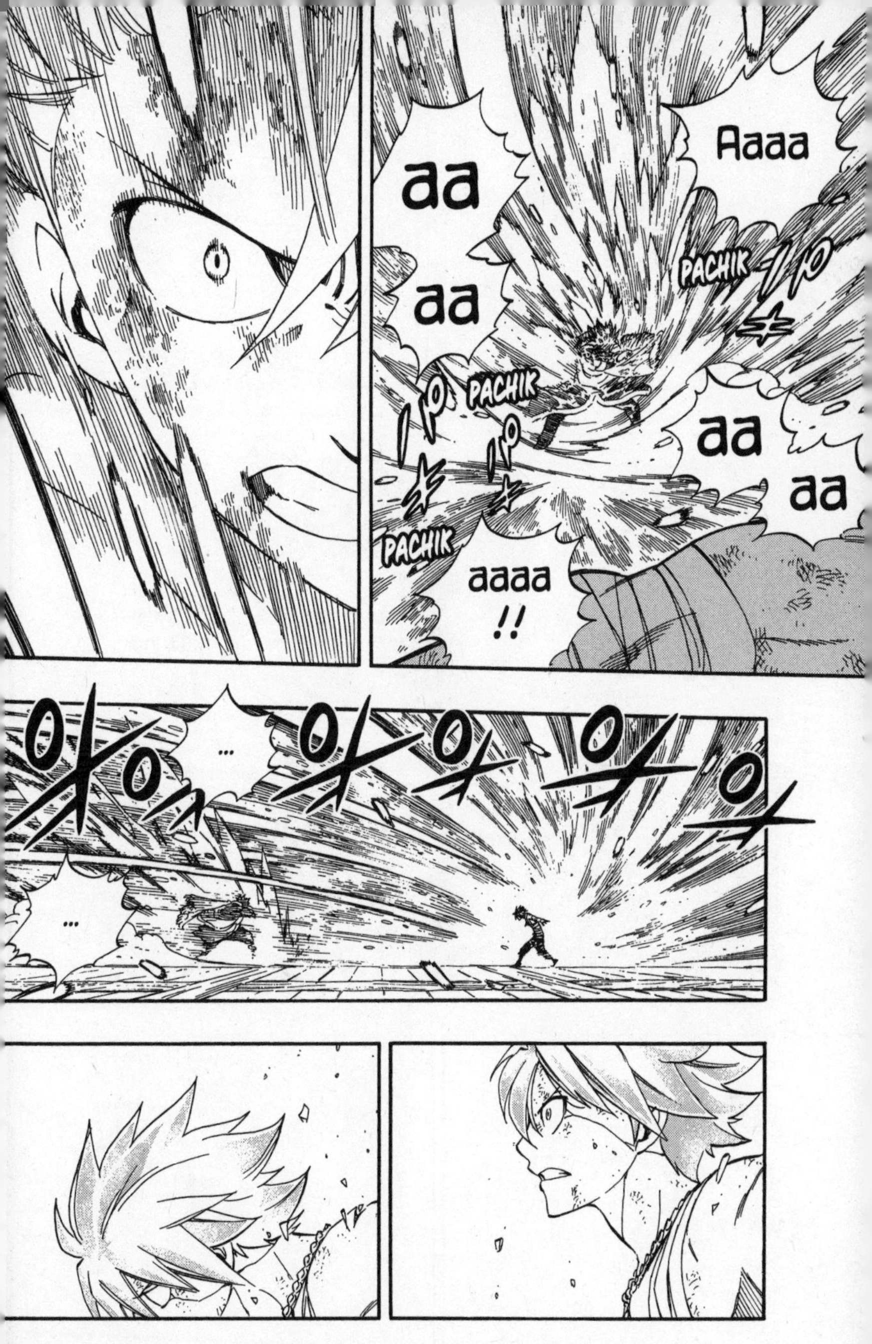
Aaaa
PACHIK
aa
aa
aa
aa
PACHIK
PACHIK
aaaa !!
...
...

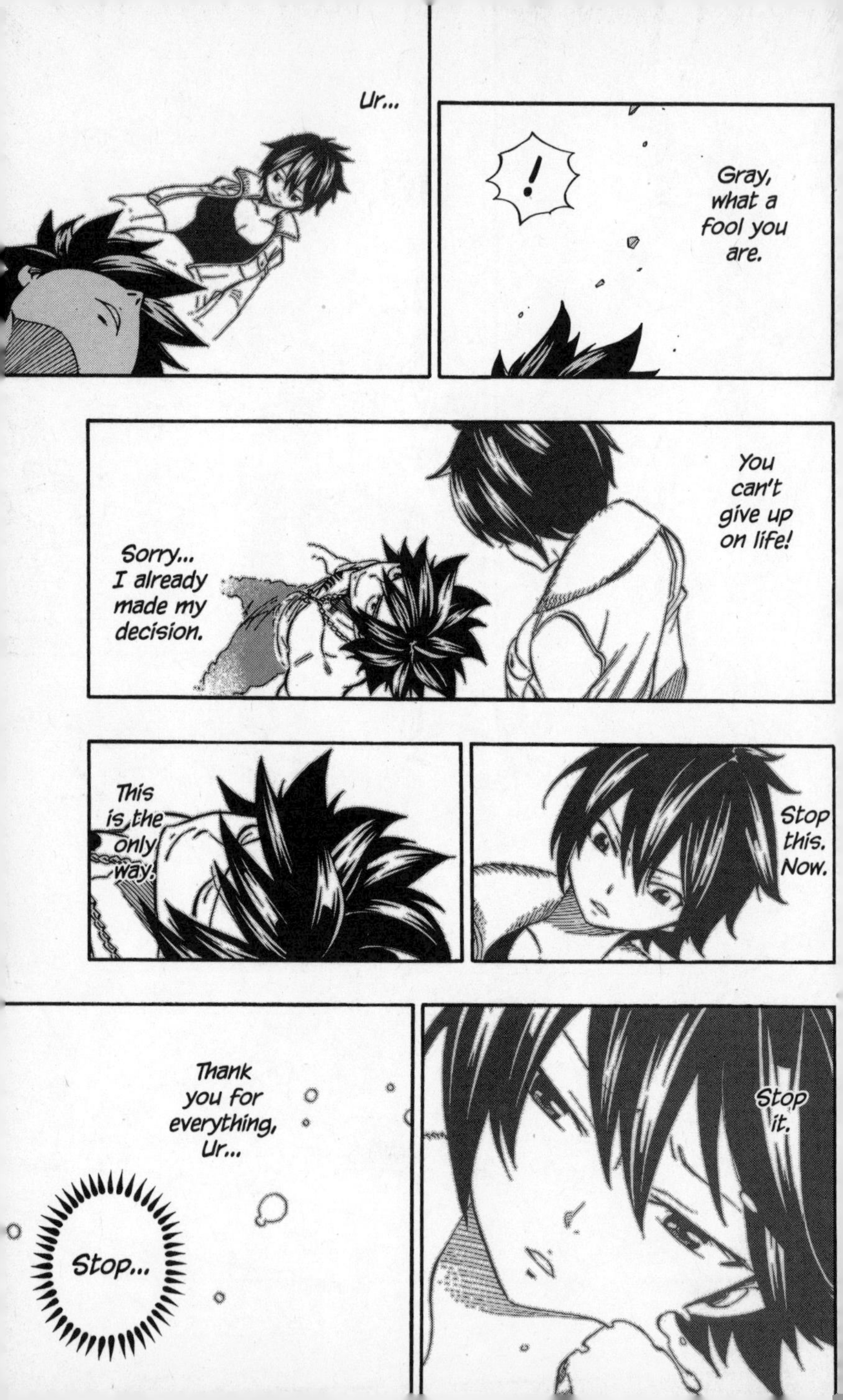
!
Gray, what a fool you are.
Ur...
You can't give up on life!
Sorry... I already made my decision.
Stop this. Now.
This is the only way.
Stop it.
Thank you for everything, Ur...
Stop...

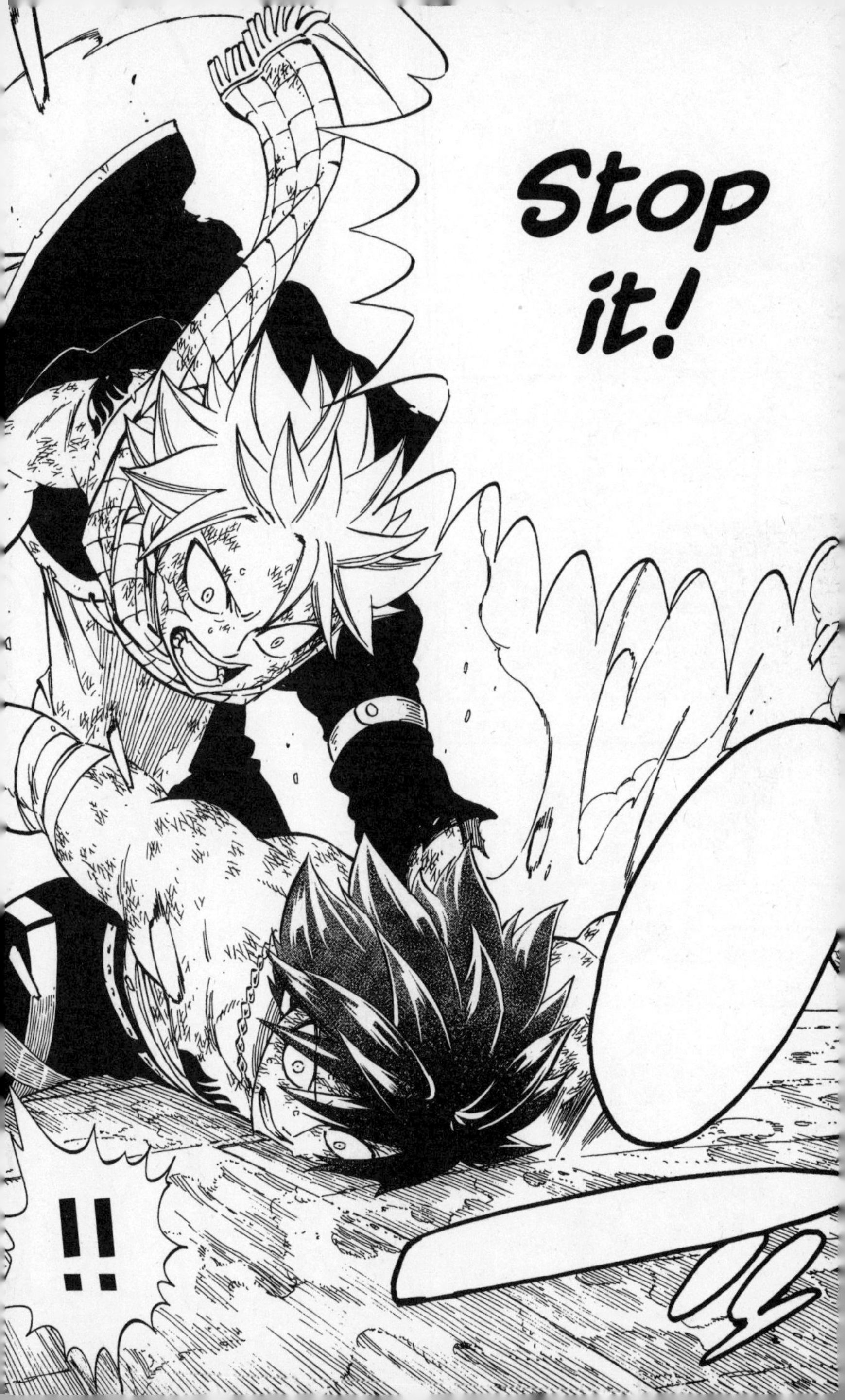
Stop it!
!!

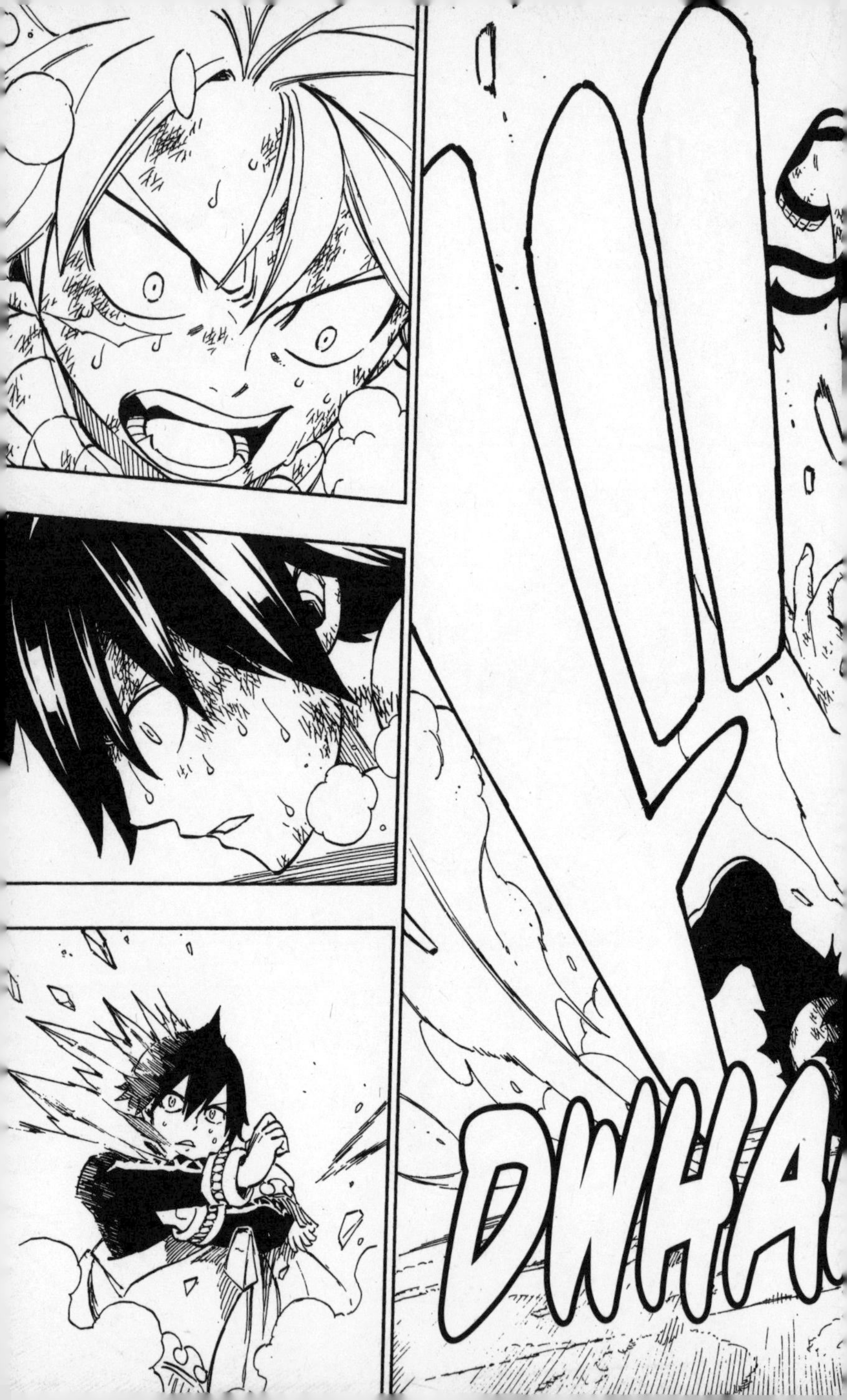
DWHA

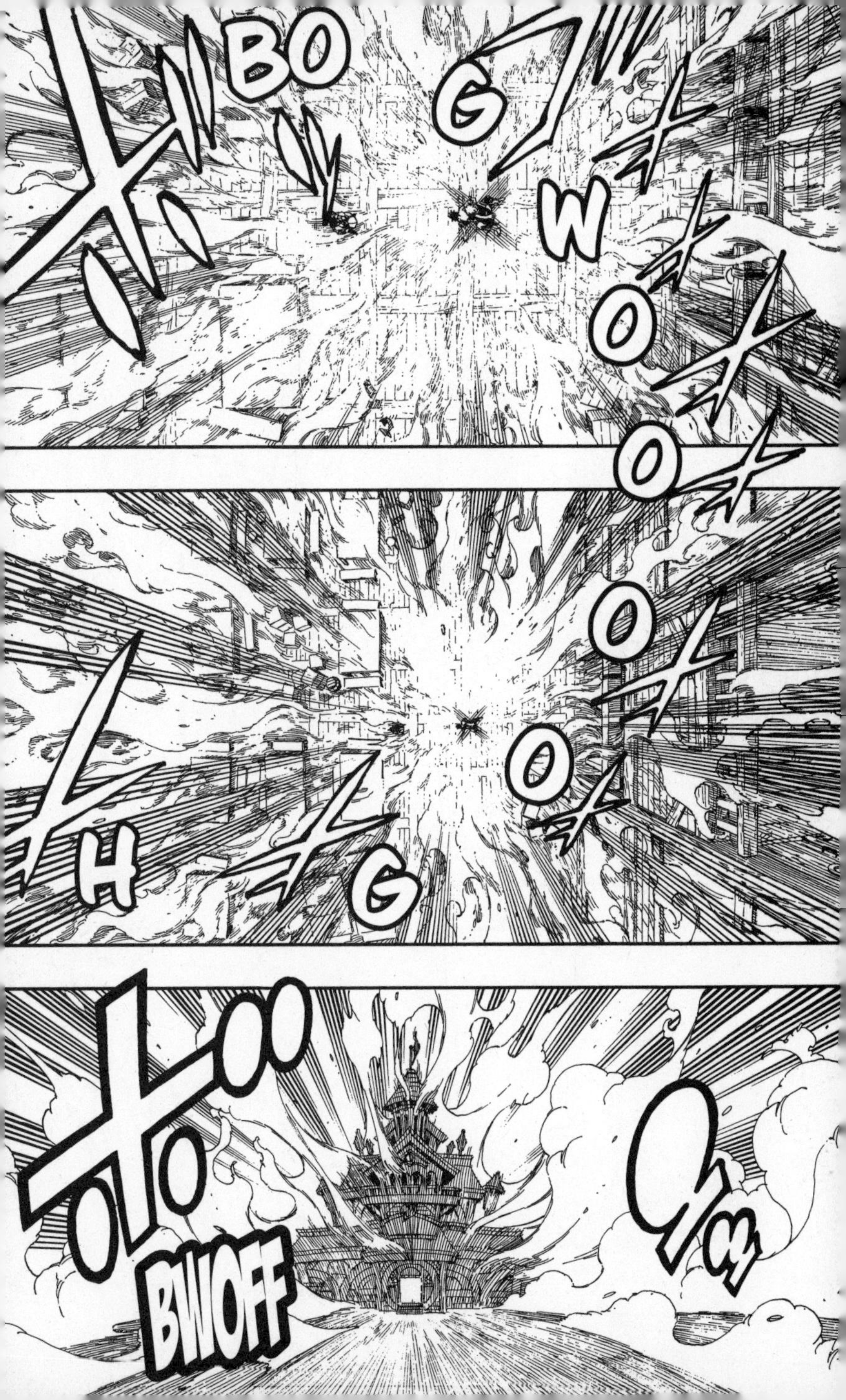
BOGWOOOOGH
BWOFF

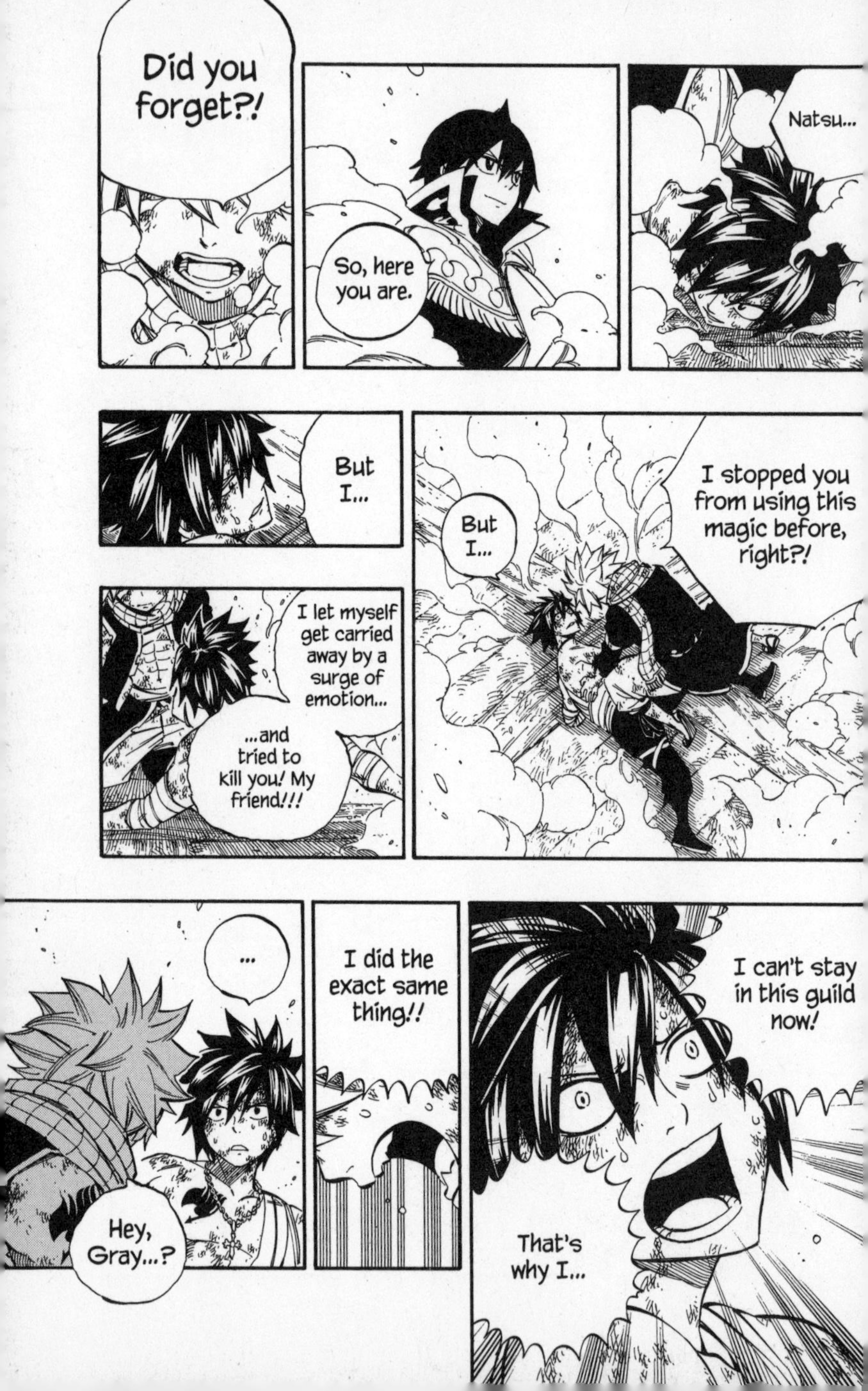

Natsu...
So, here you are.
Did you forget?!
I stopped you from using this magic before, right?!
But I...
But I...
I let myself get carried away by a surge of emotion...
...and tried to kill you! My friend!!!
I can't stay in this guild now!
That's why I...
I did the exact same thing!!
...
Hey, Gray...?

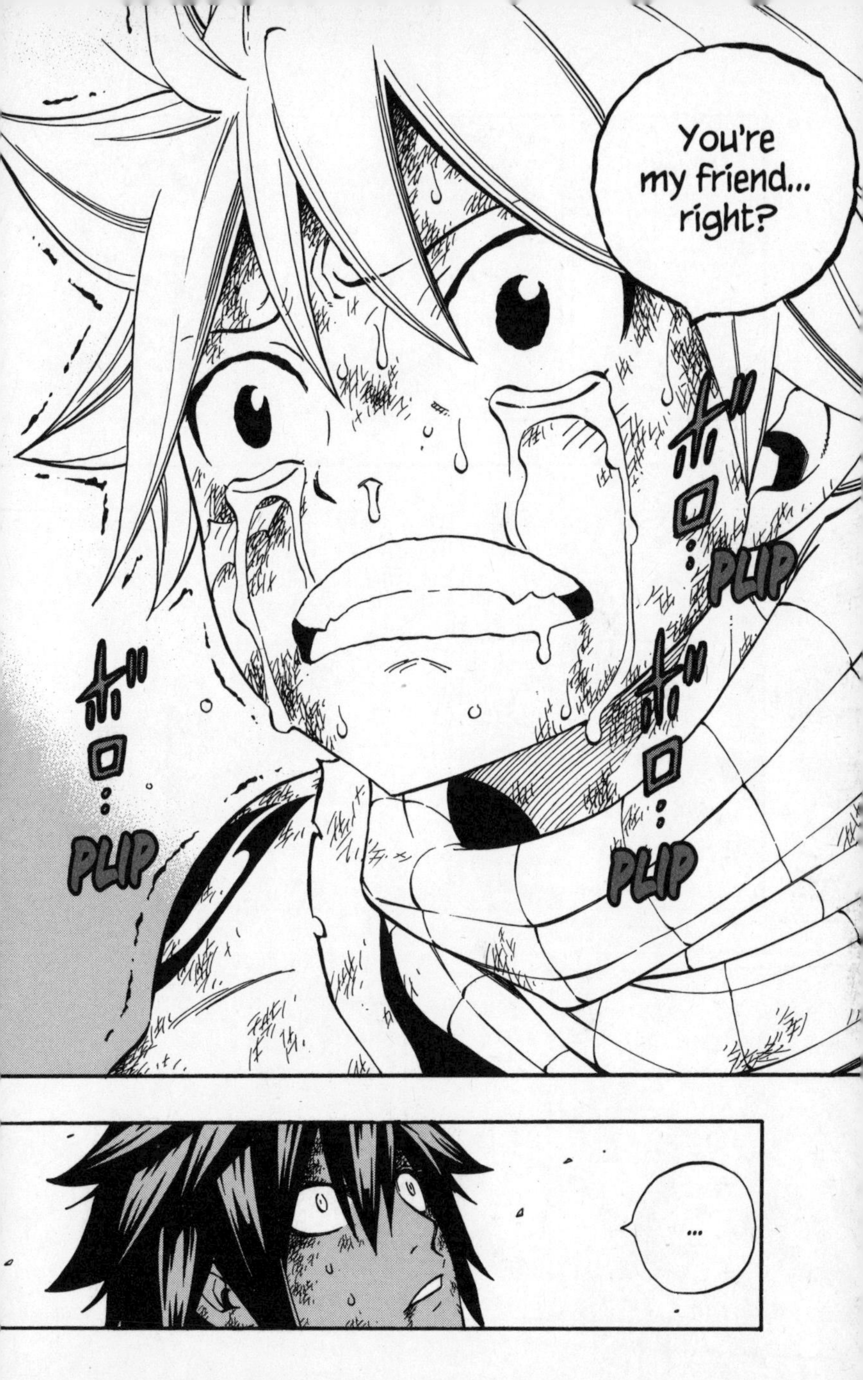

You're my friend... right?
ボロ…
PLIP
ボロ…
PLIP
ボロ…
PLIP
...

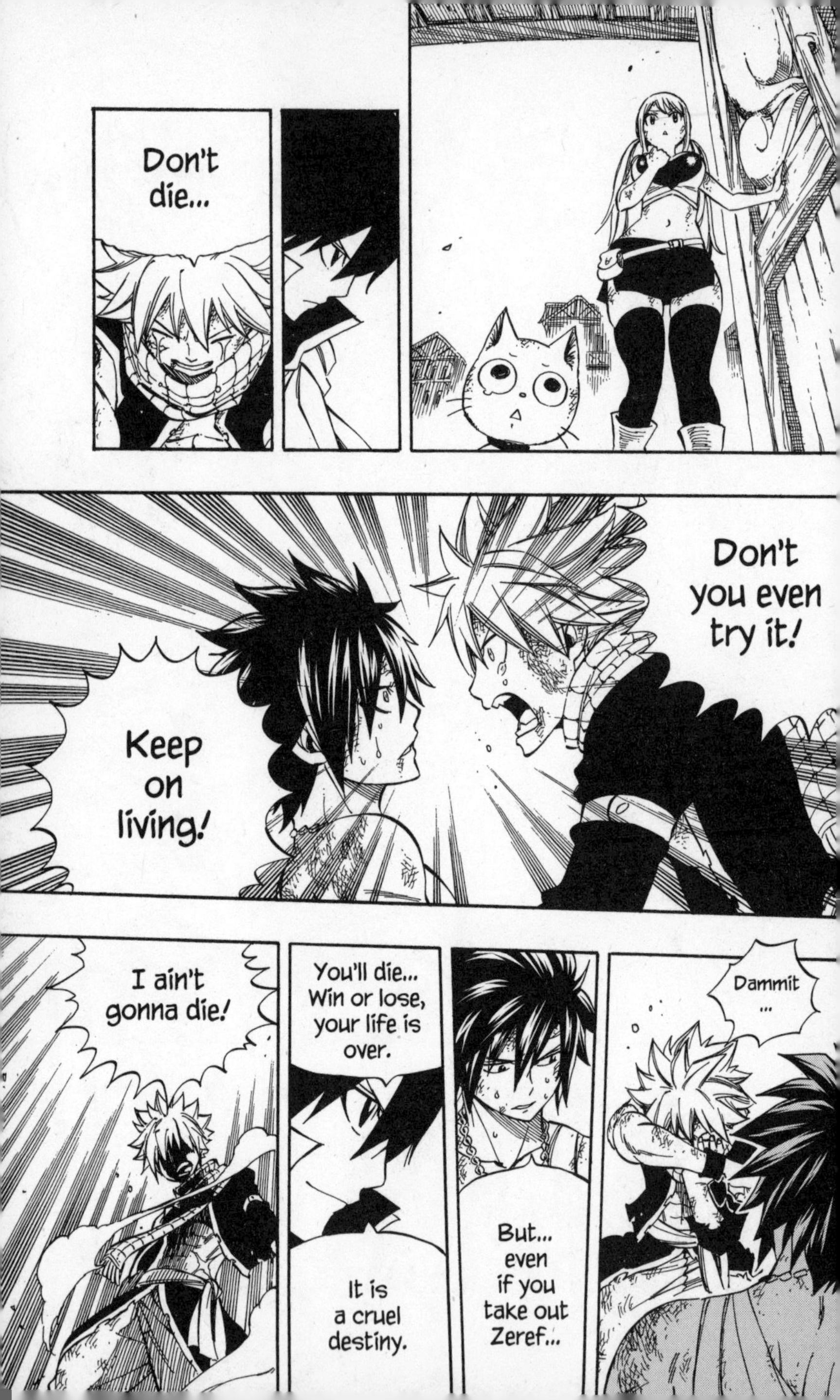
Don't die...
Don't you even try it!
Keep on living!
Dammit ...
But... even if you take out Zeref...
You'll die... Win or lose, your life is over.
It is a cruel destiny.
I ain't gonna die!

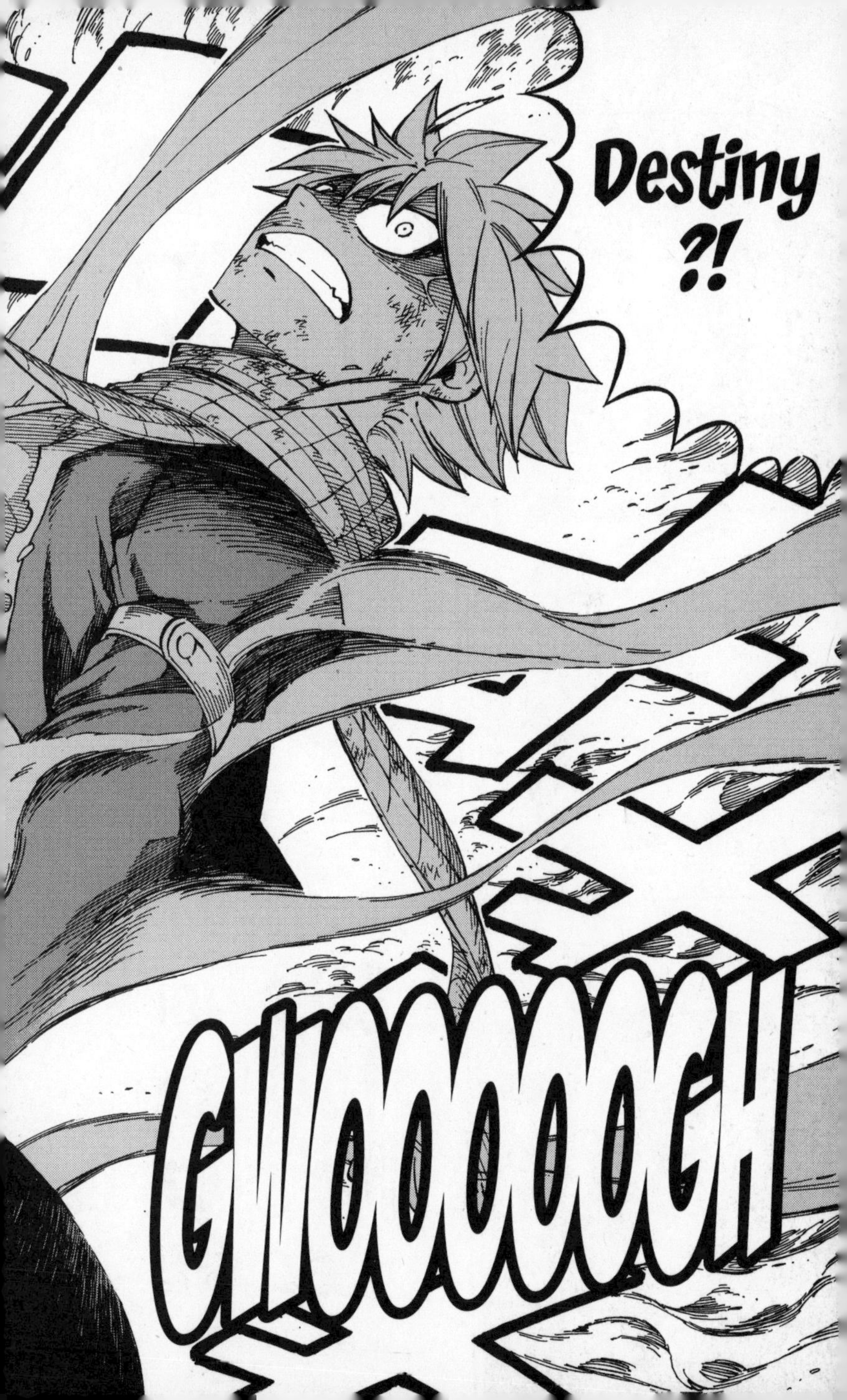
Destiny ?!
GWOOOOOCH

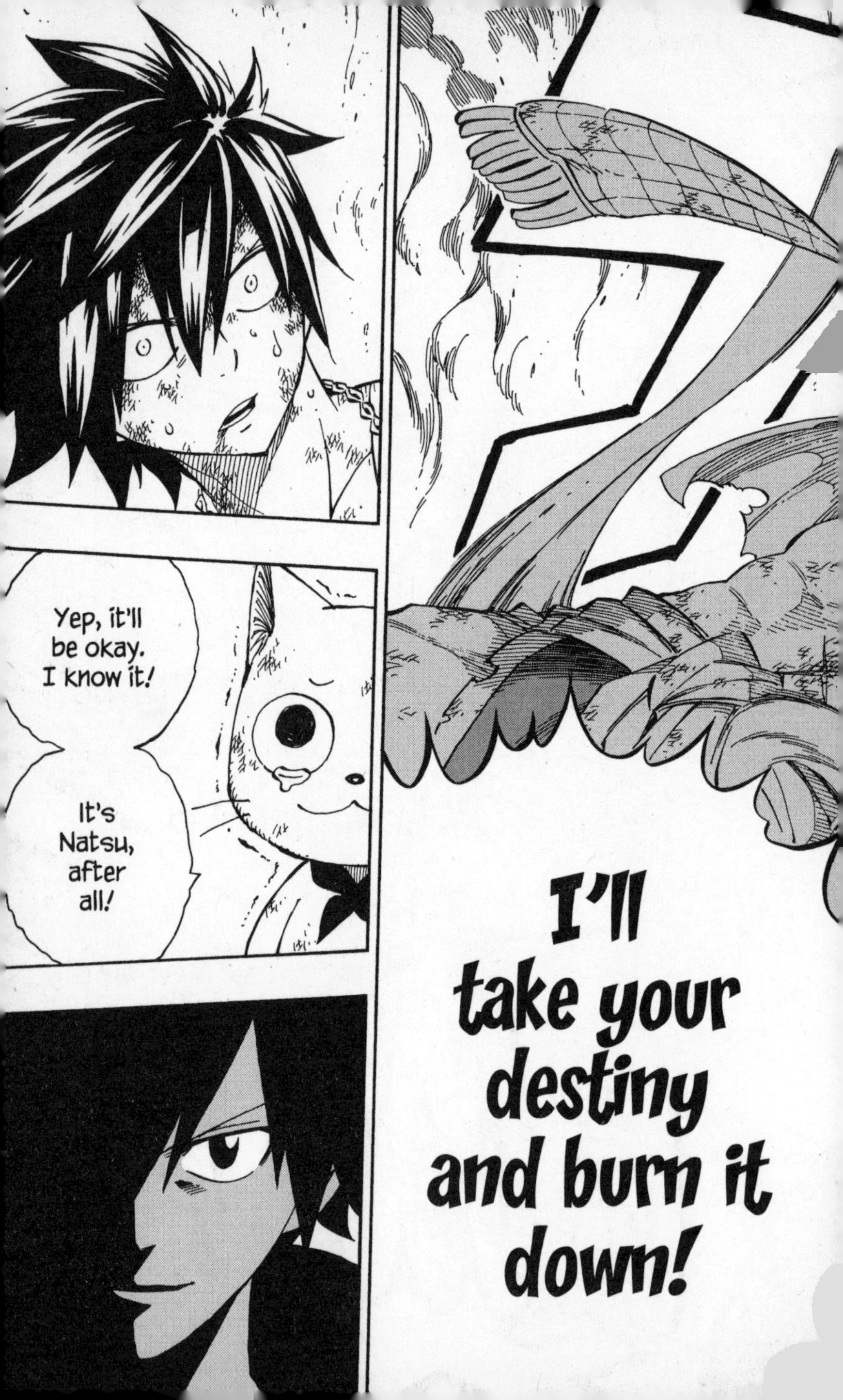
I'll take your destiny and burn it down!
Yep, it'll be okay. I know it!
It's Natsu, after all!

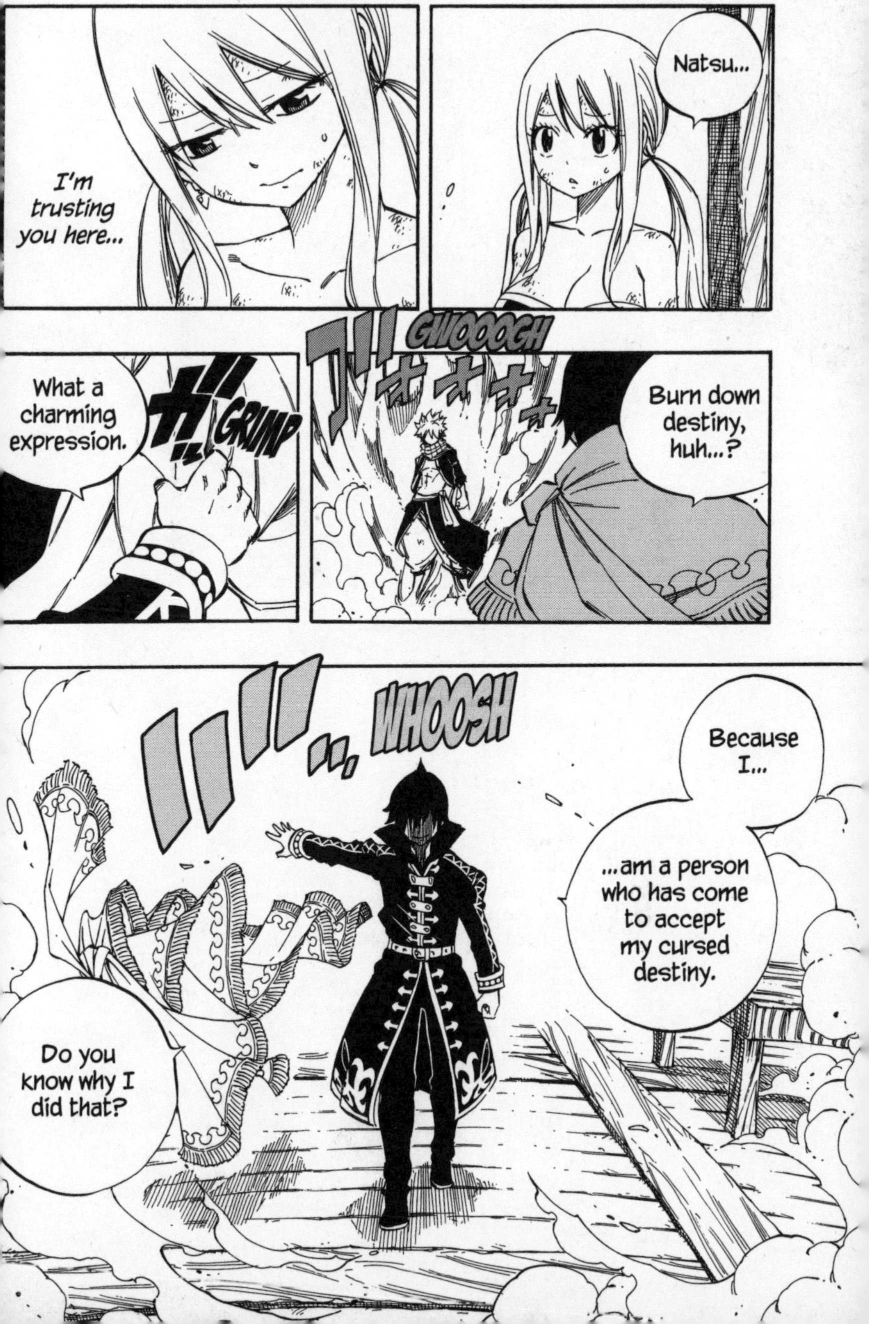
Natsu...
I'm trusting you here...
GWOOOGH
Burn down destiny, huh...?
GRUMP
What a charming expression.
Because I...
WHOOSH
...am a person who has come to accept my cursed destiny.
Do you know why I did that?

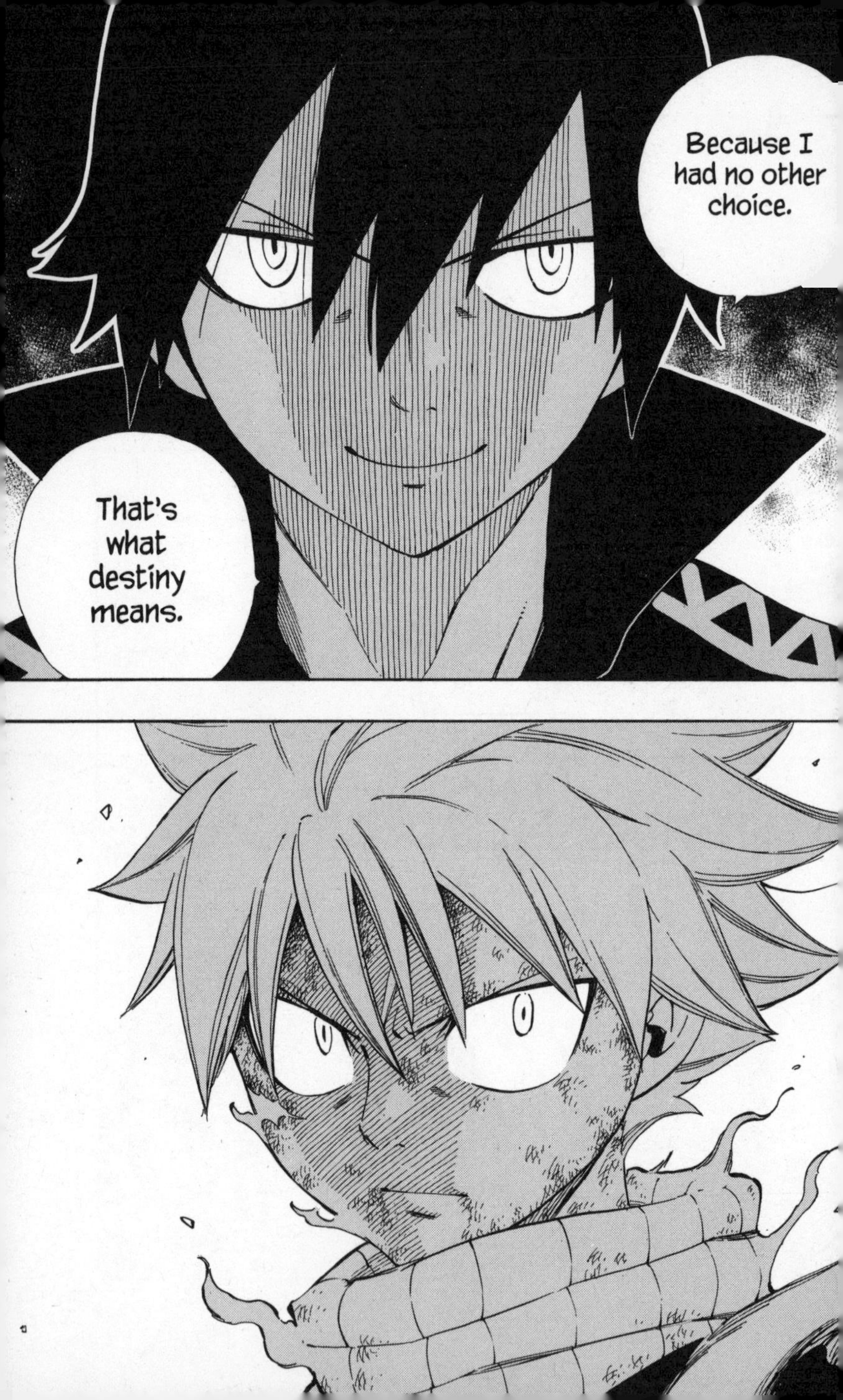
Because I had no other choice.
That's what destiny means.

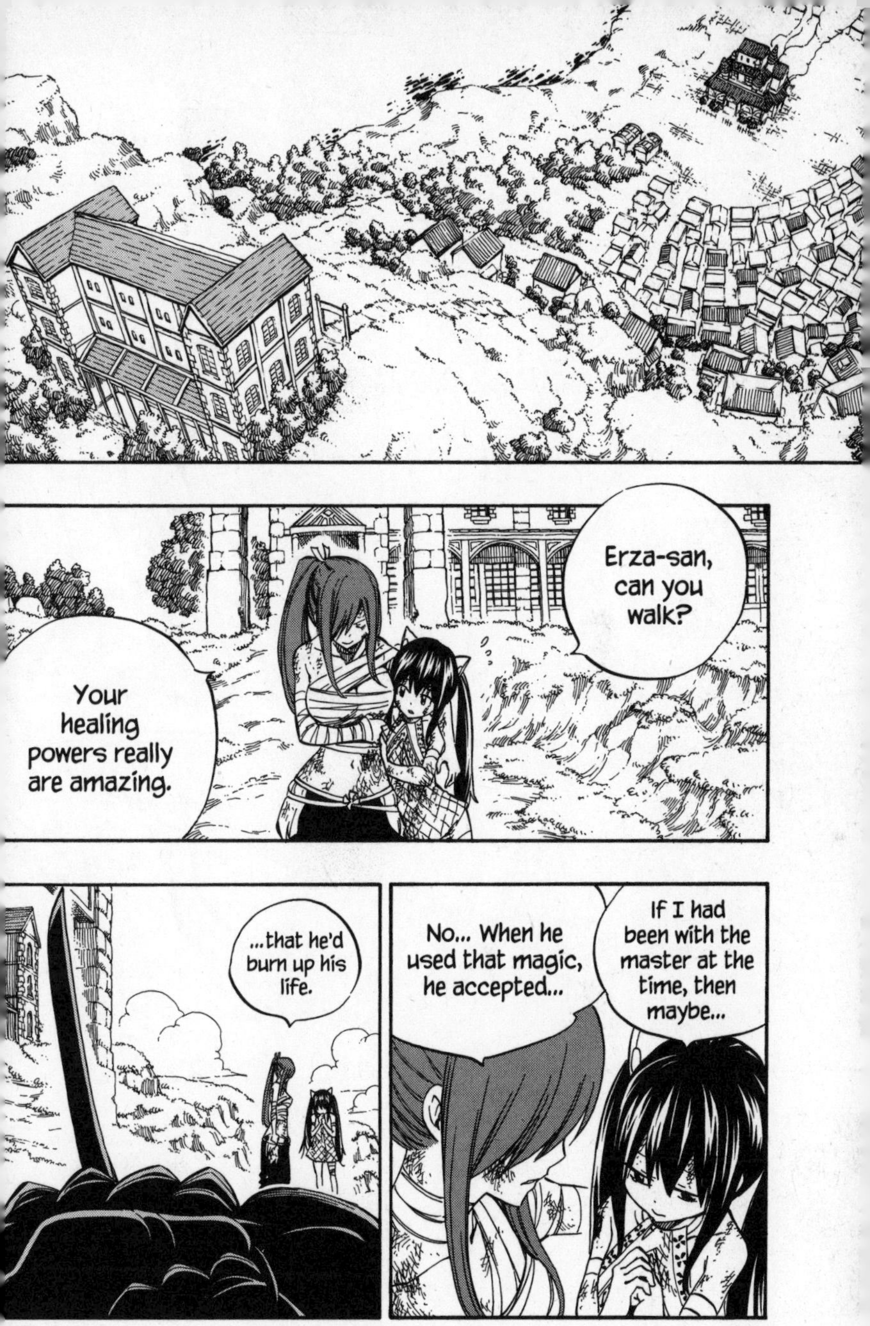
Erza-san, can you walk?
Your healing powers really are amazing.
If I had been with the master at the time, then maybe...
No... When he used that magic, he accepted...
...that he'd burn up his life.

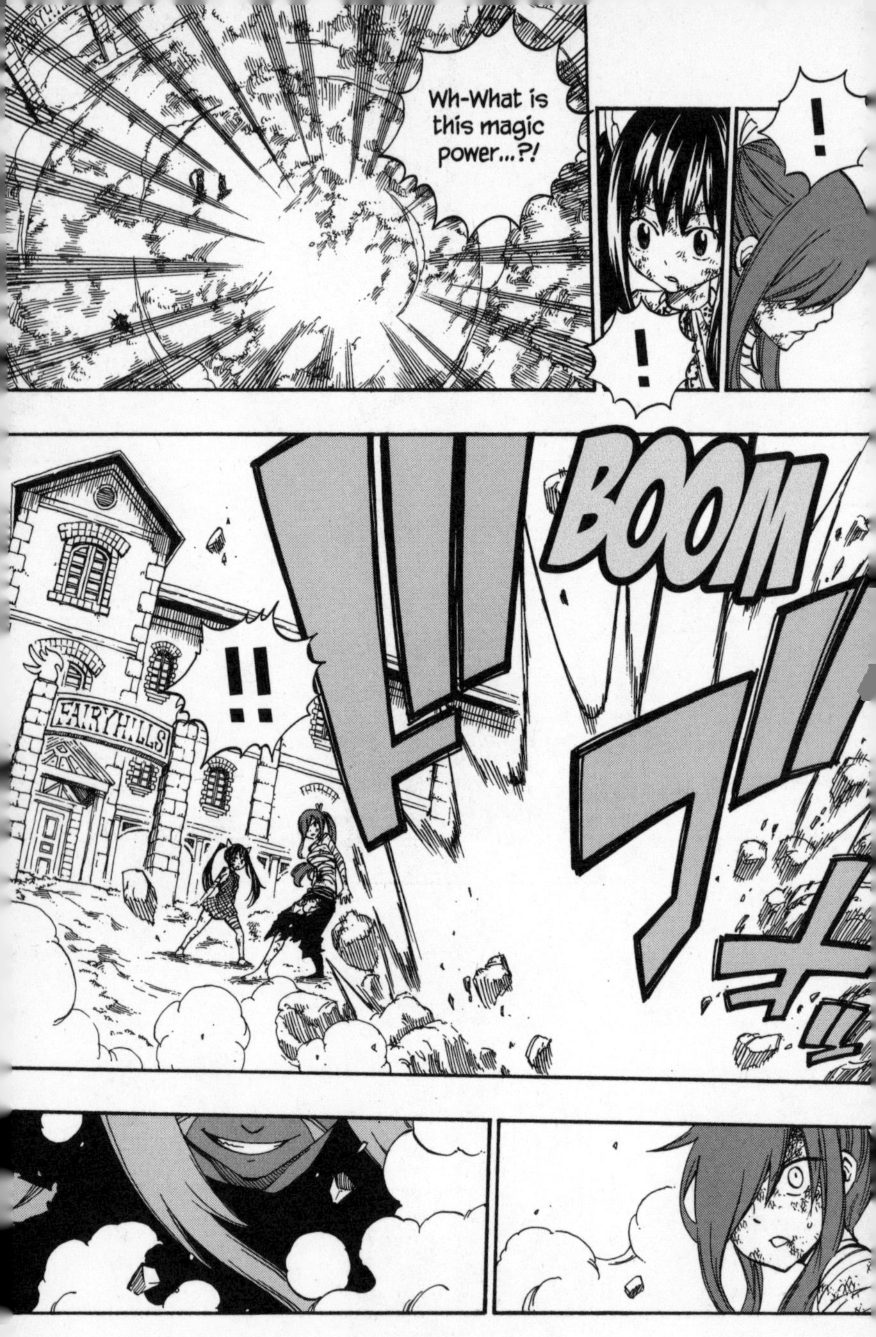
!
!
Wh-What is this magic power...?!
BOOM
!!

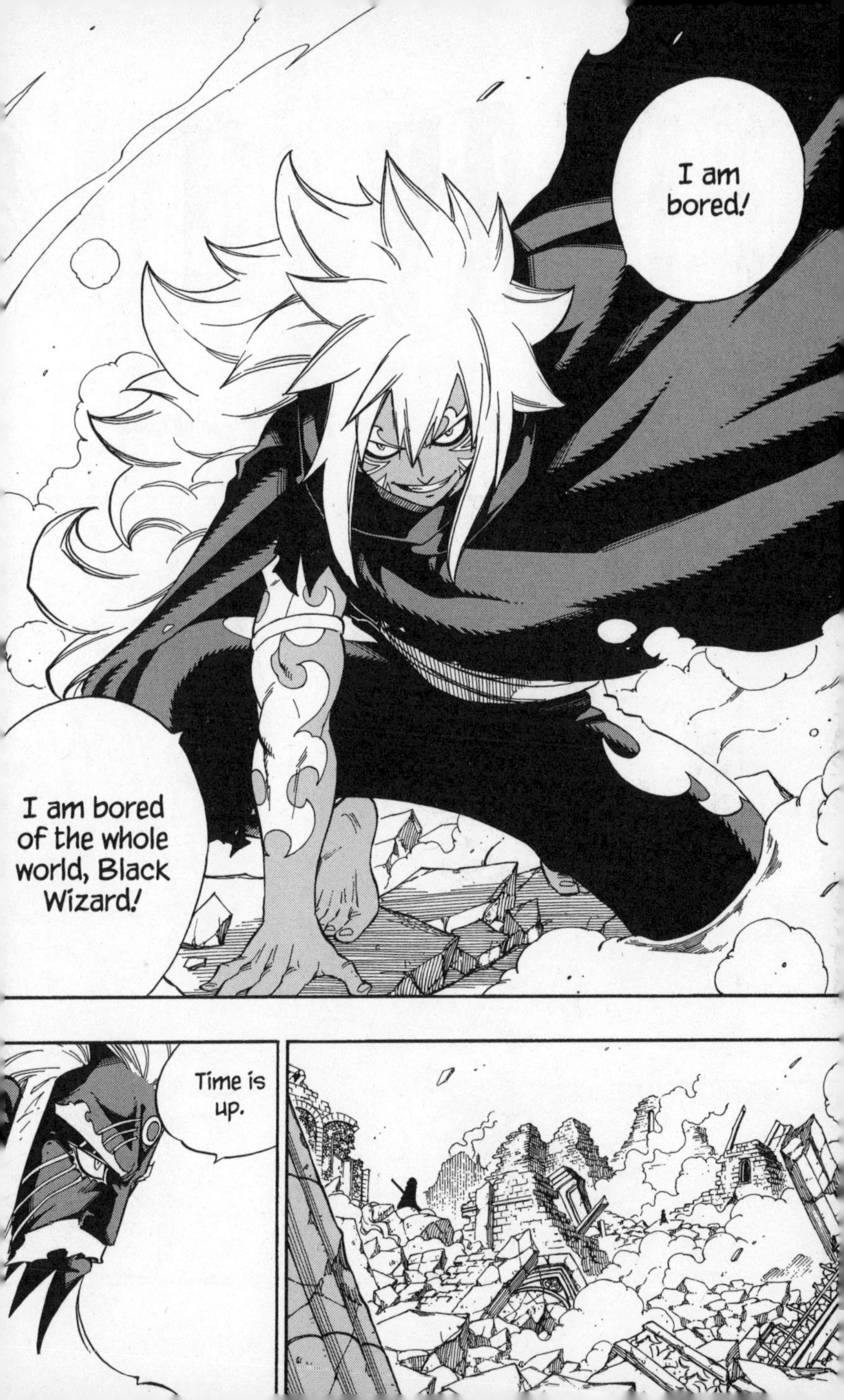
I am bored!
I am bored of the whole world, Black Wizard!
Time is up.

FAIRY TAIL

フェアリーテイル

# Chapter 524: The Black Future

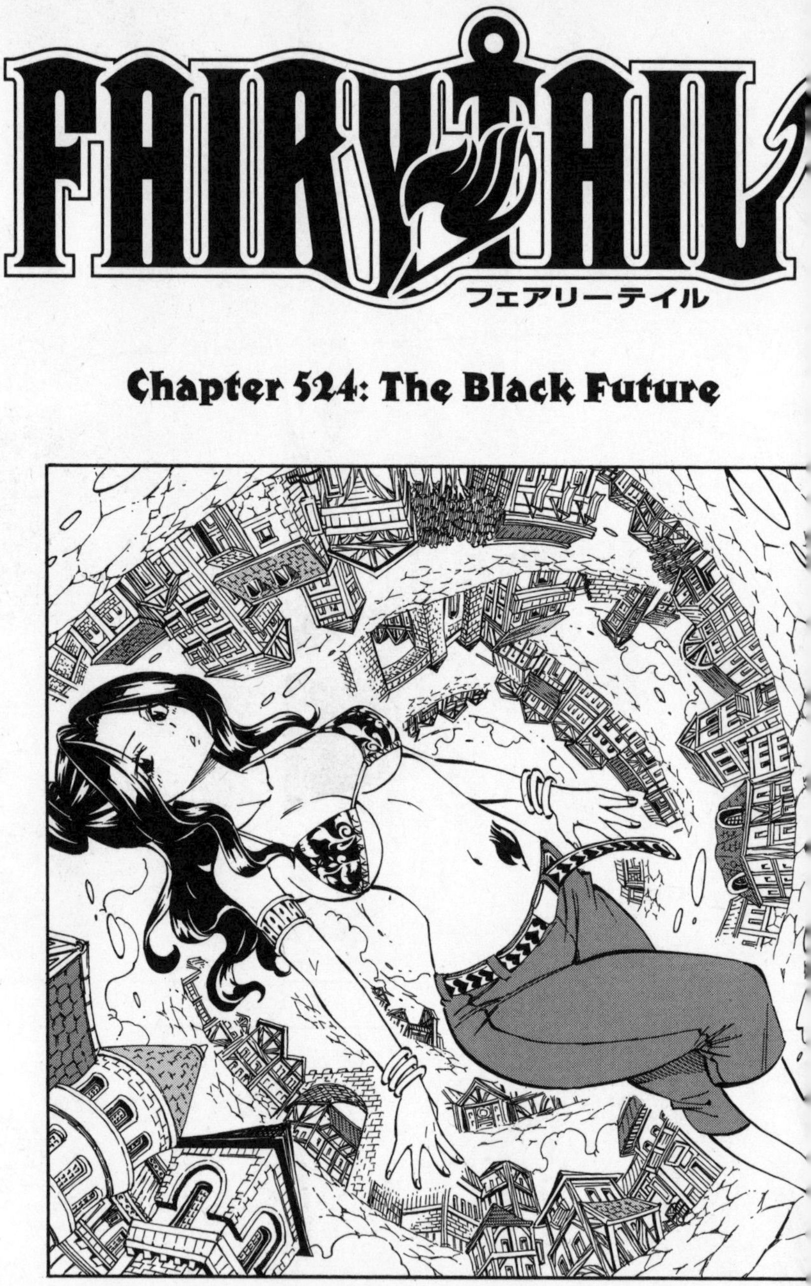

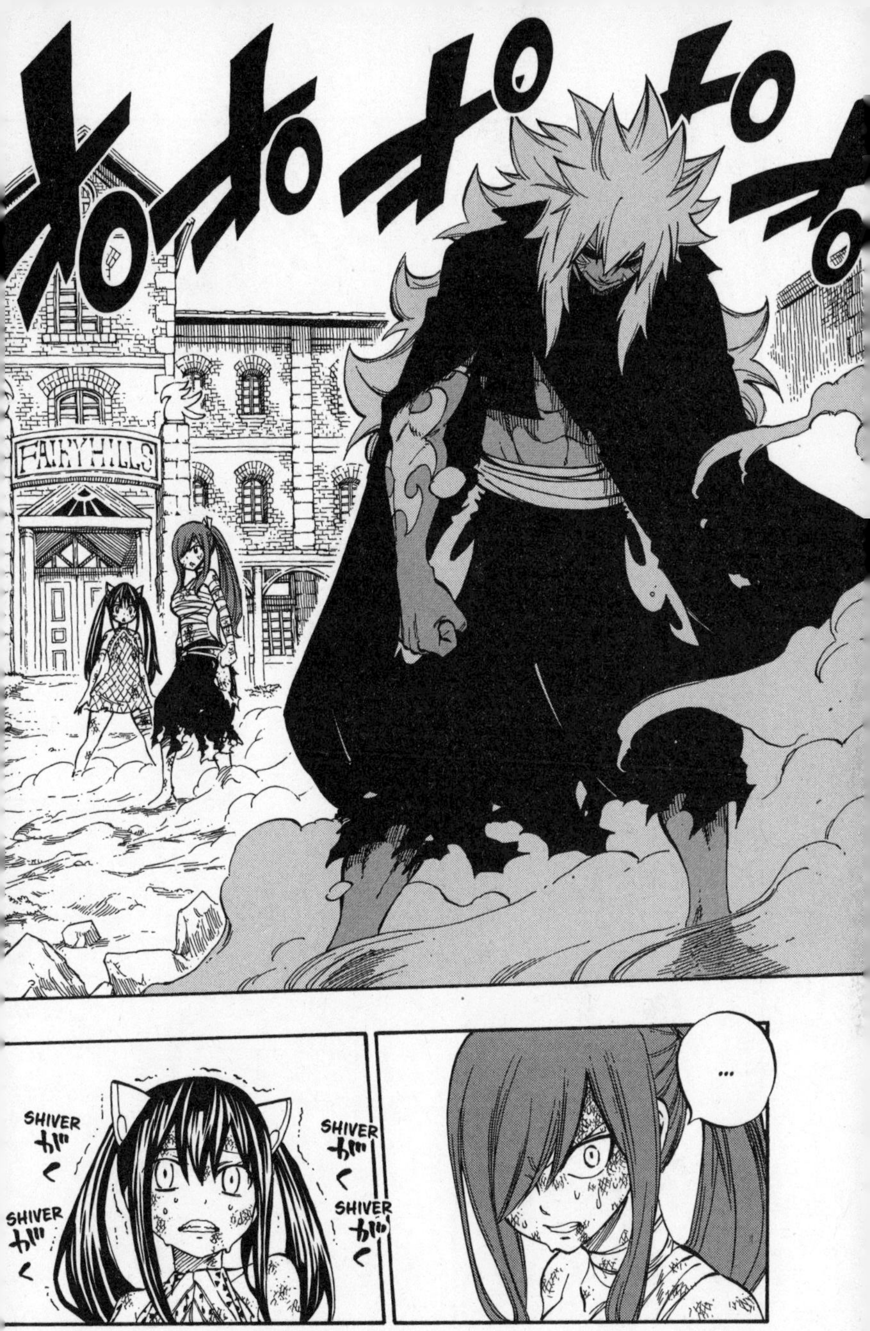
FAIRYHILLS
...
SHIVER
SHIVER
SHIVER
SHIVER

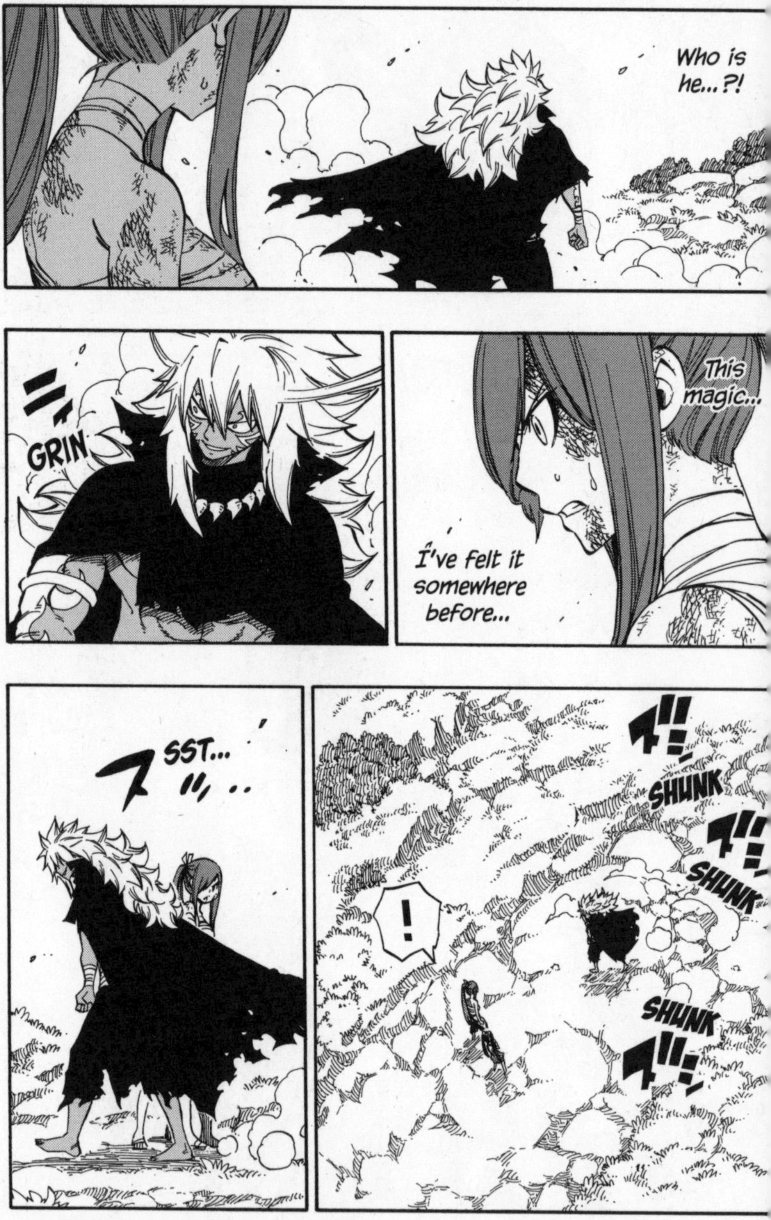
Who is he...?!
This magic...
I've felt it somewhere before...
GRIN
SHUNK
SHUNK
!
SHUNK
SST...

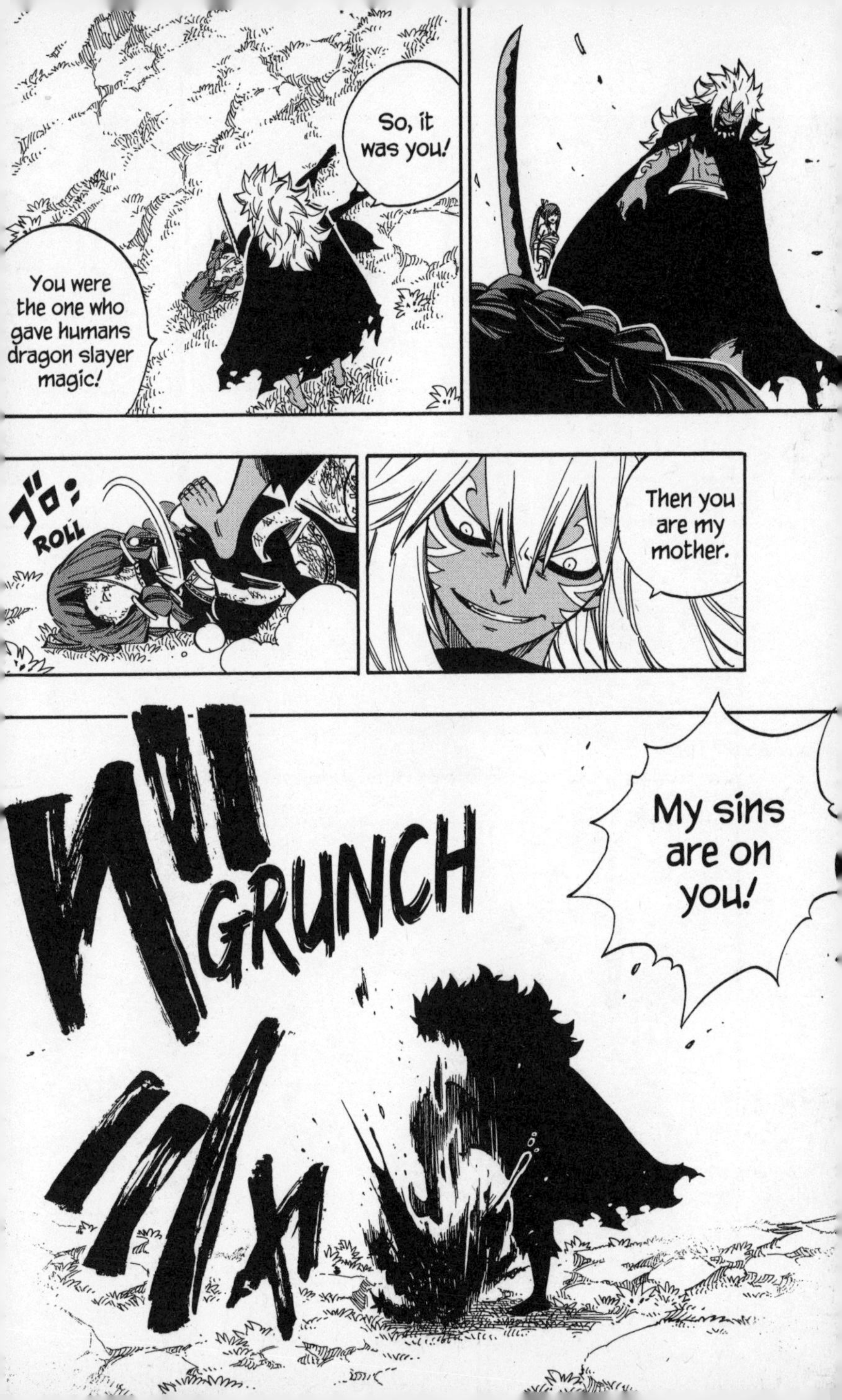
So, it was you!
You were the one who gave humans dragon slayer magic!
Then you are my mother.
ゴロ…
ROLL
My sins are on you!
グシャ
GRUNCH

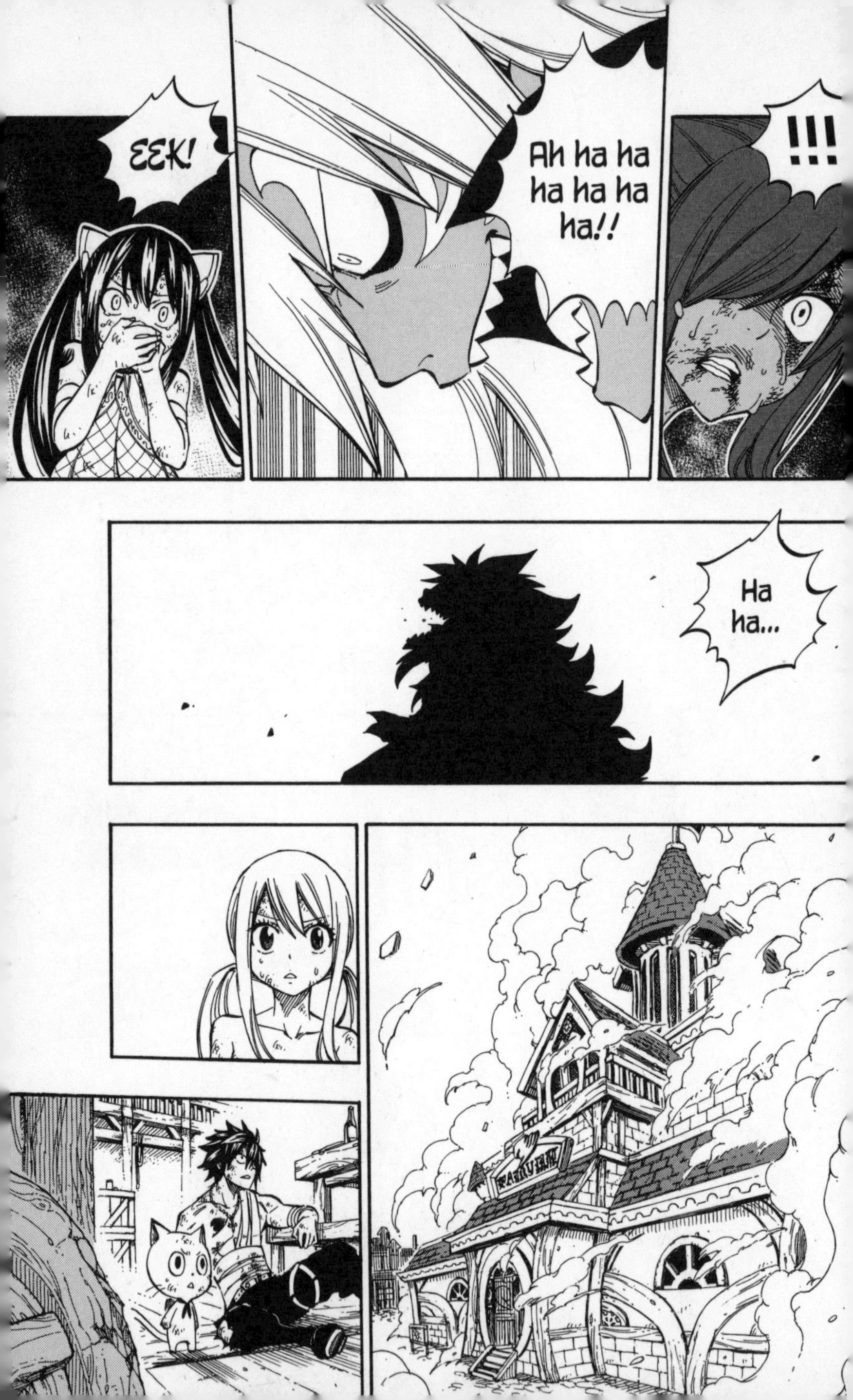
!!!
Ah ha ha ha ha ha ha!!
EEK!
Ha ha...

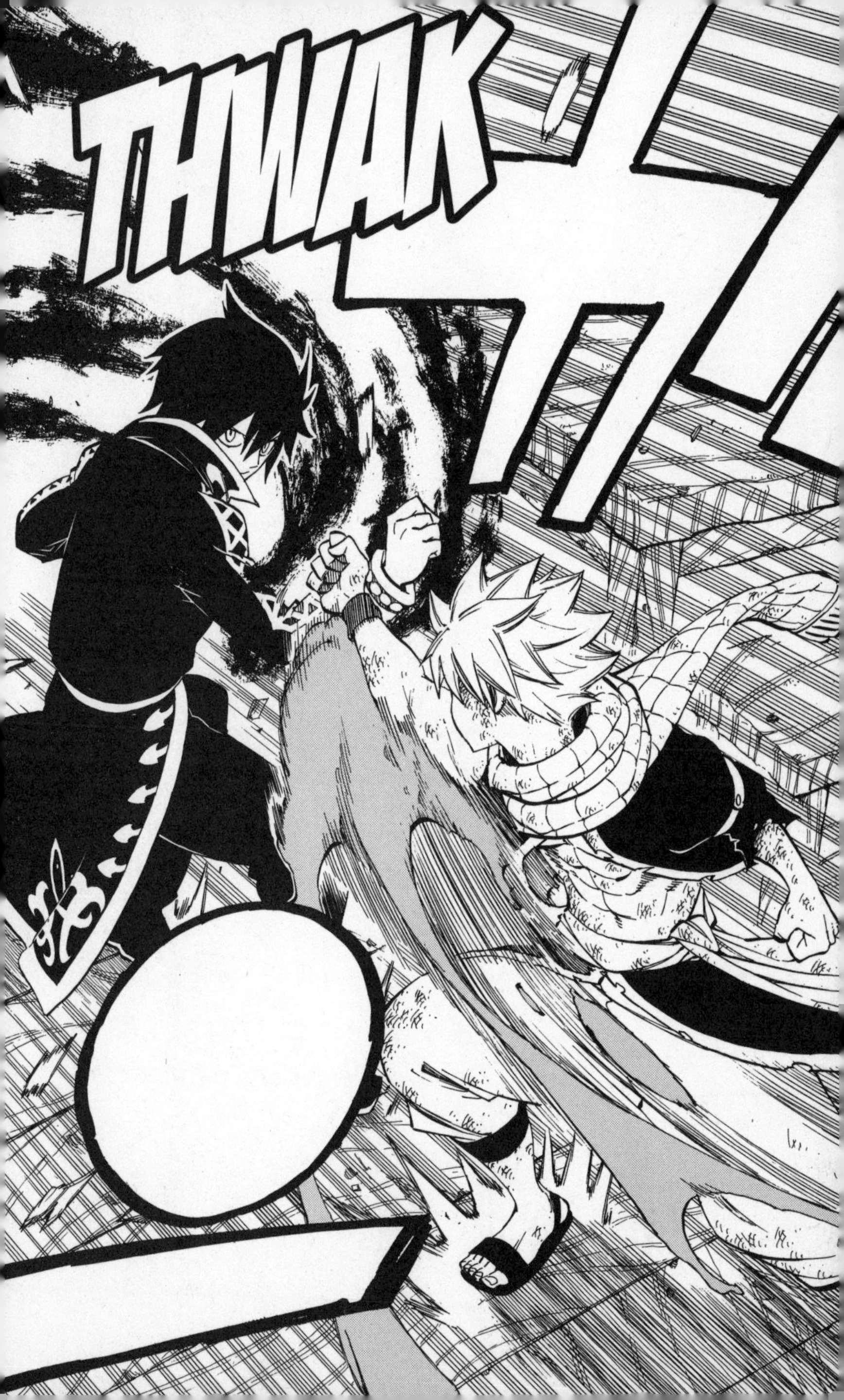
THWAK

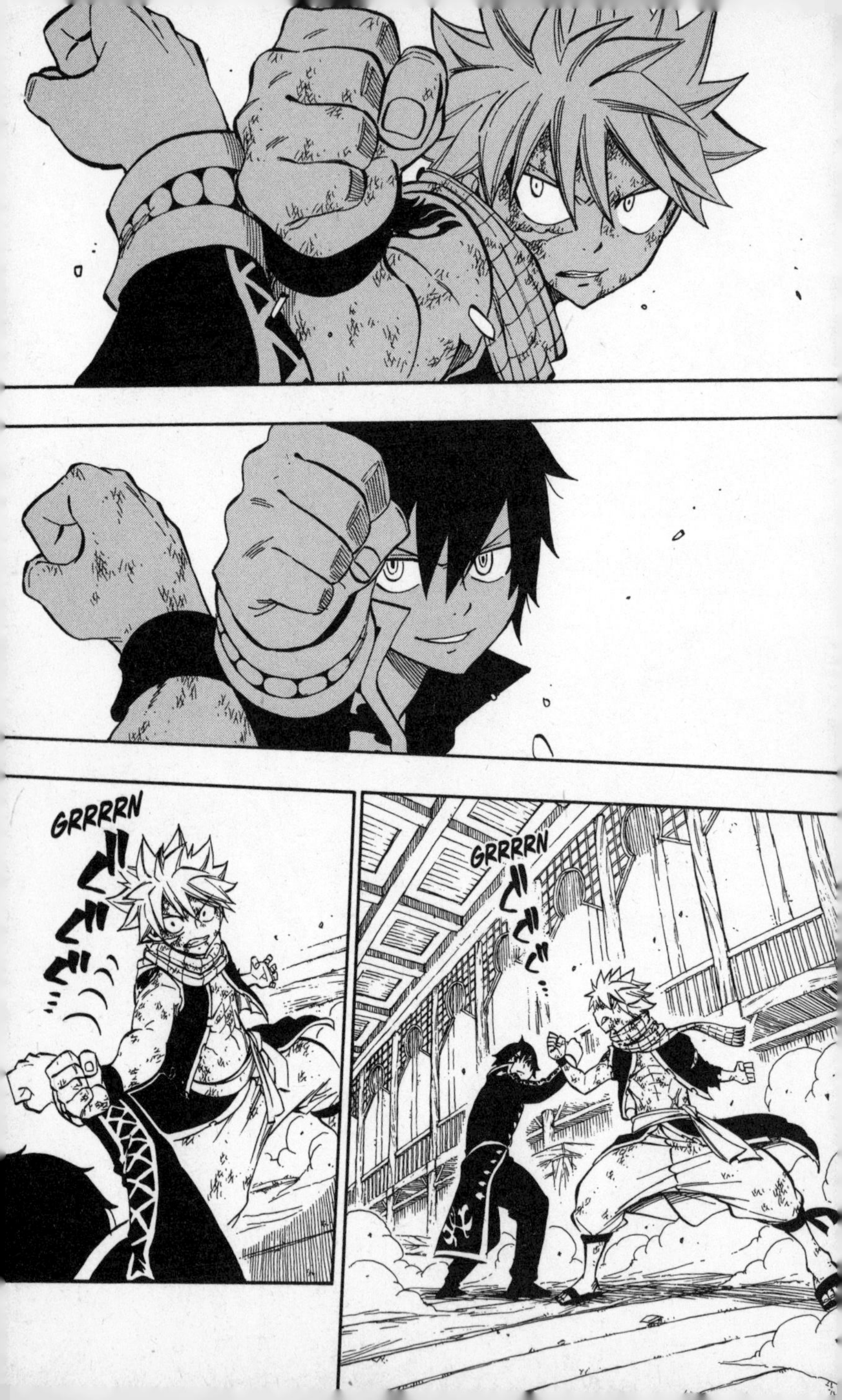
GRRRRN
GRRRRN

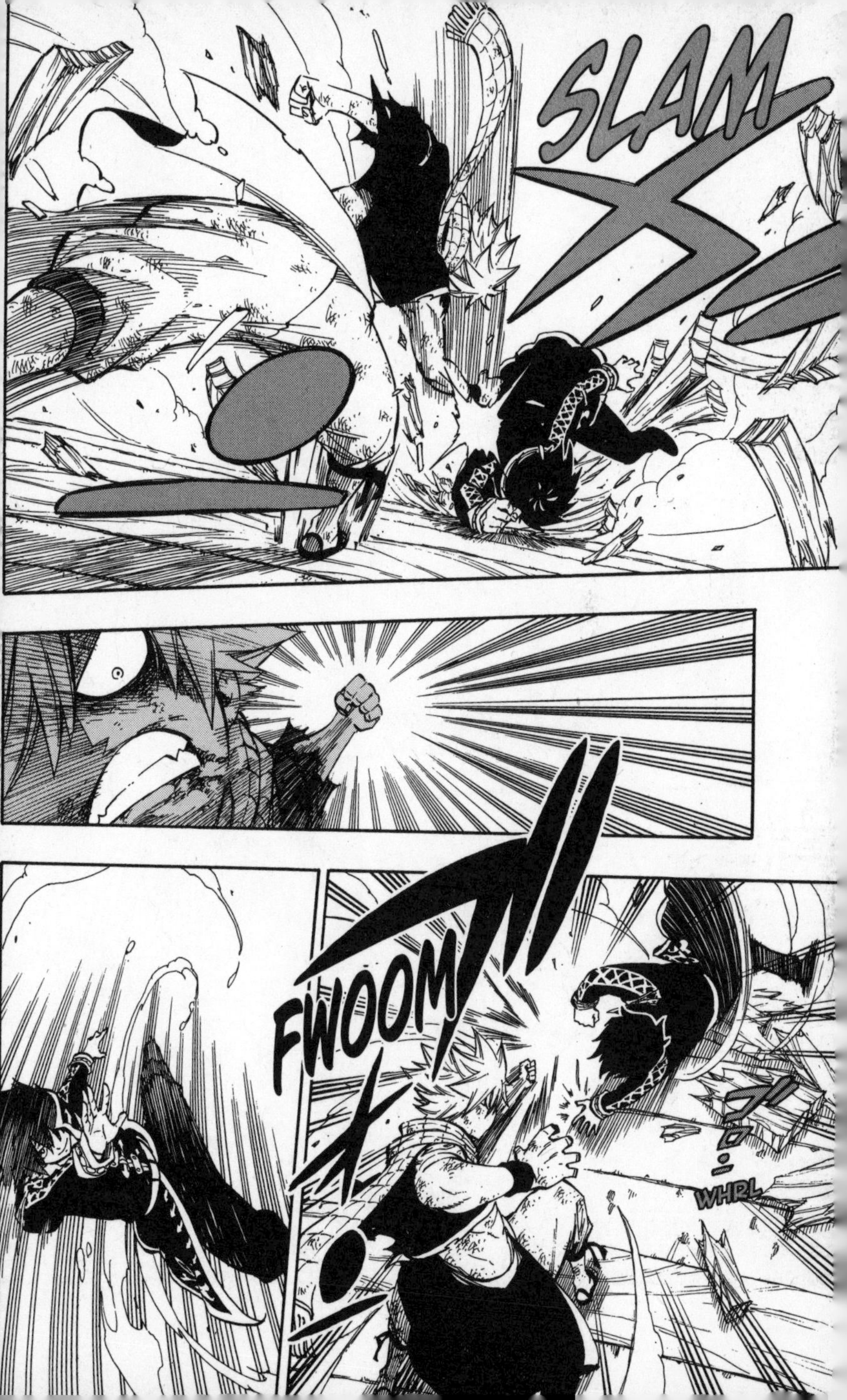
SLAM
FWOOM
WHRL

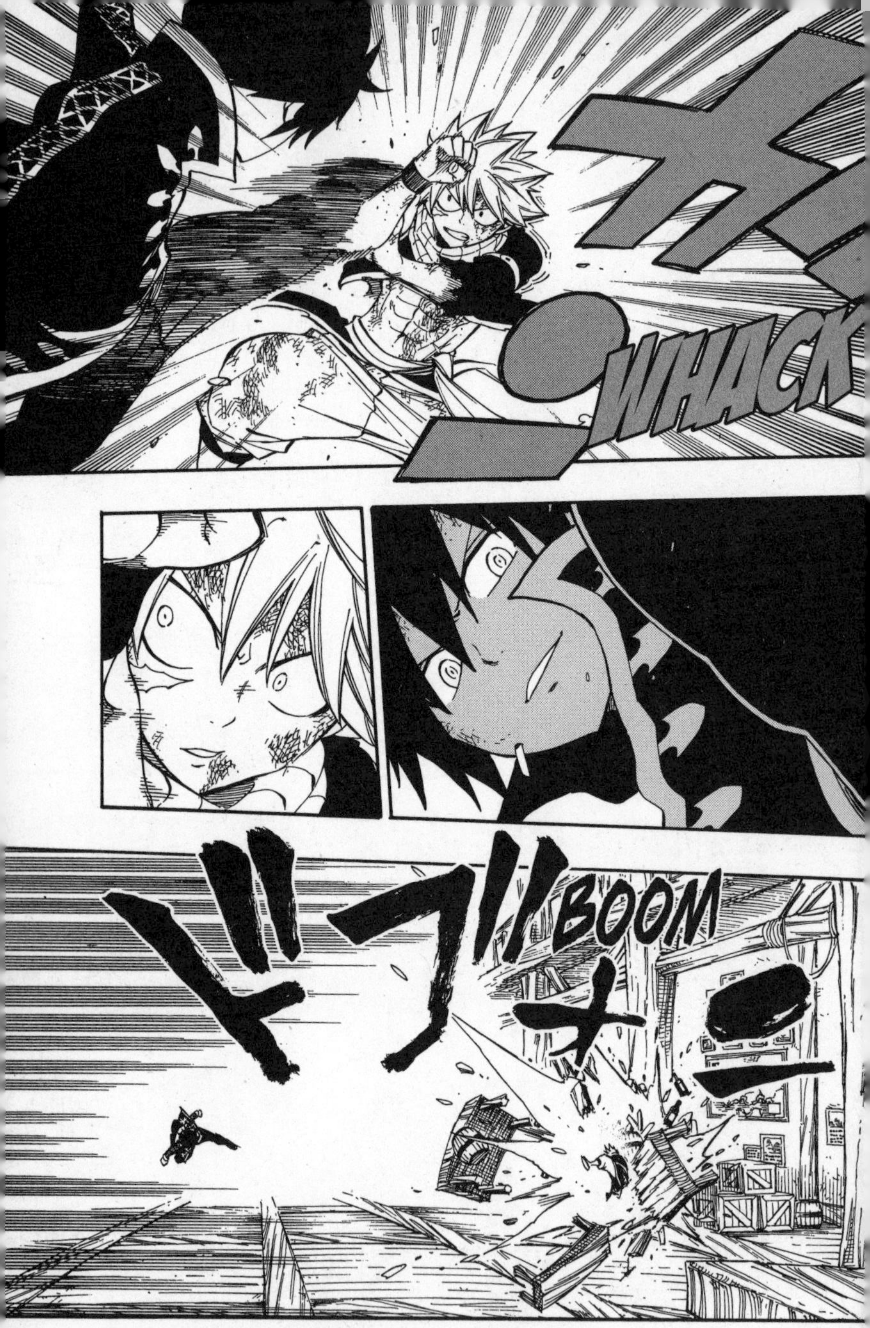
WHACK
BOOM

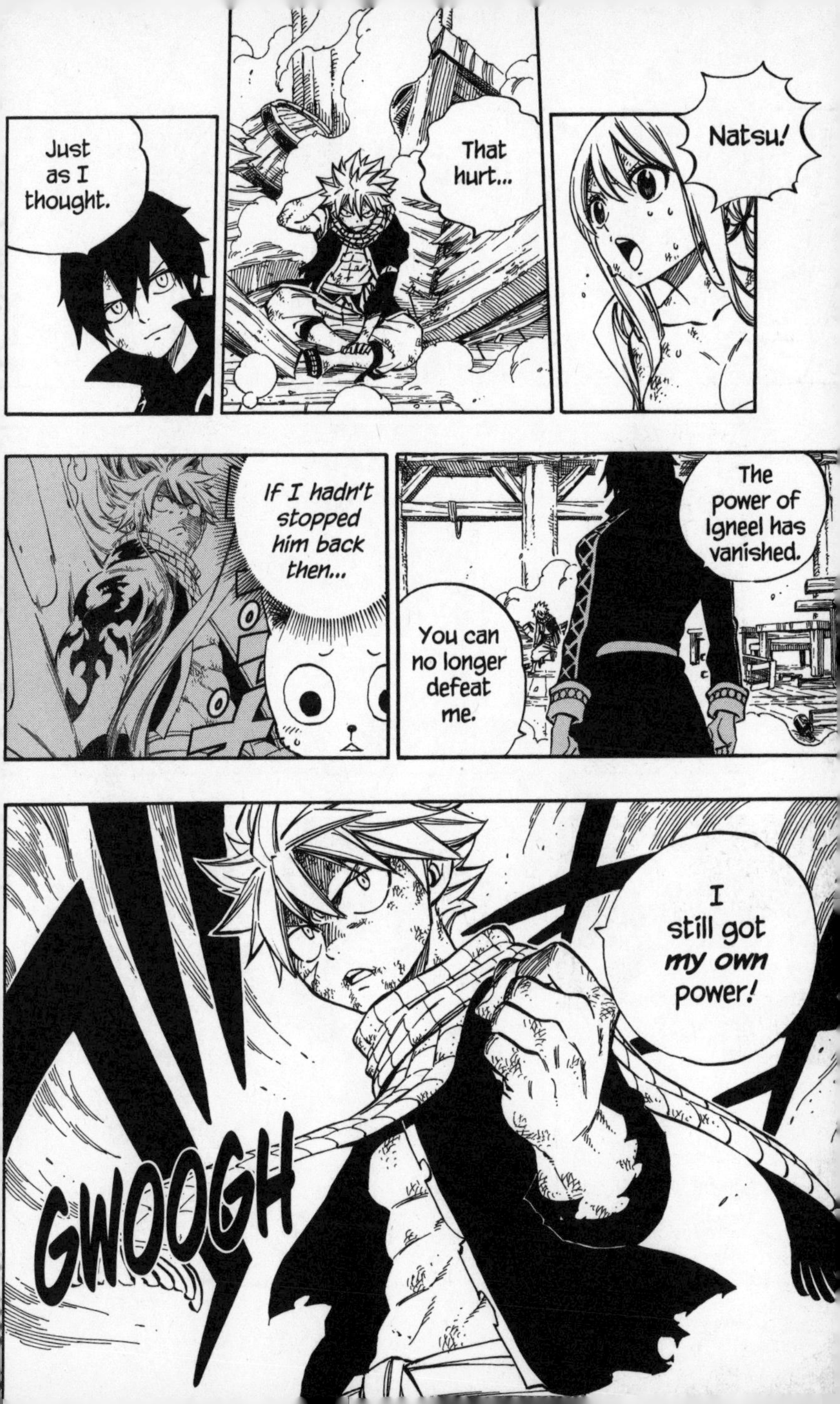
Natsu!
That hurt...
Just as I thought.
The power of Igneel has vanished.
You can no longer defeat me.
If I hadn't stopped him back then...
I still got *my own* power!
GWOOGH

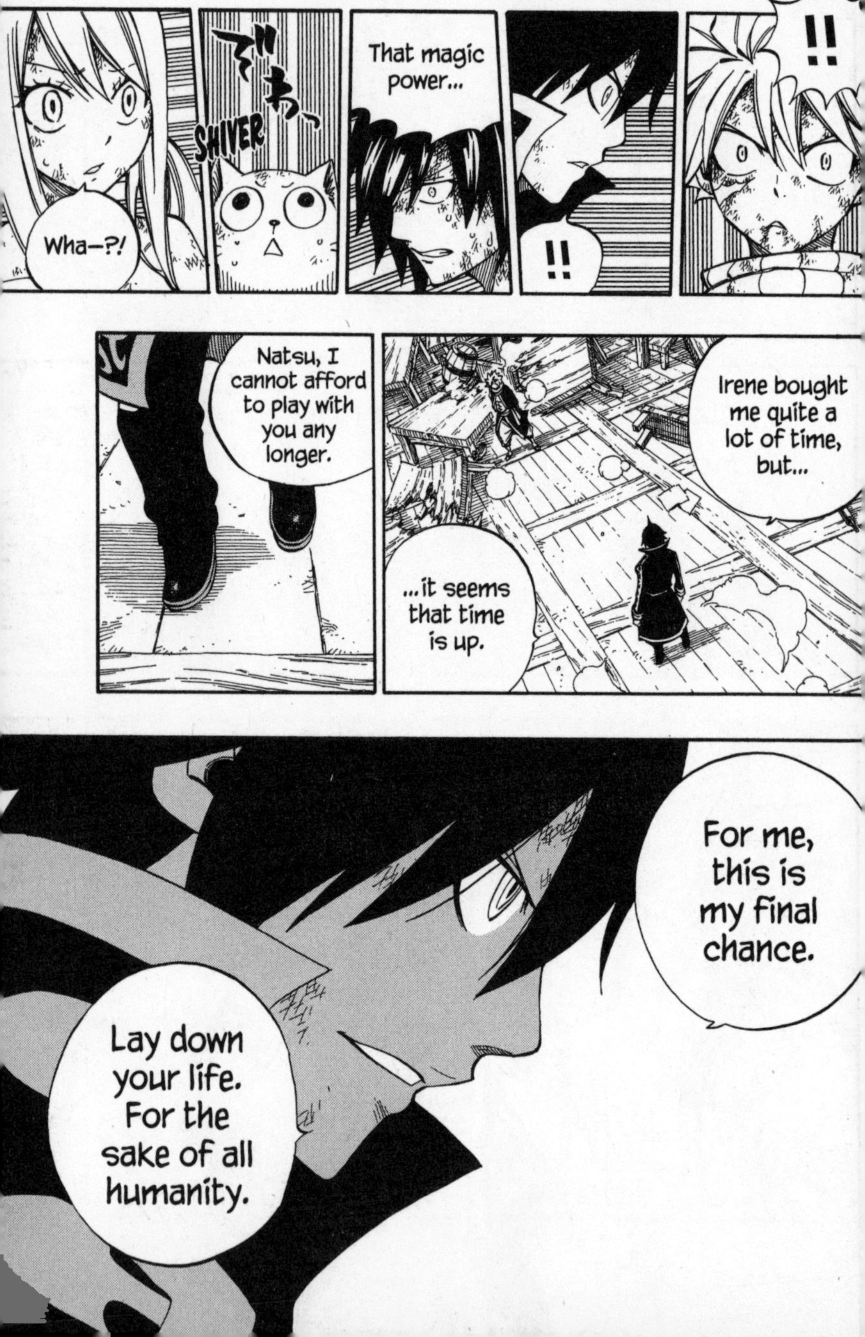
!!
!!
That magic power...
SHIVER
Wha-?!
Irene bought me quite a lot of time, but...
...it seems that time is up.
Natsu, I cannot afford to play with you any longer.
For me, this is my final chance.
Lay down your life. For the sake of all humanity.

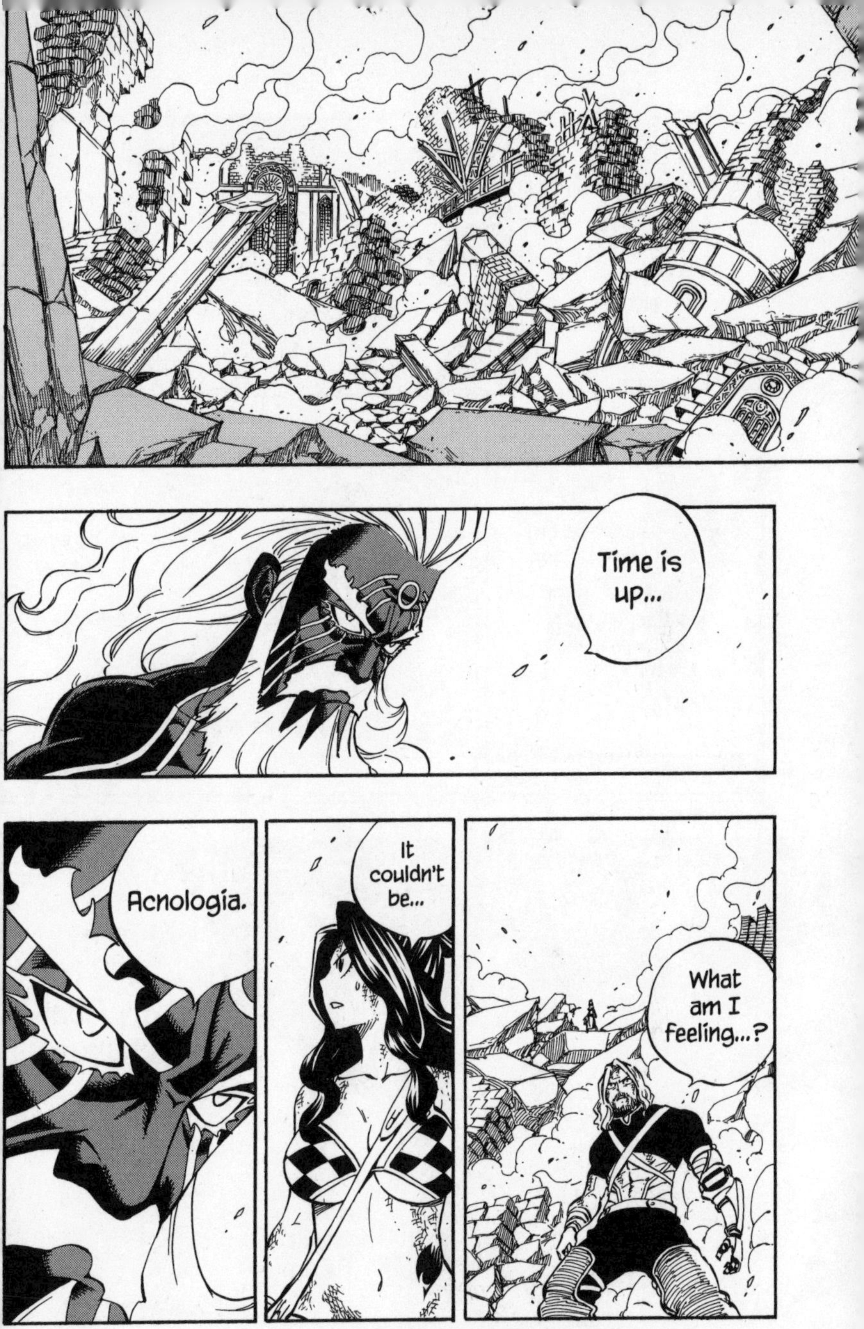
Time is up...
What am I feeling...?
It couldn't be...
Acnologia.

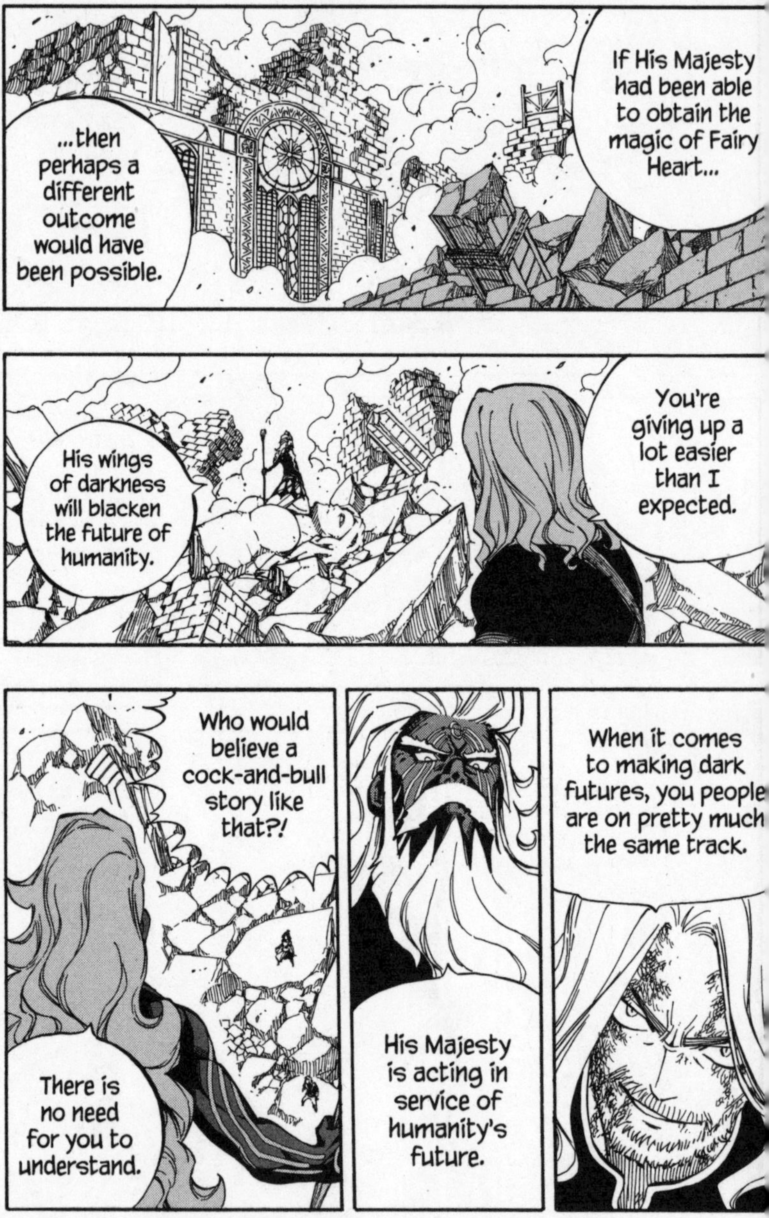
If His Majesty had been able to obtain the magic of Fairy Heart...
...then perhaps a different outcome would have been possible.
You're giving up a lot easier than I expected.
His wings of darkness will blacken the future of humanity.
When it comes to making dark futures, you people are on pretty much the same track.
His Majesty is acting in service of humanity's future.
Who would believe a cock-and-bull story like that?!
There is no need for you to understand.

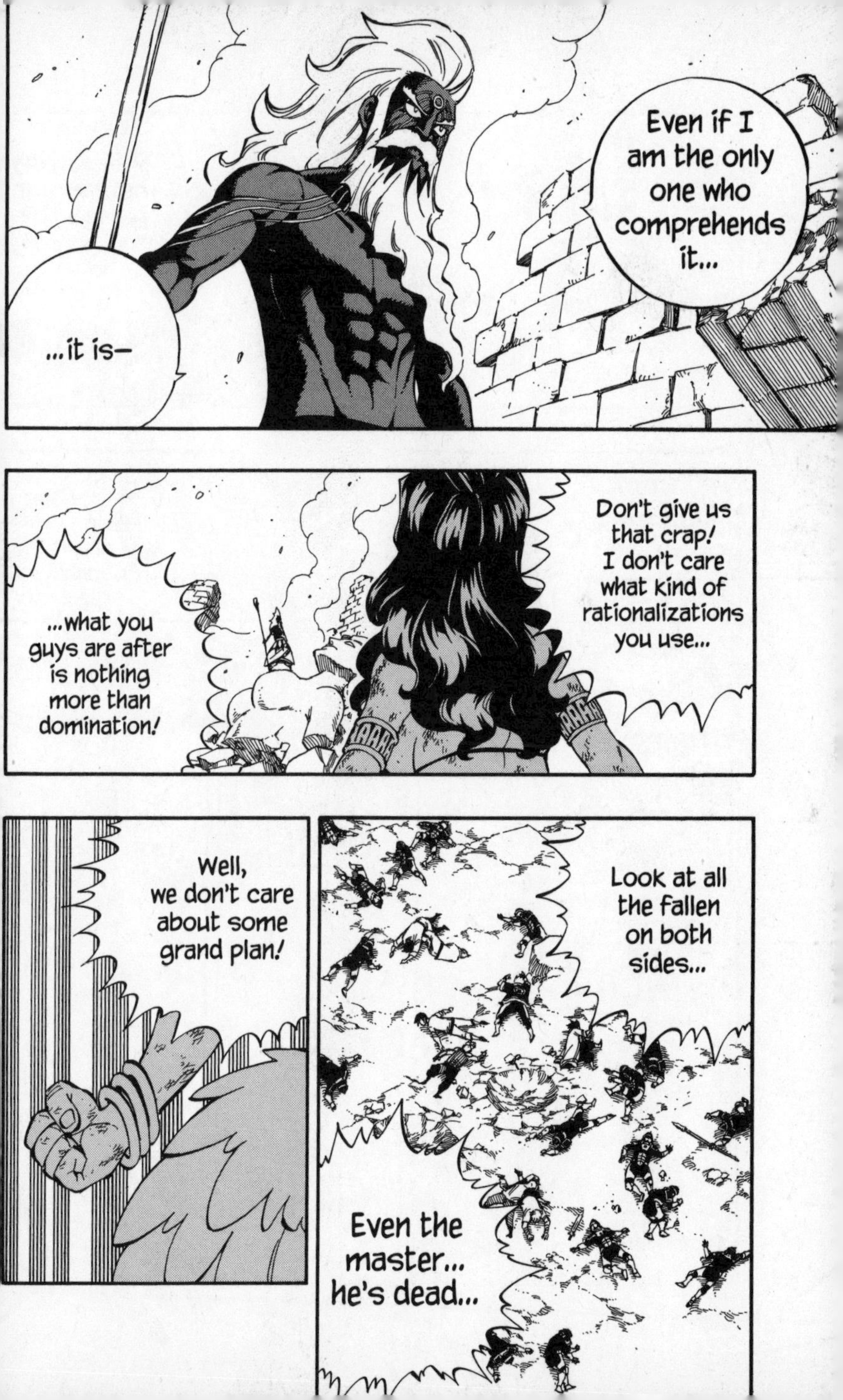
Even if I am the only one who comprehends it...
...it is—
Don't give us that crap! I don't care what kind of rationalizations you use...
...what you guys are after is nothing more than domination!
Look at all the fallen on both sides...
Even the master... he's dead...
Well, we don't care about some grand plan!

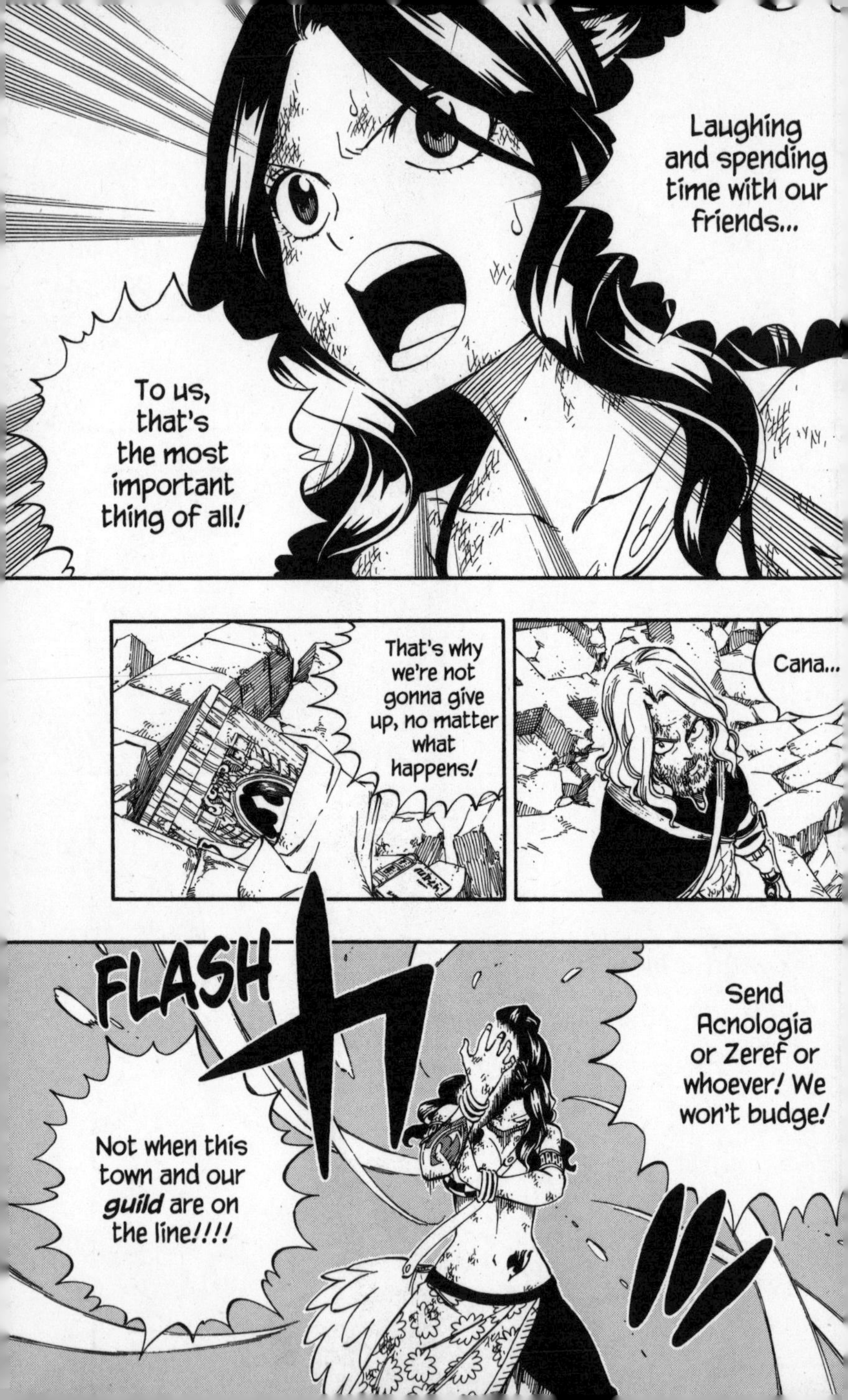
Laughing and spending time with our friends...
To us, that's the most important thing of all!
Cana...
That's why we're not gonna give up, no matter what happens!
Send Acnologia or Zeref or whoever! We won't budge!
FLASH
Not when this town and our *guild* are on the line!!!!

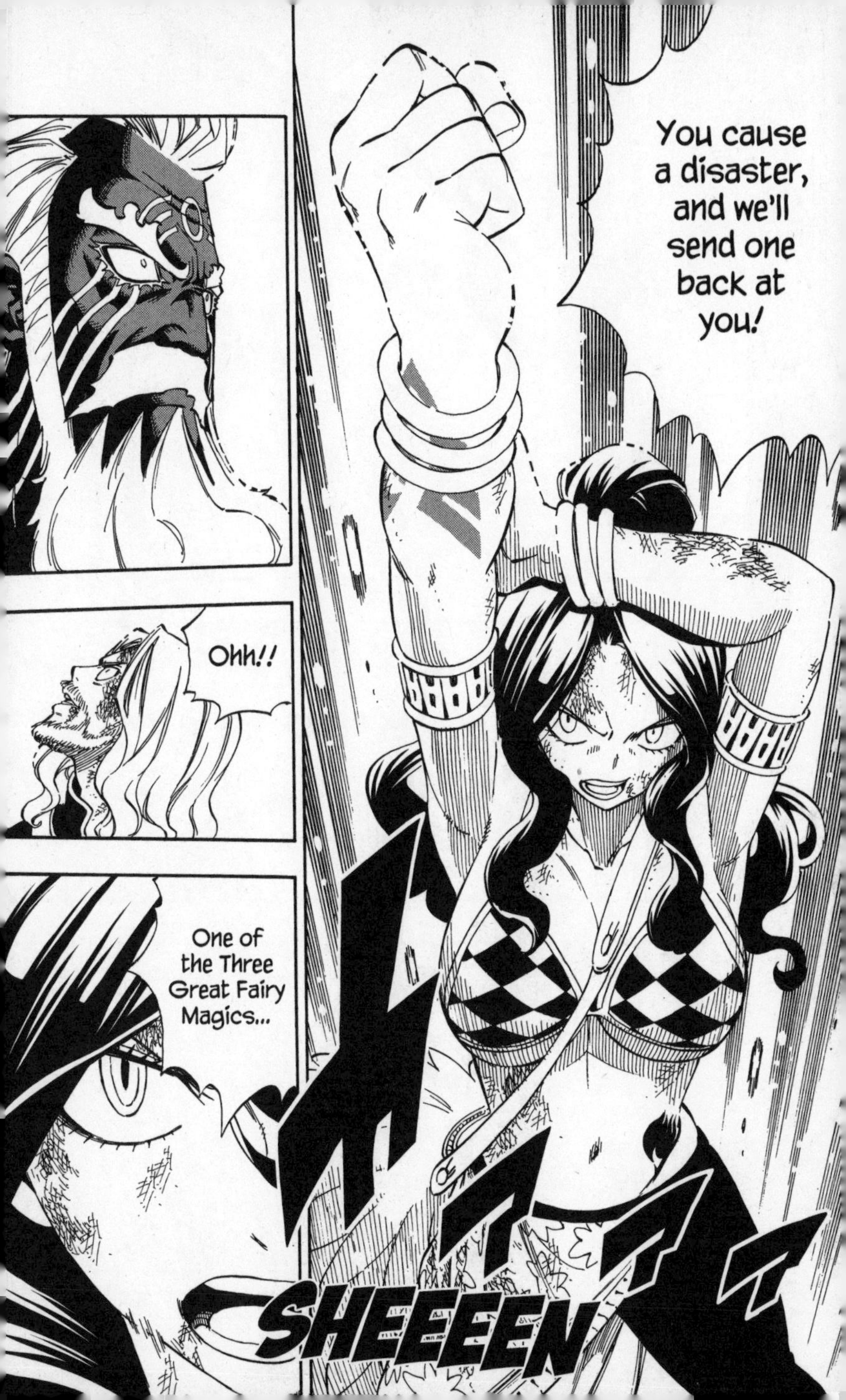
You cause a disaster, and we'll send one back at you!
SHEEEEN
Ohh!!
One of the Three Great Fairy Magics...

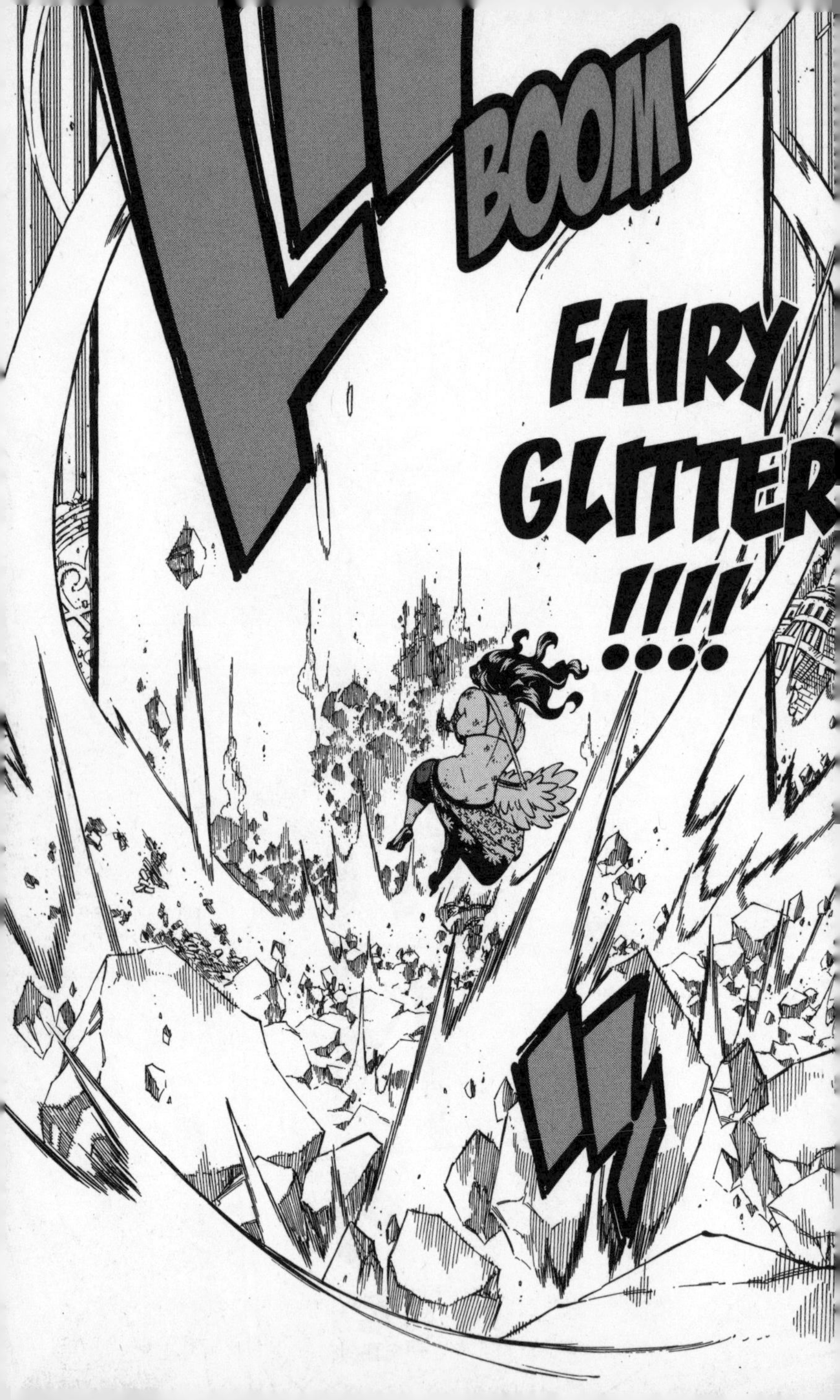
BOOM
FAIRY GLITTER!!!!

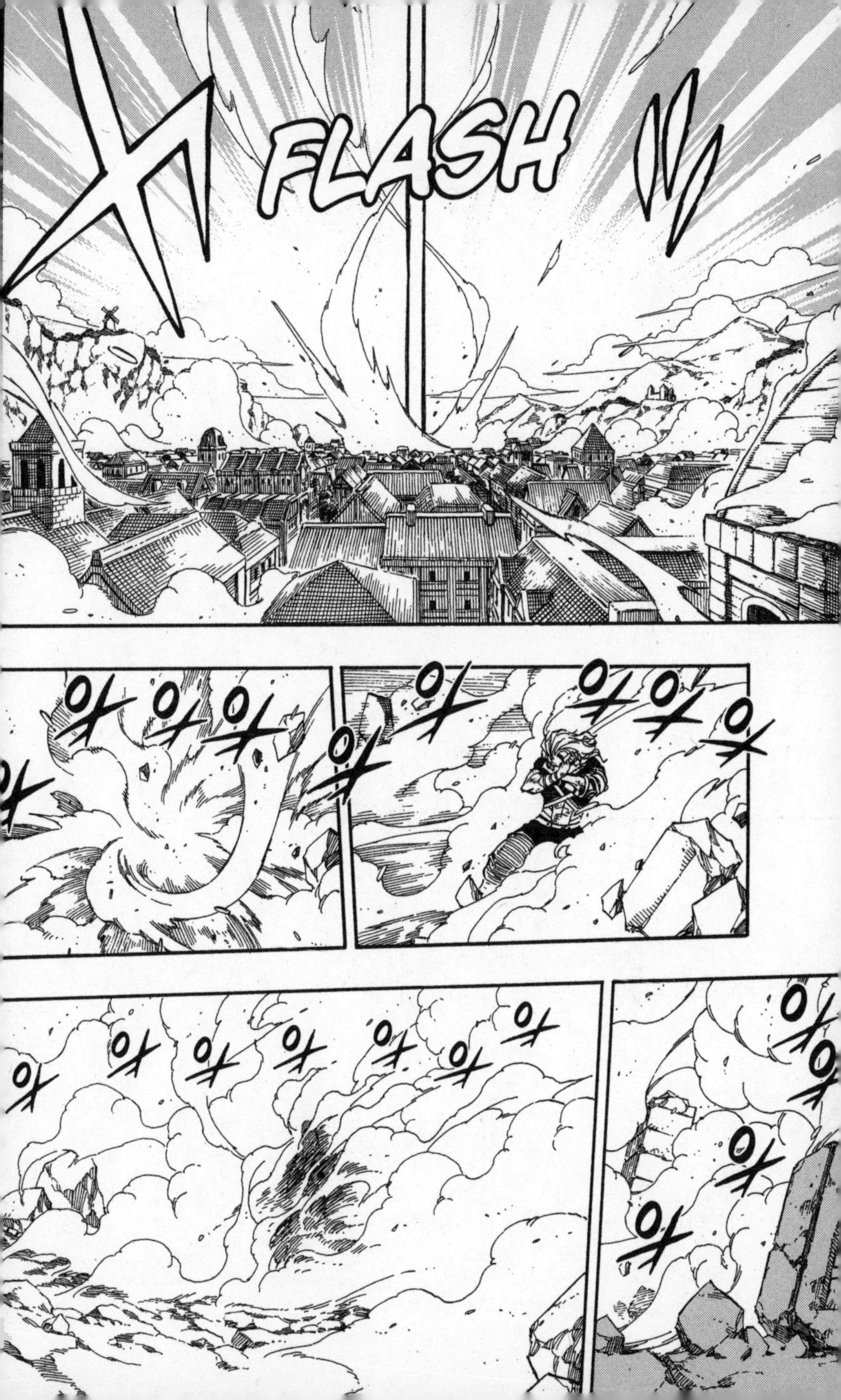
FLASH

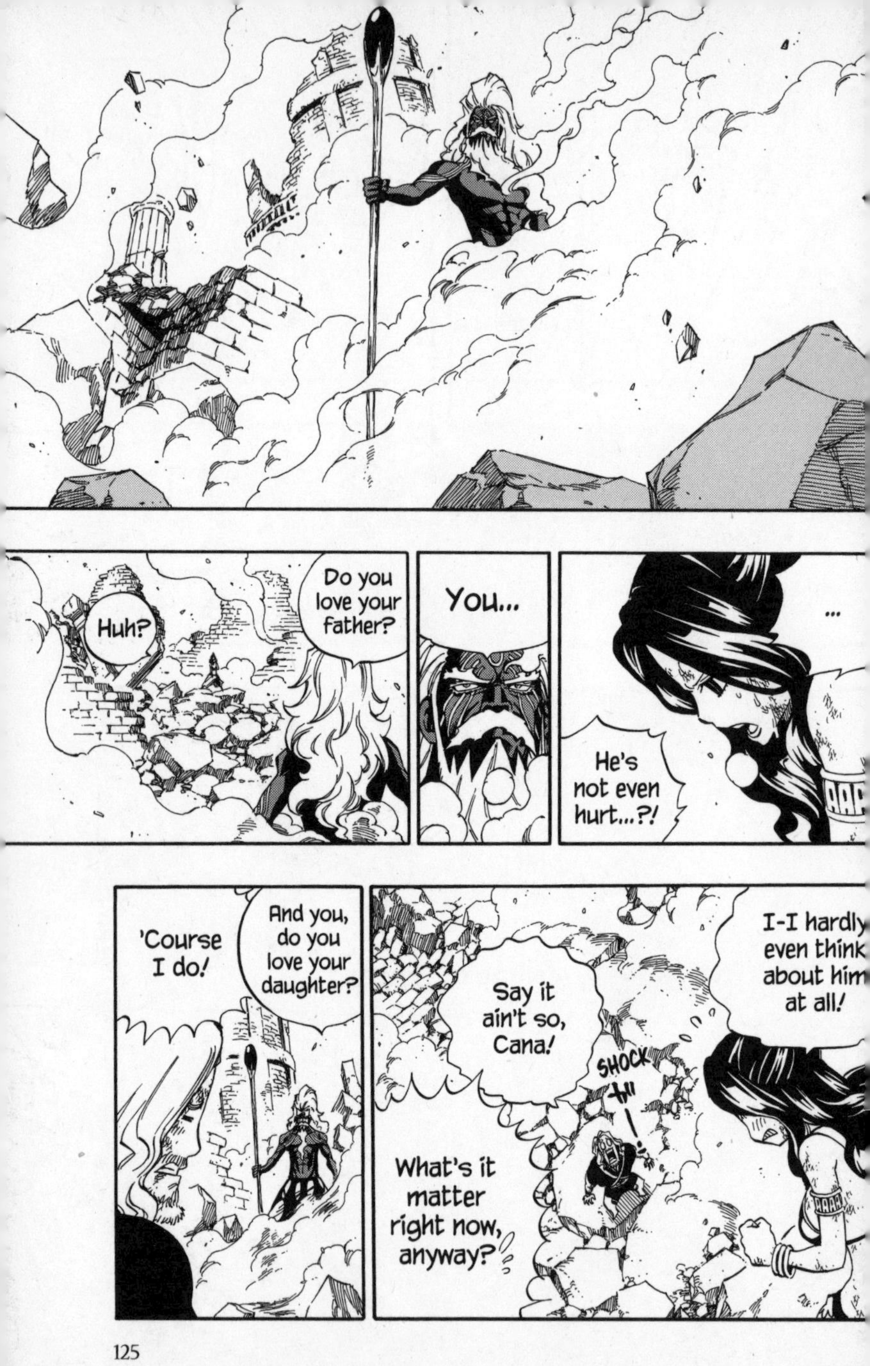
...
He's not even hurt...?!
You...
Do you love your father?
Huh?
I-I hardly even think about him at all!
Say it ain't so, Cana!
SHOCK
What's it matter right now, anyway?
And you, do you love your daughter?
'Course I do!

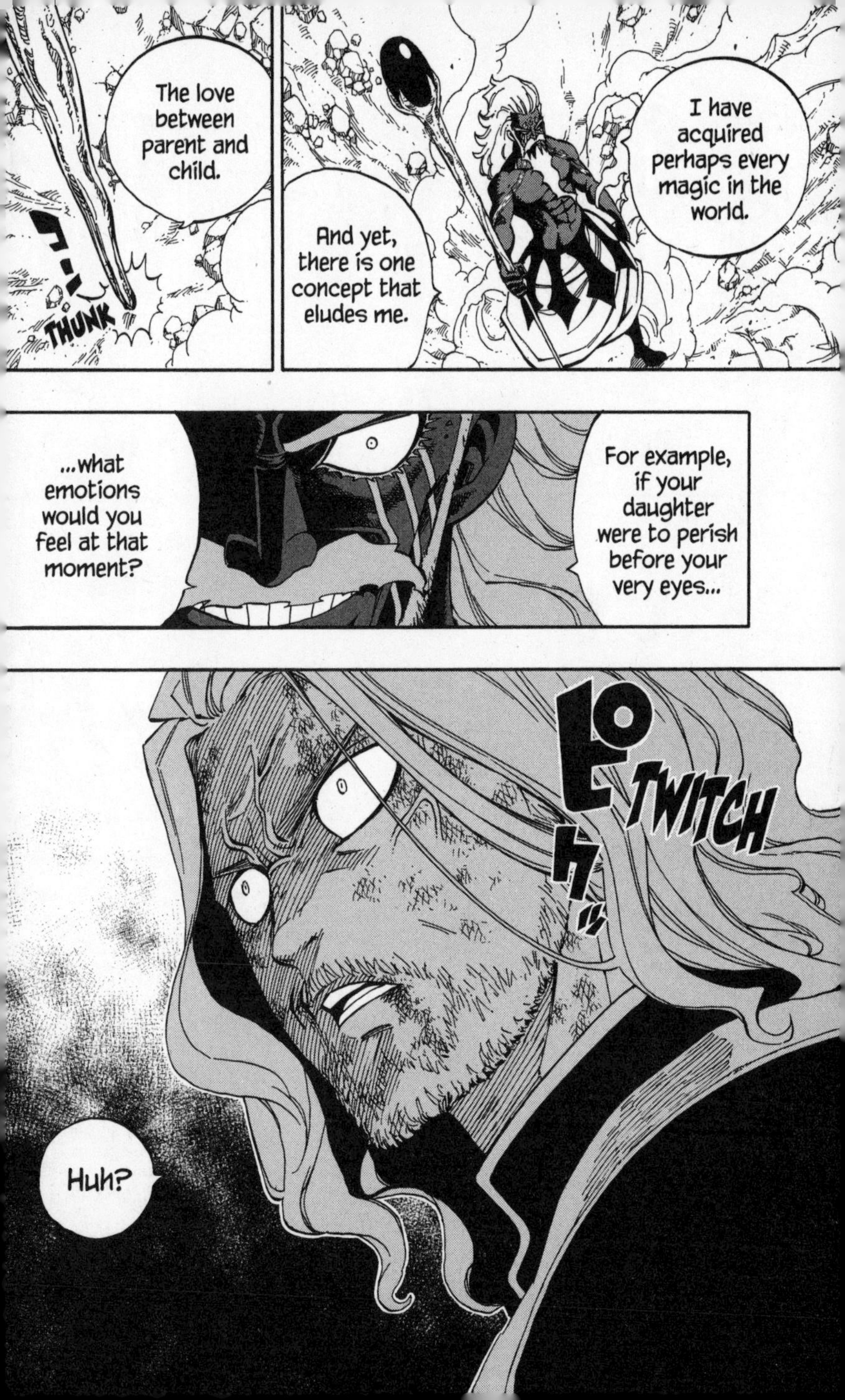
I have acquired perhaps every magic in the world.
And yet, there is one concept that eludes me.
The love between parent and child.
THUNK
For example, if your daughter were to perish before your very eyes...
...what emotions would you feel at that moment?
TWITCH
Huh?

# FAIRY TAIL

フェアリーテイル

## Chapter 525: Why Did the Emperor Never Love His Child?

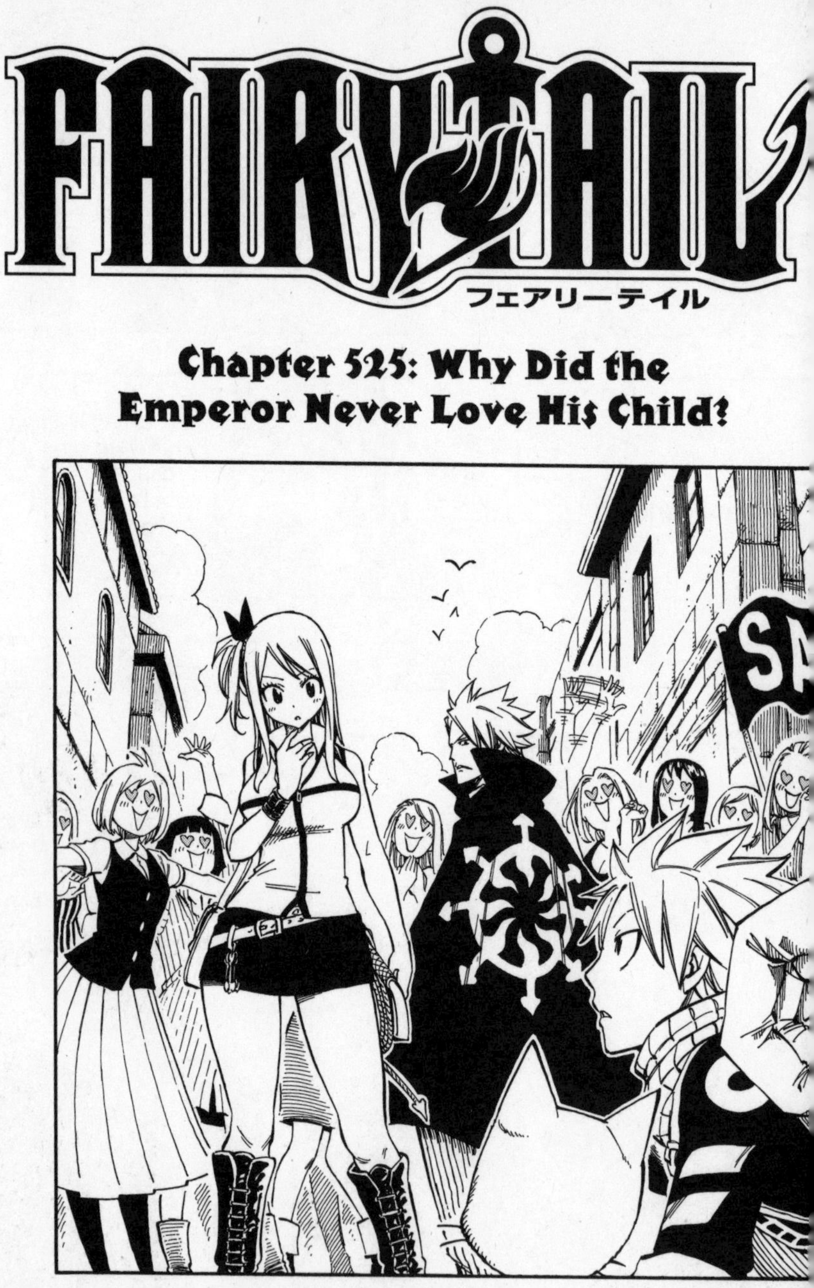

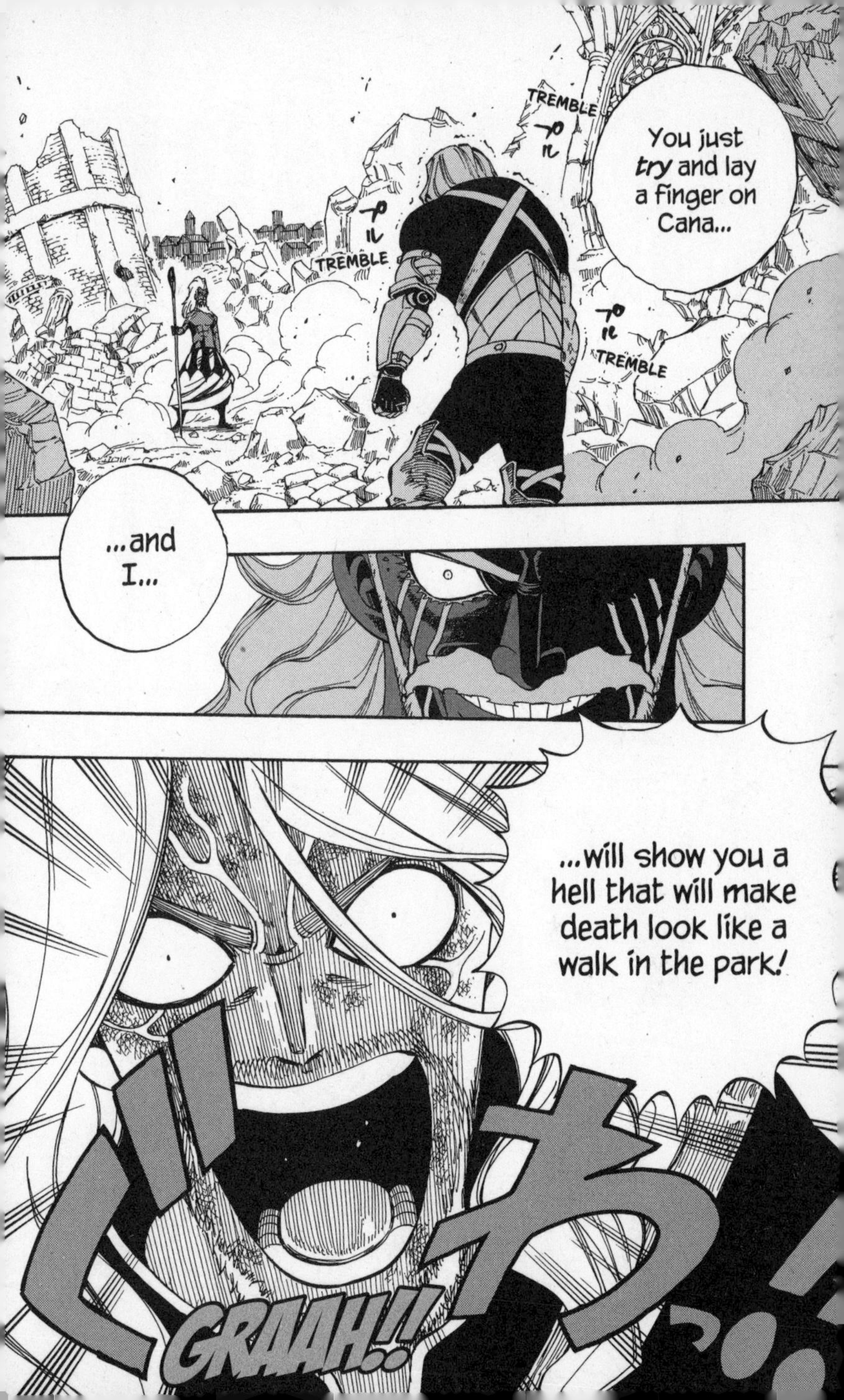
You just *try* and lay a finger on Cana...
TREMBLE
TREMBLE
TREMBLE
...and I...
...will show you a hell that will make death look like a walk in the park!
GRAAH!!

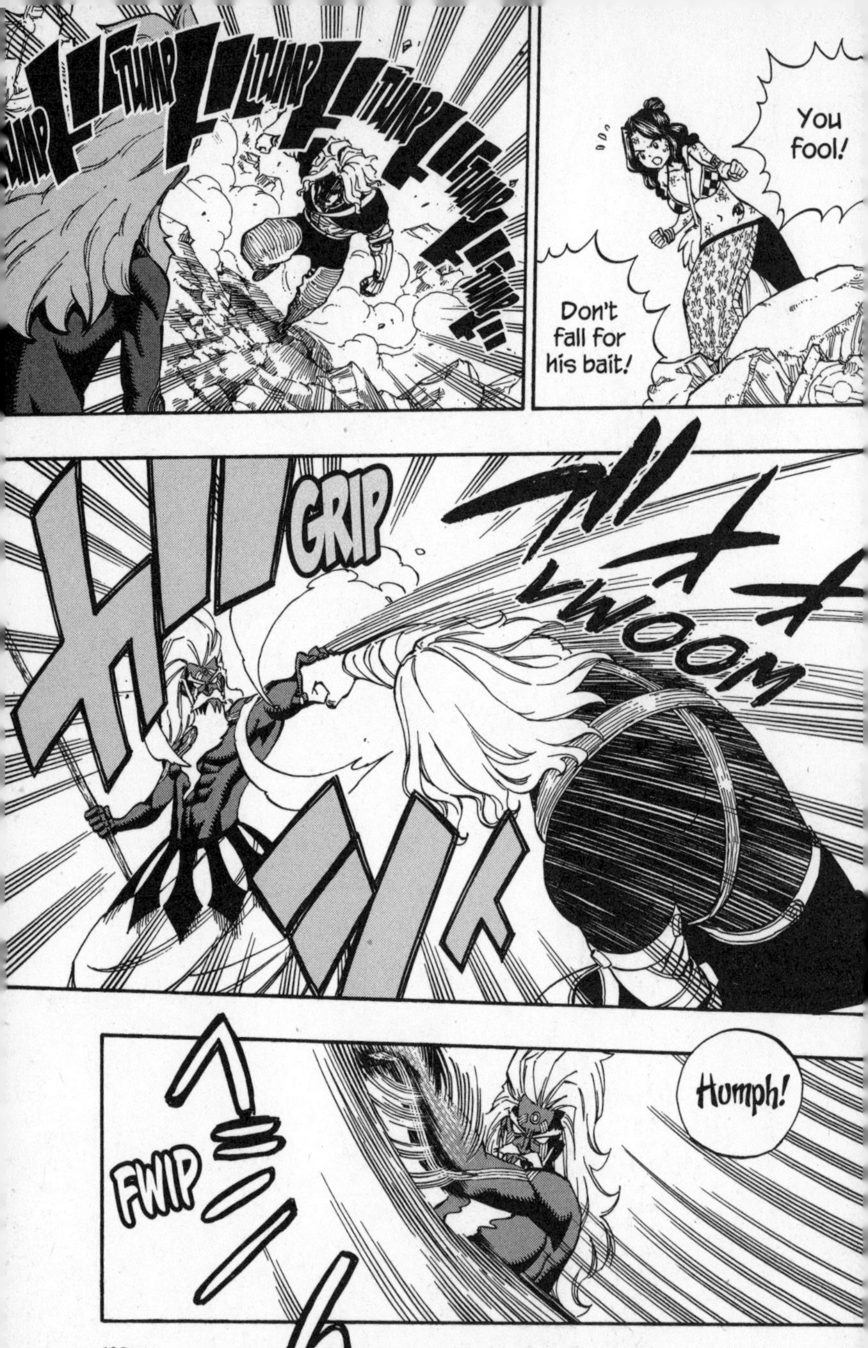

You fool!
Don't fall for his bait!
TUMP
TUMP
TUMP
TUMP
TUMP
TUMP!!
GRIP
VWOOM
Humph!
FWIP

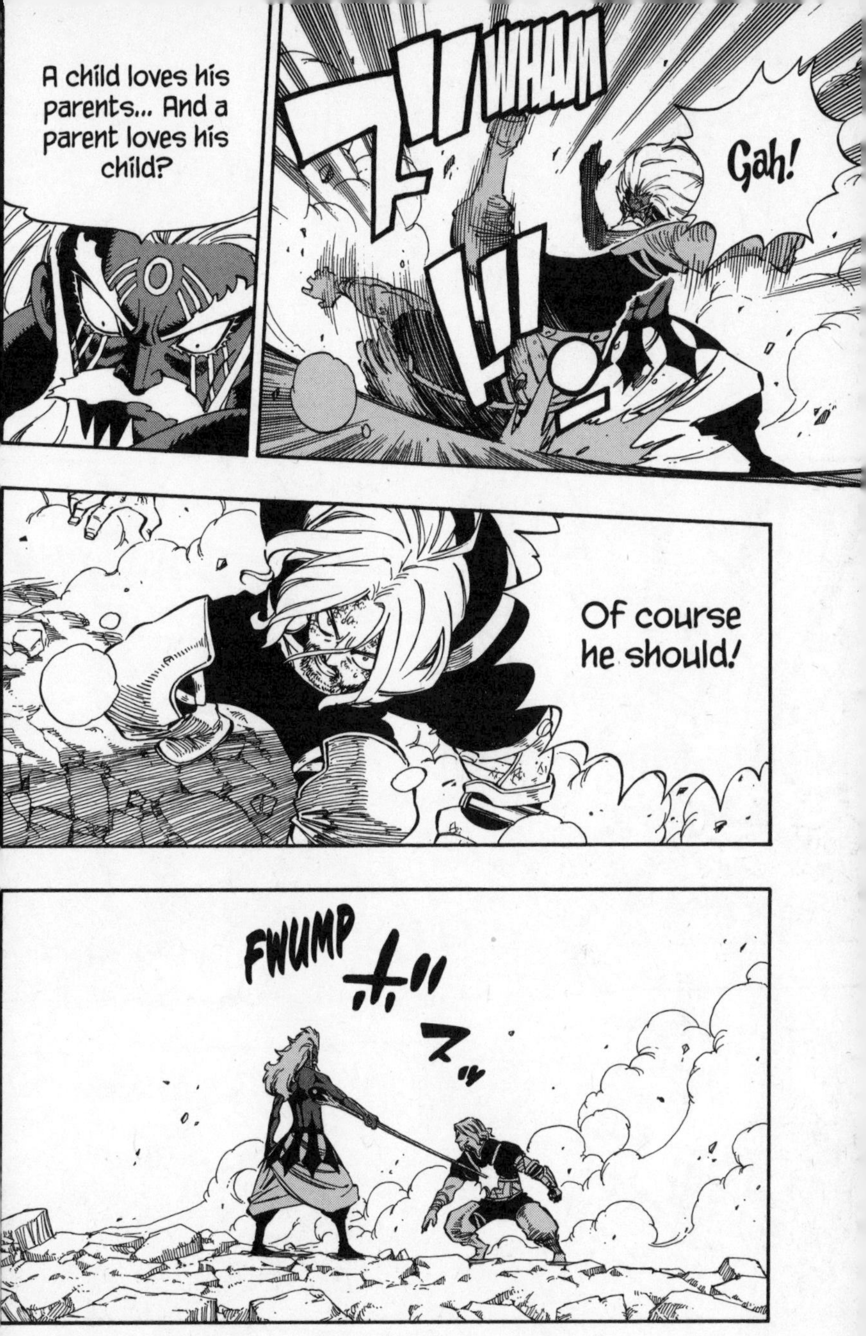
WHAM
Gah!
A child loves his parents... And a parent loves his child?
Of course he should!
FWUMP

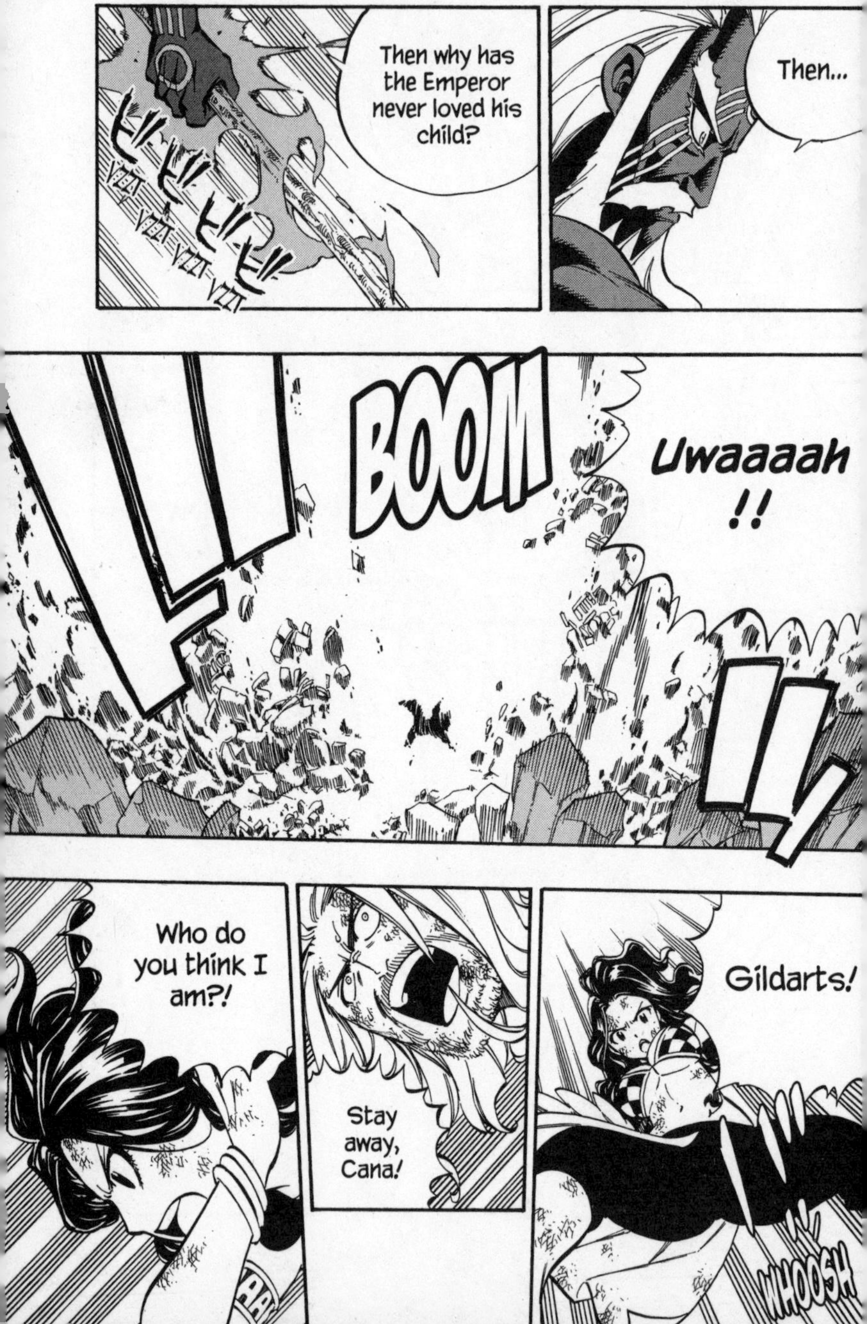
Then...
Then why has the Emperor never loved his child?
VZZT
VZZT
VZZT
VZZT
BOOM
Uwaaaah!!
Gildarts!
WHOOSH
Stay away, Cana!
Who do you think I am?!

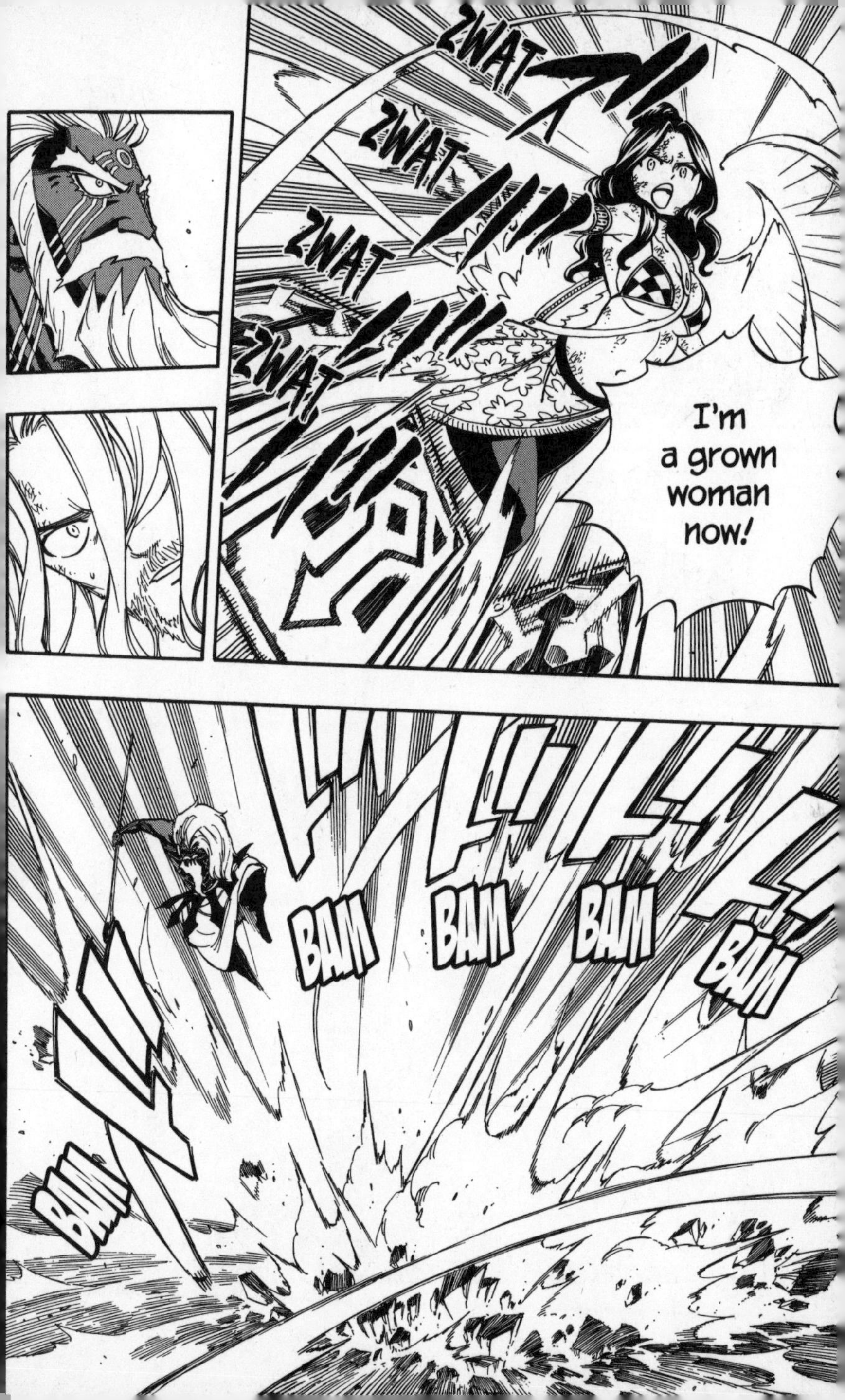
ZWAT
ZWAT
ZWAT
ZWAT
I'm a grown woman now!
BAM
BAM
BAM
BAM
BAM

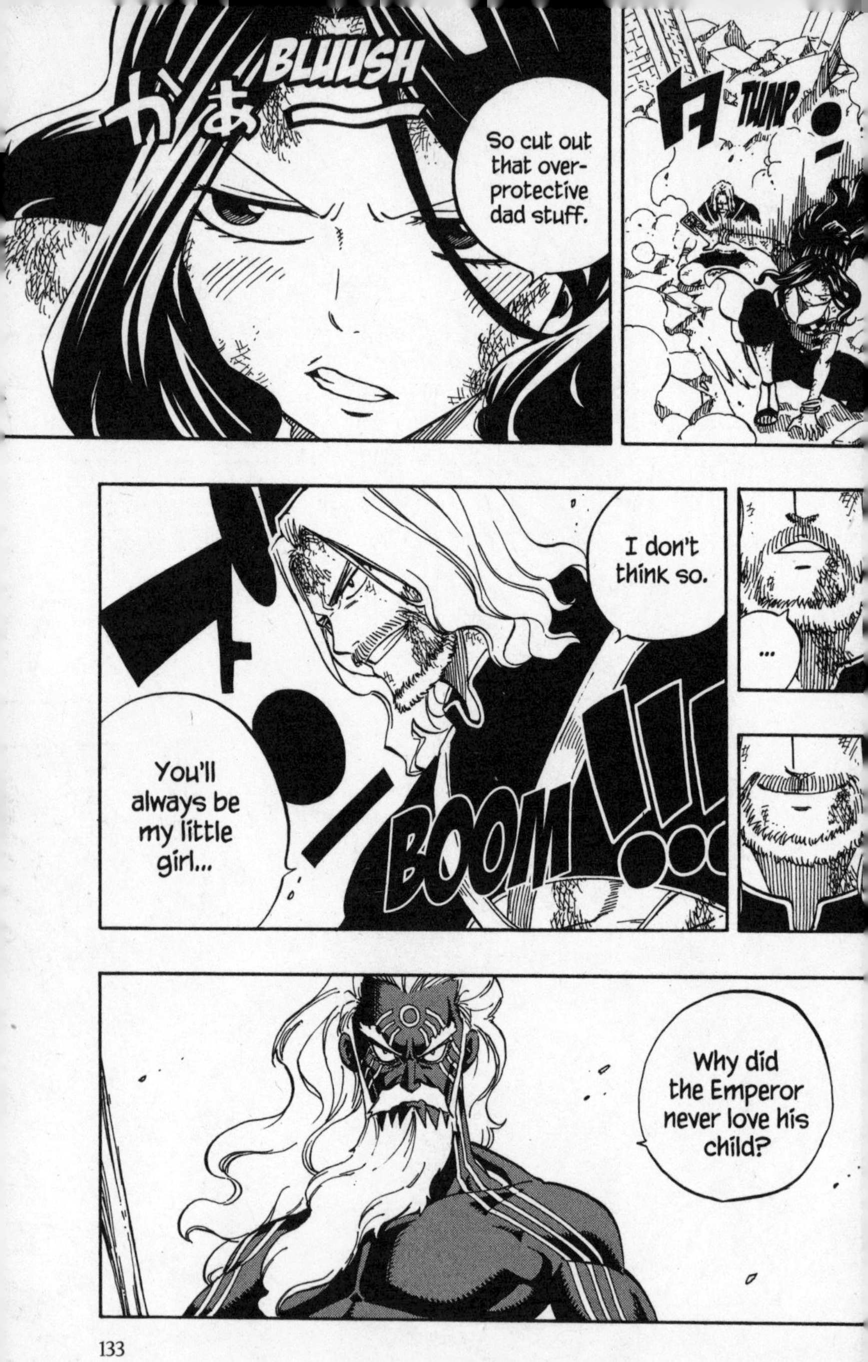
TUMP
BLUUSH
がぁー
So cut out that over-protective dad stuff.
...
I don't think so.
BOOM!!!
You'll always be my little girl...
Why did the Emperor never love his child?

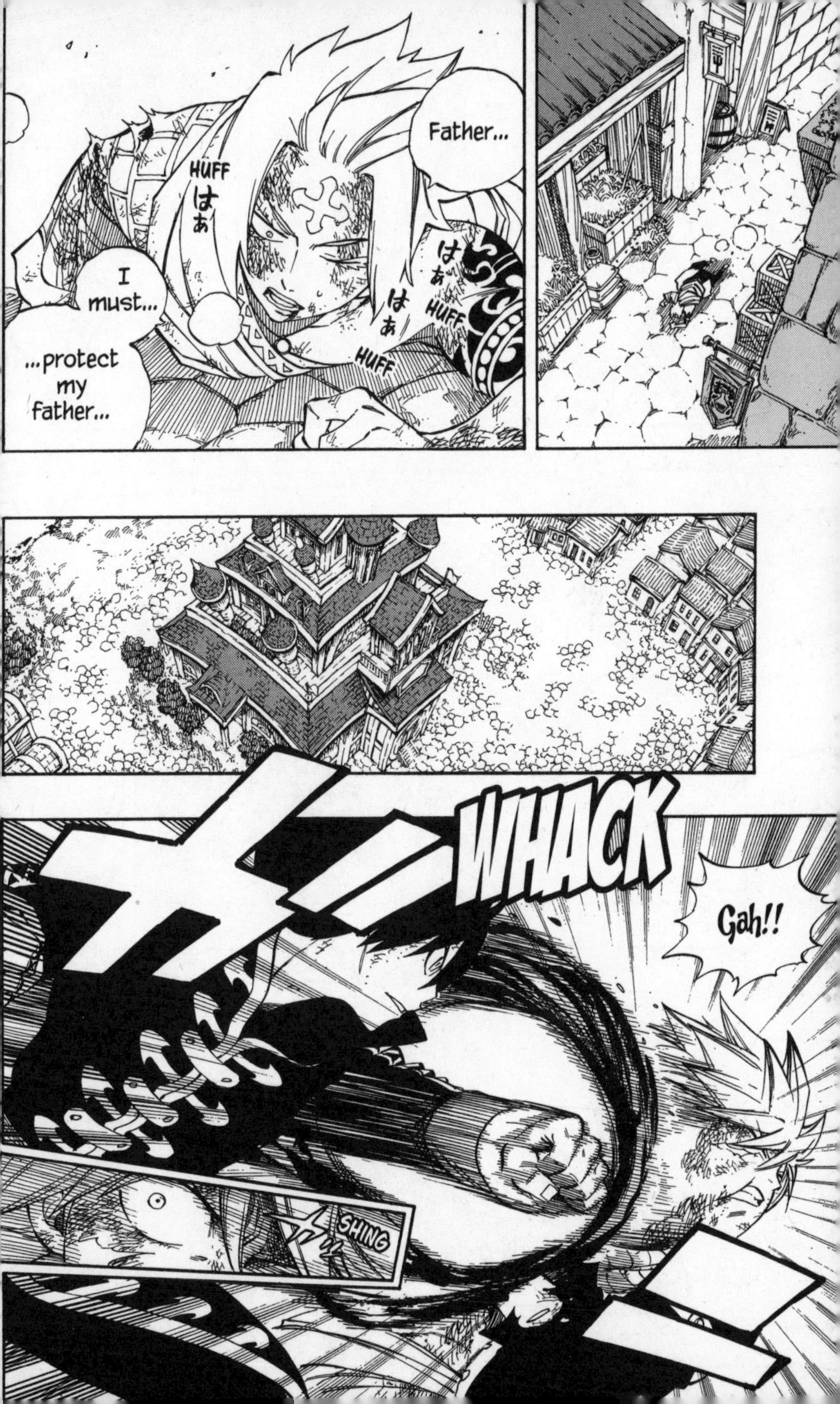
Father...
HUFF はぁ
はぁ HUFF
はぁ HUFF
I must...
...protect my father...
WHACK
Gah!!
SHING

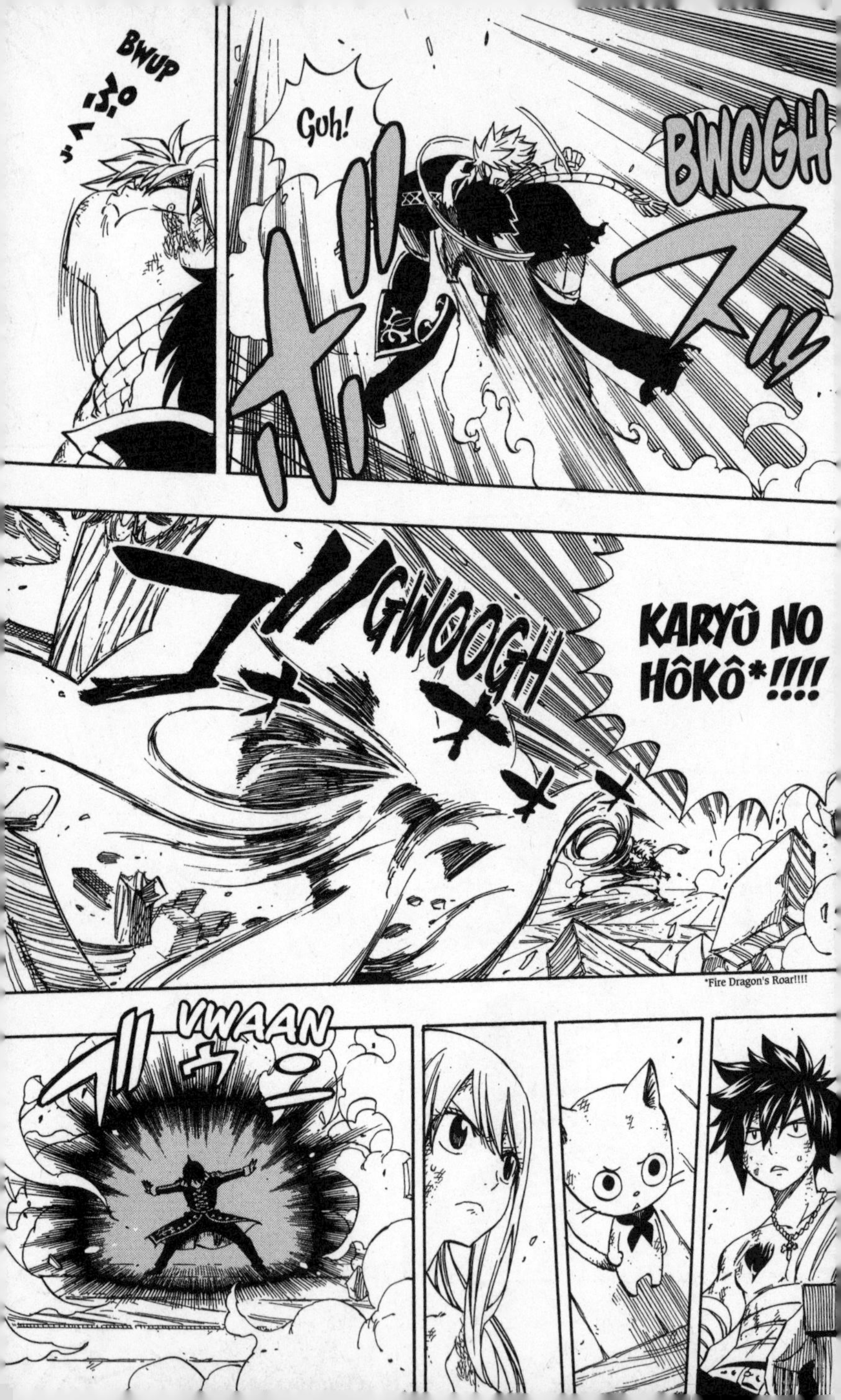
BWOGH
Guh!
BWUP
KARYÛ NO HÔKÔ*!!!!
GWOOGH
VWAAN
*Fire Dragon's Roar!!!!

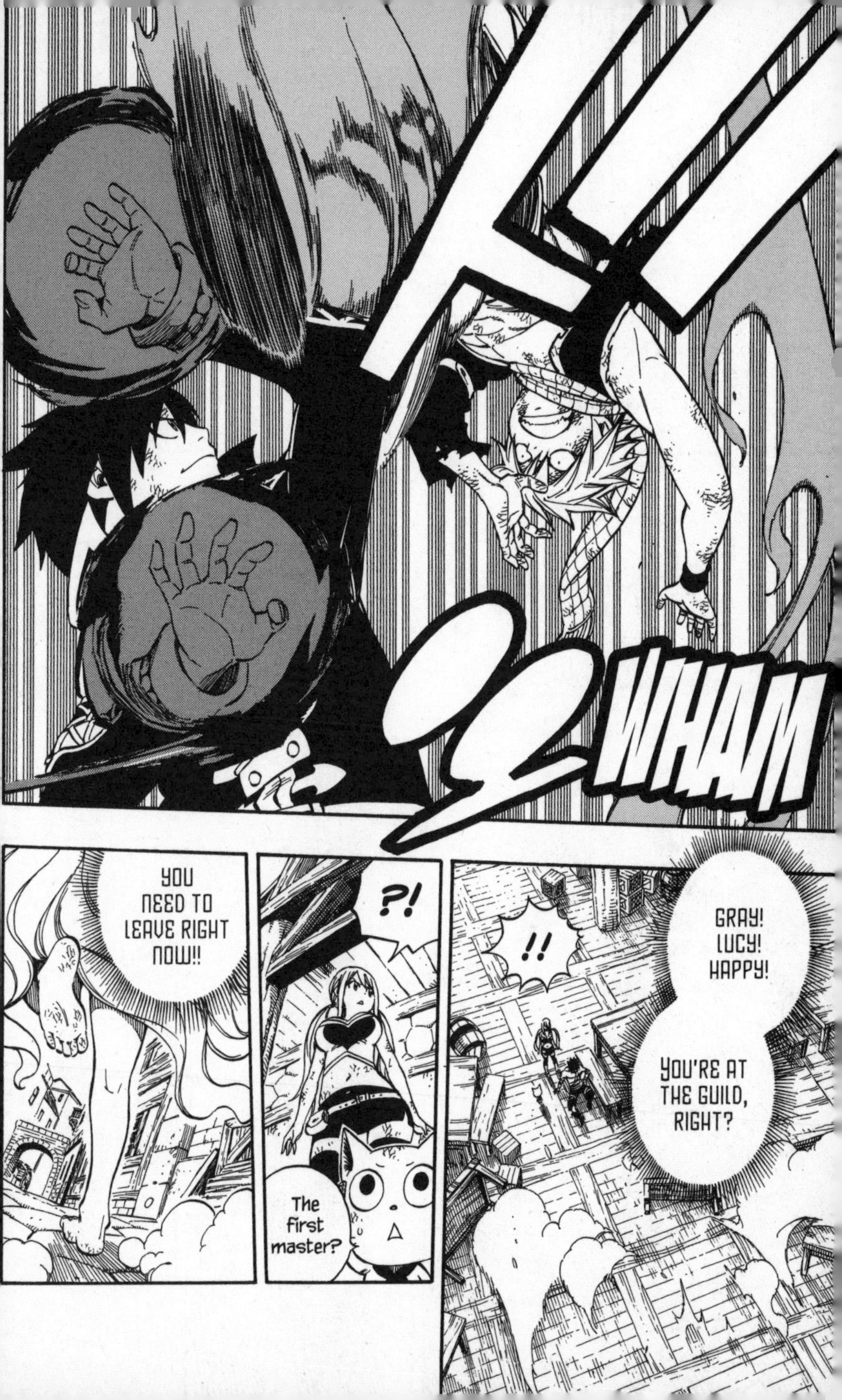
WHAM
!!
GRAY! LUCY! HAPPY!
YOU'RE AT THE GUILD, RIGHT?
?!
The first master?
YOU NEED TO LEAVE RIGHT NOW!!

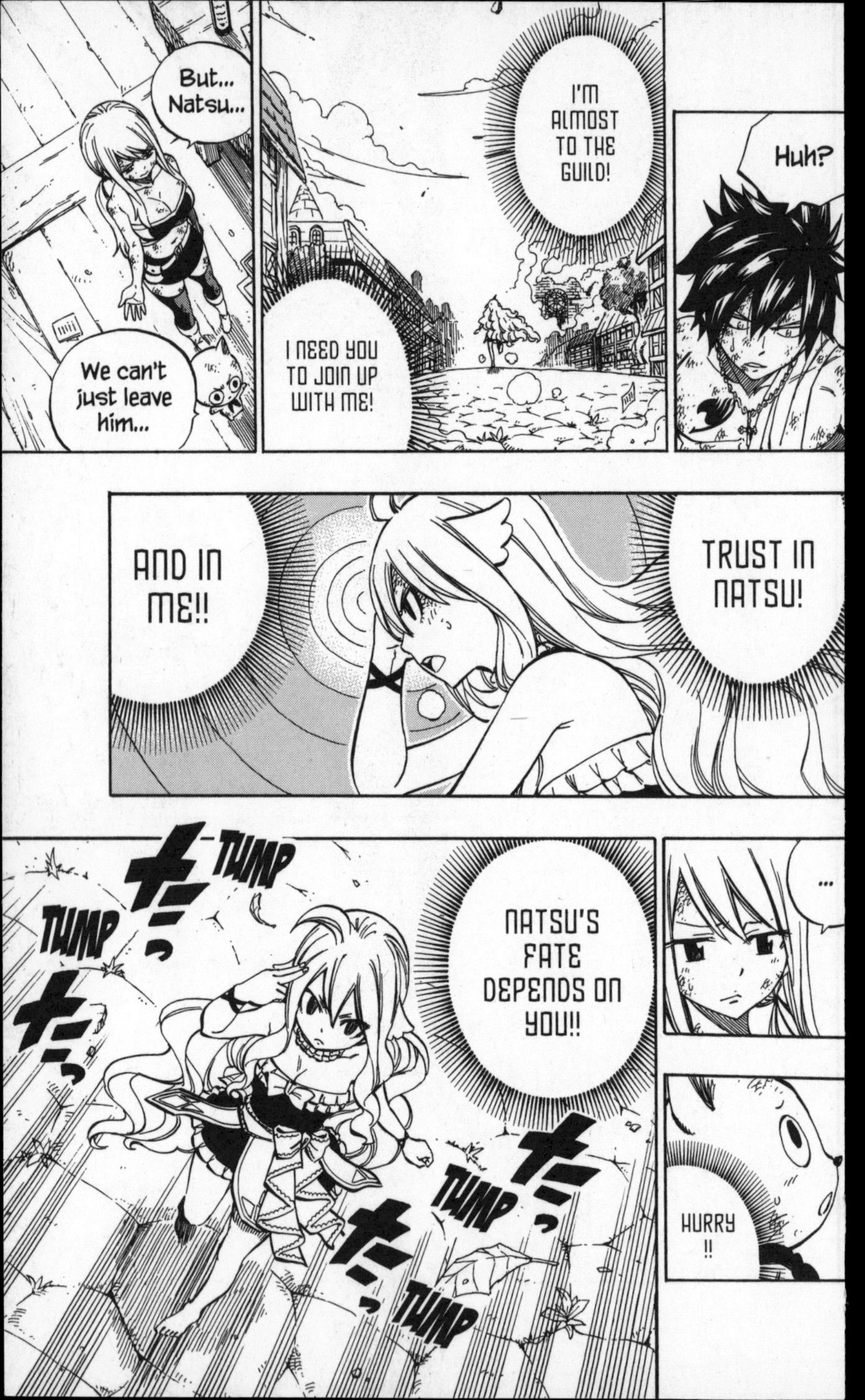

Huh?
I'M ALMOST TO THE GUILD!
I NEED YOU TO JOIN UP WITH ME!
But... Natsu...
We can't just leave him...
TRUST IN NATSU!
AND IN ME!!
...
HURRY !!
NATSU'S FATE DEPENDS ON YOU!!
TUMP
TUMP
TUMP
TUMP

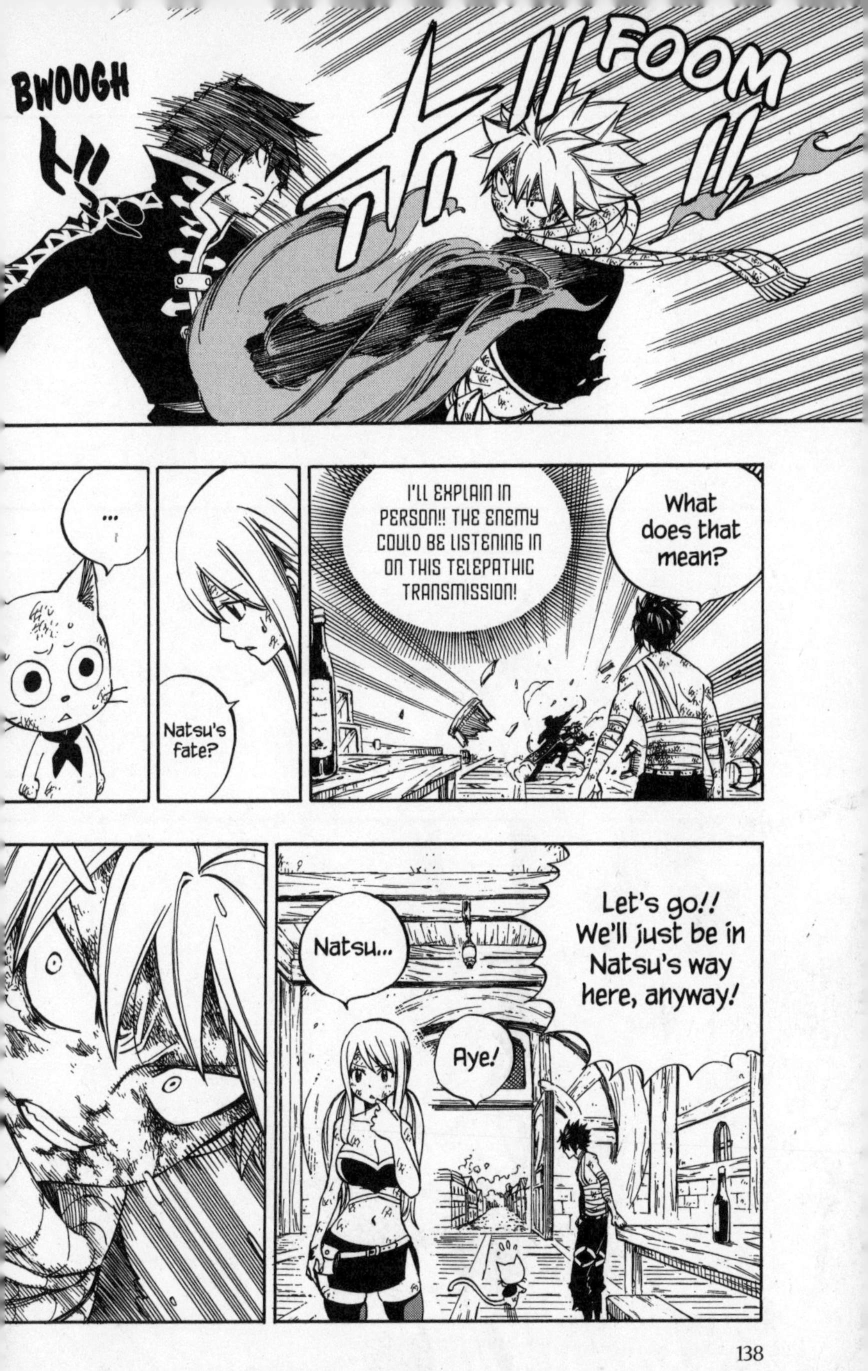
FOOM
BWOOGH
What does that mean?
I'LL EXPLAIN IN PERSON!! THE ENEMY COULD BE LISTENING IN ON THIS TELEPATHIC TRANSMISSION!
Natsu's fate?
...
Let's go!! We'll just be in Natsu's way here, anyway!
Natsu...
Aye!

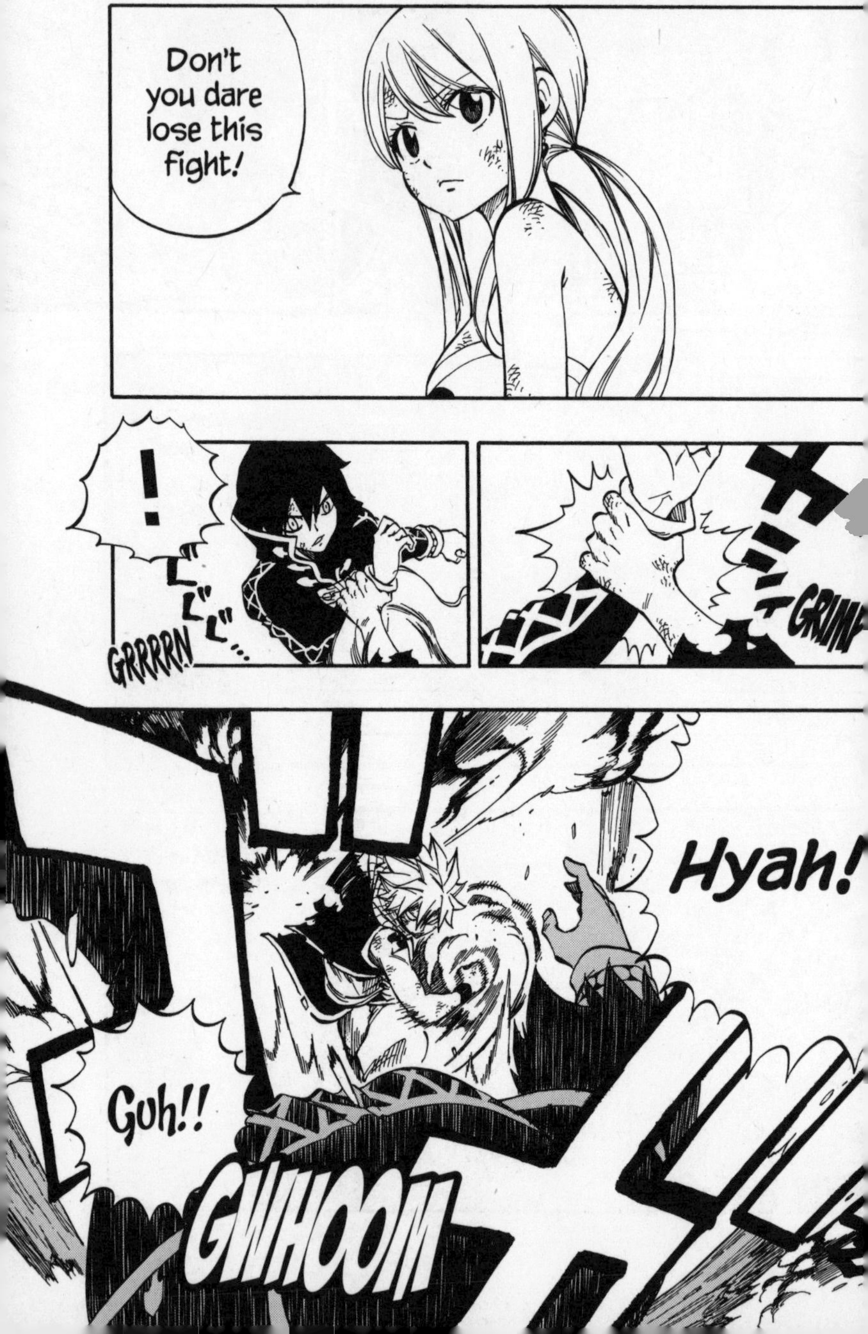
Don't you dare lose this fight!
GRINF
!
GRRRRN
Hyah!
Guh!!
GWHOOM

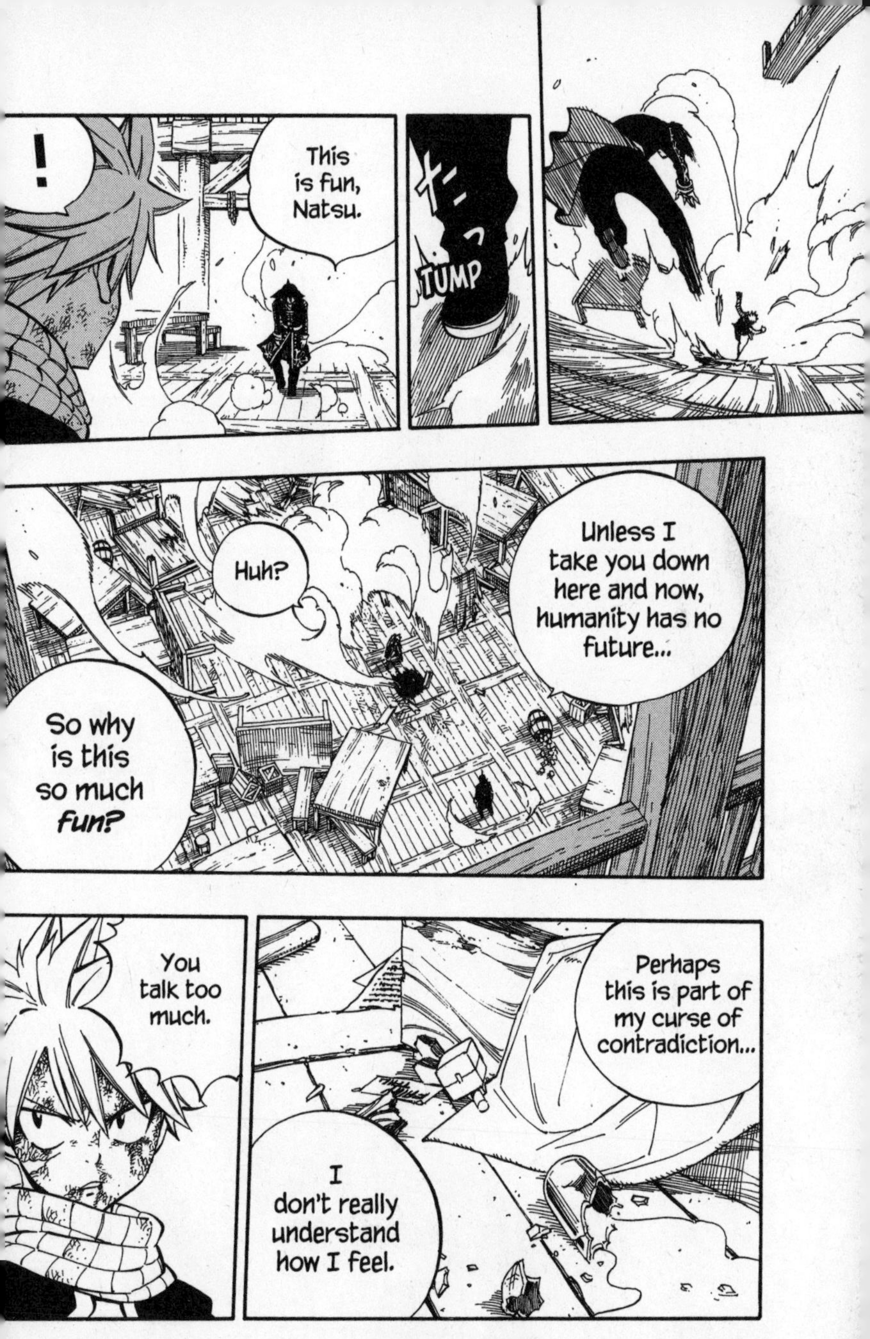
TUMP
This is fun, Natsu.
!
Unless I take you down here and now, humanity has no future...
Huh?
So why is this so much *fun?*
Perhaps this is part of my curse of contradiction...
I don't really understand how I feel.
You talk too much.

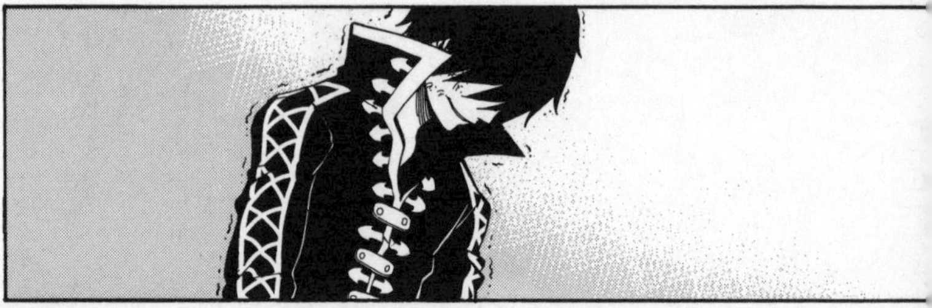

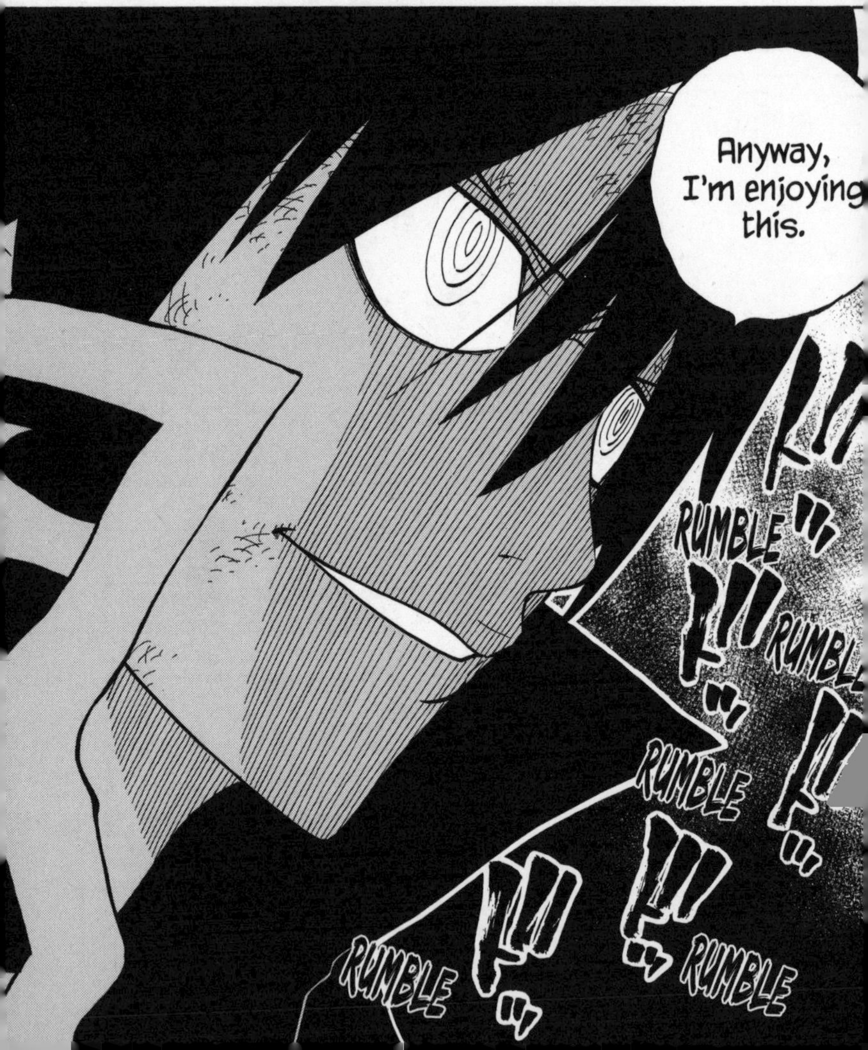
Anyway, I'm enjoying this.
RUMBLE
RUMBLE
RUMBLE
RUMBLE
RUMBLE

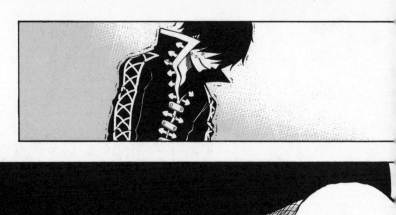

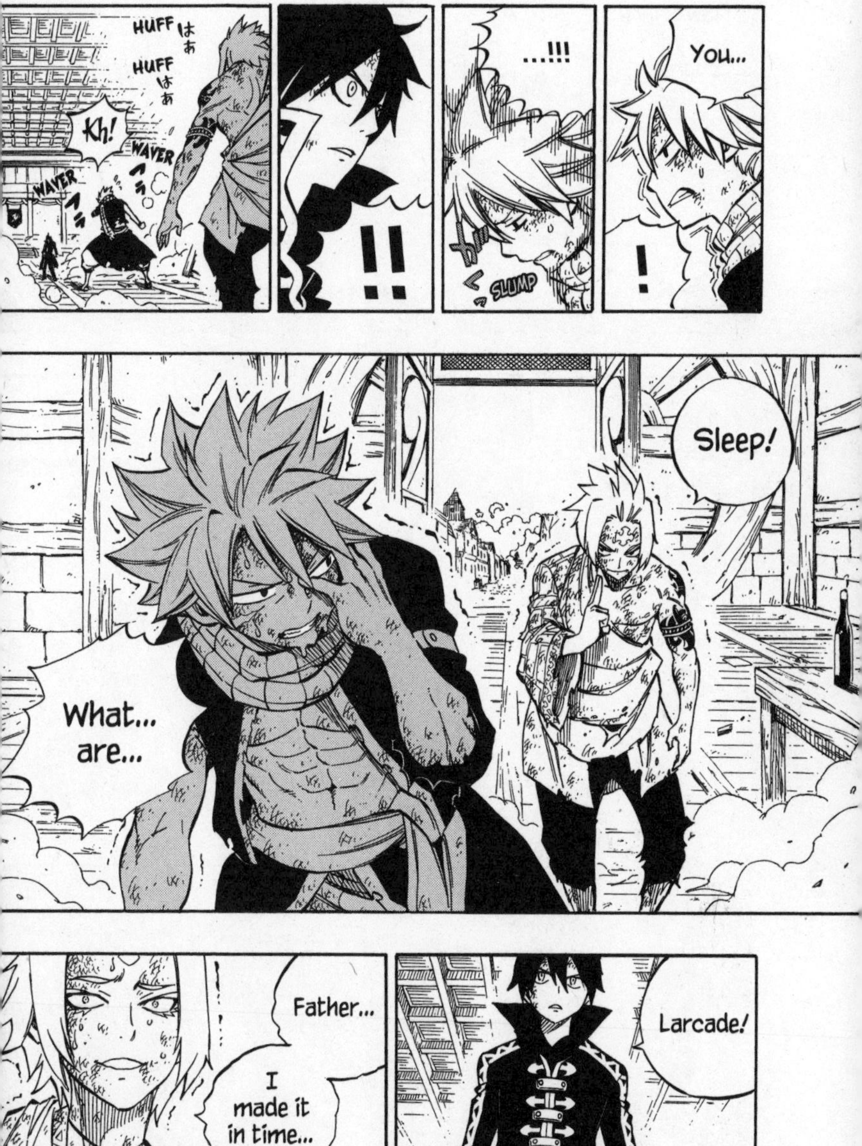
You...
!
...!!!
SLUMP
!!
HUFF はぁ
HUFF はぁ
Kh!
WAVER フラ
WAVER フラ
Sleep!
What... are...
Larcade!
Father...
I made it in time...

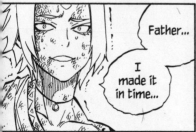

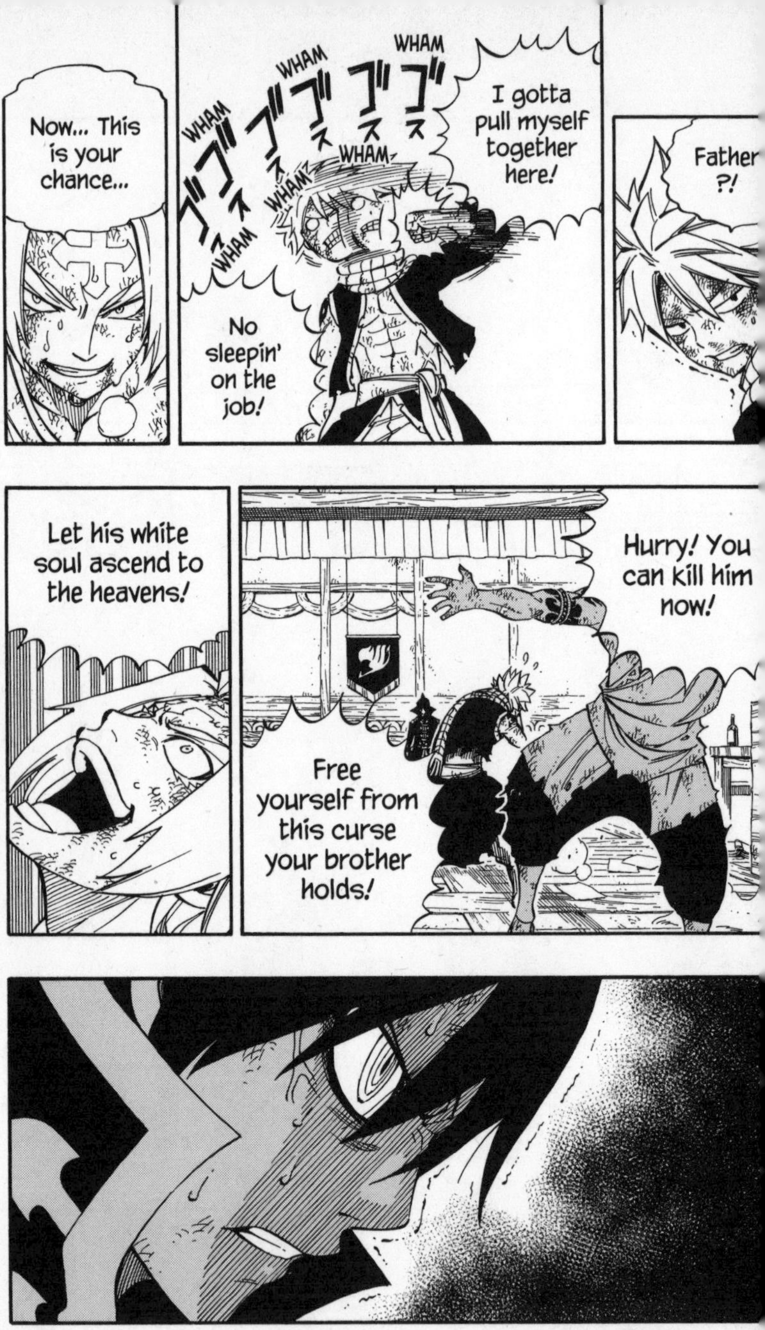
Father ?!
WHAM
WHAM
WHAM
WHAM
WHAM
WHAM
I gotta pull myself together here!
No sleepin' on the job!
Now... This is your chance...
Hurry! You can kill him now!
Free yourself from this curse your brother holds!
Let his white soul ascend to the heavens!

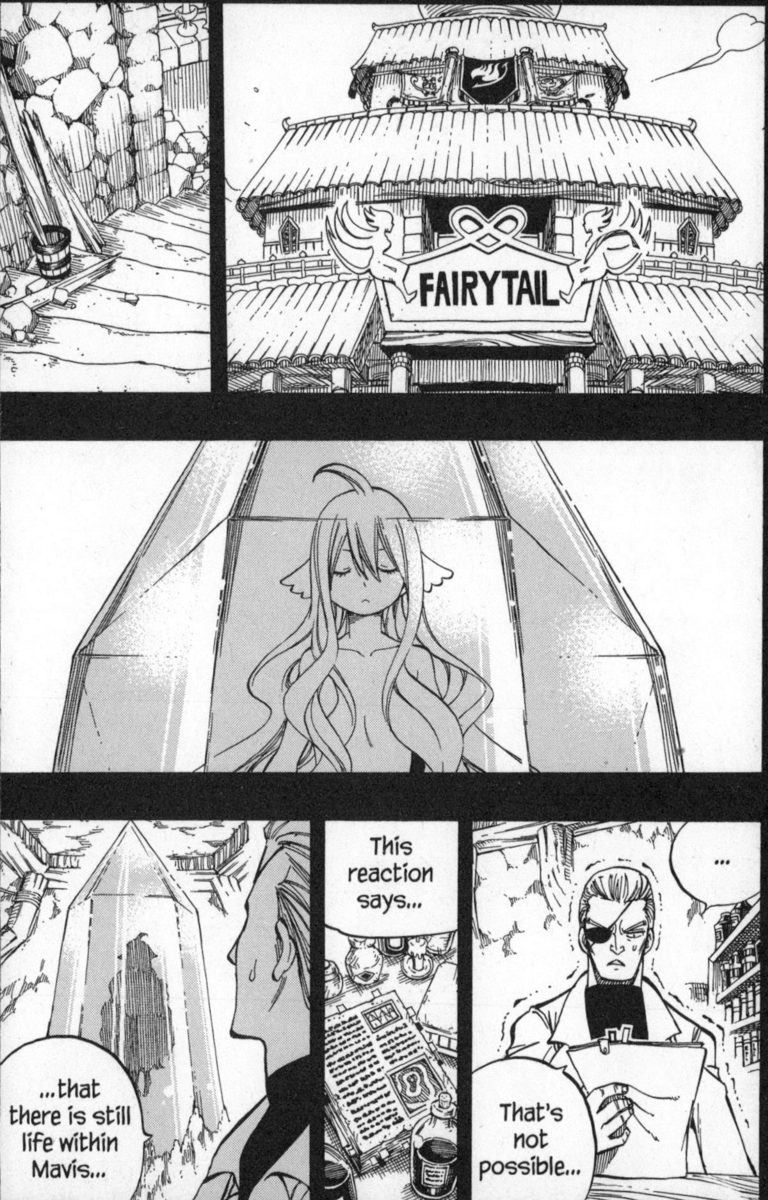
FAIRYTAIL
...
That's not possible...
This reaction says...
...that there is still life within Mavis...

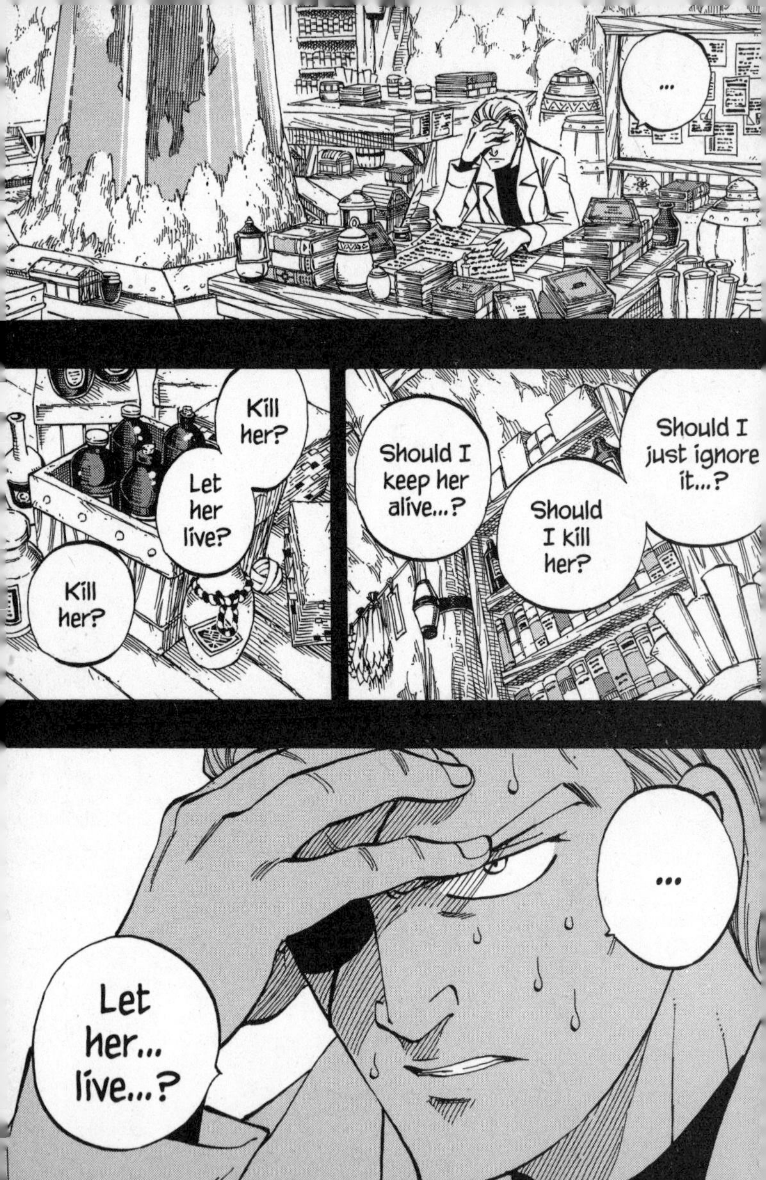
...
Should I just ignore it...?
Should I kill her?
Should I keep her alive...?
Kill her?
Let her live?
Kill her?
...
Let her... live...?

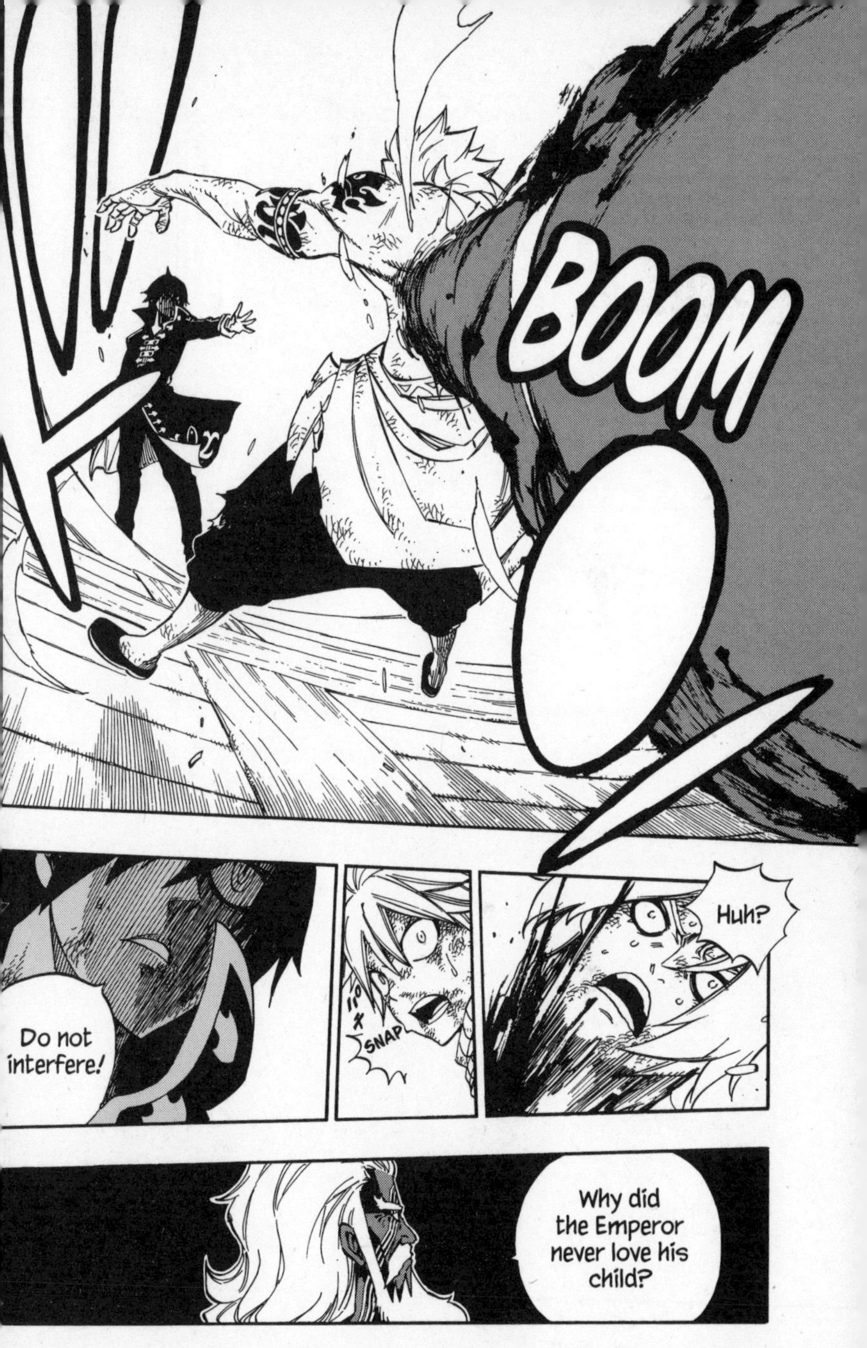
BOOM
Huh?
SNAP
Do not interfere!
Why did the Emperor never love his child?

# FAIRY TAIL

フェアリーテイル

## Chapter 526: My Name Is...

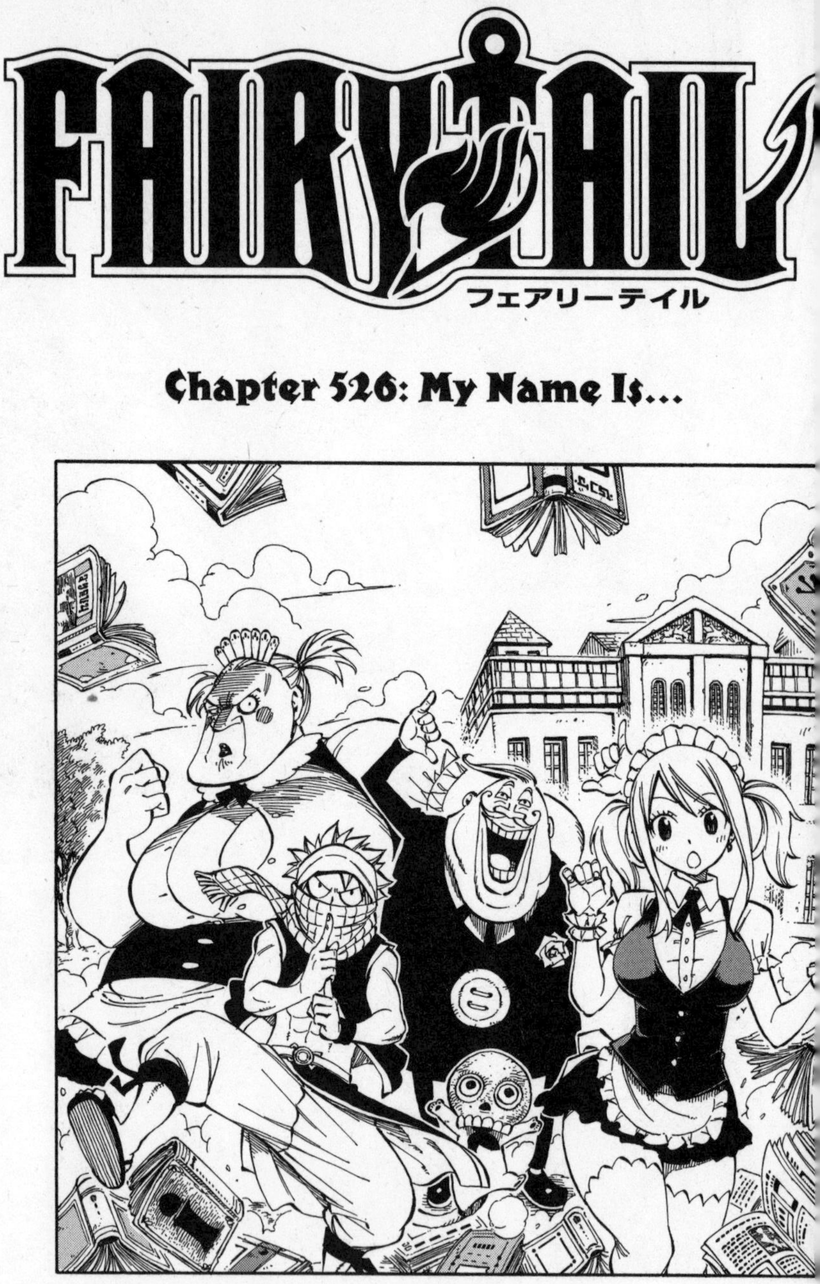

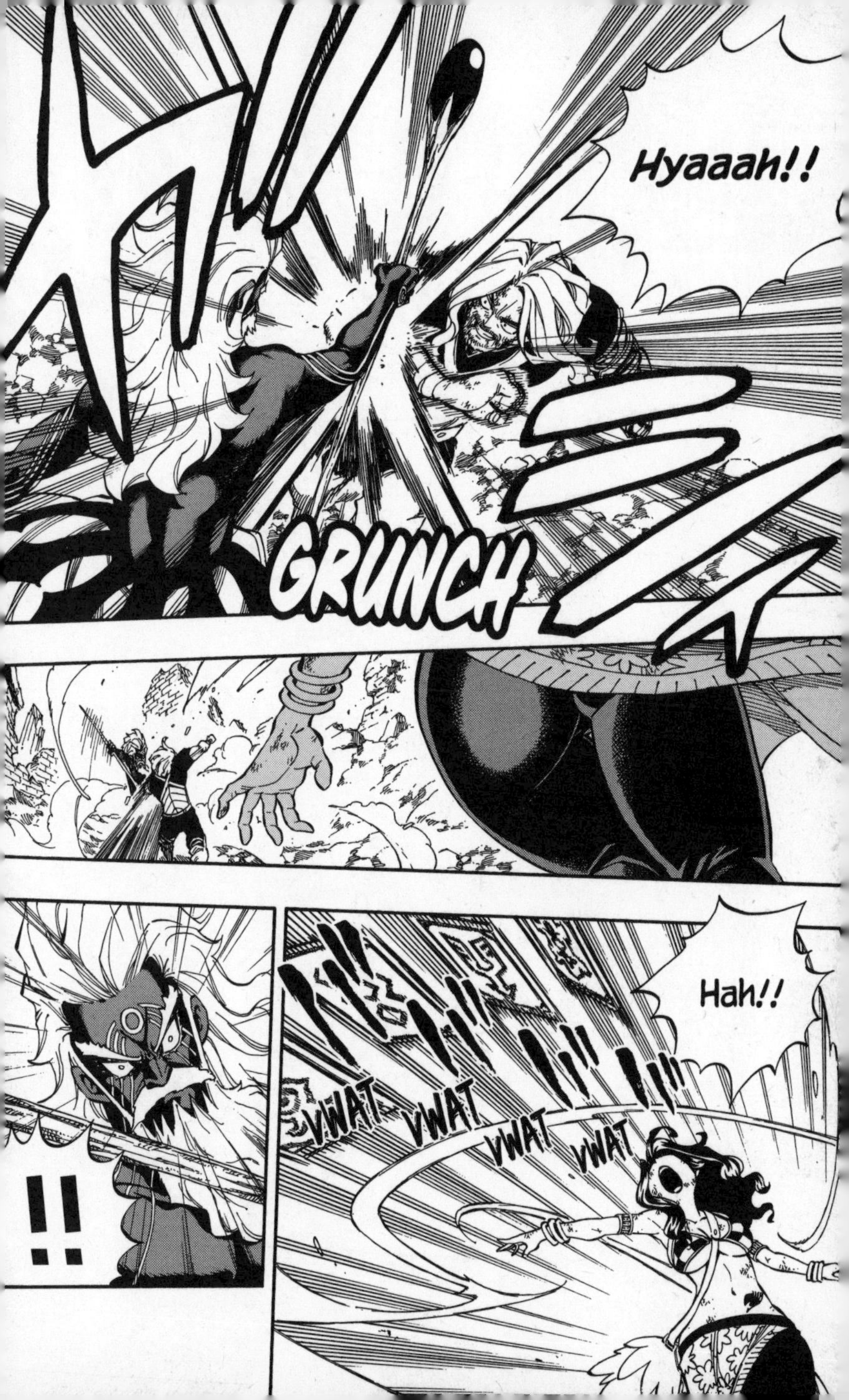
Hyaaah!!
GRUNCH
Hah!!
VWAT VWAT VWAT VWAT
!!

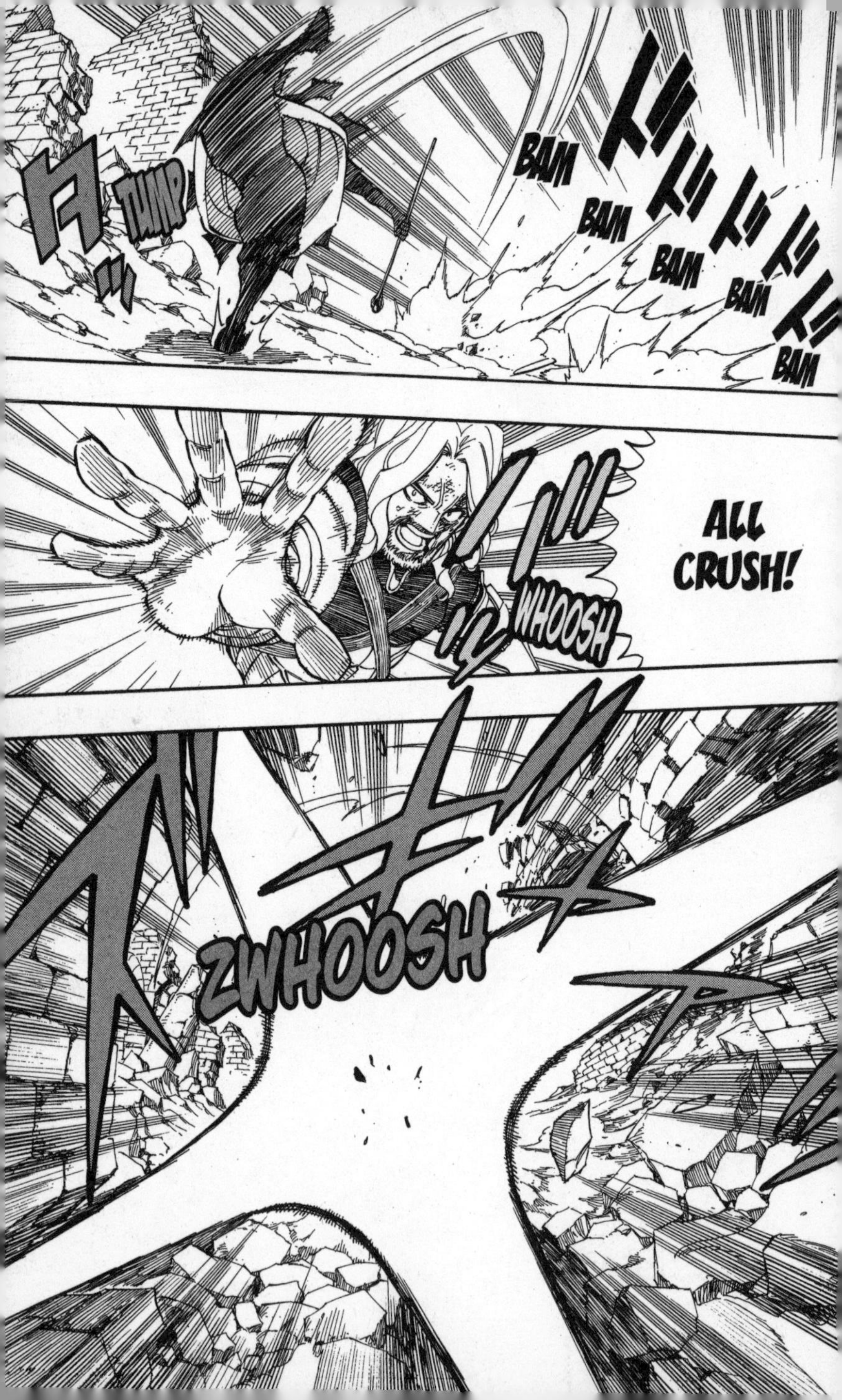
BAM
BAM
BAM
BAM
BAM
TUMP
ALL CRUSH!
WHOOSH
ZWHOOSH

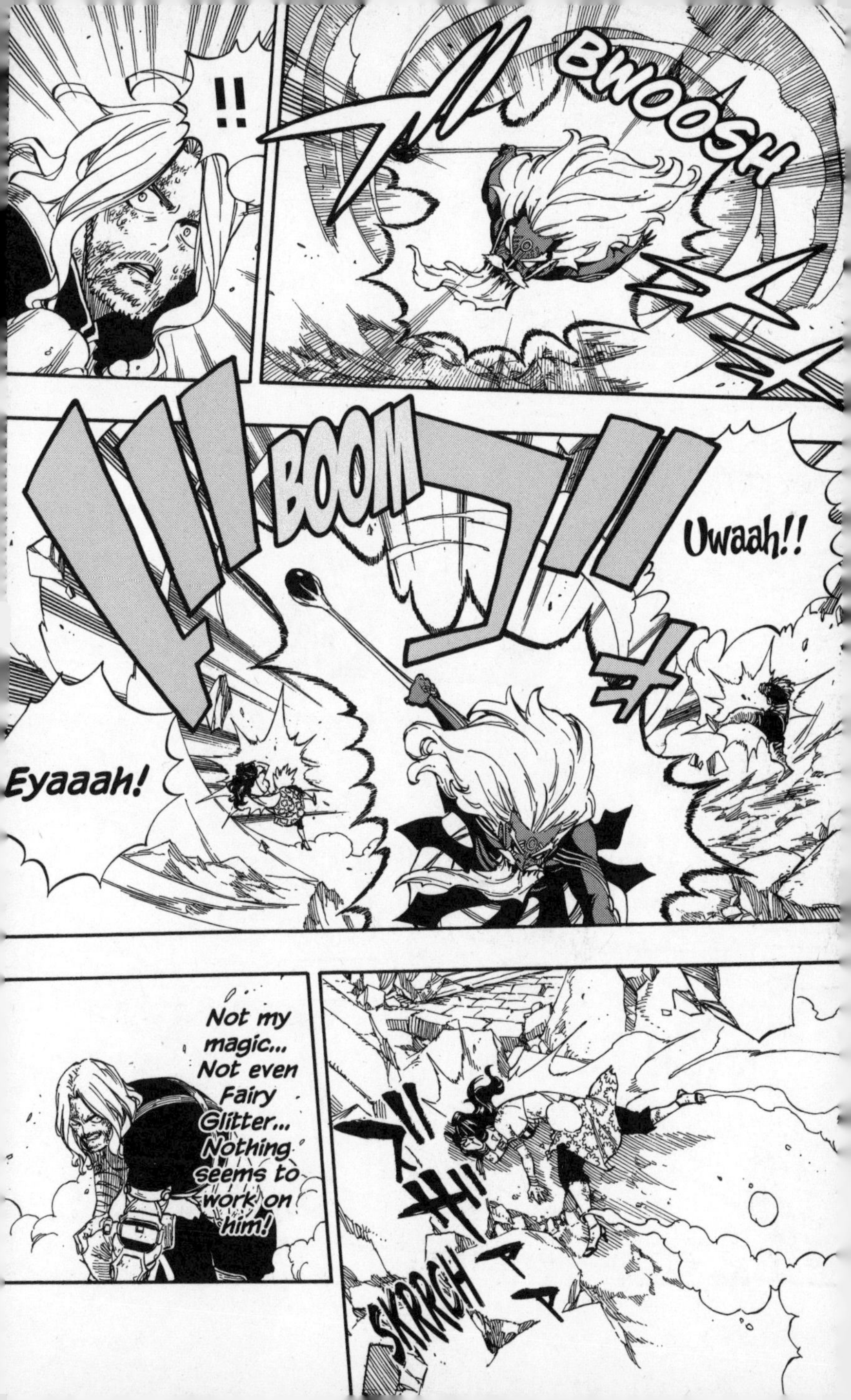
BWOOSH
!!
BOOM
Uwaah!!
Eyaaah!
SKRRCH
Not my magic... Not even Fairy Glitter... Nothing seems to work on him!

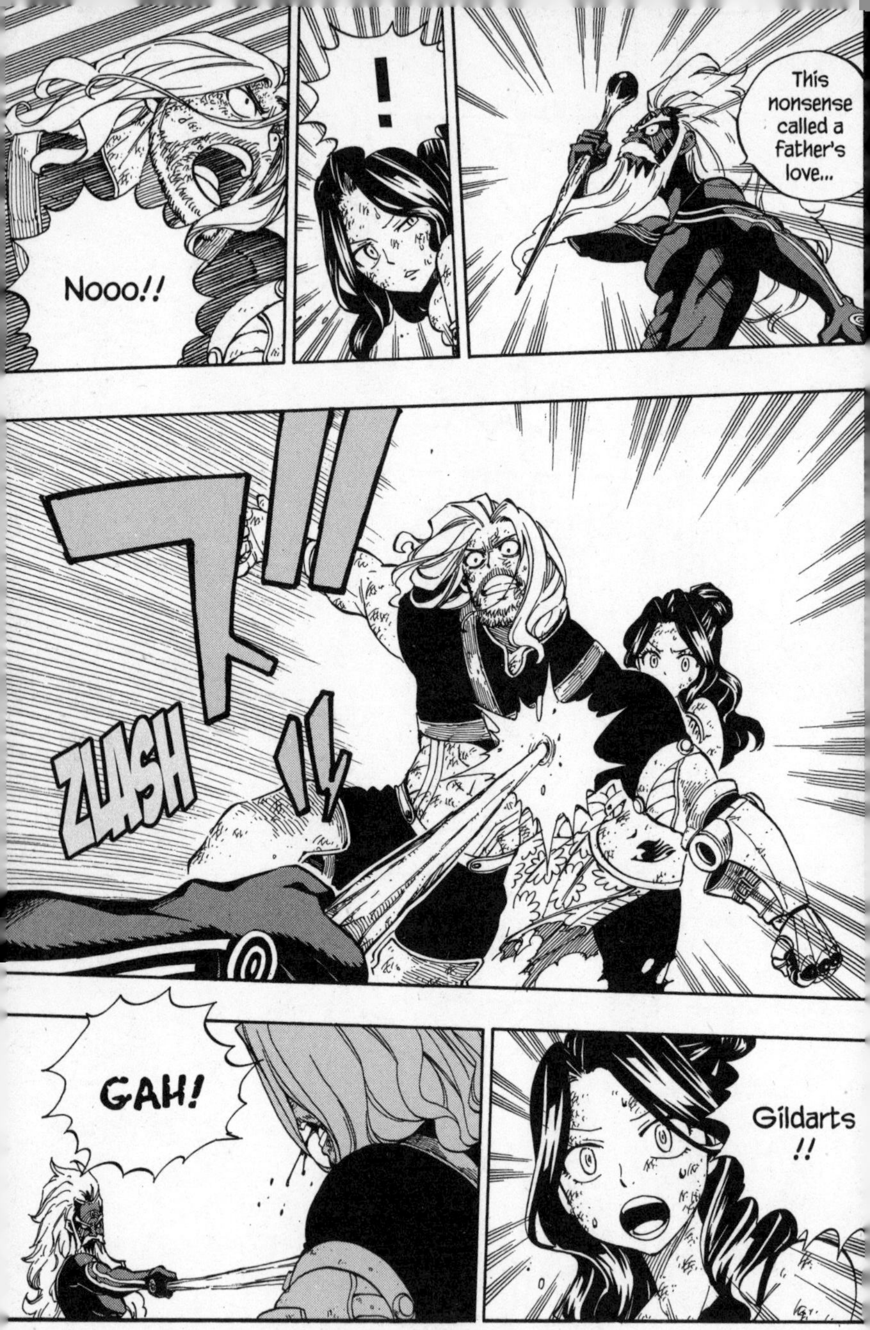
This nonsense called a father's love...
!
Nooo!!
ZLASH
Gildarts !!
GAH!

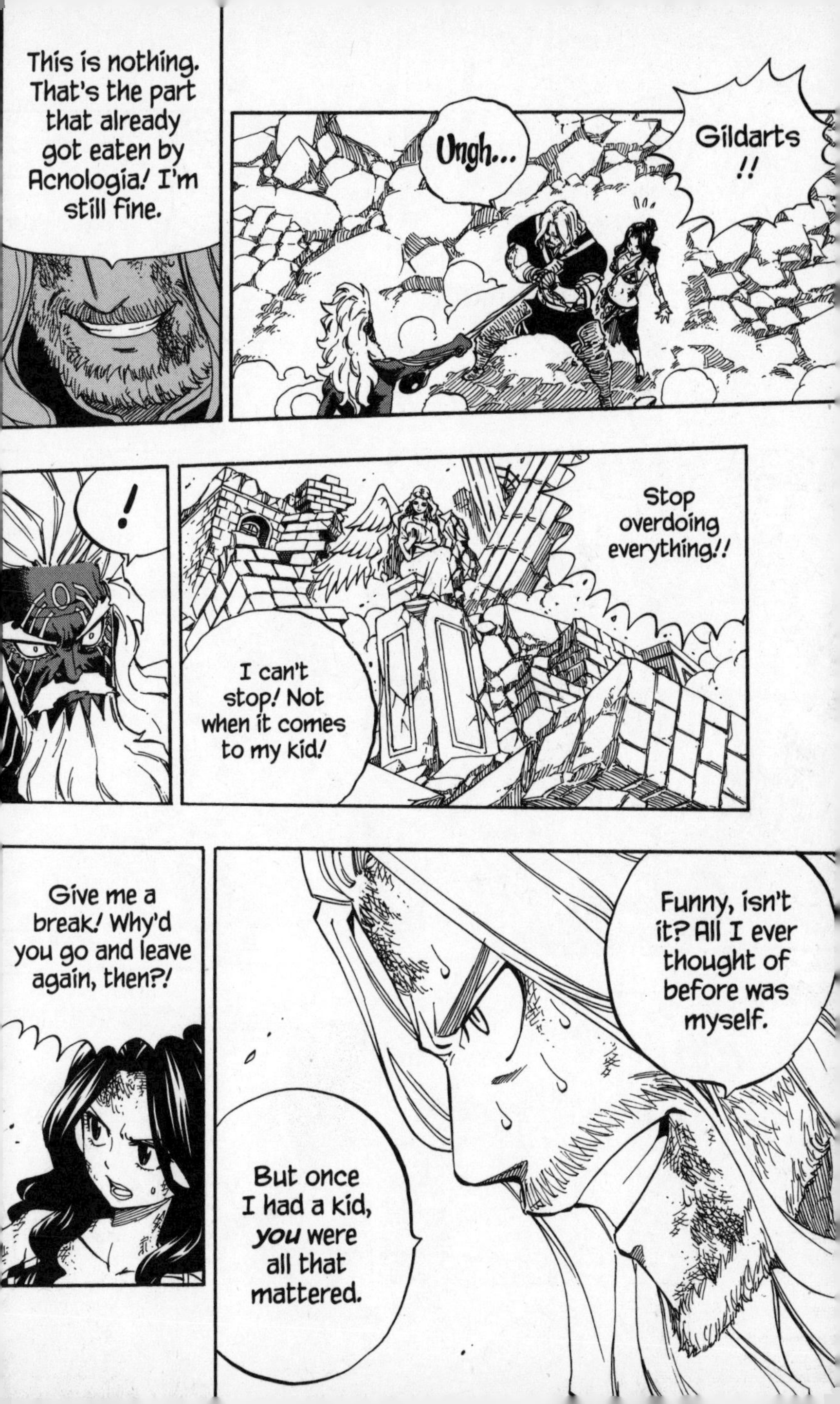

Gildarts!!
Ungh...
This is nothing. That's the part that already got eaten by Acnologia! I'm still fine.
Stop overdoing everything!!
I can't stop! Not when it comes to my kid!
!
Funny, isn't it? All I ever thought of before was myself.
But once I had a kid, *you* were all that mattered.
Give me a break! Why'd you go and leave again, then?!

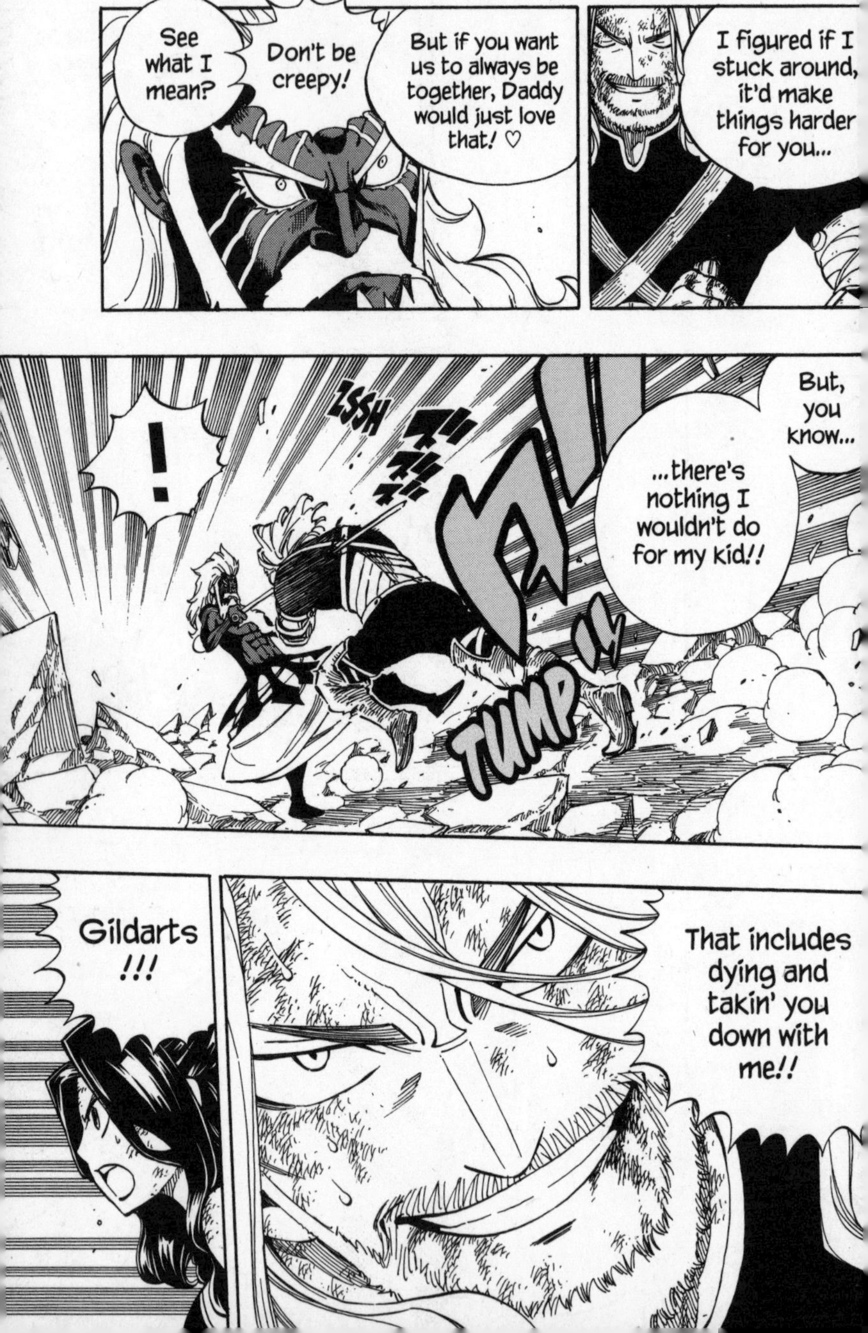
I figured if I stuck around, it'd make things harder for you...
But if you want us to always be together, Daddy would just love that! ♡
Don't be creepy!
See what I mean?
But, you know...
...there's nothing I wouldn't do for my kid!!
ZSSH
!
TUMP
That includes dying and takin' you down with me!!
Gildarts!!!

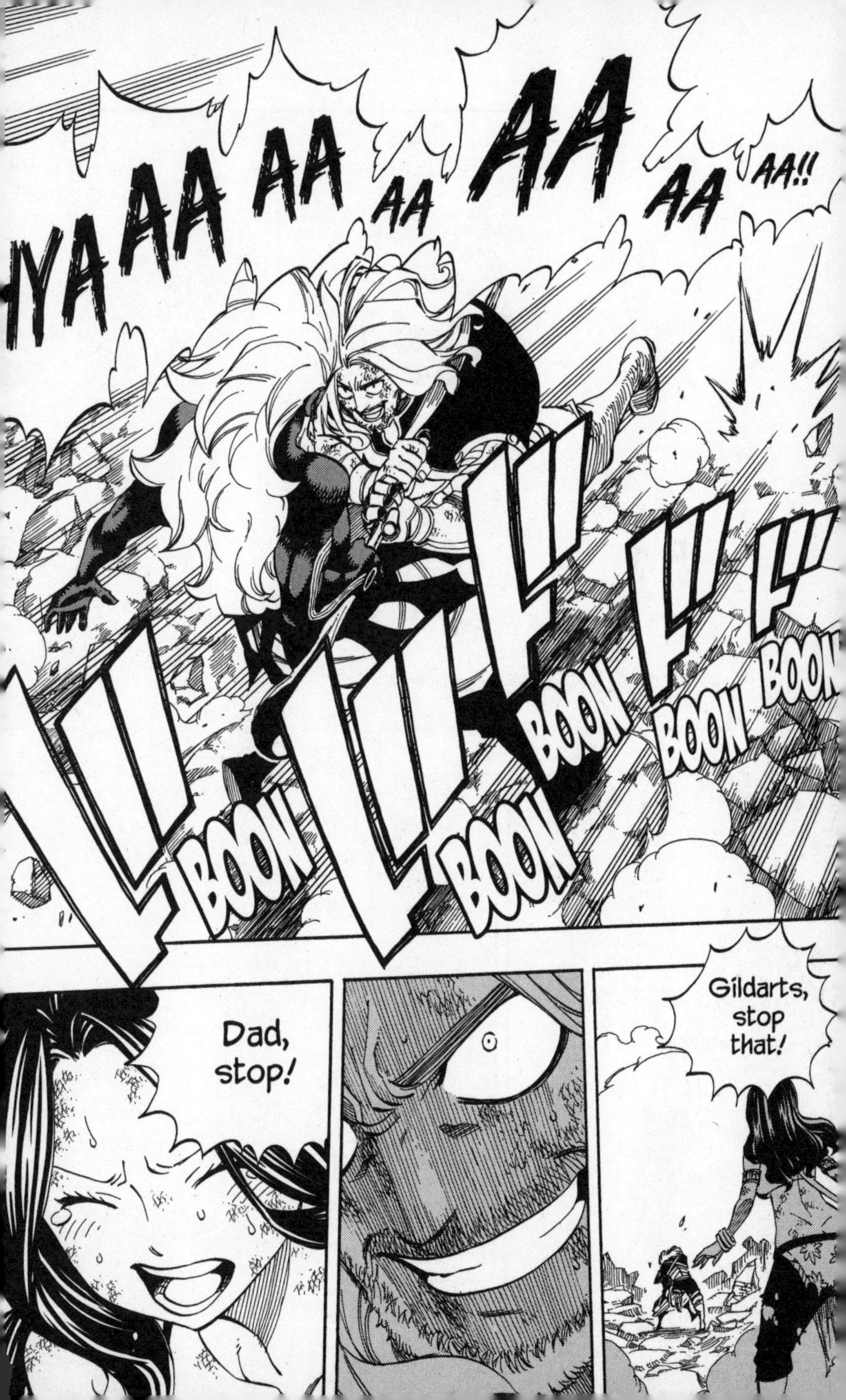
HYAAA AA AA AA AA AA!!
BOON BOON BOON BOON BOON BOON
Gildarts, stop that!
Dad, stop!

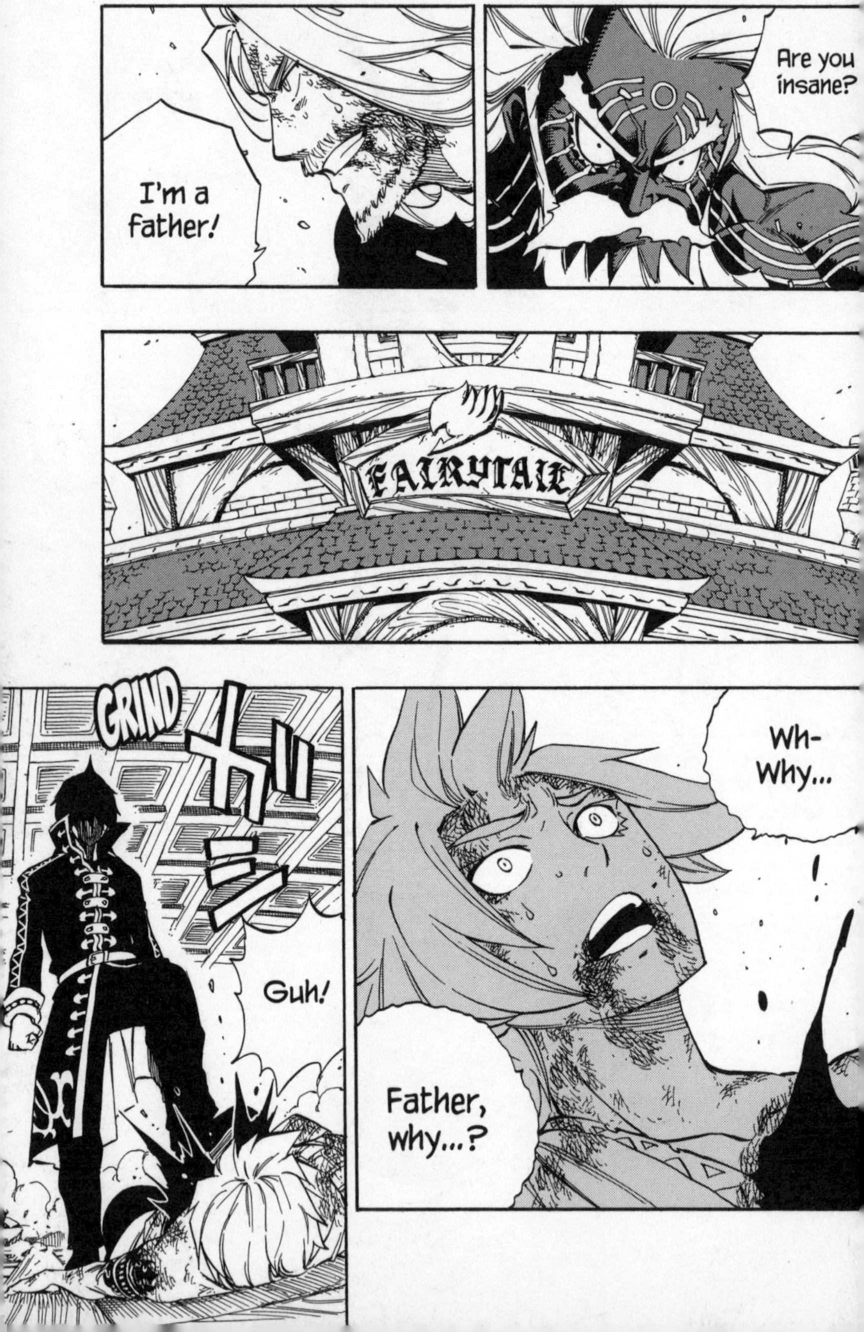
Are you insane?
I'm a father!
FAIRY TAIL
Wh- Why...
Father, why...?
GRIND
Guh!

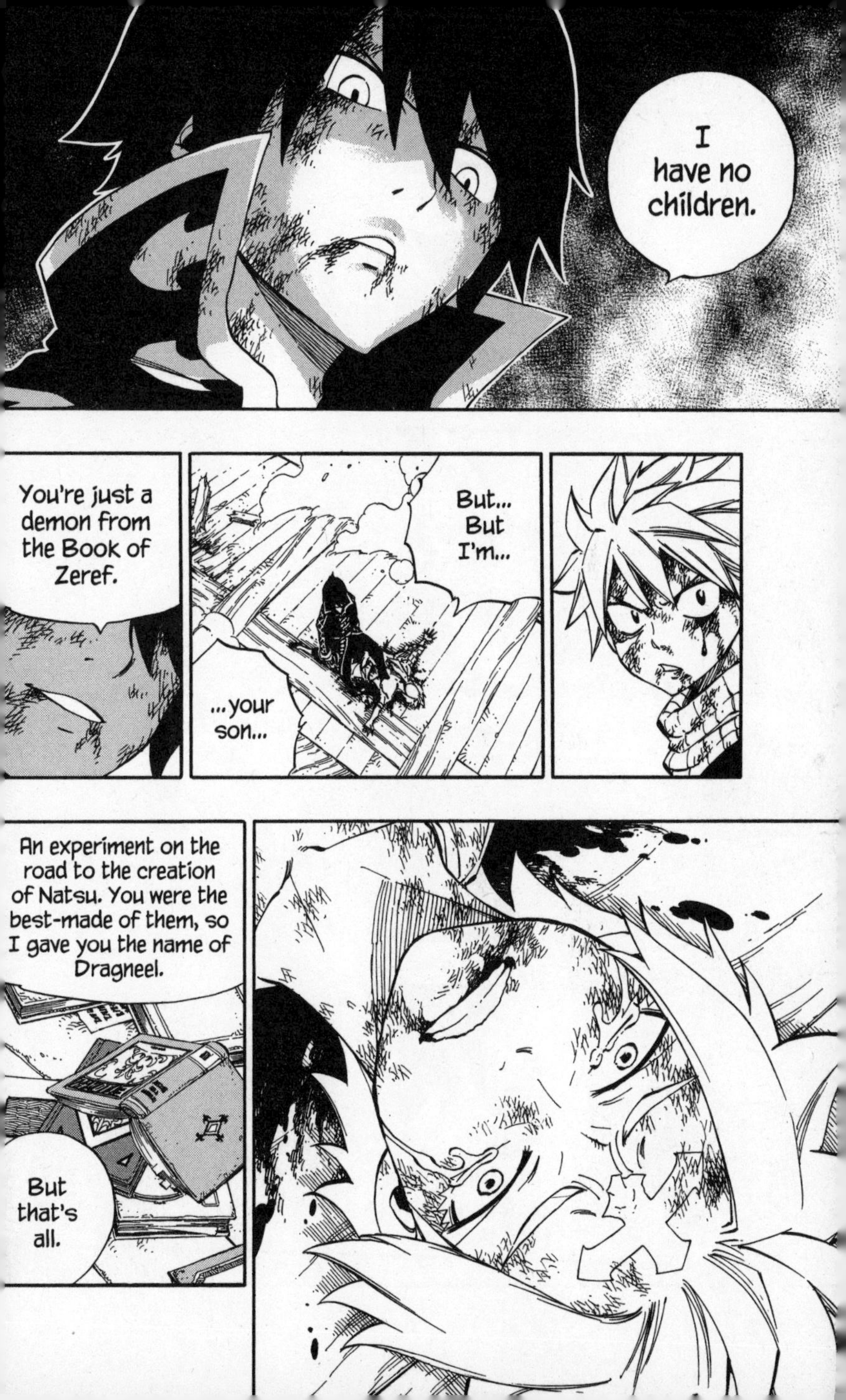
I have no children.
But... But I'm...
...your son...
You're just a demon from the Book of Zeref.
An experiment on the road to the creation of Natsu. You were the best-made of them, so I gave you the name of Dragneel.
But that's all.

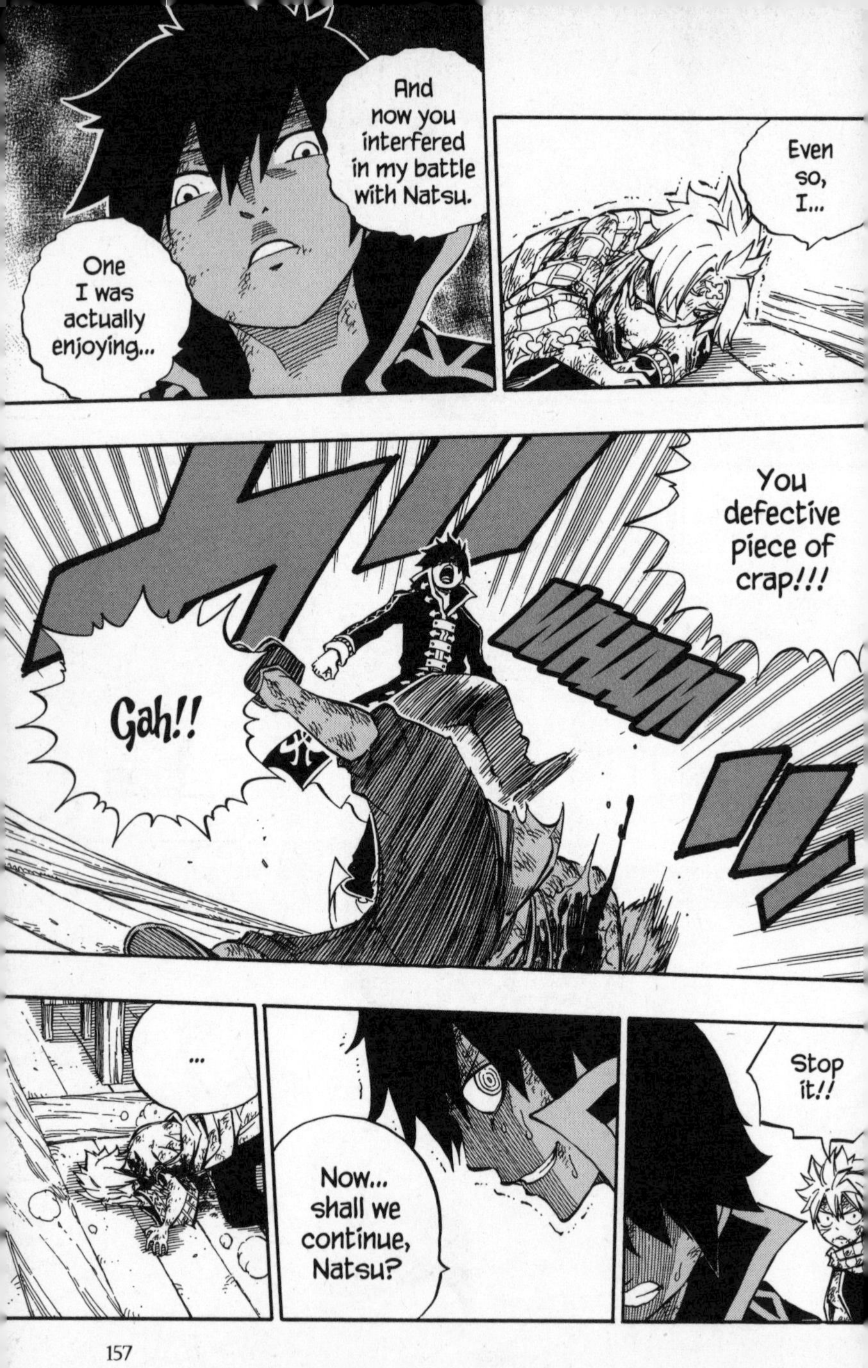
Even so, I...
And now you interfered in my battle with Natsu.
One I was actually enjoying...
You defective piece of crap!!!
WHAM
Gah!!
Stop it!!
Now... shall we continue, Natsu?
...

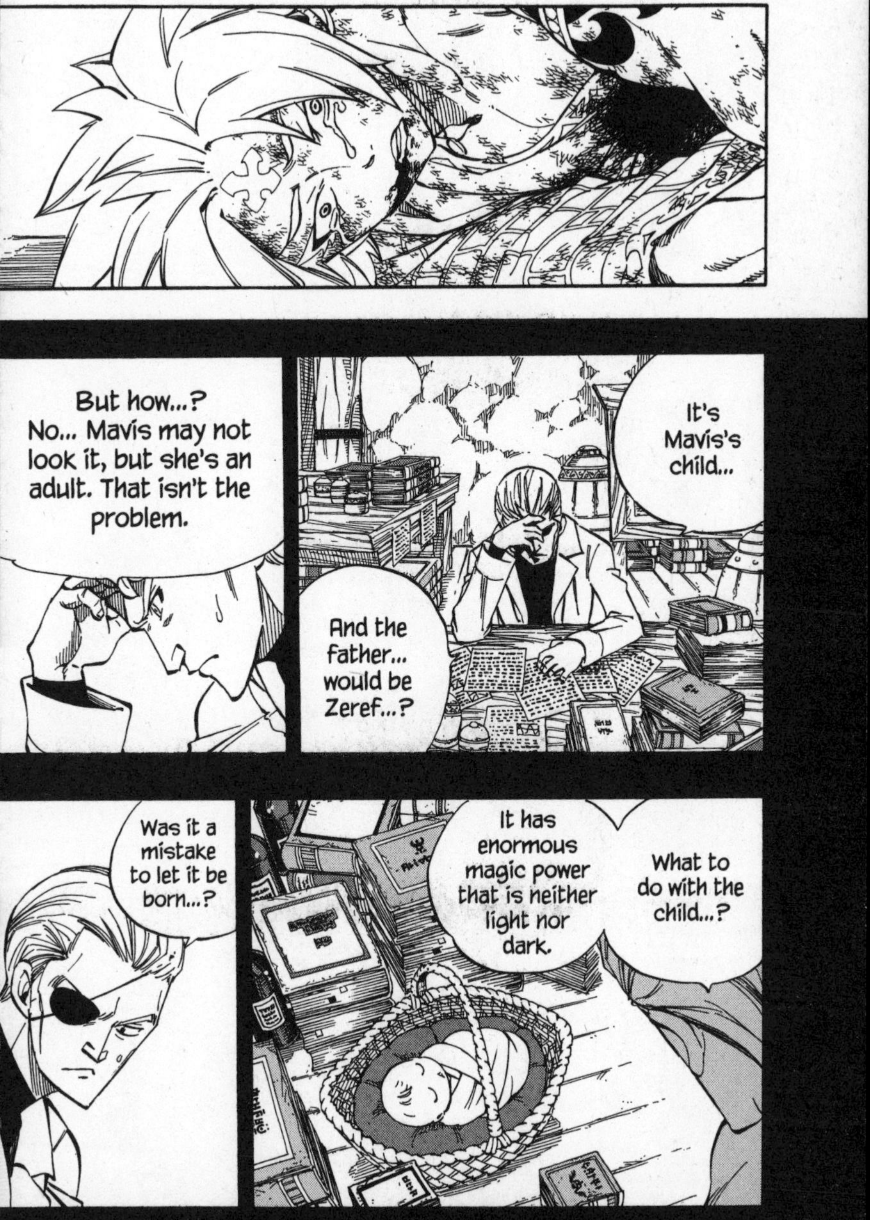
It's Mavis's child...
And the father... would be Zeref...?
But how...? No... Mavis may not look it, but she's an adult. That isn't the problem.
What to do with the child...?
It has enormous magic power that is neither light nor dark.
Was it a mistake to let it be born...?

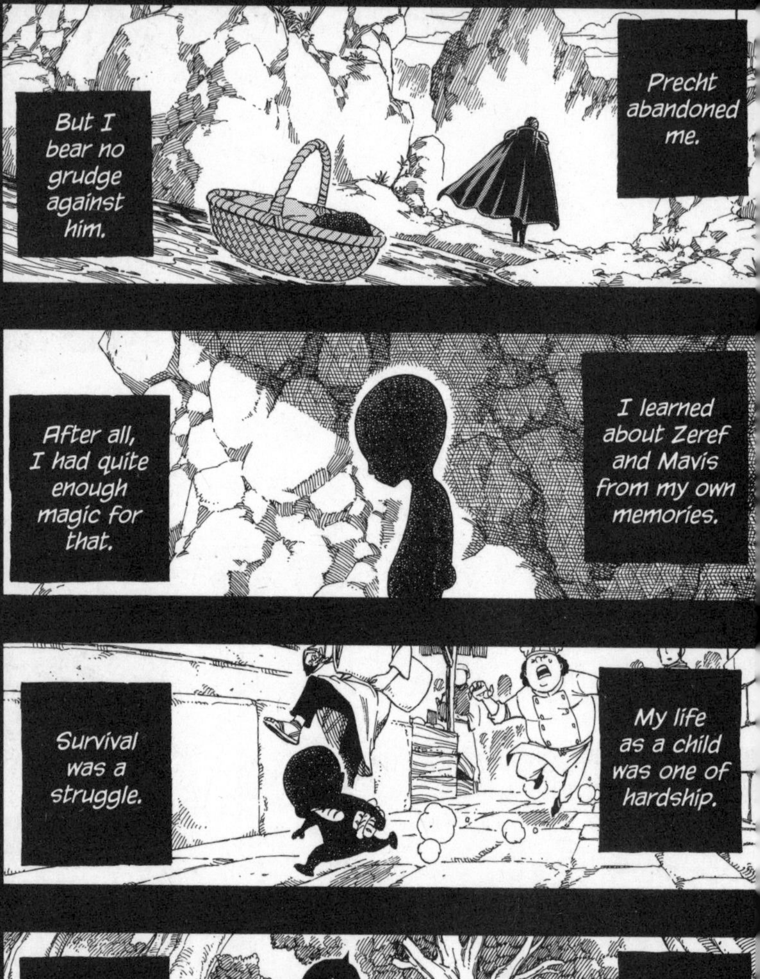
Precht abandoned me.
But I bear no grudge against him.
I learned about Zeref and Mavis from my own memories.
After all, I had quite enough magic for that.
My life as a child was one of hardship.
Survival was a struggle.
But the one who finally saved me was...
...my own father.

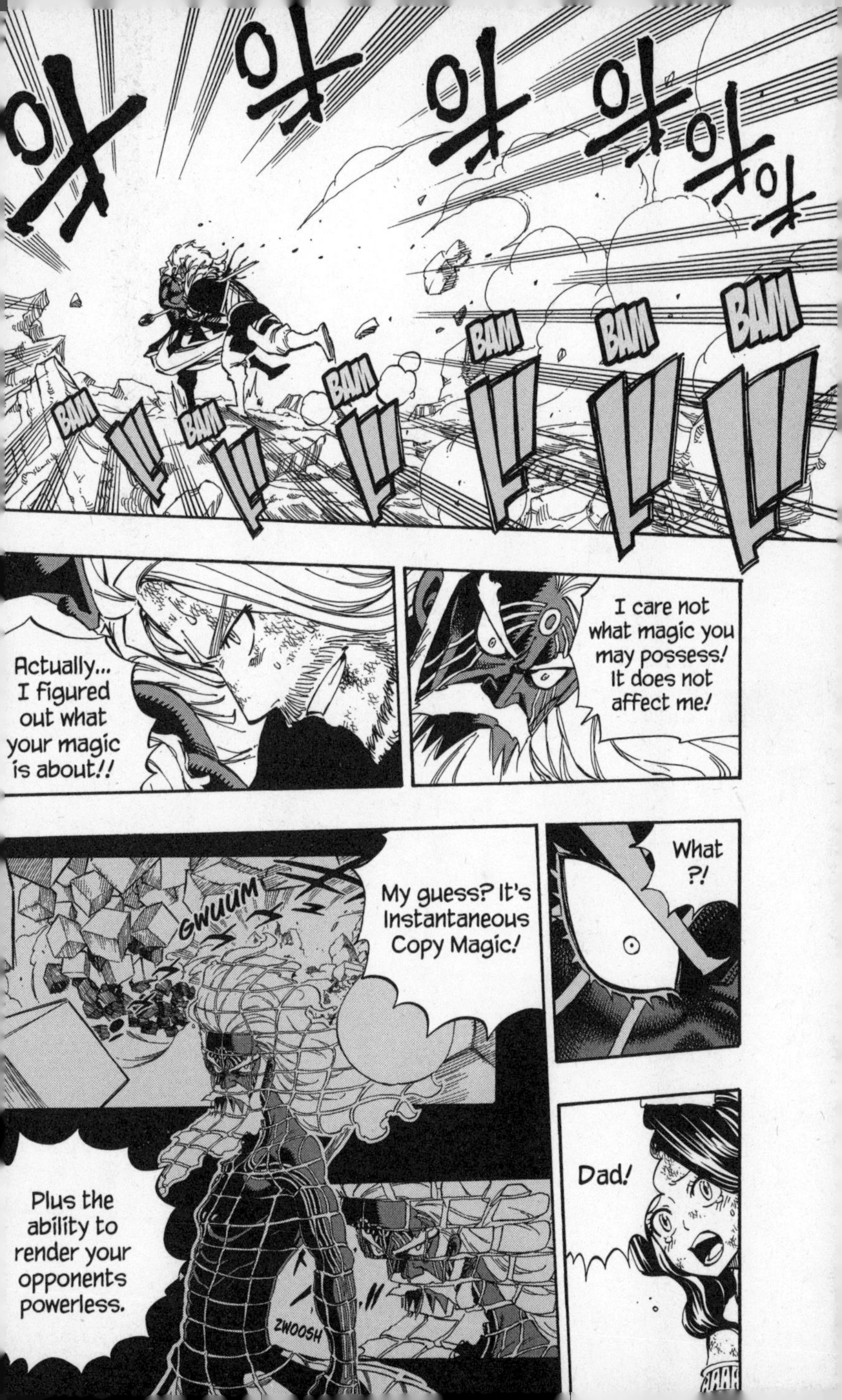
BAM
BAM
BAM
BAM
BAM
BAM
I care not what magic you may possess! It does not affect me!
Actually... I figured out what your magic is about!!
What ?!
Dad!
My guess? It's Instantaneous Copy Magic!
GWUUM
Plus the ability to render your opponents powerless.
ZWOOSH

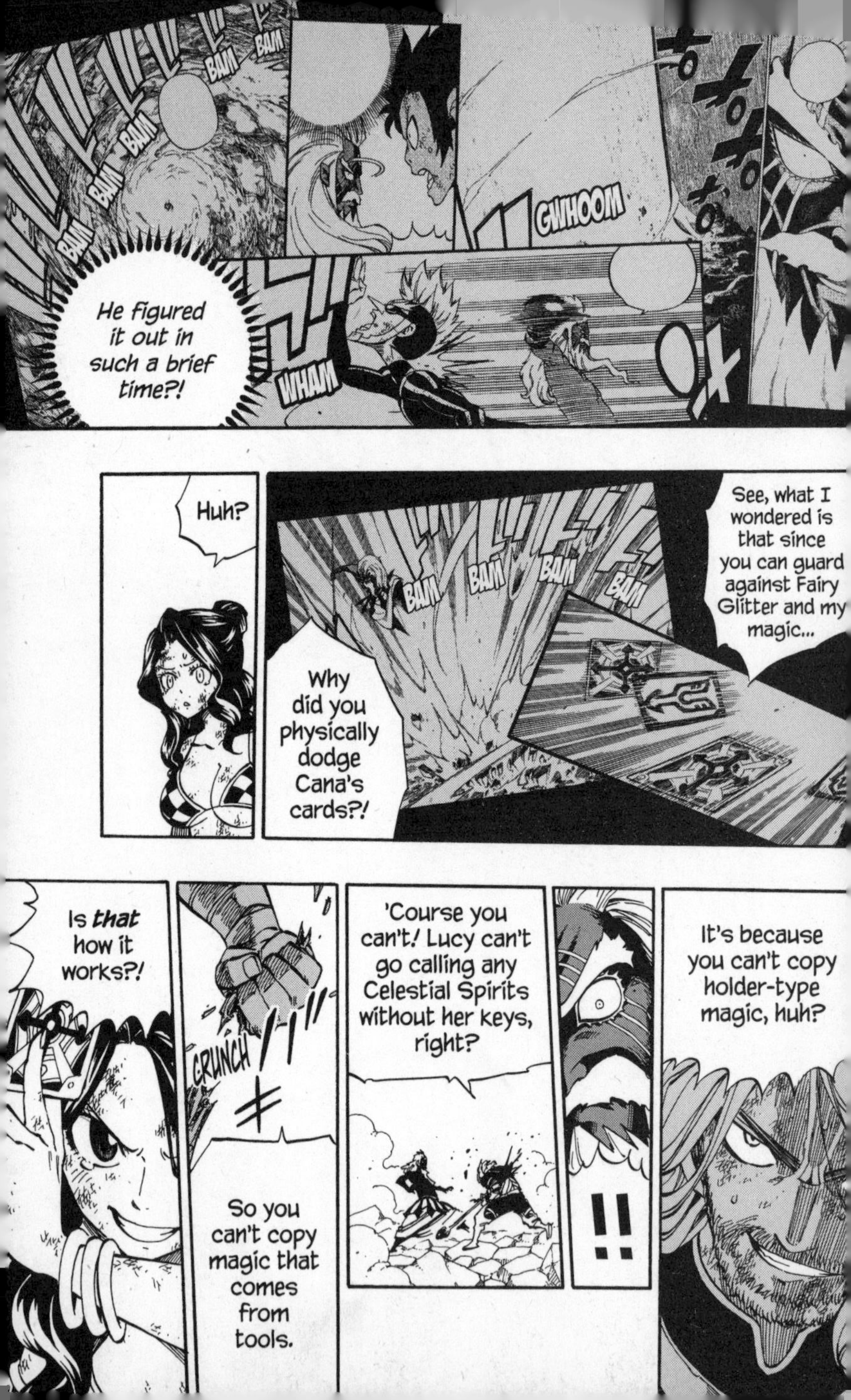

GWHOOM
BAM BAM BAM BAM BAM BAM
WHAM
He figured it out in such a brief time?!
See, what I wondered is that since you can guard against Fairy Glitter and my magic...
Why did you physically dodge Cana's cards?!
BAM BAM BAM BAM
Huh?
It's because you can't copy holder-type magic, huh?
!!
'Course you can't! Lucy can't go calling any Celestial Spirits without her keys, right?
CRUNCH
So you can't copy magic that comes from tools.
Is *that* how it works?!

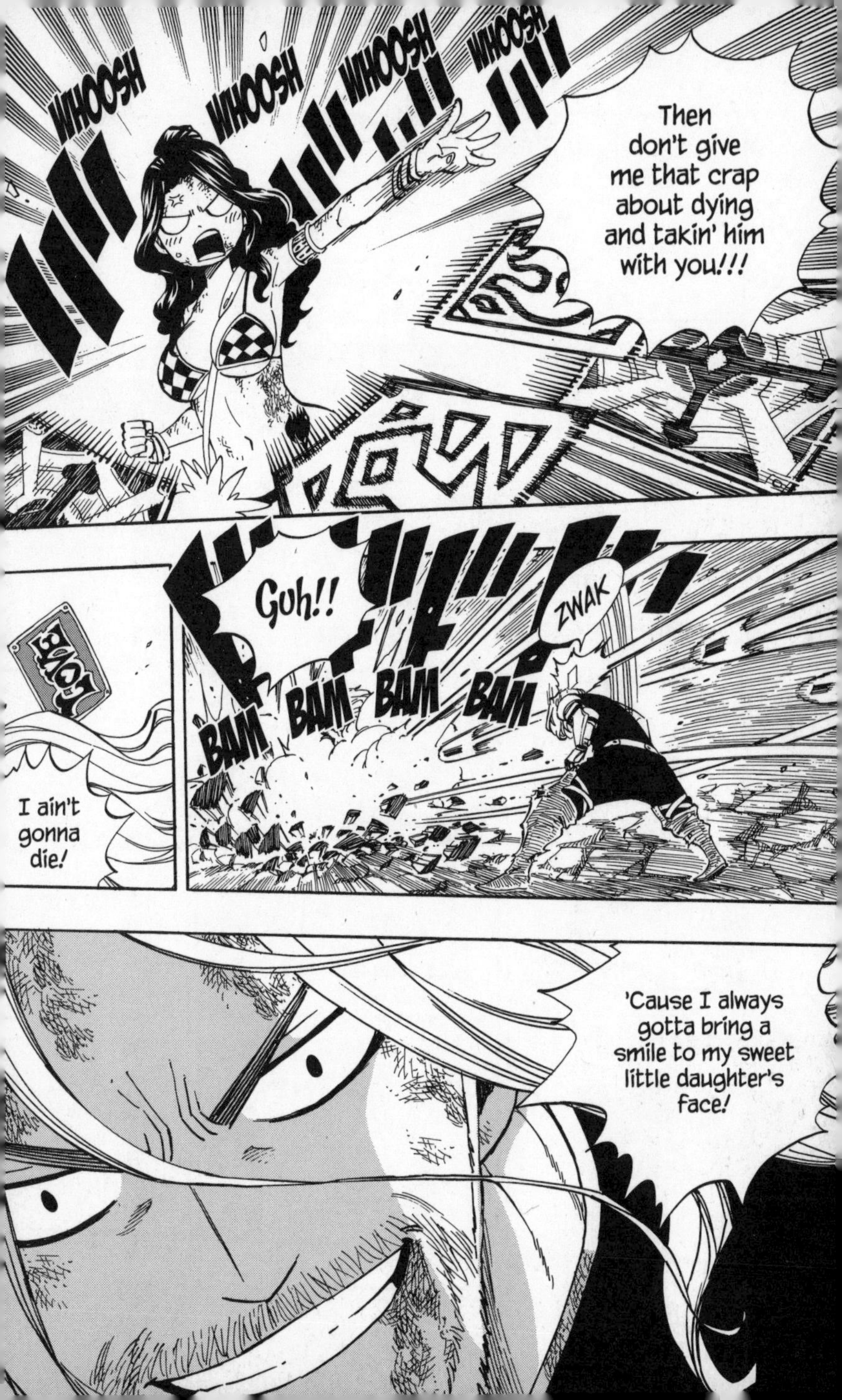
Then don't give me that crap about dying and takin' him with you!!!
WHOOSH
WHOOSH
WHOOSH
WHOOSH
ZWAK
Guh!!
BAM
BAM
BAM
BAM
I ain't gonna die!
'Cause I always gotta bring a smile to my sweet little daughter's face!

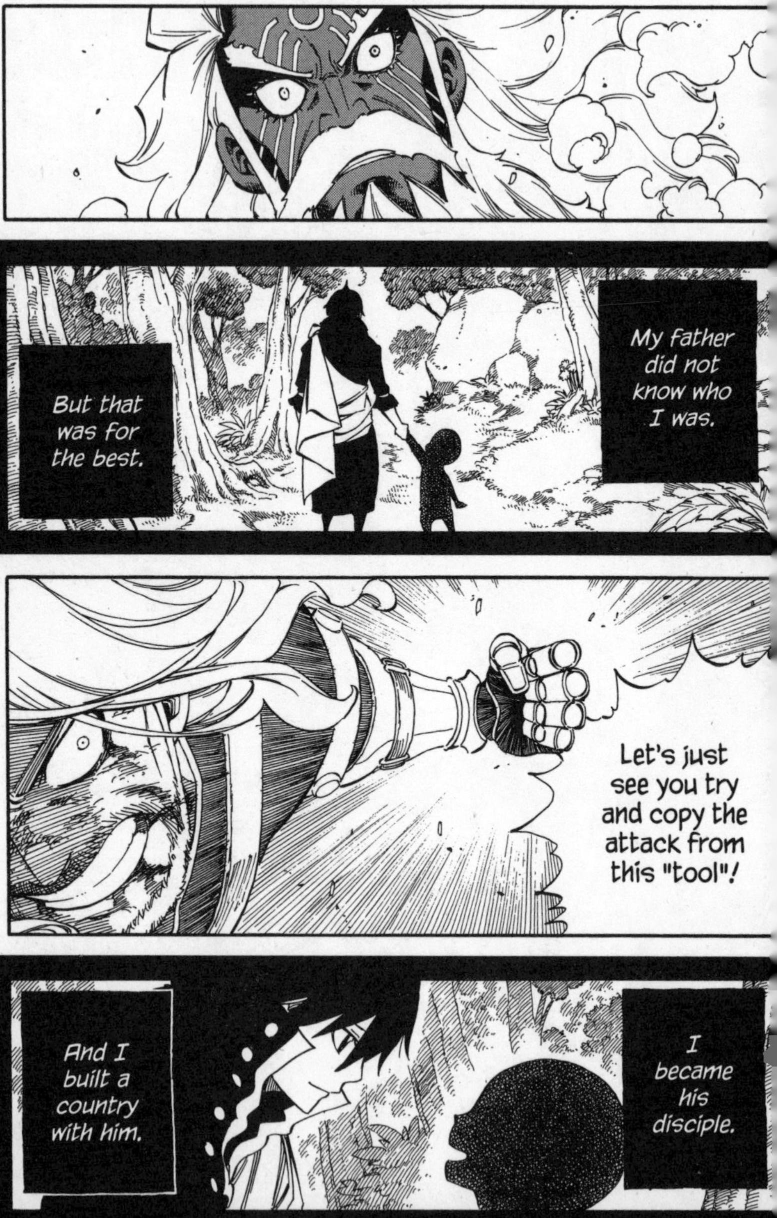
My father did not know who I was.
But that was for the best.
Let's just see you try and copy the attack from this "tool"!
I became his disciple.
And I built a country with him.

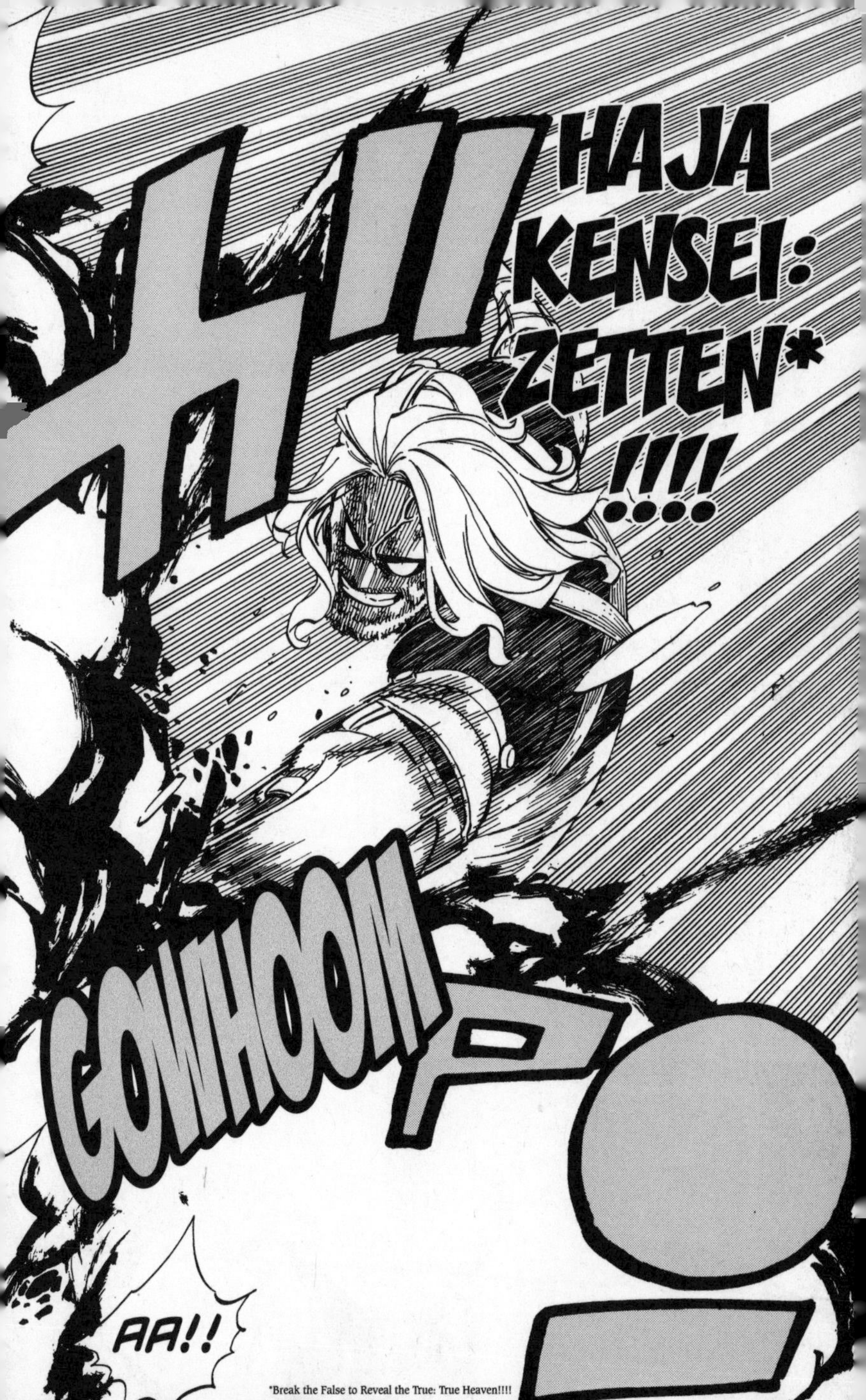
HAJA KENSEI: ZETTEN*!!!!
GOWHOOM
AA!!

*Break the False to Reveal the True: True Heaven!!!!

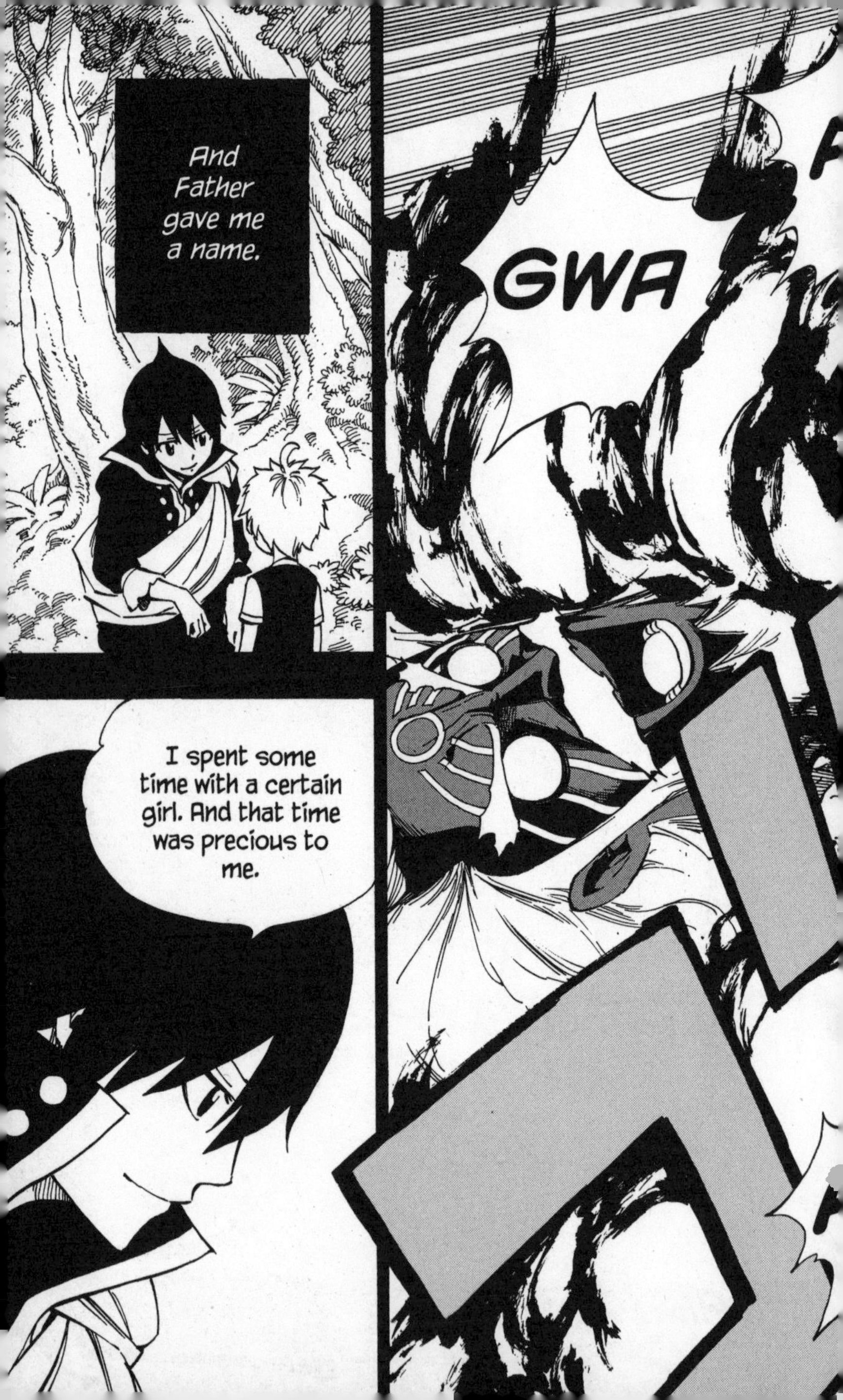
GWA
And Father gave me a name.
I spent some time with a certain girl. And that time was precious to me.

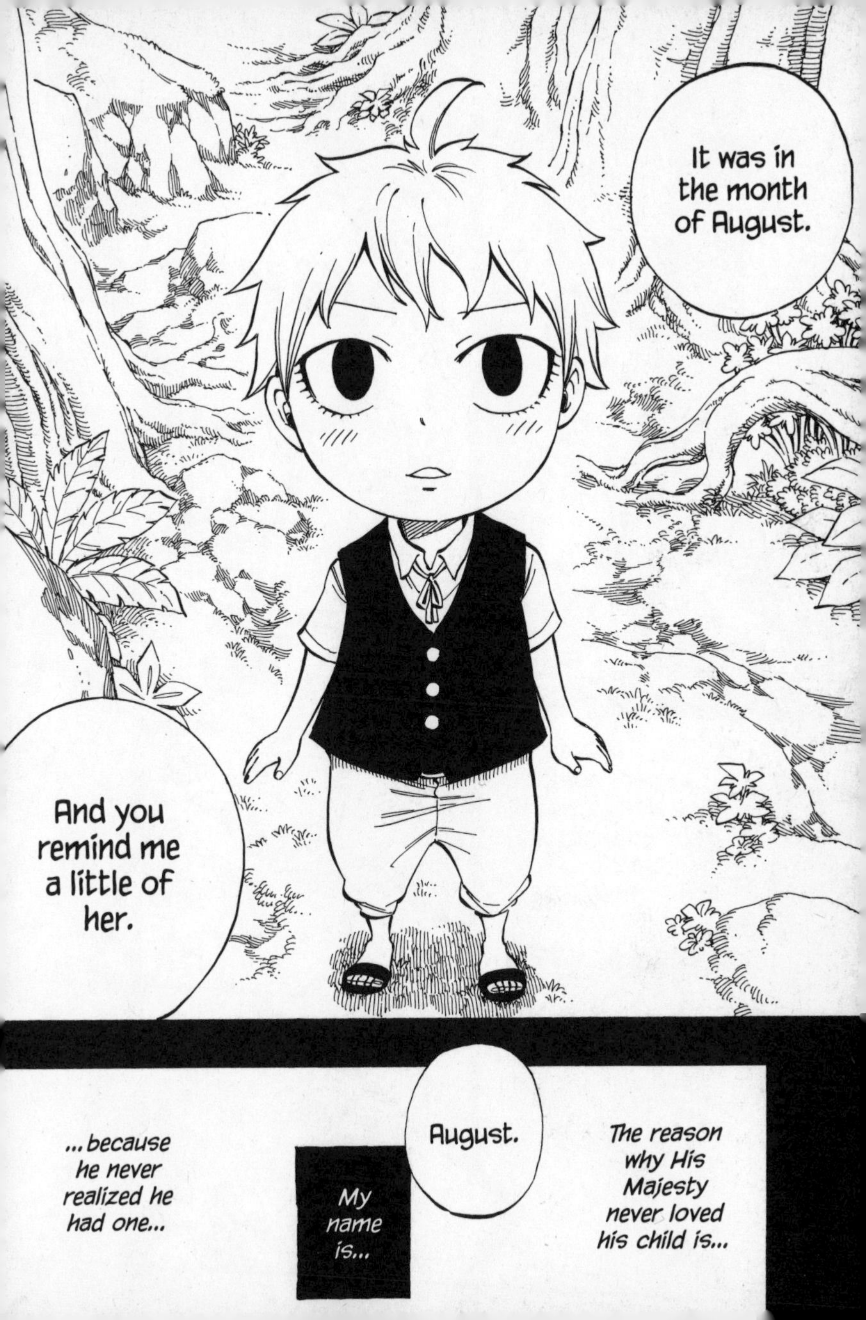
It was in the month of August.
And you remind me a little of her.
The reason why His Majesty never loved his child is...
...because he never realized he had one...
My name is...
August.

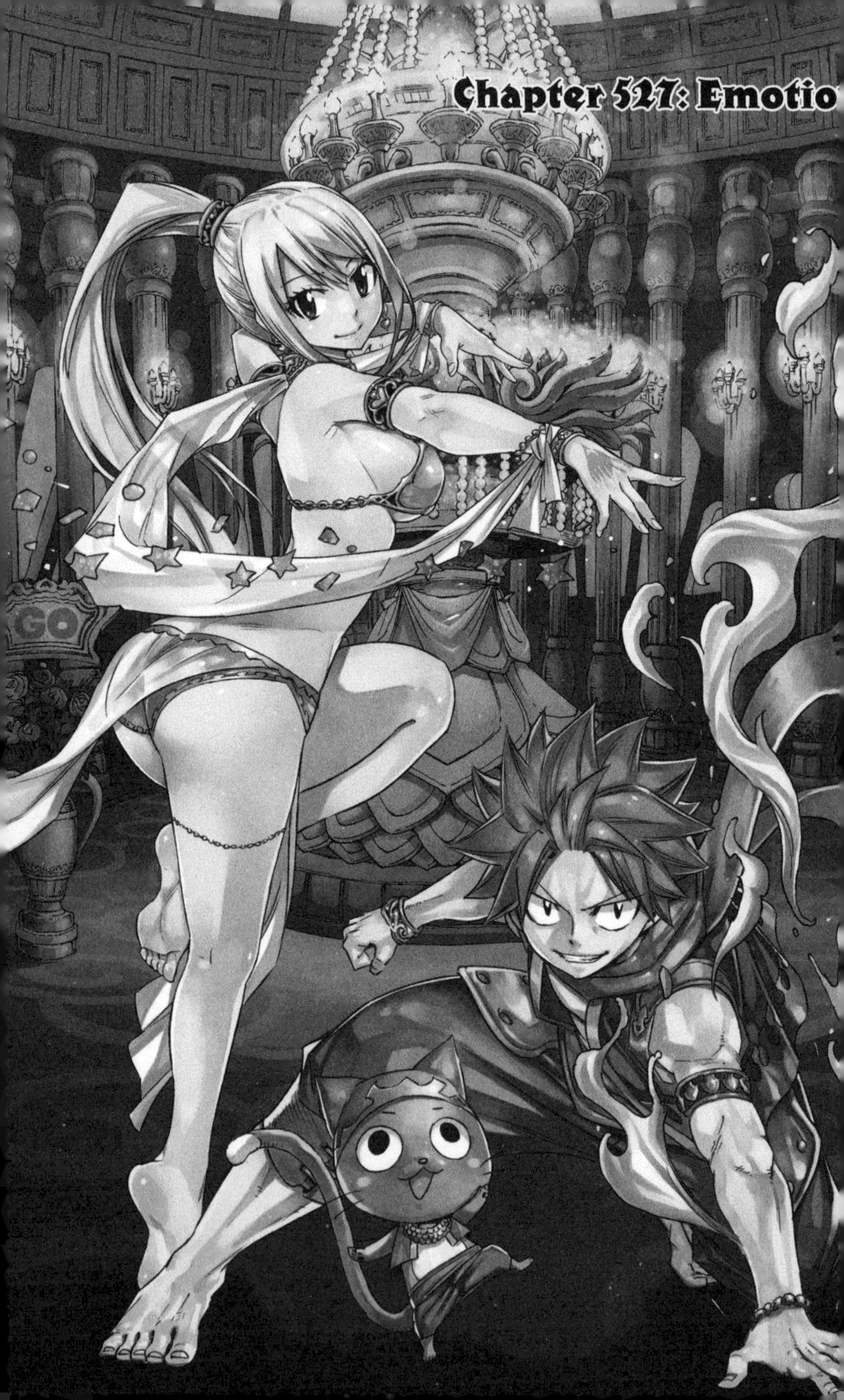
Chapter 527: Emotio

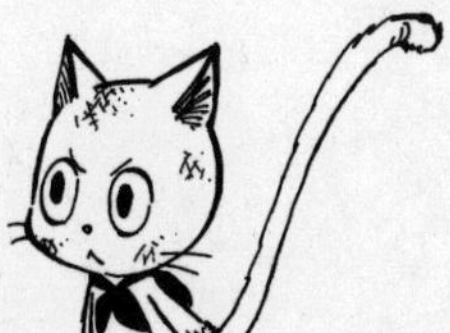

FAIRY TAIL

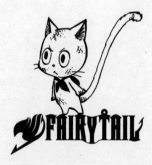

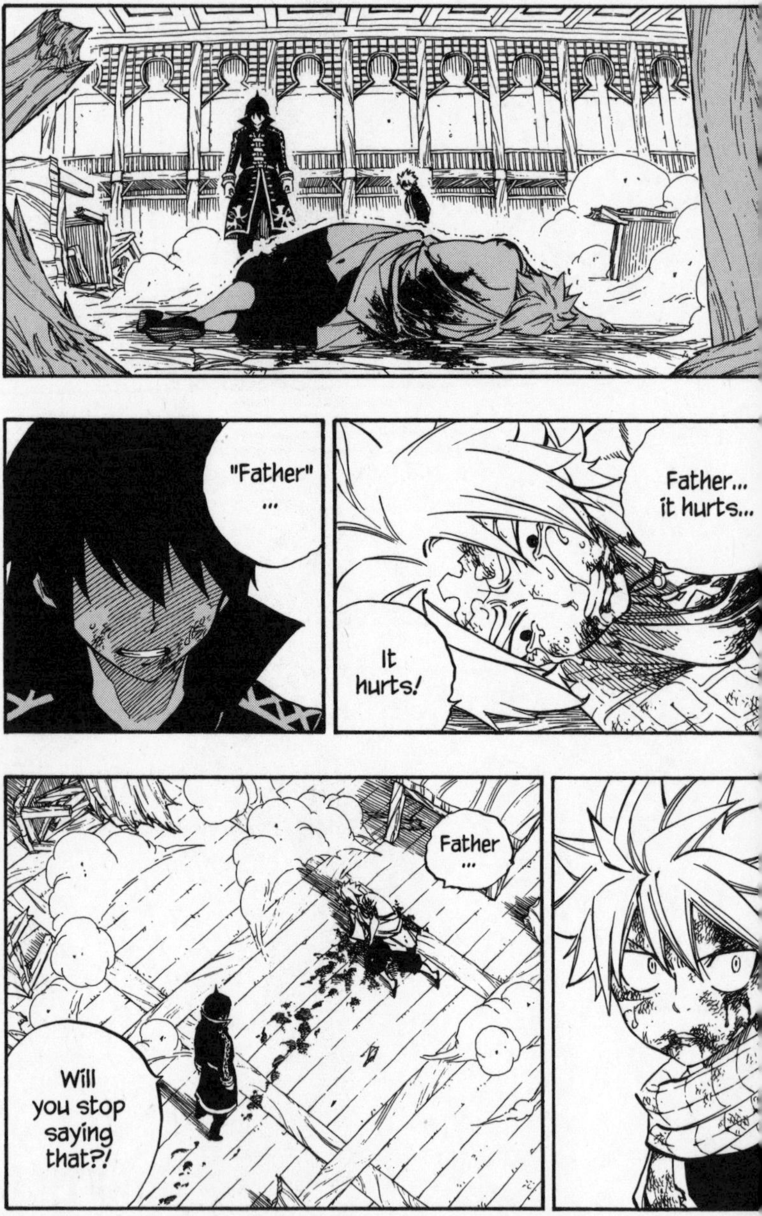
Father... it hurts...
It hurts!
"Father" ...
Father ...
Will you stop saying that?!

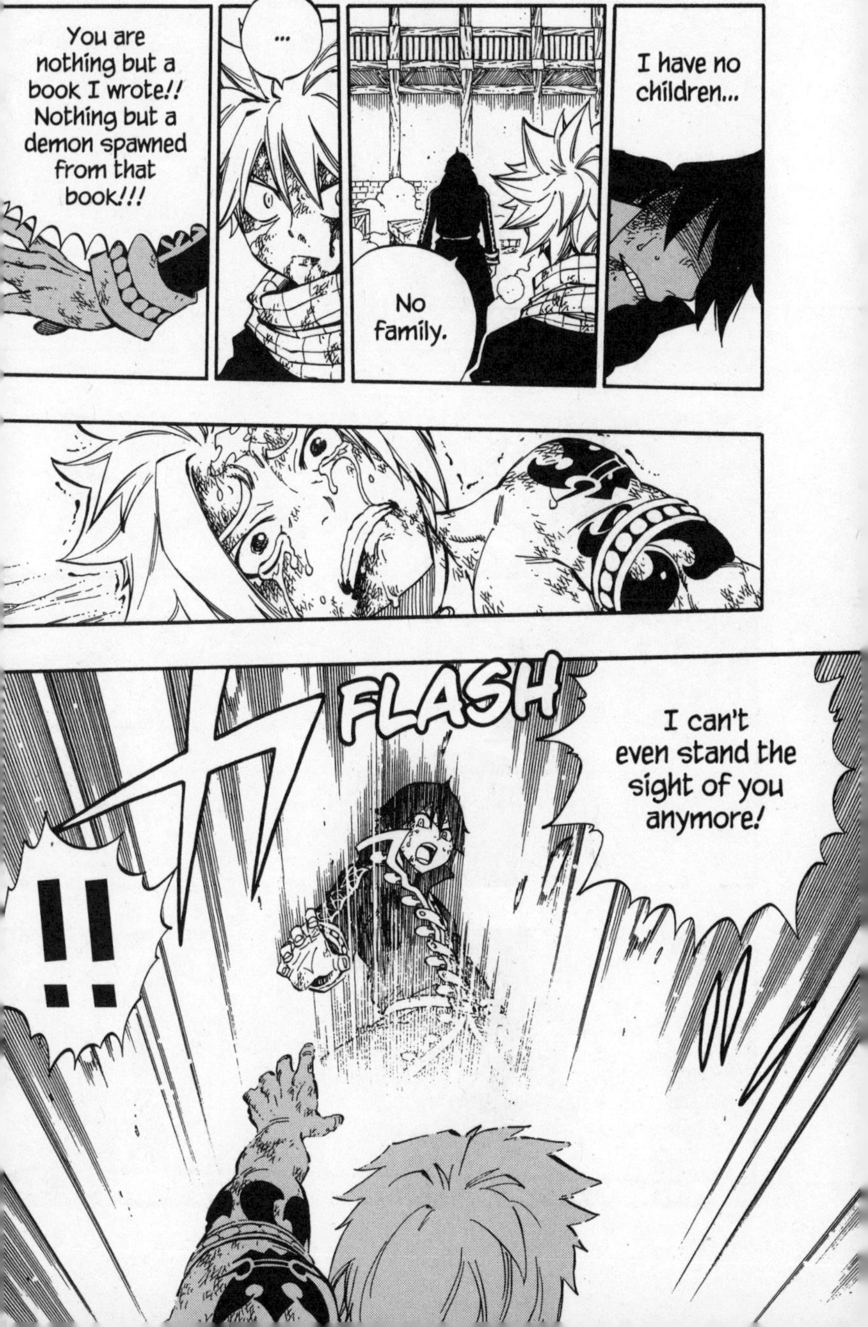
I have no children...
No family.
...
You are nothing but a book I wrote!! Nothing but a demon spawned from that book!!!
I can't even stand the sight of you anymore!
FLASH
!!

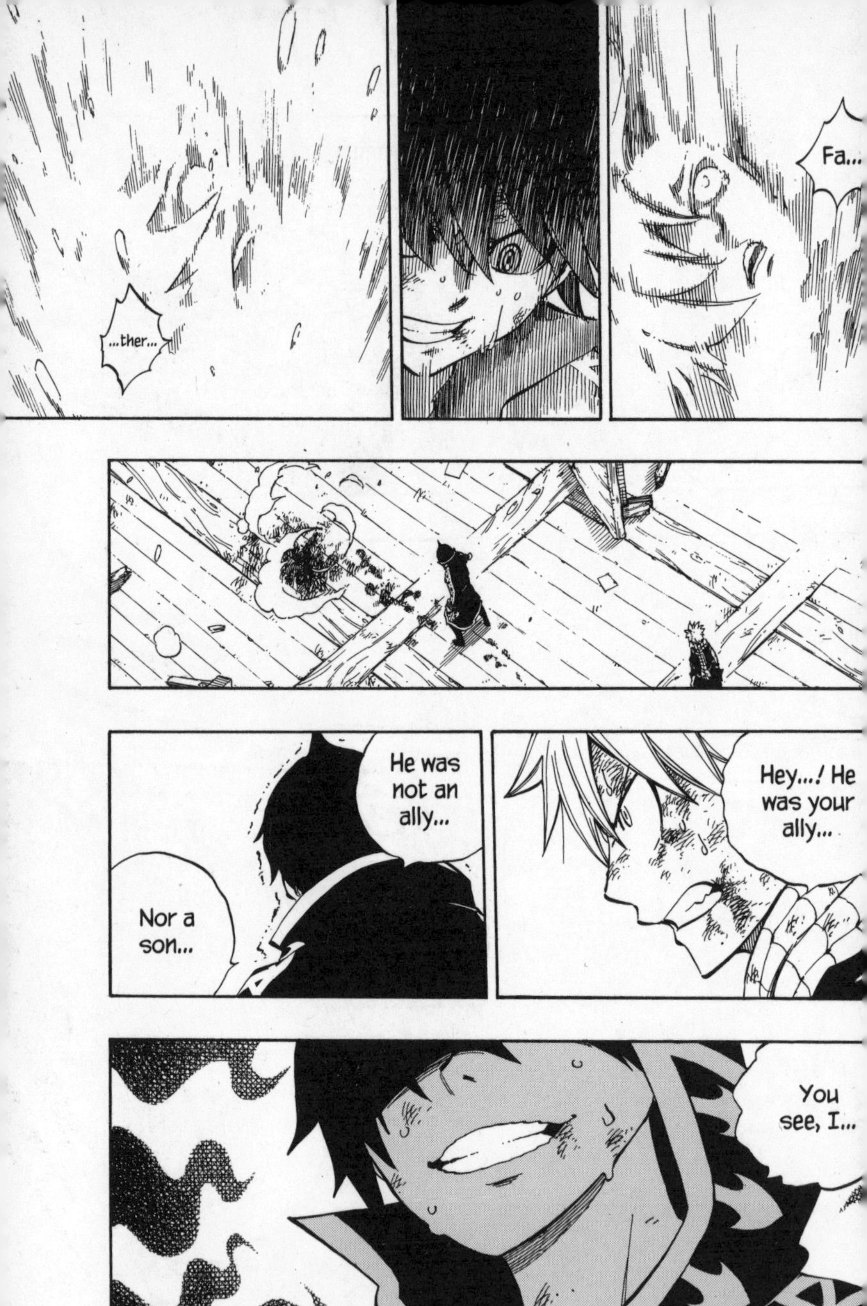
Fa...
...ther...
Hey...! He was your ally...
He was not an ally...
Nor a son...
You see, I...

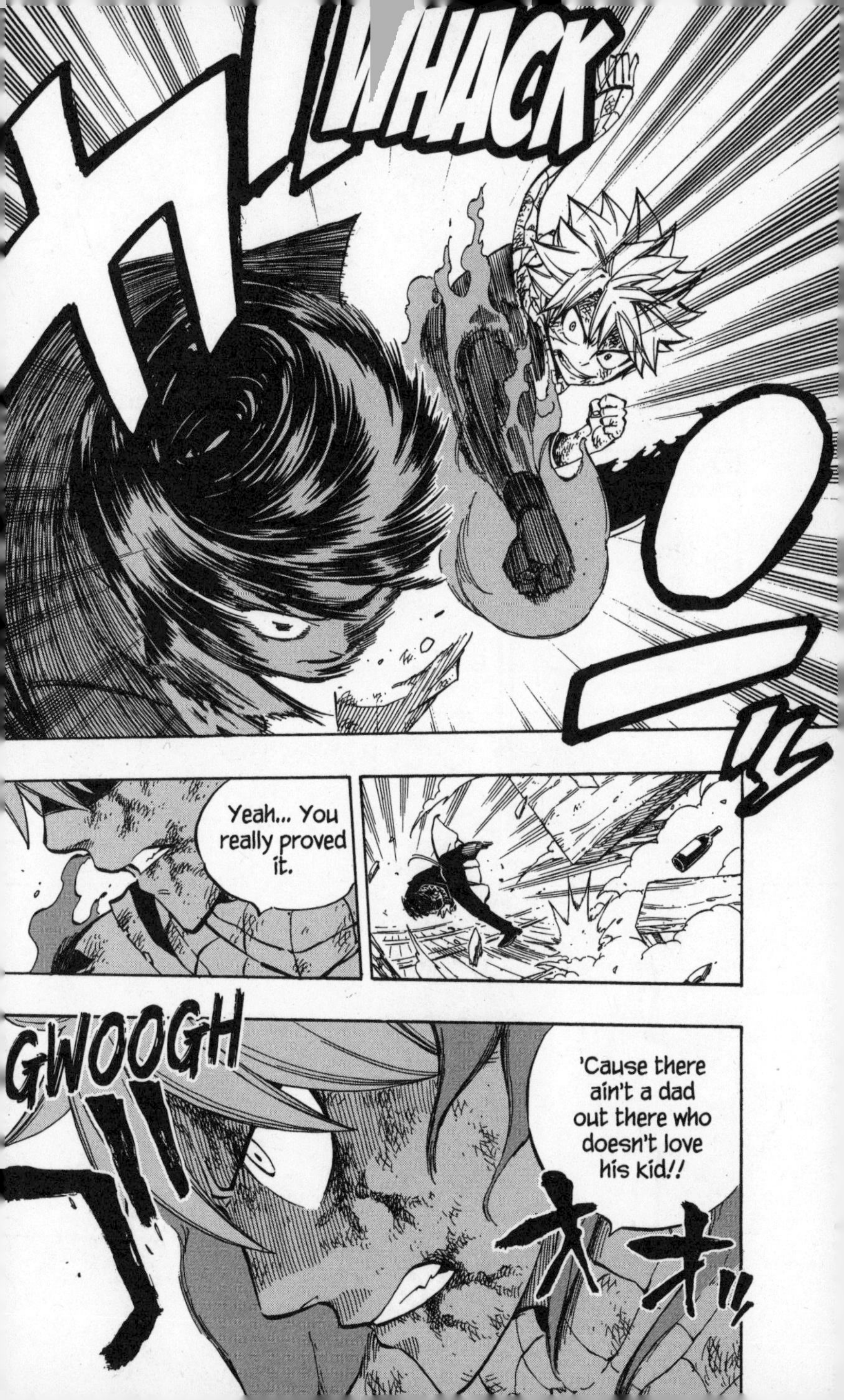
WHACK
Yeah... You really proved it.
'Cause there ain't a dad out there who doesn't love his kid!!
GWOOGH

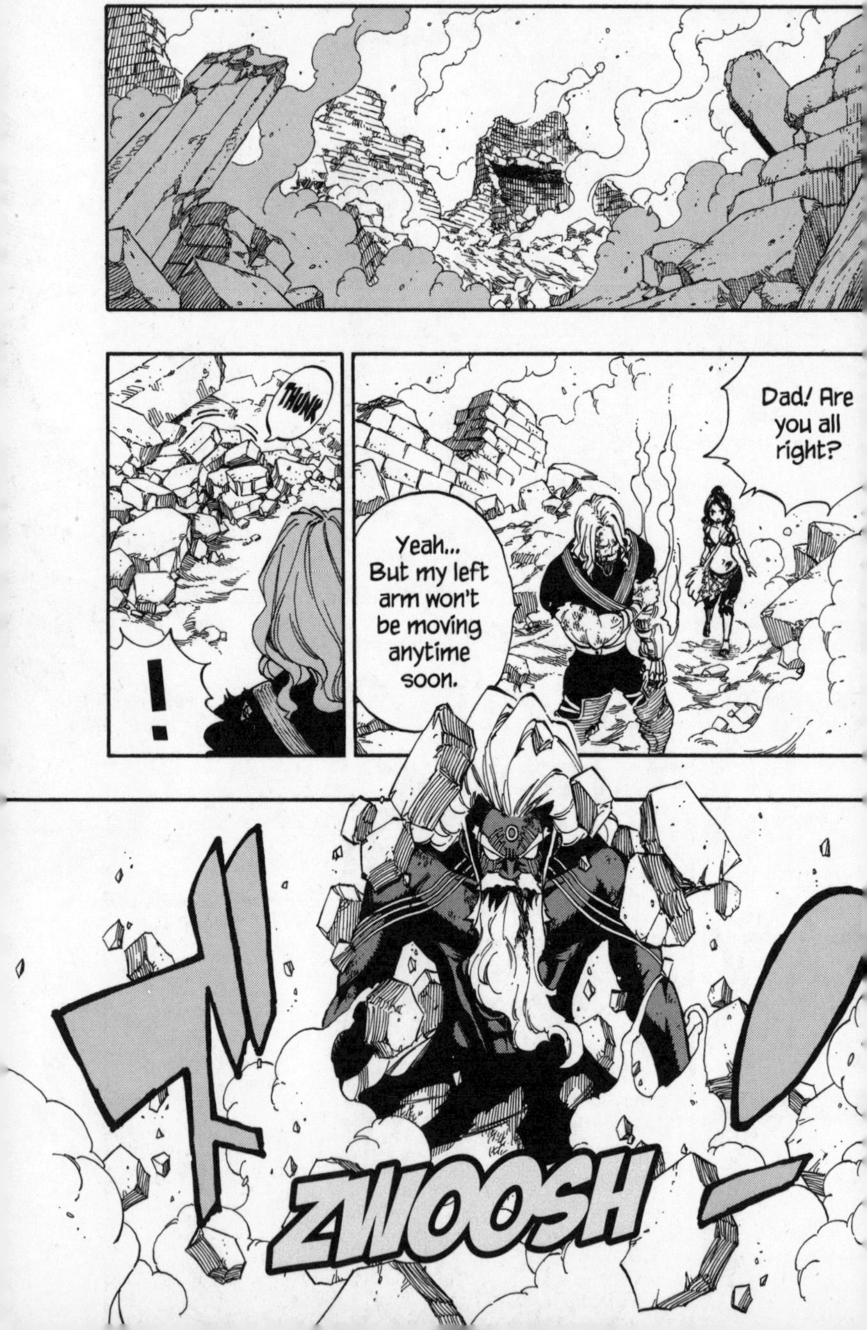
Dad! Are you all right?
Yeah... But my left arm won't be moving anytime soon.
THUNK
!
ZWOOSH

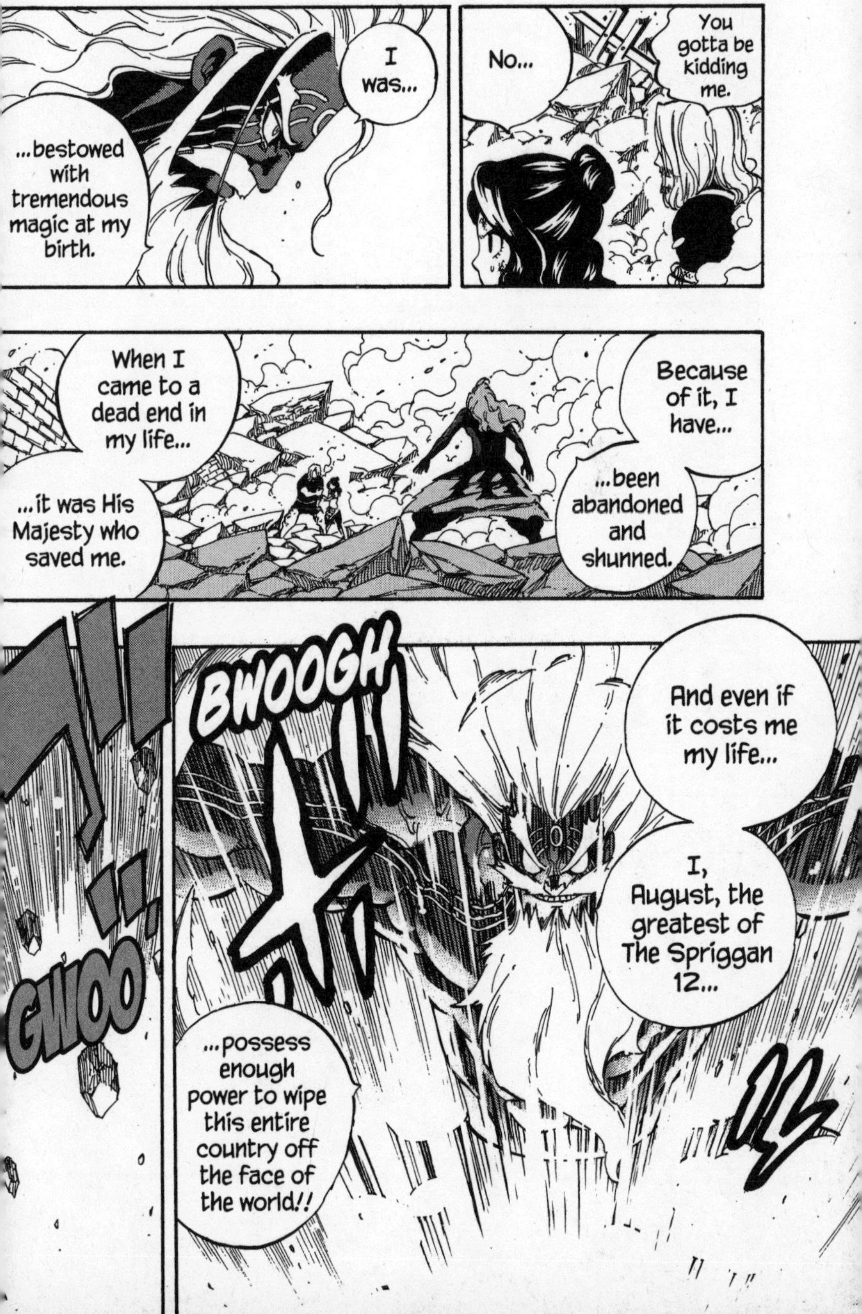
You gotta be kidding me.
No...
I was...
...bestowed with tremendous magic at my birth.
Because of it, I have...
...been abandoned and shunned.
When I came to a dead end in my life...
...it was His Majesty who saved me.
And even if it costs me my life...
BWOOGH
I, August, the greatest of The Spriggan 12...
...possess enough power to wipe this entire country off the face of the world!!
GWOO

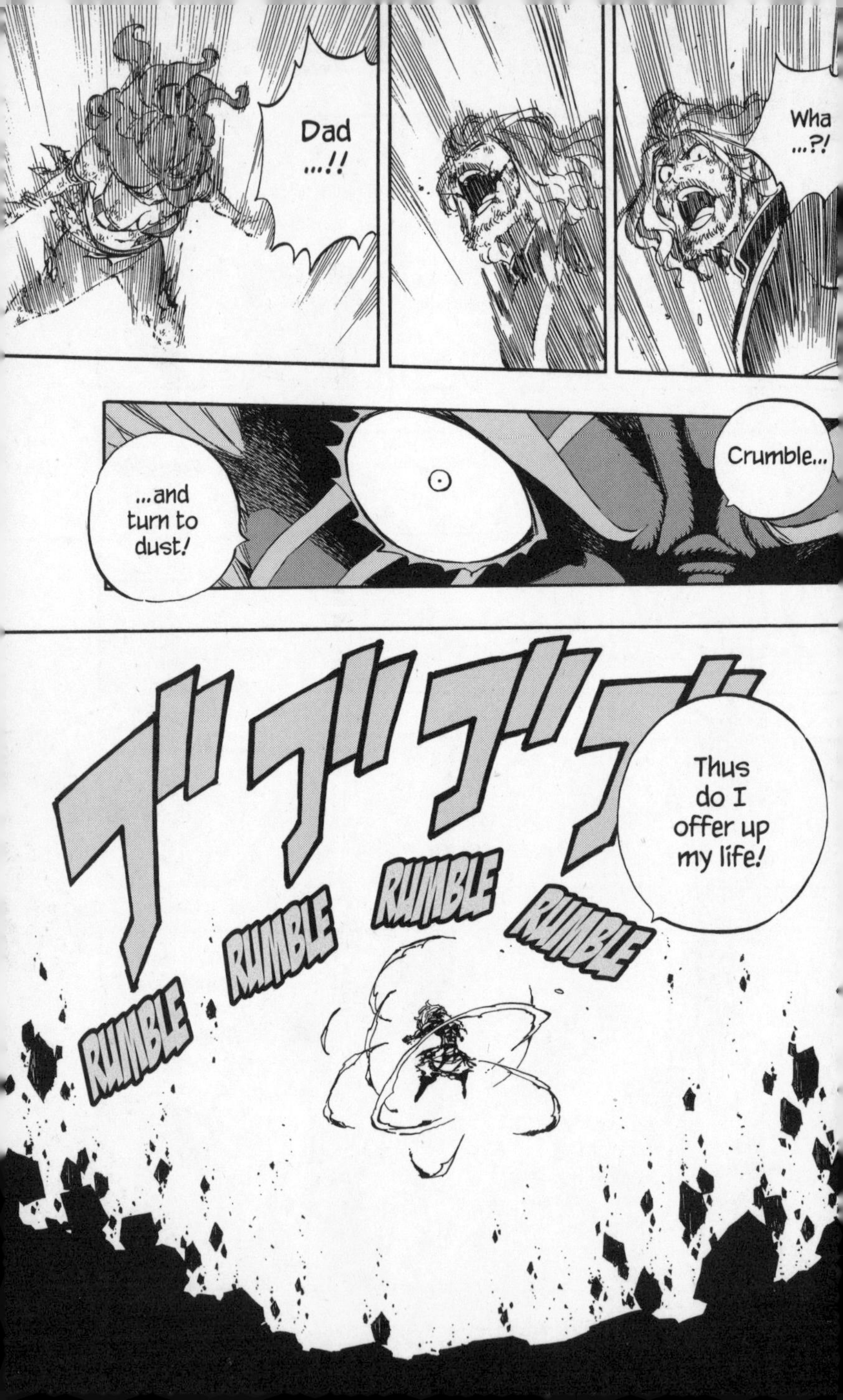
Wha ...?!
Dad ...!!
Crumble...
...and turn to dust!
Thus do I offer up my life!
RUMBLE
RUMBLE
RUMBLE
RUMBLE

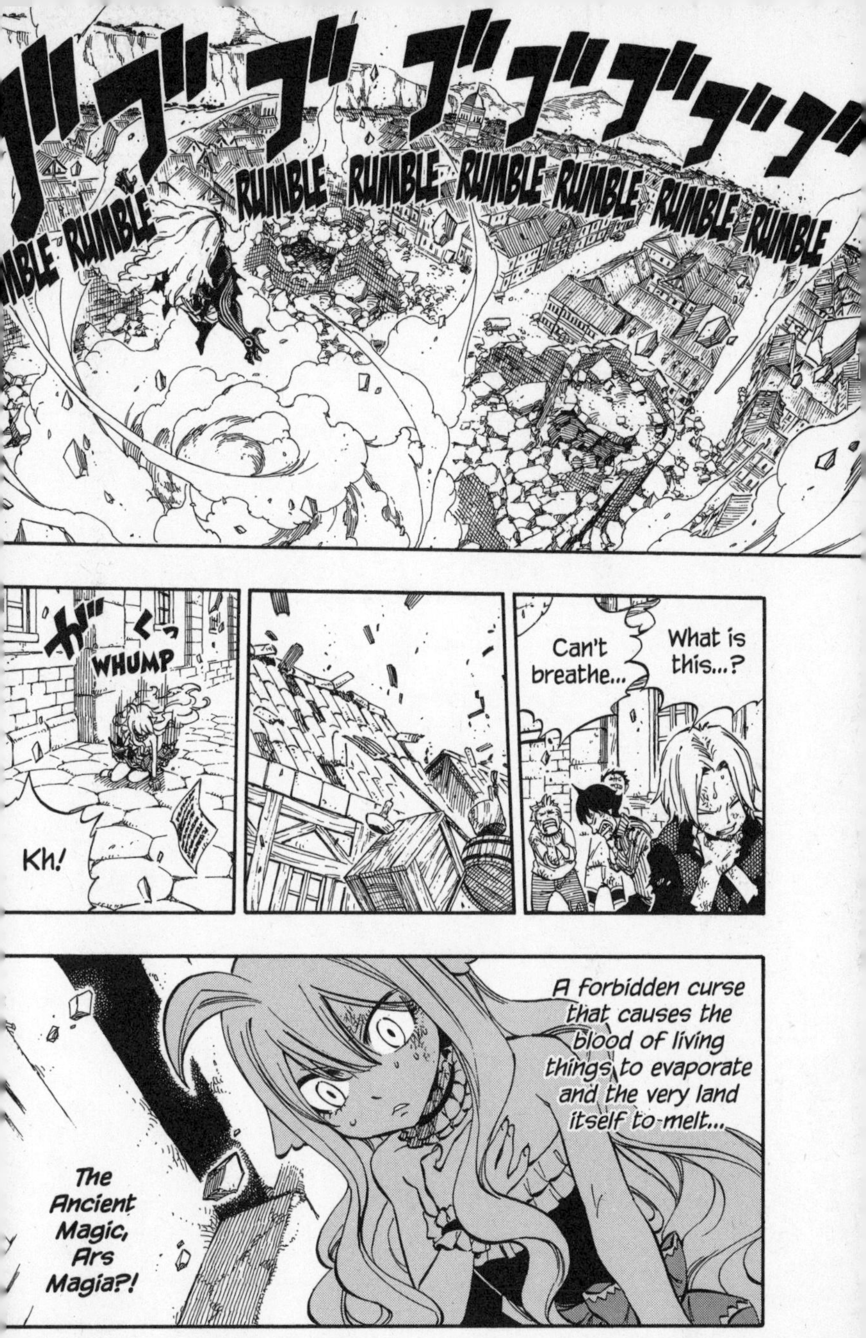
RUMBLE RUMBLE RUMBLE RUMBLE RUMBLE RUMBLE RUMBLE RUMBLE
What is this...?
Can't breathe...
WHUMP
Kh!
A forbidden curse that causes the blood of living things to evaporate and the very land itself to melt...
The Ancient Magic, Ars Magia?!

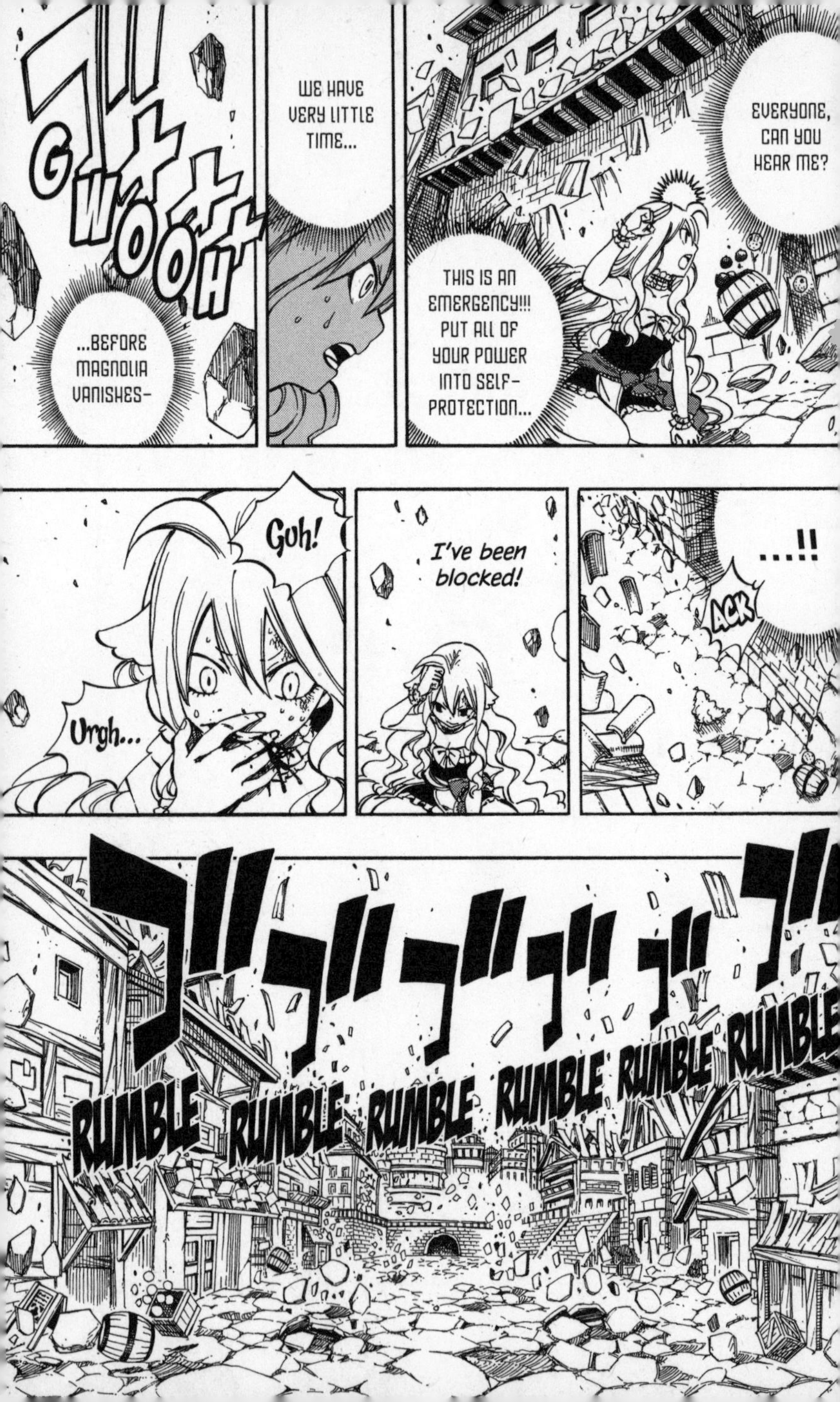
EVERYONE, CAN YOU HEAR ME?
THIS IS AN EMERGENCY!!! PUT ALL OF YOUR POWER INTO SELF-PROTECTION...
WE HAVE VERY LITTLE TIME...
GWOOOH
...BEFORE MAGNOLIA VANISHES–
...!!
ACK
I've been blocked!
Goh!
Urgh...
RUMBLE RUMBLE RUMBLE RUMBLE RUMBLE RUMBLE

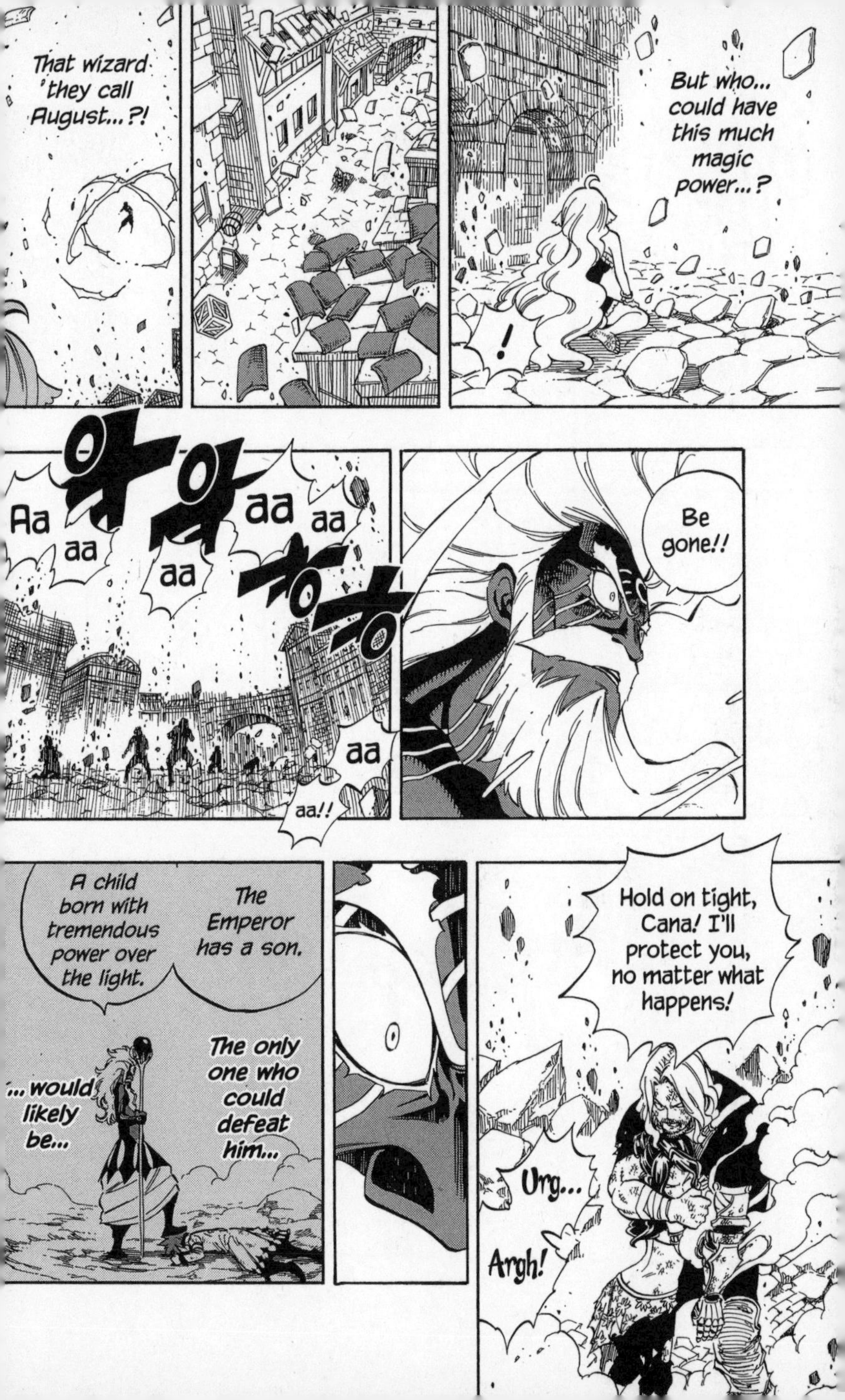
But who... could have this much magic power...?
!
That wizard they call August...?!
Be gone!!
Aa
aa
aa
aa
aa
aa
aa
aa!!
Hold on tight, Cana! I'll protect you, no matter what happens!
Urg...
Argh!
The Emperor has a son.
A child born with tremendous power over the light.
The only one who could defeat him...
...would likely be...

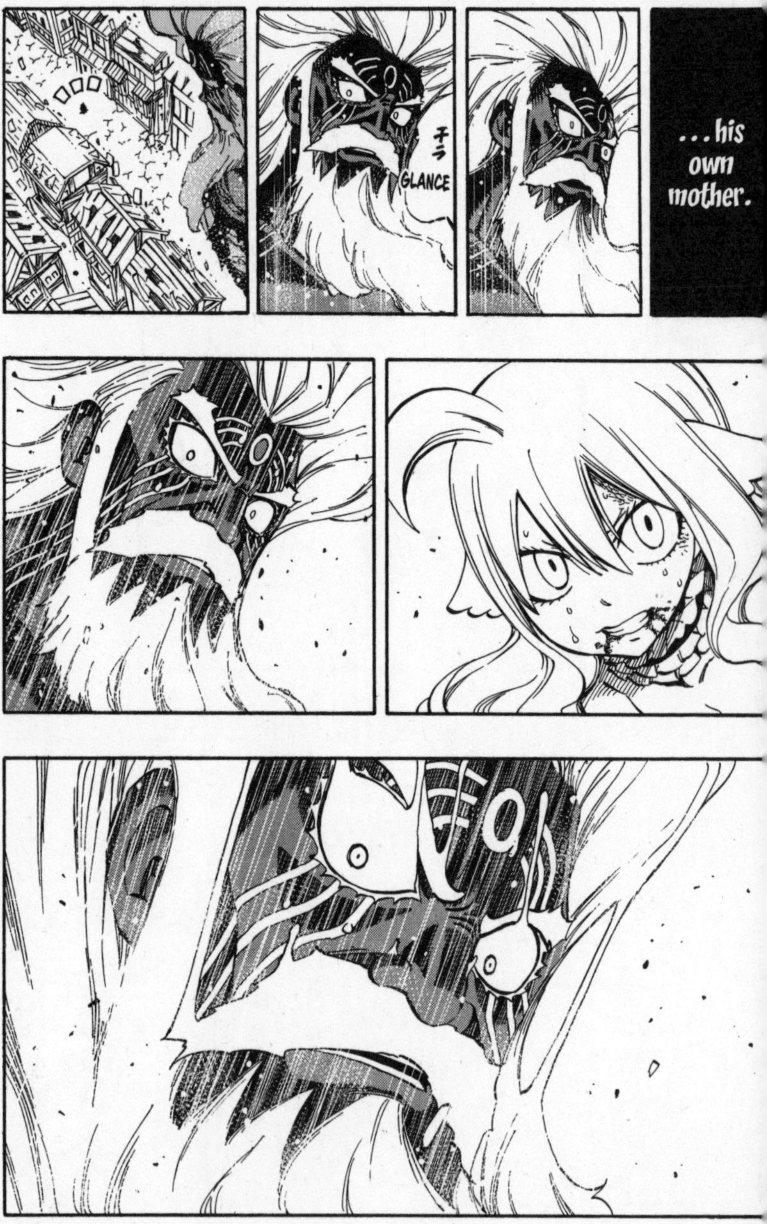
...his own mother.
チラ
GLANCE

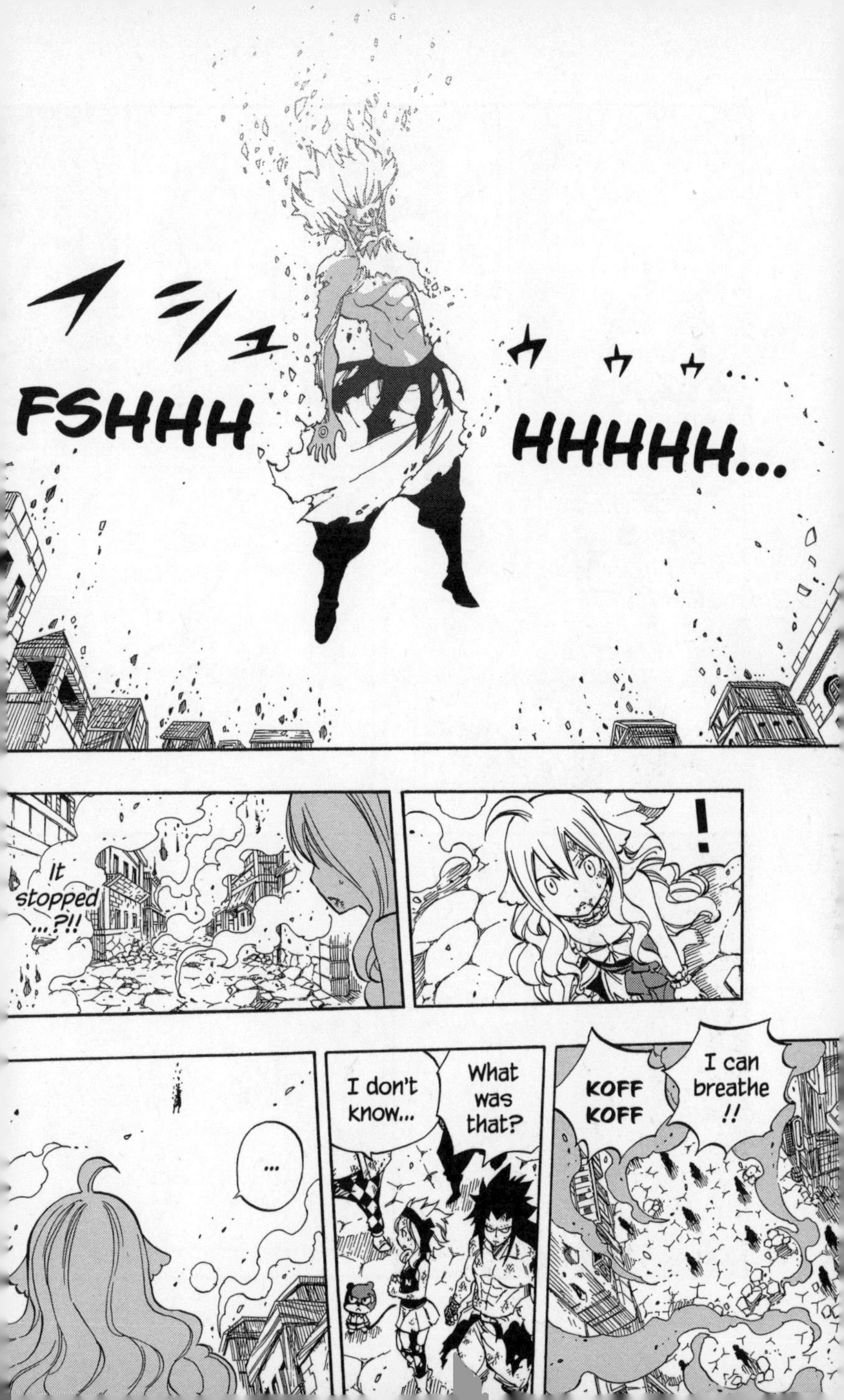
FSHHH
HHHHH...
!
It stopped ...?!!
I can breathe !!
KOFF KOFF
What was that?
I don't know...
...

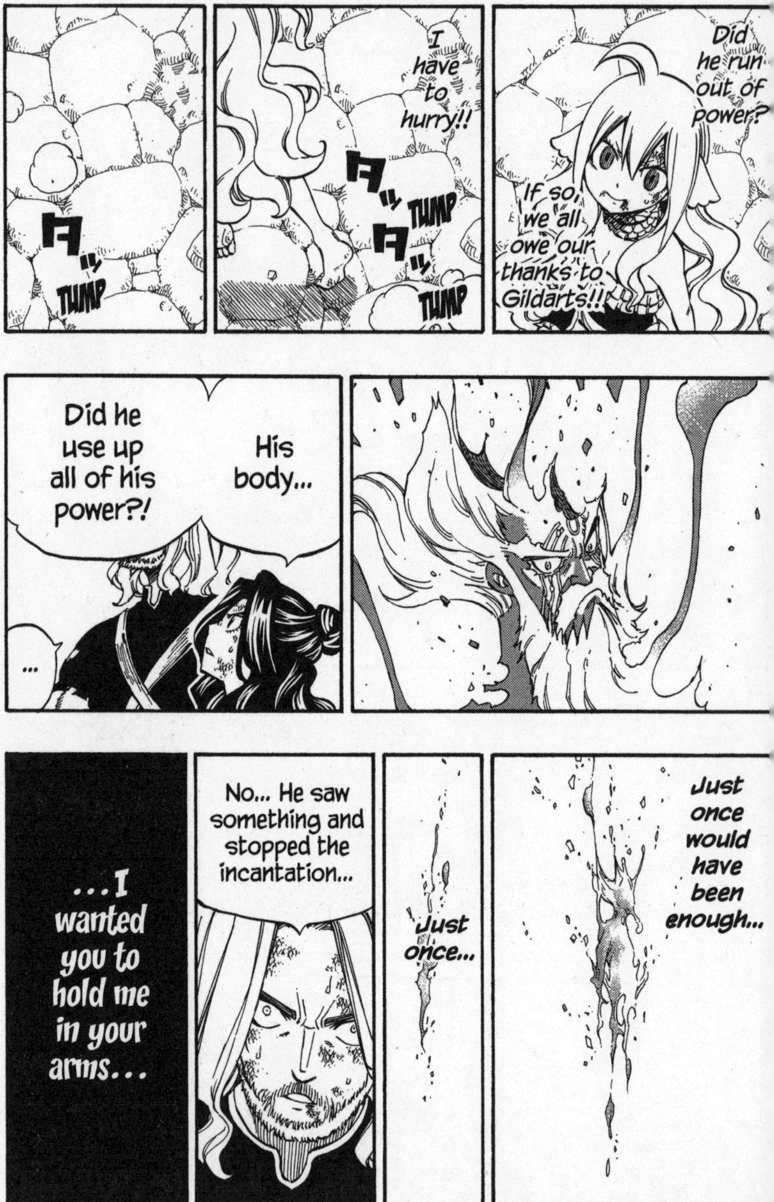
Did he run out of power?
If so, we all owe our thanks to Gildarts!!
I have to hurry!!
タッ
TUMP
タッ
TUMP
タッ
TUMP
His body...
Did he use up all of his power?!
...
Just once would have been enough...
Just once...
No... He saw something and stopped the incantation...
...I wanted you to hold me in your arms...

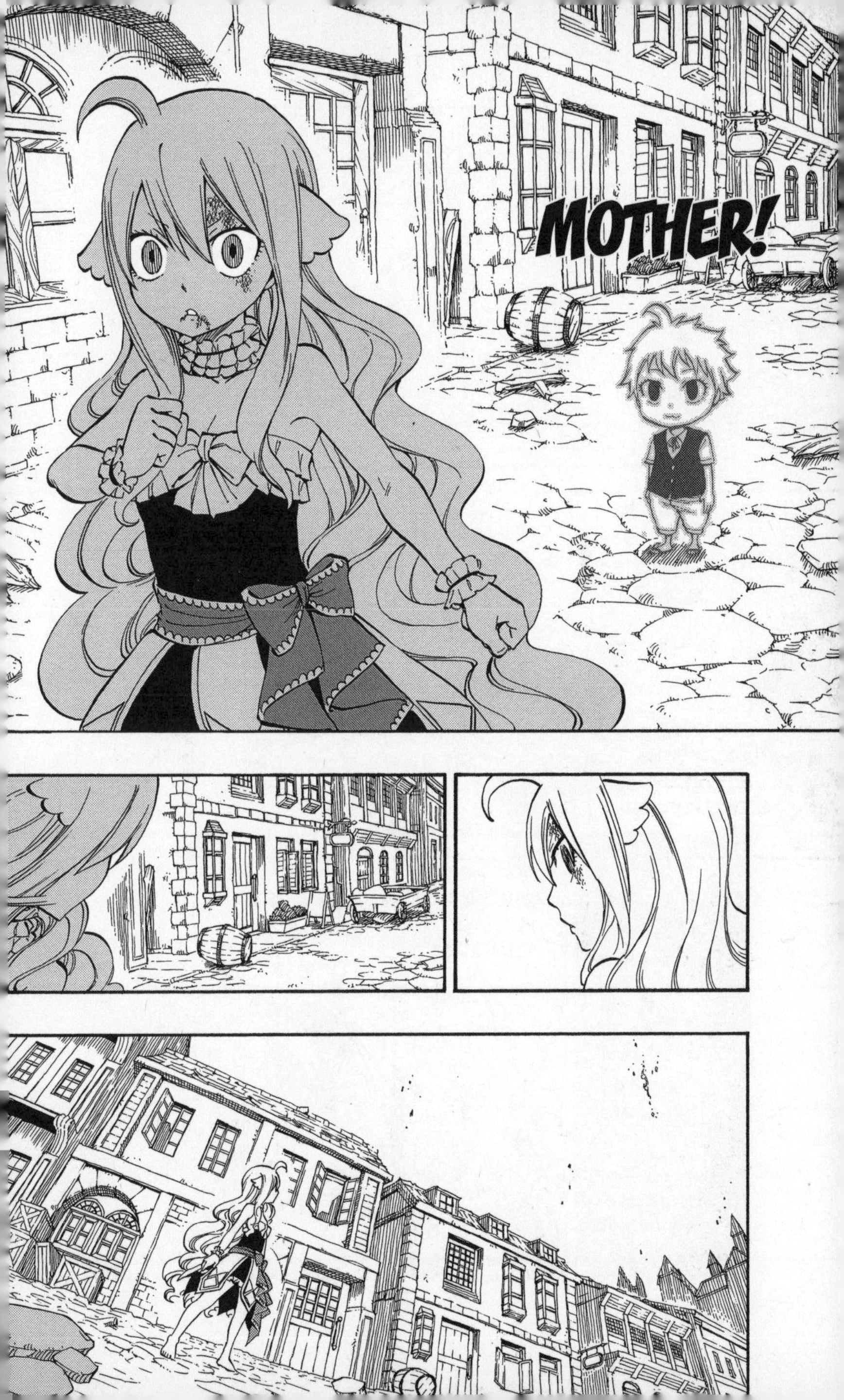
MOTHER!

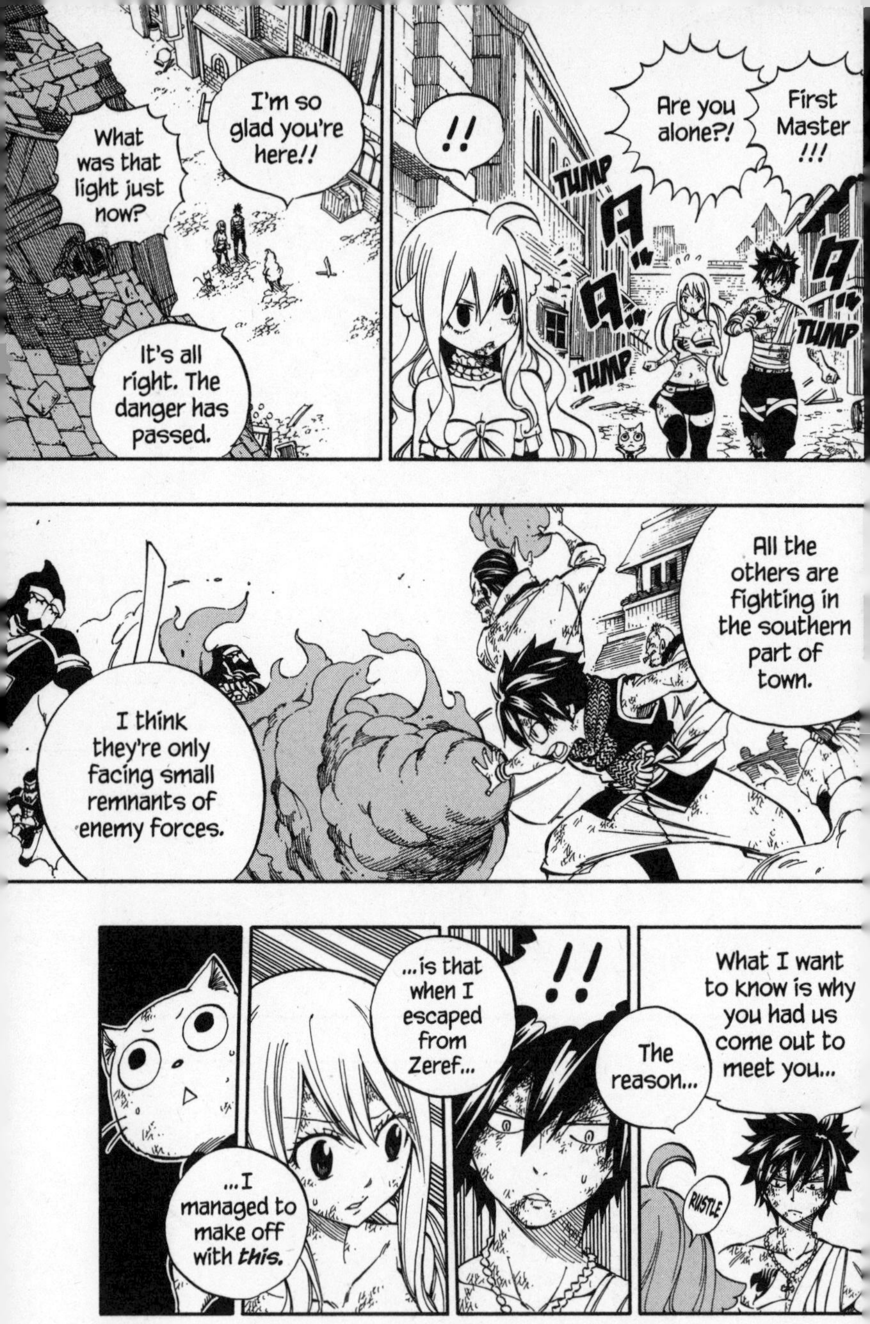
First Master!!!
Are you alone?!
!!
TUMP
TUMP
TUMP
TUMP
I'm so glad you're here!!
What was that light just now?
It's all right. The danger has passed.
All the others are fighting in the southern part of town.
I think they're only facing small remnants of enemy forces.
What I want to know is why you had us come out to meet you...
The reason...
RUSTLE
!!
...is that when I escaped from Zeref...
...I managed to make off with *this.*

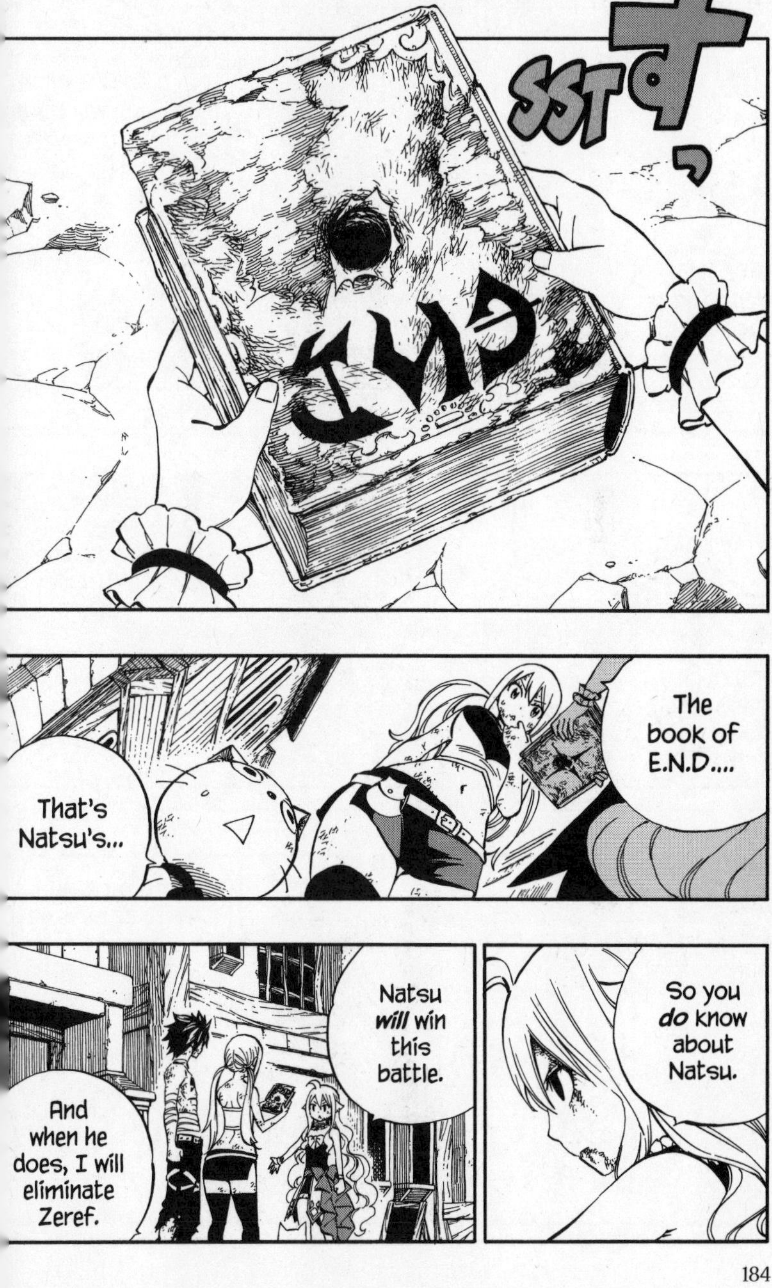
SST
The book of E.N.D....
That's Natsu's...
So you *do* know about Natsu.
Natsu *will* win this battle.
And when he does, I will eliminate Zeref.

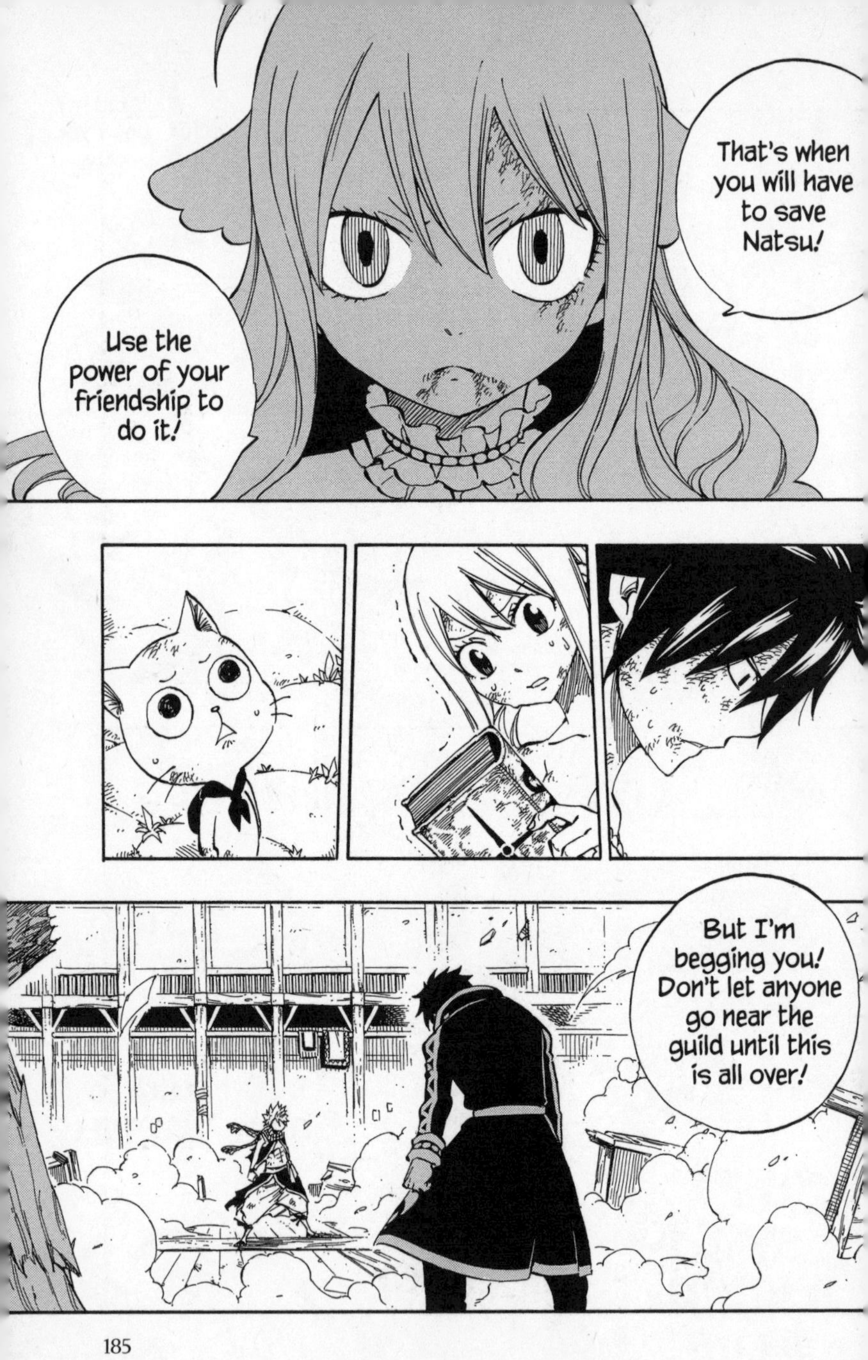
That's when you will have to save Natsu!
Use the power of your friendship to do it!
But I'm begging you! Don't let anyone go near the guild until this is all over!

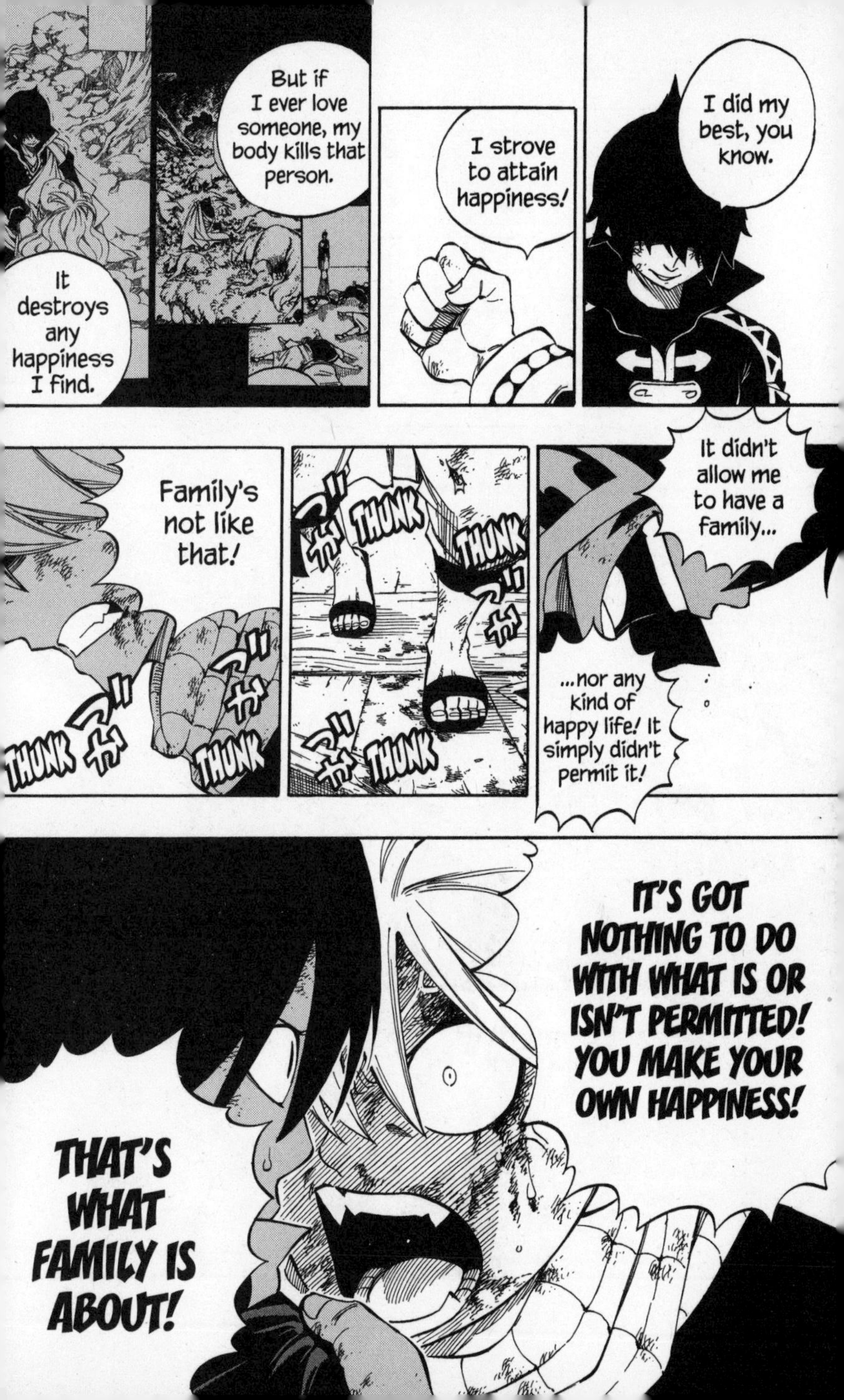
I did my best, you know.
I strove to attain happiness!
But if I ever love someone, my body kills that person.
It destroys any happiness I find.
It didn't allow me to have a family...
...nor any kind of happy life! It simply didn't permit it!
THUNK
THUNK
THUNK
Family's not like that!
THUNK
THUNK
IT'S GOT NOTHING TO DO WITH WHAT IS OR ISN'T PERMITTED! YOU MAKE YOUR OWN HAPPINESS!
THAT'S WHAT FAMILY IS ABOUT!

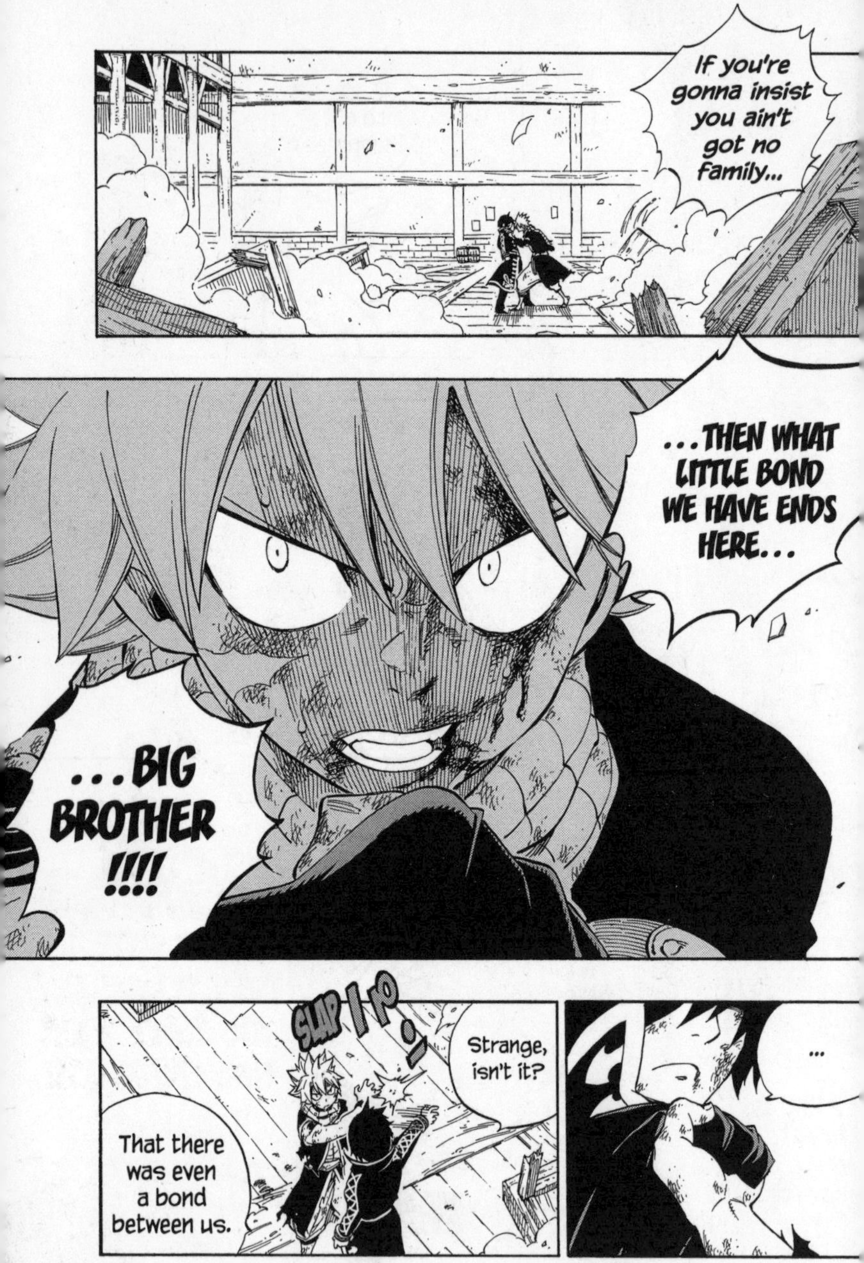
If you're gonna insist you ain't got no family...
...THEN WHAT LITTLE BOND WE HAVE ENDS HERE...
...BIG BROTHER!!!!
...
SLAP
Strange, isn't it?
That there was even a bond between us.

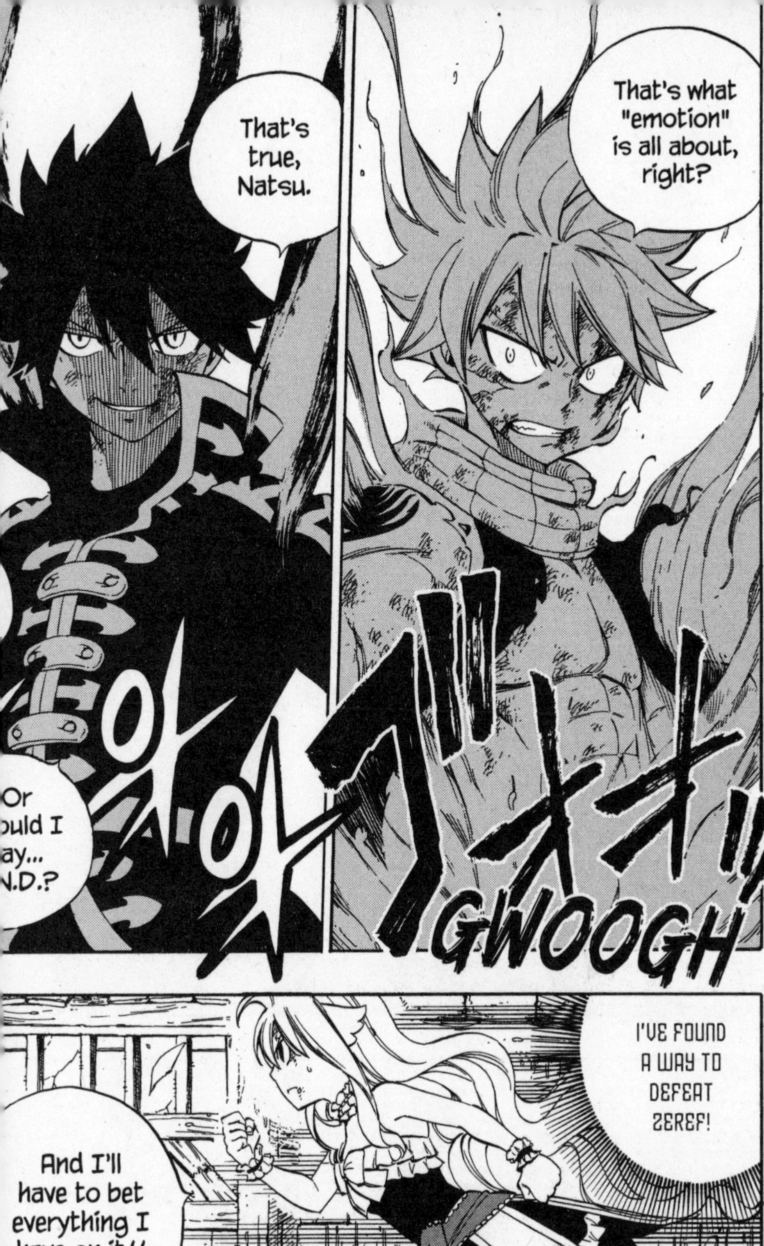
That's what "emotion" is all about, right?
That's true, Natsu.
Or
ould I
ay...
N.D.?
ゴオオ!!
GWOOGH
I'VE FOUND A WAY TO DEFEAT ZEREF!
And I'll have to bet everything I have on it!!

TO BE CONTINUED

# あとがき

## Afterword

Is the full-fledged final decisive battle unravelling well...? (sweats). In the very beginning, the story was never envisioned to be this big, so whenever I'm writing the heavier parts of the story, I always worry if what I'm doing is working well.

Just some fun adventures, and solving a couple problems here and there—that's how this whole series started. But when a series goes on for a while, that alone will become a bit bland to read, so you know, I've been adding lots of other things.

The series I did before this had some pretty heavy themes, so I remember that my stance at the start of all this was that I wanted this story to be lighter. But before I knew it, it had blown up into a huge story about war... A big difference between my last work and this one is that Natsu and the guild aren't fighting for world peace. The previous one was a story where youth were fighting to save the world. This time, the characters do it for their guild. They fight only to protect their community. During the Edolas arc, you might remember that Natsu said, "We entered our guild to survive. What the "world" needs ain't up to us!"

That's not something you usually hear from the main character of a shonen manga, but I think that's a vital part of the concept of this story. They're fighting for survival. They're fighting for their friends. And something like that may have nothing to do with world peace. But that's what drives Natsu and his guild mates to heroism—that's their everything. And I love Natsu and his friends who are this way. So much that I'm tempted to keep on drawing their story forever... But I want to make a new world, new characters, and a new story. So, Fairy Tail will come to an end in two more volumes. And yes, I'm sad about that, but you see, I'm also brimming with the anticipation of new things. So, you! Yes, you, with the tears welling up! Thank you so much!! I'm planning on starting the new story very soon after this, so please watch over the Fairies' final performance.

# TAIL de ART

Those chosen to be published will get a signed mini poster! ♪

▼ What a cute expression on Natsu! It's like he's doing an "Eh heh heh" chuckle.

Tokyo, Risa Ono

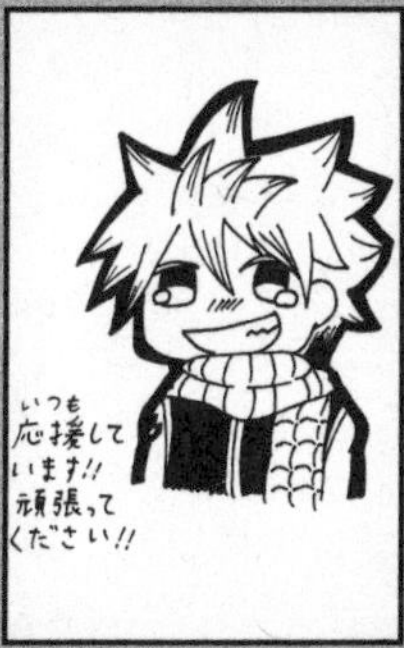
いつも
応援しています!!
頑張ってください!!

Shizuoka Prefecture, Yūna Serizawa

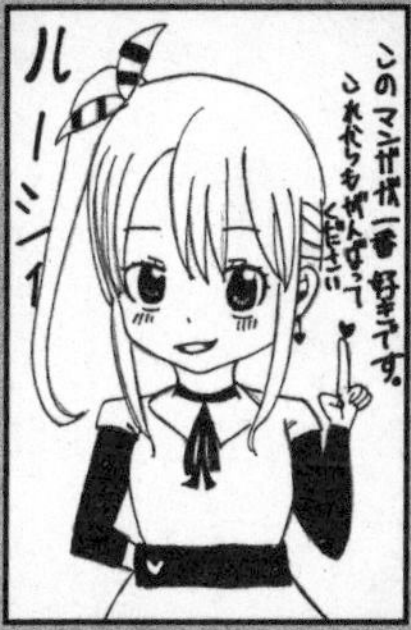
ルーシィ
このマンガが一番好きです。
これからもがんばってください

▲ Yaay! Thanks for the really nice message!!

▼ I hope the bond between their parents can be passed down to their children!

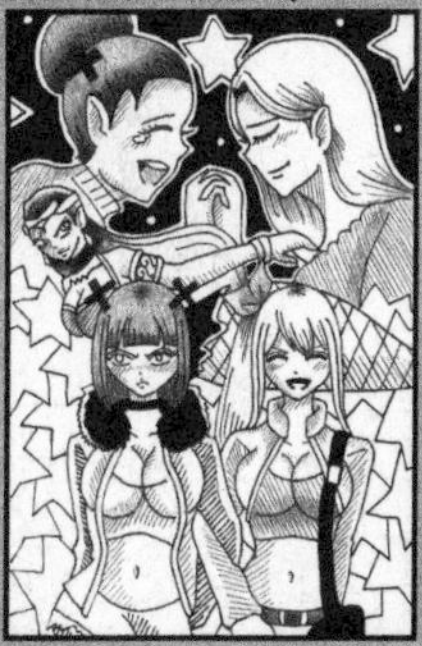

Hyogo Prefecture, Nyan

Kanagawa Prefecture, Kurione

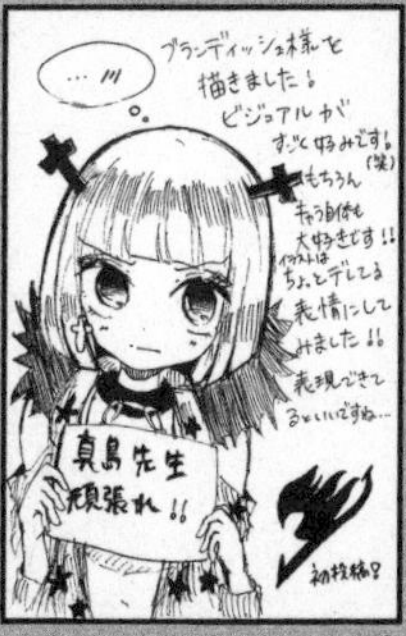
…!!!
ブランディッシュ様を
描きました！
ビジュアルが
すごく好みです！(笑)
もちろん
キャラ自体も
大好きです!!
イラストは
ちょっとデレてる
表情にして
みました!!
表現できてるといいですね…
真島先生
頑張れ!!
初投稿?

▲ Brandish is more popular than I expected. I like her, too!

▶ Thanks! I'm doing my best!! The answer to that is coming very soon.

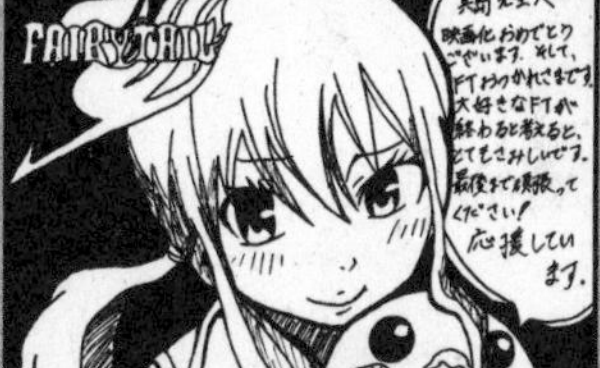
FAIRY TAIL
真島先生へ
映画化おめでとうございます。そして、
FTおつかれさまです。
大好きなFTが
終わると考えると、
とてもさみしいです。
最後まで頑張って
ください！
応援しています。

Okayama, Cheru

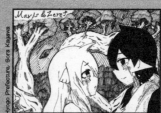

Hyogo Prefecture, Sora Kagawa

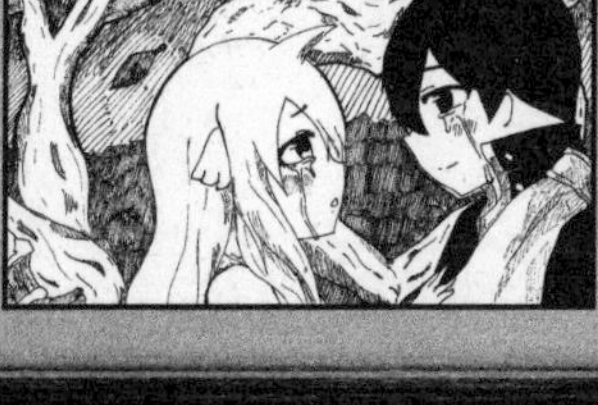
Mavis & Zeref

◀ Hey, there have been a lot of post cards with Mavis and Zeref recently.

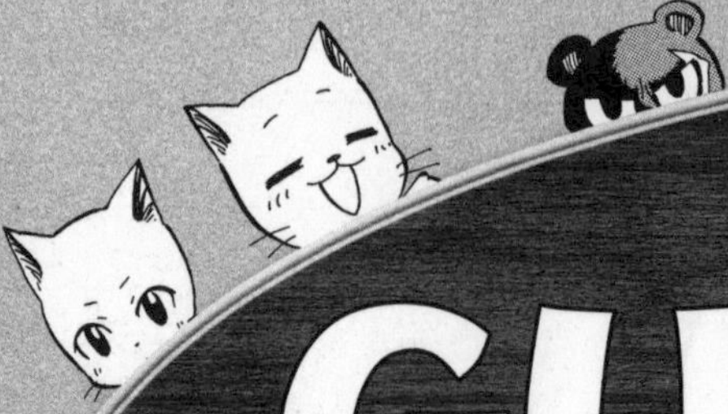

# FAIRY GUILD

▼ The pair look? I think it looks surprisingly good.

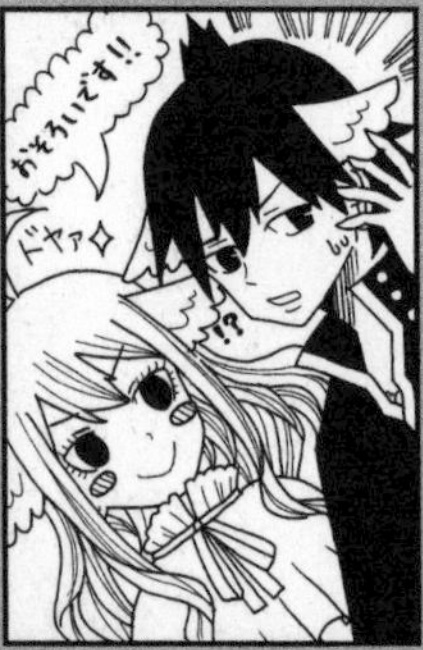
おそろいです!!
ドヤァ♢
!?

Hiroshima Prefecture, Mai Tokuda

Osaka, Noroka Nagai

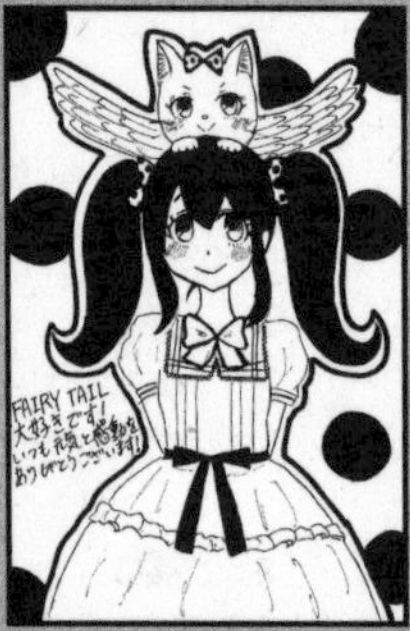
FAIRY TAIL

▲ Cute!! That type of dress looks good on her!

▼ Uwa ha ha! A Rogue-Fro, and tiny too!

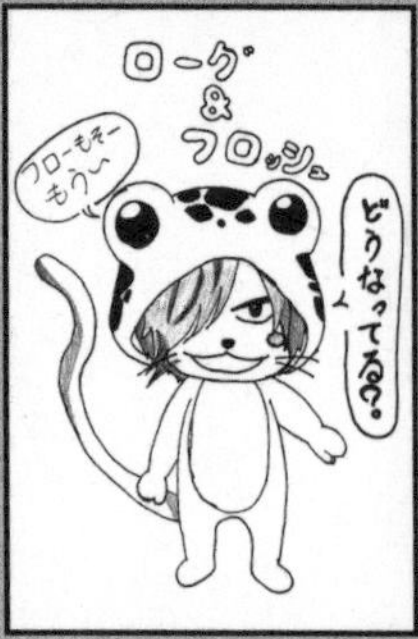
ローグ
&
フロッシュ
フローもそーもう〜
どうなってる?。

Shiga Prefecture, Akari Sumi

REJECTION CORNER

Tokyo, Satsuki Nakama

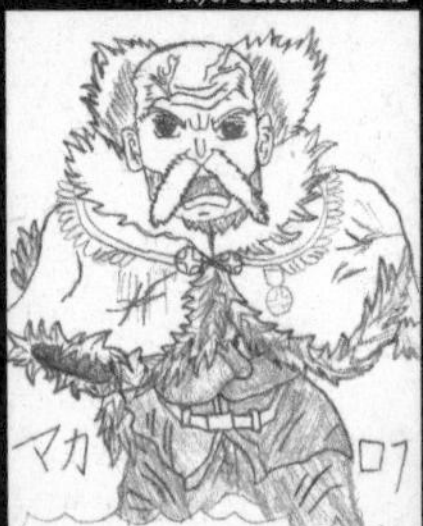
マカロフ
のせて

◀ I-I don't think there's a choice. If the master says he wants to ride, he gets to ride. Handsome man!

▶ Lucy taking a selfie with Erza! Erza's kind of cute here!

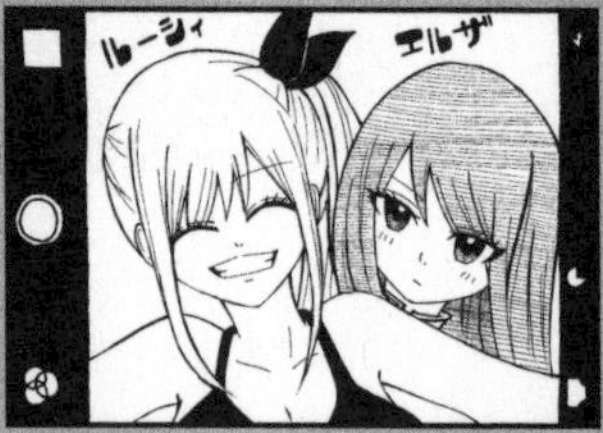
ルーシィ
エルザ

Kanagawa Prefecture, Rei

Nagasaki Prefecture, Nana Nakahara

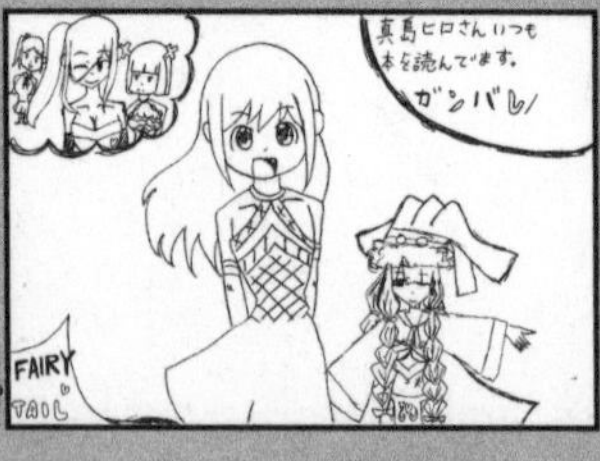
真島ヒロさんいつも本を読んでます。
ガンバレ!
FAIRY TAIL

◀ This is pretty cute! Especially Wendy's expression!

Only two
volumes left
until the end!!

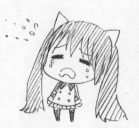

# FAIRY TAIL
フェアリーテイル

61

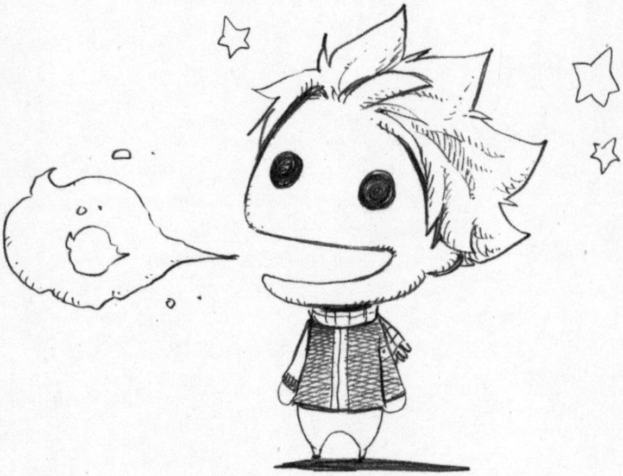

HIRO 真島ヒロ MASHIMA

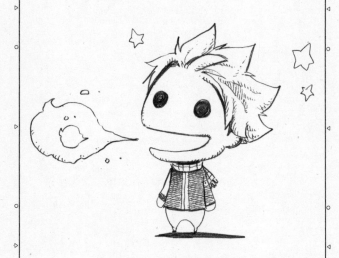

## FROM HIRO MASHIMA

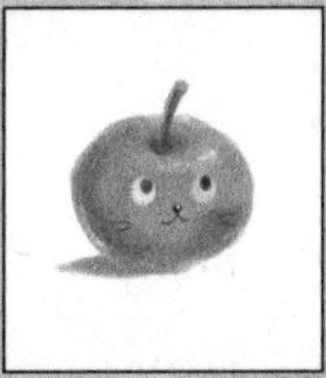

The second theatrical production of a Fairy Tail movie has been released!!
It's been a long time since the original announcement, but it's now taken full form.
They call me an executive producer, but to tell the truth, I didn't do anything.
I gave them the rough drawings of the story, and then I requested some images be better drawn, but that was all.
So this is just between us, but...
I really didn't do anything.

Original Jacket Design: Hisao Ogawa

# Translation Notes:

Japanese is a difficult language and translation is often more art than science. For your edification and reading pleasure, here are notes on some of the places where we could have gone in a different direction with our translation of the work, or where a Japanese cultural reference is used.

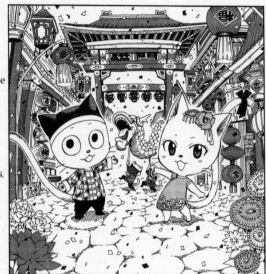

### Page 87, Chinese New Years

Since this chapter was originally published to coincide with the Chinese New Year, the image on this title page presents quite a few customs connected with the Chinese New Year. The lanterns and signs read: Good Fortune, Happiness, Longevity, Treasure, and Celebration. The gate to the temple also says, "Cat Gate."

### Page 164, Haja Kensei: Zetten

*Haja kensei* is a concept in martial arts, which tasks one to break through any evil to reveal what is right and true. Although that evil is in the form of the villains in *Fairy Tail*, a big part of this concept is breaking through evil within oneself. *Zetten* is made up of the *kanji* for "absolute" and "heavens," so it can refer to a "true heaven."

### Page 176, Ars Magia

Ars Magia in Latin can mean "The Art of Magic."

**The award-winning manga about what happens inside you!**

"Far more entertaining than it ought to be... what kid doesn't want to think that every time they sneeze a torpedo shoots out their nose?"
–Anime News Network

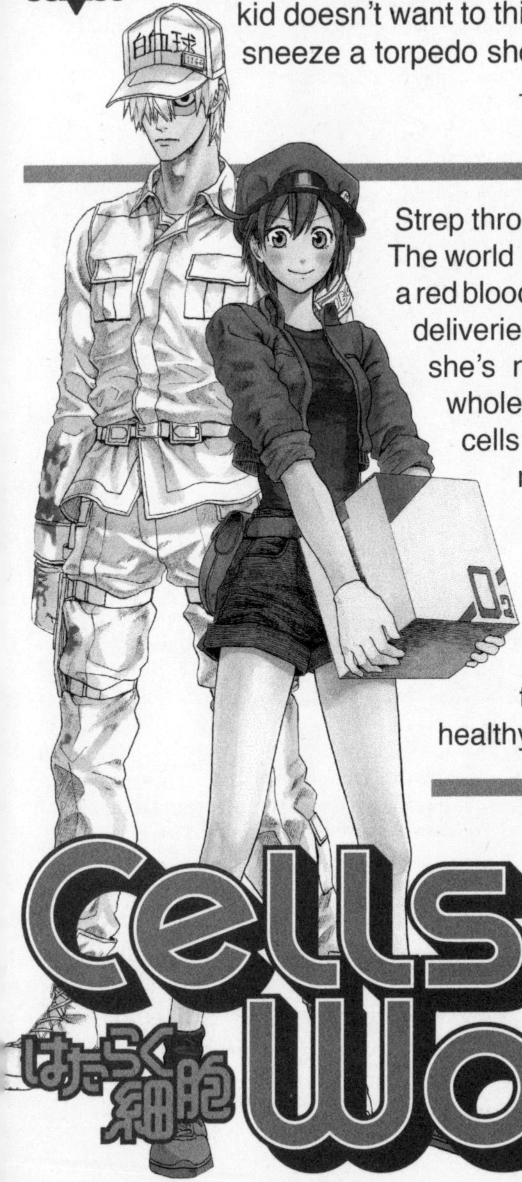

Strep throat! Hay fever! Influenza! The world is a dangerous place for a red blood cell just trying to get her deliveries finished. Fortunately, she's not alone...she's got a whole human body's worth of cells ready to help out! The mysterious white blood cells, the buff and brash killer T cells, even the cute little platelets— everyone's got to come together if they want to keep you healthy!

# Cells at Work!

By Akane Shimizu

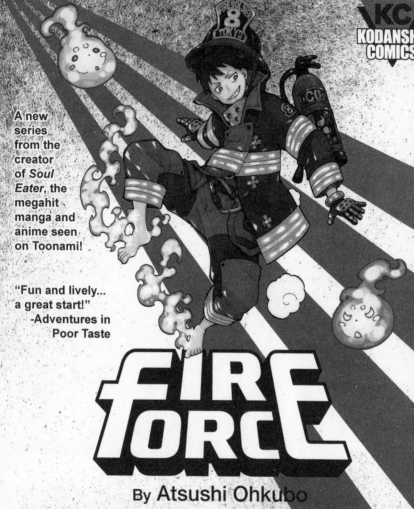

A new series from the creator of *Soul Eater*, the megahit manga and anime seen on Toonami!

"Fun and lively... a great start!"
-Adventures in Poor Taste

# FIRE FORCE

By Atsushi Ohkubo

The city of Tokyo is plagued by a deadly phenomenon: spontaneo[us] human combustion! Luckily, a special team is there to quench th[e] inferno: The Fire Force! The fire soldiers at Special Fire Cathedra[l] are about to get a unique addition. Enter Shinra, a boy who possess[es] the power to run at the speed of a rocket, leaving behind the famo[us] "devil's footprints" (and destroying his shoes in the proces[s]) Can Shinra and his colleagues discover the source of this strang[e] epidemic before the city burns to ashes?

# KC
## KODANSHA COMICS

Japan's most powerful spirit medium delves into the ghost world's greatest mysteries!

Story by Kyo Shirodaira, famed author of mystery fiction and creator of *Spiral*, *Blast of Tempest*, and *The Record of a Fallen Vampire*.

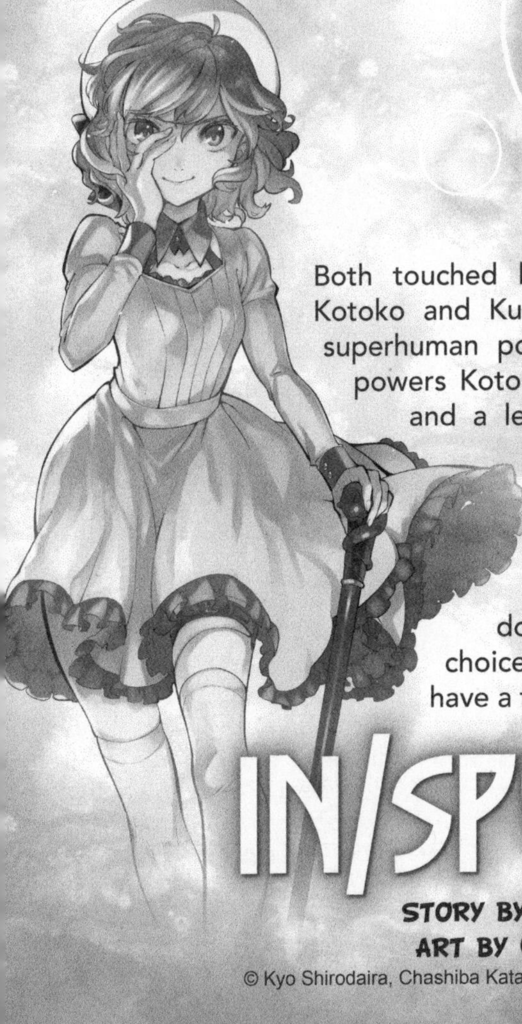

Both touched by spirits called yôkai, Kotoko and Kurô have gained unique superhuman powers. But to gain her powers Kotoko has given up an eye and a leg, and Kurô's personal life is in shambles. So when Kotoko suggests they team up to deal with renegades from the spirit world, Kurô doesn't have many other choices, but Kotoko might just have a few ulterior motives...

# IN/SPECTRE

### STORY BY KYO SHIRODAIRA
### ART BY CHASHIBA KATASE

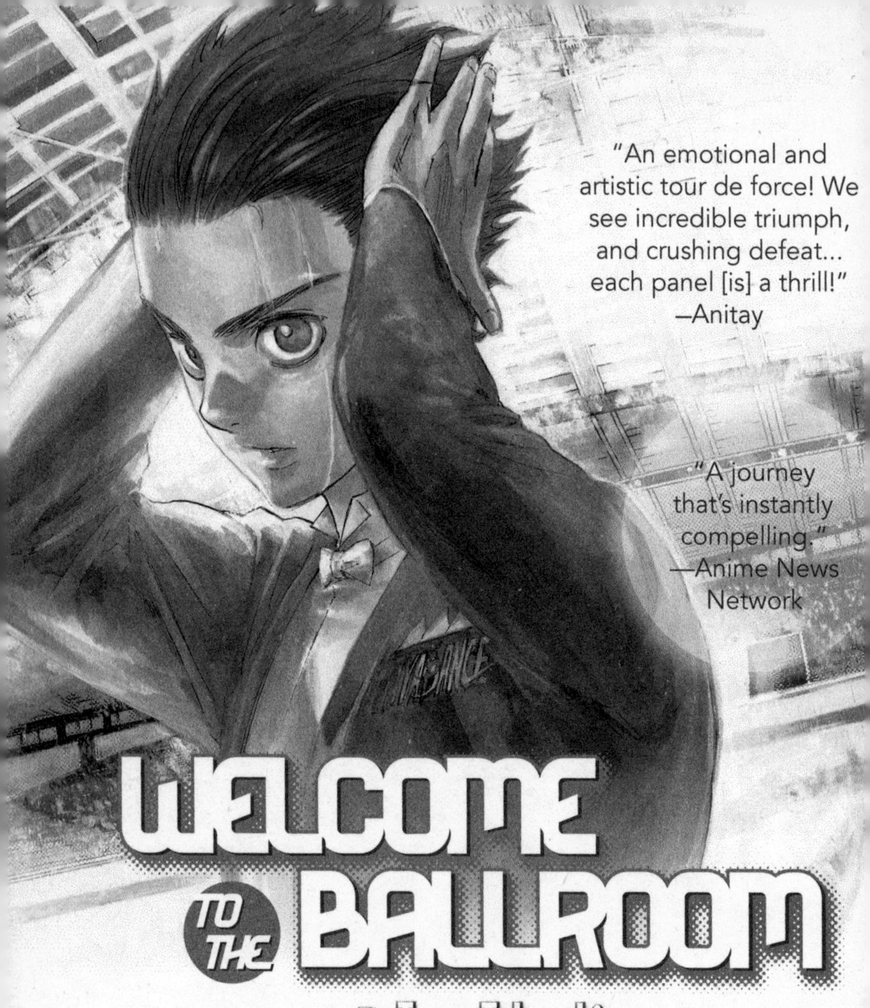

"An emotional and artistic tour de force! We see incredible triumph, and crushing defeat... each panel [is] a thrill!"
—Anitay

"A journey that's instantly compelling."
—Anime News Network

# WELCOME TO THE BALLROOM

**By Tomo Takeuchi**

Feckless high school student Tatara Fujita wants to be good something—anything. Unfortunately, he's about as average as a slouc teen can be. The local bullies know this, and make it a habit to hit him for cash, but all that changes when the debonair Kaname Sengoku sen them packing. Sengoku's not the neighborhood watch, though. He's professional ballroom dancer. And once Tatara Fujita gets pulled into the world of ballroom, his life will never be the same.

KC KODANSH COMICS

KC
KODANSHA
COMICS

*New action series from Hiroyuki Takei, creator of the classic shonen franchise Shaman King!*

In medieval Japan, a bell hanging on the collar is a sign that a cat has a master. Norachiyo's bell hangs from his katana sheath, but he is nonetheless a stray — a ronin. This one-eyed cat samurai travels across a dishonest world, cutting through pretense and deception with his blade.

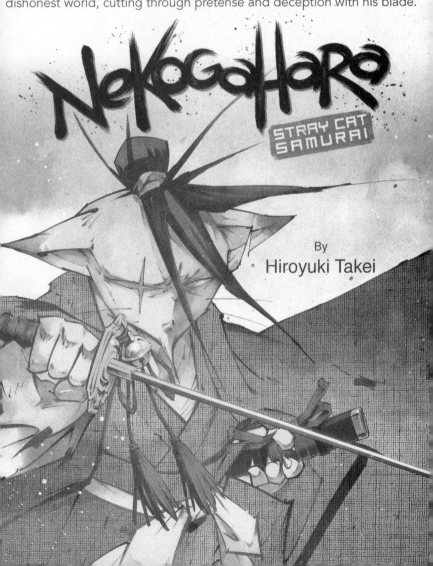

# NEKOGAHARA

## STRAY CAT SAMURAI

By
Hiroyuki Takei

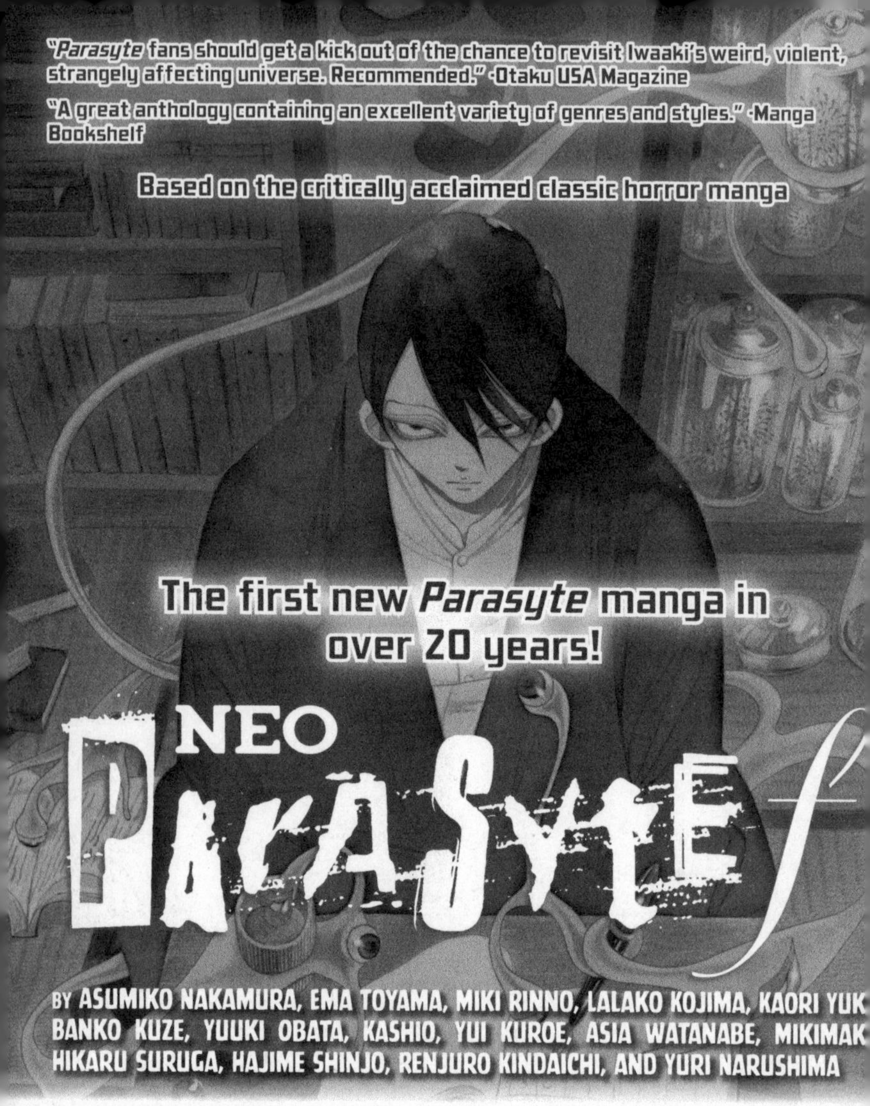

**Based on the critically acclaimed classic horror manga**

# The first new *Parasyte* manga in over 20 years!

# NEO PARASYTE f

BY ASUMIKO NAKAMURA, EMA TOYAMA, MIKI RINNO, LALAKO KOJIMA, KAORI YUK
BANKO KUZE, YUUKI OBATA, KASHIO, YUI KUROE, ASIA WATANABE, MIKIMAK
HIKARU SURUGA, HAJIME SHINJO, RENJURO KINDAICHI, AND YURI NARUSHIMA

A collection of chilling new *Parasyte* stories from Japan's top shojo artists!

Parasites: shape-shifting aliens whose only purpose is to assimilate with and consum the human race... but do these monsters have a different side? A parasite becomes prince to save his romance-obsessed female host from a dangerous stalker. Anothe hosts a cooking show, in which the real monsters are revealed. These and 13 mor stories, from some of the greatest shojo manga artists alive today, together make up a chilling, funny, and entertaining tribute to one of manga's horror classics!

KC
KODANSH
COMICS

**KC**

**KODANSHA COMICS**

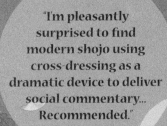

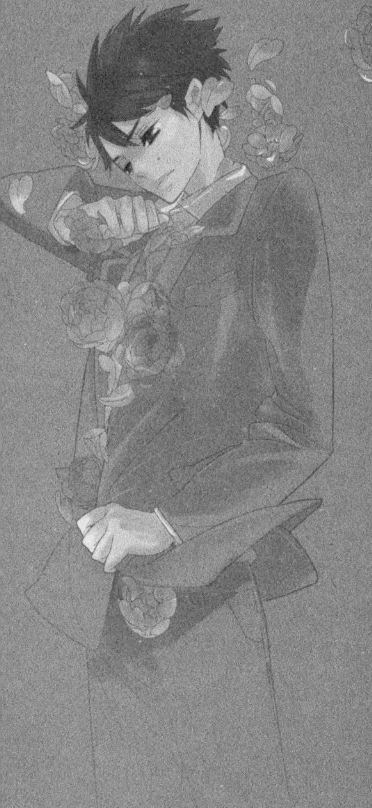

# The prince in his dark days

By **Hico Yamanaka**

A drunkard for a father, a household of poverty... For 17-year-old Atsuko, misfortune is all she knows and believes in. Until one day, a chance encounter with Itaru-the wealthy heir of a huge corporation-changes everything. The two look identical, uncannily so. When Itaru curiously goes missing, Atsuko is roped into being his stand-in. There, in his shoes, Atsuko must parade like a prince in a palace. She encounters many new experiences, but at what cost...?

# HAPPINESS

## —ハピネス—

**By Shuzo Oshimi**

**From the creator of *The Flowers of Evil***

Nothing interesting is happening in Makoto Ozaki's first year of hig school. HIs life is a series of quiet humiliations: low-grade bullie unreliable friends, and the constant frustration of his adolescent lust. Bu one night, a pale, thin girl knocks him to the ground in an alley and offer him a choice.

Now everything is different. Daylight is searingly bright. Food taste awful. And worse than anything is the terrible, consuming thirst...

**Praise for Shuzo Oshimi's *The Flowers of Evil***

"A shockingly readable story that vividly—one might even say queasily—evokes the fe and confusion of discovering one's own sexuality. Recommended." —The Manga Critic

"A page-turning tale of sordid middle school blackmail." —Otaku USA Magazine

"A stunning new horror manga." —Third Eye Comics

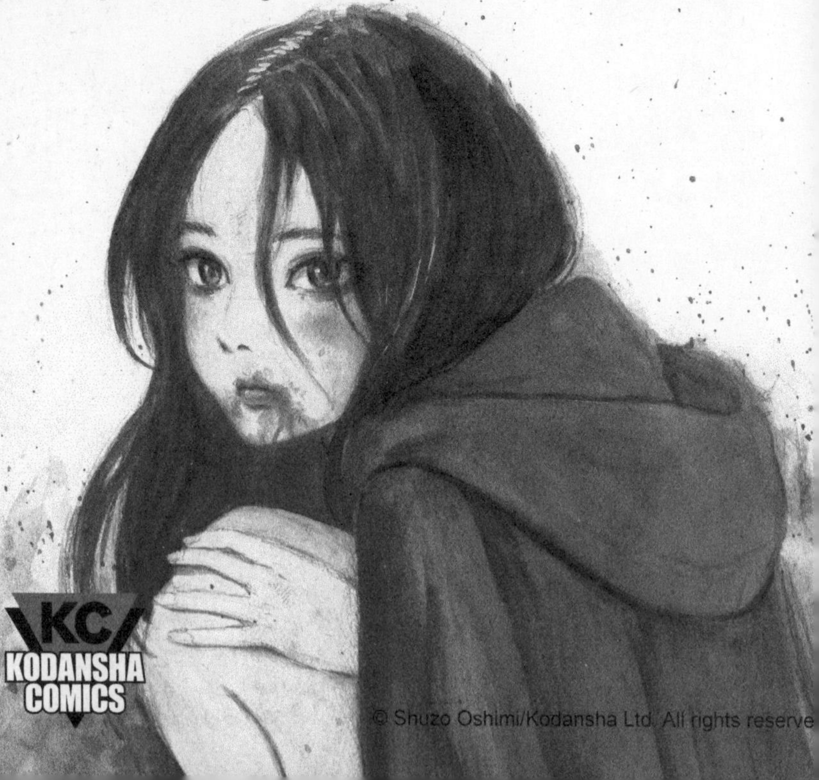
KC
KODANSHA COMICS

aving lost his wife, high school teacher Kōhei Inuzuka is doing his best to raise his young
aughter Tsumugi as a single father. He's pretty bad at cooking and doesn't have a huge
ppetite to begin with, but chance brings his little family together with one of his students, the
nely Kotori. The three of them are anything but comfortable in the kitchen, but the healing
ower of home cooking might just work on their grieving hearts.

his season's number-one feel-good anime!" —Anime News Network

 beautifully-drawn story about comfort food and family and grief. Recommended." —Otaku
SA Magazine

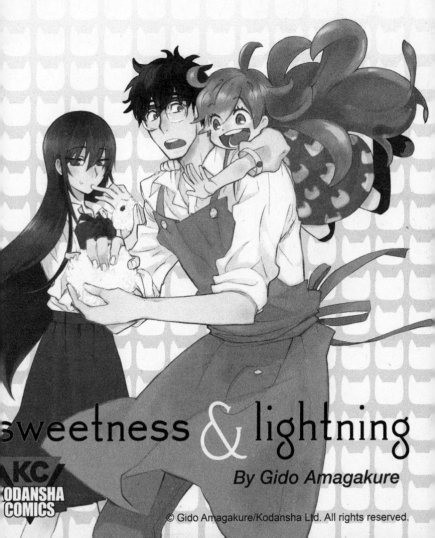

sweetness & lightning

By Gido Amagakure

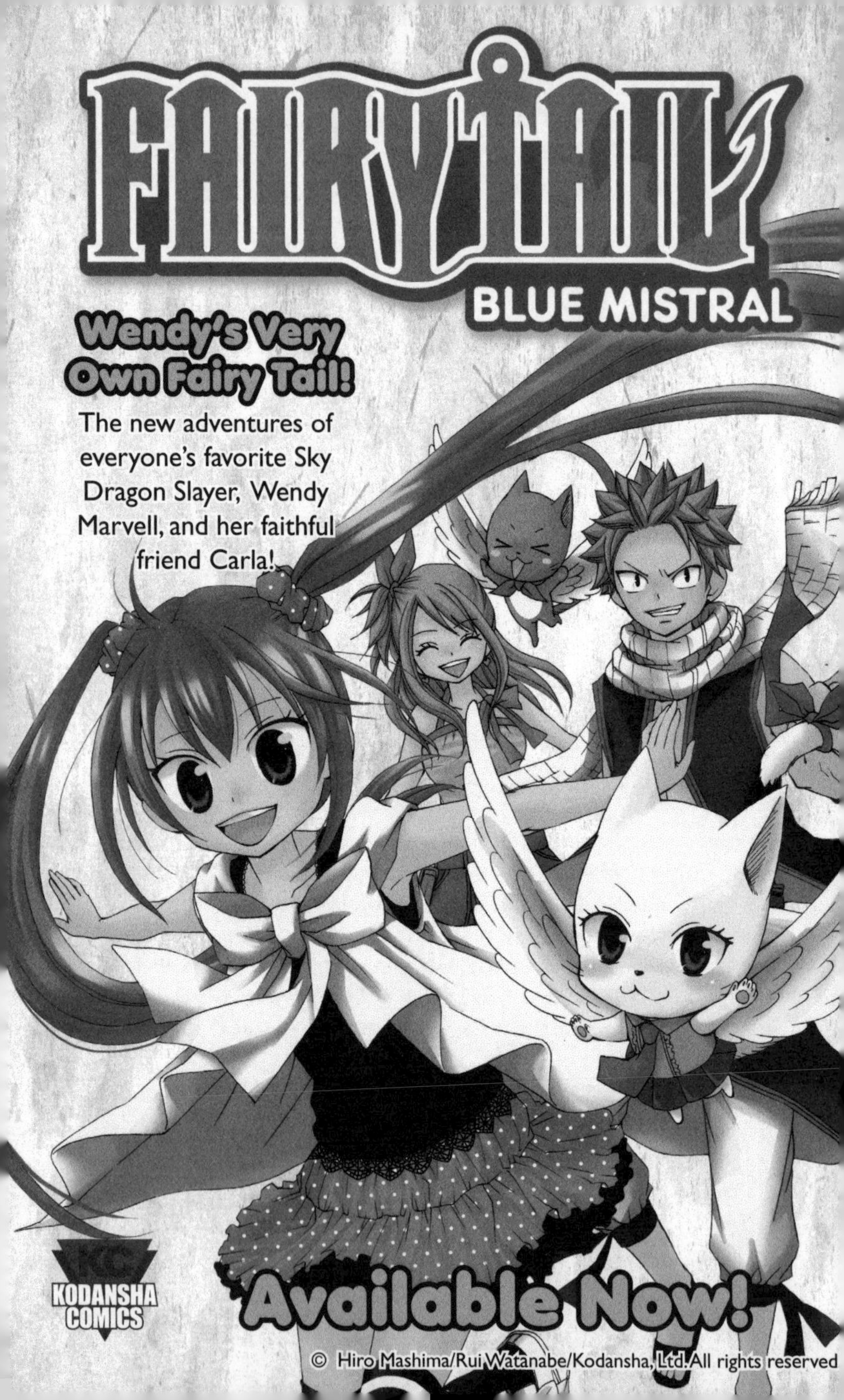
FAIRY TAIL
BLUE MISTRAL
Wendy's Very Own Fairy Tail!
The new adventures of everyone's favorite Sky Dragon Slayer, Wendy Marvell, and her faithful friend Carla!
KC
KODANSHA COMICS
Available Now!
© Hiro Mashima/Rui Watanabe/Kodansha, Ltd. All rights reserved

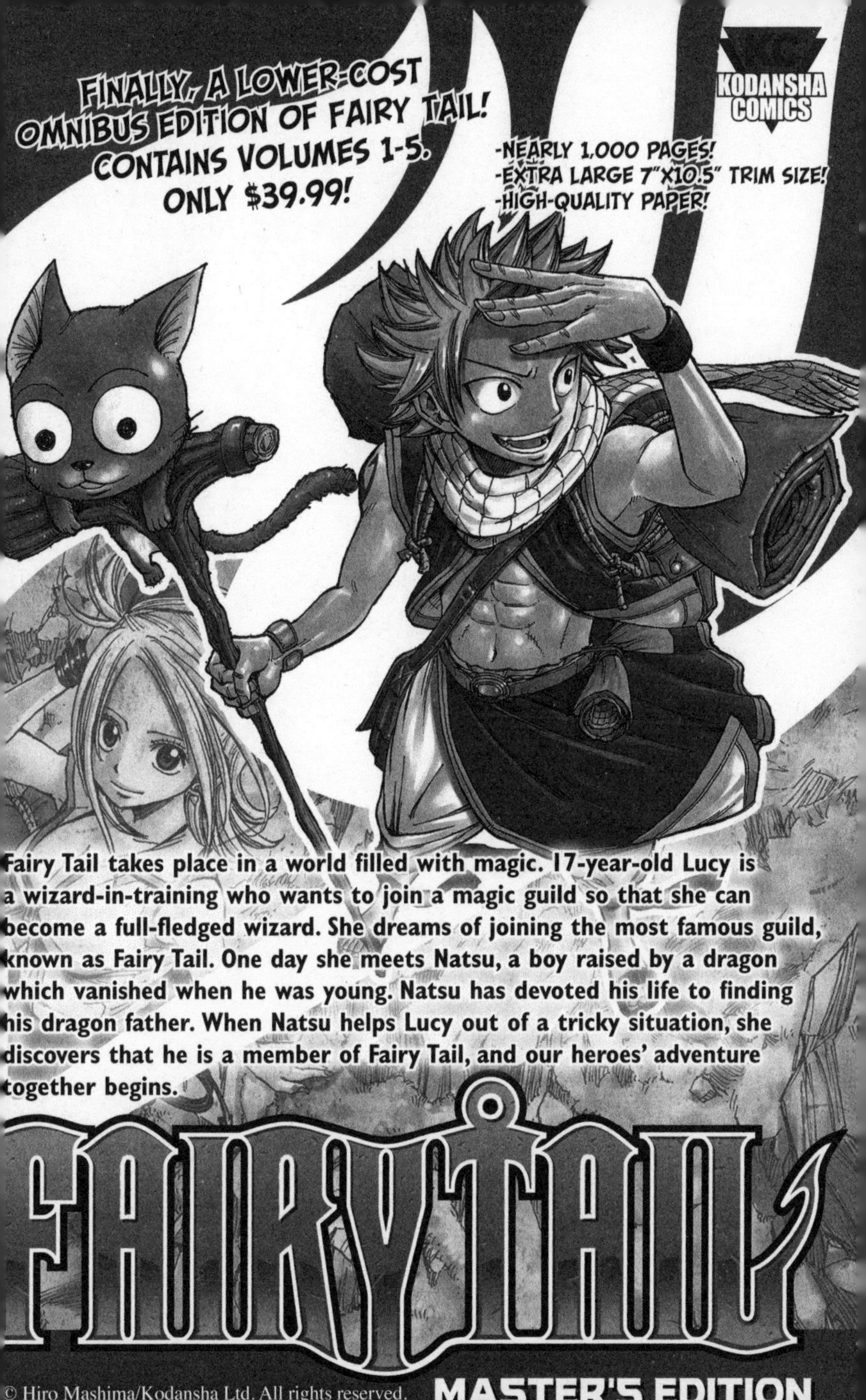
FINALLY, A LOWER-COST OMNIBUS EDITION OF FAIRY TAIL! CONTAINS VOLUMES 1-5. ONLY $39.99!
KODANSHA COMICS
-NEARLY 1,000 PAGES!
-EXTRA LARGE 7"X10.5" TRIM SIZE!
-HIGH-QUALITY PAPER!
Fairy Tail takes place in a world filled with magic. 17-year-old Lucy is a wizard-in-training who wants to join a magic guild so that she can become a full-fledged wizard. She dreams of joining the most famous guild, known as Fairy Tail. One day she meets Natsu, a boy raised by a dragon which vanished when he was young. Natsu has devoted his life to finding his dragon father. When Natsu helps Lucy out of a tricky situation, she discovers that he is a member of Fairy Tail, and our heroes' adventure together begins.
FAIRY TAIL
MASTER'S EDITION

*Fairy Tail* volume 61 is a work of fiction. Names, characters, places, and incidents are the products of the author's imagination or are used fictitiously. Any resemblance to actual events, locales, or persons, living or dead, is entirely coincidental.

A Kodansha Comics Trade Paperback Original.



Published in the United States by Kodansha Comics, an imprint of Kodansha USA Publishing, LLC, New York.

Publication rights for this English edition arranged through Kodansha Ltd., Tokyo.

First published in Japan in 2017 by Kodansha Ltd., Tokyo
ISBN 978-1-63236-430-2

Printed in the United States of America.

www.kodanshacomics.com

9 8 7 6 5 4 3 2 1

Translation: William Flanagan
Lettering: AndWorld Design
Editing: Haruko Hashimoto
Kodansha Comics edition cover design by Phil Balsman

# TOMARE!

止まれ

[STOP!]

You're going the wrong way!

Manga is a completely different type of reading experience.

To start at the beginning, go to the end!

at's right! Authentic manga is read the traditional Japanese way— m right to left, exactly the opposite of how American books are d. It's easy to follow: Just go to the other end of the book and read ch page—and each panel—from right side to left side, starting at e top right. Now you're experiencing manga as it was meant to be!